Stochastic Simulation and Applications in Finance with MATLAB® Programs

For other titles in the Wiley Finance Series
please see www.wiley.com/finance

Stochastic Simulation and Applications in Finance with MATLAB® Programs

Huu Tue Huynh,
Van Son Lai
and
Issouf Soumaré

A John Wiley and Sons, Ltd, Publication

Telephone (+44) 1243 779777

Email (for orders and customer service enquiries): cs-books@wiley.co.uk
Visit our Home Page on www.wiley.com

Reprinted June 2010

Other Wiley Editorial Offices

John Wiley & Sons Inc., 111 River Street, Hoboken, NJ 07030, USA

Jossey-Bass, 989 Market Street, San Francisco, CA 94103-1741, USA

Wiley-VCH Verlag GmbH, Boschstr. 12, D-69469 Weinheim, Germany

John Wiley & Sons Australia Ltd, 42 McDougall Street, Milton, Queensland 4064, Australia

John Wiley & Sons (Asia) Pte Ltd, 2 Clementi Loop #02-01, Jin Xing Distripark, Singapore 129809

John Wiley & Sons Canada Ltd, 6045 Freemont Blvd, Mississauga, ONT, L5R 4J3, Canada

Wiley also publishes its books in a variety of electronic formats. Some content that appears in print may not be available in electronic books.

Library of Congress Cataloging-in-Publication Data

Huynh, Huu Tue.
Stochastic simulation and applications in finance with MATLAB programs / Huu Tue Huynh, Van Son Lai, and Issouf Soumaré.
p. cm.—(The Wiley finance series)
Includes bibliographical references and index.
ISBN 978-0-470-72538-2 (cloth)
1. Finance—Mathematical models. 2. Stochastic models. I. Lai, Van Son. II. Soumaré, Issouf. III. Title.
HG106.H89 2008
332.01′51923—dc22

2008038608

British Library Cataloguing in Publication Data

A catalogue record for this book is available from the British Library

ISBN 978-0-470-72538-2 (H/B)

Typeset in 10/12pt Times by Aptara Inc., New Delhi, India
Printed and bound in Great Britain by CPI Antony Rowe, Chippenham, Wiltshire

Huu Tue Huynh: To my late parents, my wife Carole, and all members of my family.

Van Son Lai: To my parents, my wife Quynh-Trang, my son Laurent Lam, and my brothers and sisters.

Issouf Soumaré: To my wife Fatou, my son Moussa, and my daughter Candia.

Contents

Preface

Since the seminal works of Black-Scholes-Merton in 1973, the world of finance has been revolutionized by the emergence of a new field known as financial engineering. On the one hand, markets (foreign exchange, interest rate, commodities, etc.) have become more volatile, which creates an increase in the demand for derivatives products (options, forwards, futures, swaps, hybrids and exotics, and credit derivatives to name a few) used to measure, control, and manage risks, as well as to speculate and take advantage of arbitrage opportunities.

On the other hand, technological advances have enabled financial institutions and other markets players to create, price and launch new products and services to not only hedge against risks, but also to generate revenues from these risks. In addition to a deep grasp of advanced financial theories, the design, analysis and development of these complex products and financial services, or financial engineering, necessitate a mastering of sophisticated mathematics, statistics and numerical computations.

By way of an integrated approach, the object of this book is to teach the reader:

- to apply stochastic calculus and simulation techniques to solve financial problems;
- to develop and/or adapt the existing contingent claims models to support financial engineering platforms and applications.

There are several books in the market covering stochastic calculus and Monte Carlo simulations in finance. These books can be roughly grouped into two categories: introductory or advanced. Unfortunately, the books at the introductory level do not answer the needs of upper-level undergraduate and graduate students and finance professionals and practitioners. Advanced books, being very sophisticated and specialized, are tailored for researchers and users with solid and esoteric scientific backgrounds in mathematics and statistics. Furthermore, these books are often biased towards the research interests of the authors, hence their scope is narrowed and their applications in finance limited. By and large, the existing books are less suitable for day-to-day use which is why there is a need for a book that can be used equally by beginners and established researchers wishing to acquire an adequate knowledge of stochastic processes and simulation techniques and to learn how to formulate and solve problems in finance.

This book, which has developed from the master programme in financial engineering at Laval University in Canada first offered in 1999, aims to reinforce several aspects of simulation techniques and their applications in finance. Building on an integrated approach, the book provides a pedagogical treatment of the material for senior undergrad and graduate students as well as professionals working in risk management and financial engineering. While initiating students into basic concepts, it covers current up-to-date problems. It is written in a clear, concise and rigorous pedagogical language, which widens accessibility to a larger audience without sacrificing mathematical rigor. By way of a gradual learning of existing theories and new developments, our goal is also to provide an approach to help the reader follow the relevant literature which continually expands at a rapid pace.

This book is intended for students in business, economics, actuarial sciences, computer sciences, general sciences, and engineering, programmers and practitioners in financial, investment/asset and risk management industries. The prerequisites for the book are some familiarity in linear algebra, differential calculus and programming.

The book introduces and trains users in the formulation and resolution of financial problems. As exercises, it provides computer programs for use with the practical examples, exercises and case studies, which give the reader specific recipes for solving problems involving stochastic processes in finance. The programming language is the MATLAB®[1] software which is easy to learn and popular among professionals and practitioners. Moreover, the programs could be readily converted for use with the platform C++. Note that, unlike the MATLAB financial toolboxes which are still limited in scope, our proposed exercises and case studies tackle the complex problems encountered routinely in finance.

Overall, the general philosophy of the book can be summarized as follows:

- keep mathematical rigor by minimizing abstracts and unnecessary jargon;
- each concept, either in finance or in computation, leads to algorithms and is illustrated by concrete examples in finance.

Therefore, after they are discussed, the topics are presented in algorithmic forms. Furthermore, some of the examples which treat current financial problems are expounded in case studies, enabling students to better comprehend the underlying financial theory and related quantitative methods.

Every effort has been made to structure the chapters in a logical and coherent manner, with a clear thread and linkage between the chapters which is not apparent in most existing books. Each chapter has been written with regard to the following four principles: pedagogy, rigor, relevance and application. Advanced readers can skip the chapters they are familiar with and go straight to those of interest.

The book starts with a refresher of basic probability and statistics which underpin random processes and computer simulation techniques introduced later. Most of the developed tools are used later to study computational problems of derivative products and risk management. The text is divided into the following four major parts. The first part (Chapters 1 to 3) reviews basic probability and statistics principles. The second part (Chapters 4 to 6) introduces the Monte Carlo and Quasi Monte Carlo simulations topics and techniques. In addition to the other commonly used variance reduction techniques, we introduce the quadratic resampling technique of Barraquand (1995) to obtain the prescribed distribution characteristics of the simulated samples, which is important to improve the quality of the simulations. We also present the Markov Chain Monte Carlo (MCMC) and important sampling methods. The third part (Chapters 7 and 8) treats random processes, stochastic calculus, Brownian bridges, jump

[1] MATLAB is a registered trademark of The MathWorks, Inc. For more information, see htt://www.mathworks.com.

processes and stochastic differential equations. Finally, the fourth part (Chapters 9 to 15) develops the applications in finance.

To price contingent claims, two equivalent approaches are used in finance: the state variables approach consisting of solving partial differential equations and the probabilistic or equivalent martingale approach. The equivalence between the two approaches is established via the Feynman-Kac theorem. Our purpose is to teach how to solve numerically stochastic differential equations using Monte Carlo simulations, which essentially constitutes the pedagogical contribution of our book.

The fourth part of the book presents different applications of stochastic processes and simulation techniques to solve problems frequently encountered in finance. This part is structured as follows. Chapter 9 lays the foundation to price and replicate contingent claims. Chapter 10 prices European, American and other complex and exotic options using Monte Carlo simulations. Chapter 11 presents modern continuous-time models of the term structure of interest rates and the pricing of interest rate derivatives. Chapters 12 and 13 develop valuation models of corporate securities and credit risk. Chapters 14 and 15 overview risk management and develop estimations of Value at Risk (VaR) by combining Monte Carlo and Quasi Monte Carlo simulations with Principal Components Analysis.

Although this is an introductory and pedagogical book, nonetheless, in Chapter 10 we explain many useful and modern simulation techniques such as the Least-Squares Method (LSM) of Longstaff and Schwartz (2001) and the dynamic programming with Stratified State Aggregation of Barraquand and Martineau (1995) to price American options, the extreme value simulation technique proposed by El Babsiri and Noel (1998) to price exotic options and the Retrieval of Volatility Method proposed by Cvitanic, Goukassian and Zapatero (2002) to estimate the option sensitivity coefficients or hedge ratios (the Greeks). Note that, to our knowledge, with the exception of LSM, this is the first book to bring to the fore these important techniques. In Chapter 11 on term structure of interest rates modeling and pricing of interest rate derivatives, we present the interest rate model of Heath, Jarrow and Morton (1992) and the industry-standard Market Model of Brace, Gatarek and Musiela (2001). An extensive treatment of corporate securities valuation and credit risk based on the structural approach of Merton (1974) is presented in chapter 12. Chapter 13 gives case studies on financial guarantees to show how the simulations techniques can be implemented, and this chapter is inspired from the research publications of the authors. As such, Chapters 12 and 13 provide indispensable fundamentals for a reader to embark on the study of structured products design and credit derivatives.

To perform a sound simulation experiment, one has to undertake roughly the following three steps: (1) modeling of the problem to be studied, (2) calibration/estimation of the model parameters, and (3) backtesting using real data and recalibration. This book focuses on the use of Monte Carlo and Quasi Monte Carlo simulations in finance for the sake of pricing and risk management assuming the dynamics of the underlying variables are known.

We do not pretend that the book provides complete coverage of all topics and issues; future editions would include application examples of the Markov Chain Monte Carlo (MCMC) simulation technique, estimation techniques of the parameters of the diffusion processes and the determination of the assets variance-covariance matrix, the spectral analysis, real options, volatility derivatives, etc.

We would like to thank Pete Baker from Wiley, our copy-editor Rachael Wilkie and anonymous reviewers for their very constructive comments which help improve this book. We also thank Noël Amenc, Didier Cossin, Rose-Anne Dana, Catherine Hersent, Lionel Martellini,

Thierry Roncalli and Yves Simon for their various contributions and comments during the gestation of this book. We reserve a special thank-you to Yves Langlois and Jean-François Carter for their valuable assistance. We extend our gratitude to André Gascon (Associate Dean Academics), Michel Gendron (Head of the Department of Finance and Insurance), Maurice Gosselin (former Associate Dean Research), Fayez Boctor (current Associate Dean Research) and Robert Mantha (Dean), all from the Faculty of Business Administration of Laval University, for their continual support and financial contribution to the production of the book.

1
Introduction to Probability

Since financial markets are very volatile, in order to model financial variables we need to characterize randomness. Therefore, to study financial phenomena, we have to use probabilities.

Once defined, we will see how to use probabilities to describe the evolution of random parameters that we later call random processes. The key step here is the quantitative construction of the events' probabilities. First, one must define the events and then the probabilities associated to these events. This is the objective of this first chapter.

1.1 INTUITIVE EXPLANATION

1.1.1 Frequencies

Here is an example to illustrate the notion of relative frequency. We toss a dice N times and observe the outcomes. We suppose that the 6 faces are identified by letters A, B, C, D, E and F. We are interested in the probability of obtaining face A. For that purpose, we count the number of times that face A appears and denote it by $n(A)$. This number represents the frequency of appearance of face A.

Intuitively, we see that the division of the number of times that face A appears, $n(A)$, by the total number N of throws, $\frac{n(A)}{N}$, is a fraction that represents the probability of obtaining face A each time that we toss the dice. In the first series of experiments when we toss the dice N times we get $n_1(A)$ and if we repeat this series of experiments another time by tossing it again N times, we obtain $n_2(A)$ of outcomes A.

It is likely that $n_1(A)$ and $n_2(A)$ are different. The fractions $\frac{n_1(A)}{N}$ and $\frac{n_2(A)}{N}$ are then different. Therefore, how can we say that this fraction quantifies the probability of obtaining face A? To find an answer, we need to continue the experiment. Even if the fractions are different, when the number N of throws becomes very large, we observe that these two fractions converge to the same value of $\frac{1}{6}$.

Intuitively, this fraction measures the probability of obtaining face A, and when N is large, this fraction goes to $\frac{1}{6}$. Thus, each time we toss the dice, it is natural to take $\frac{1}{6}$ as the probability of obtaining face A.

Later, we will see that from the law of large numbers these fractions converge to this limit. This limit, $\frac{1}{6}$, corresponds to the concept of the ratio of the number of favorable cases over the total number of cases.

1.1.2 Number of Favorable Cases Over The Total Number of Cases

When we toss a dice, there is a total of 6 possible outcomes, $\{1, 2, 3, 4, 5, 6\}$, corresponding to the letters on faces $\{A, B, C, D, E, F\}$. If we wish to obtain face A and we have only one such case, then the probability of getting face A is quantified by the fraction $\frac{1}{6}$. However, we may be interested in the event {"the observed face is even"}. What does this mean? The even face can be 2, 4 or 6. Each time that one of these three faces appears, we have a realization of the event {"the observed face is even"}. This means that when we toss a dice, the total number of possible cases is always 6 and the number of favorable cases associated to even events is 3. Therefore, the probability of obtaining an even face is simply $\frac{3}{6}$ and intuitively this appears to be correct.

From this consideration, in the following section we construct in an axiomatic way the mechanics of what is happening. However, we must first establish what is an event, and then we must define the probabilities associated with an event.

1.2 AXIOMATIC DEFINITION

Let's define an universe in which we can embed all these intuitive considerations in an axiomatic way.

1.2.1 Random Experiment

A random experiment is an experiment in which we cannot precisely predict the outcome. Each result obtained from this experiment is random *a priori* (before the realization of the experiment). Each of these results is called a simple event. This means that each time that we realize this experiment we can obtain only one simple event. Further we say that all simple events are exclusive.

Example 2.1 Tossing a dice is a random experiment because before the toss, we cannot exactly predict the future result. The face that is shown can be 1, 2, 3, 4, 5 or 6. Each of these results is thus a simple event. All these 6 simple events are mutually exclusive.

We denote by Ω the set of all simple events. The number of elements in Ω can be finite, countably infinite, uncountably infinite, etc. The example with the dice corresponds to the first case (the case of a "finite number of results", $\Omega = \{1, 2, 3, 4, 5, 6\}$).

Example 2.2 We count the number of phone calls to one center during one hour. The number of calls can be 0, 1, 2, 3, etc. up to infinity. An infinite number of calls is evidently an event that will never occur. However, to consider it in the theoretical development allows us to build useful models in a relatively simple fashion. This phone calls example corresponds to the countably infinite case ($\Omega = \{ 0, 1, 2, 3, \ldots, \infty\}$).

Example 2.3 When we throw a marble on the floor of a room, the position on which the marble will stop is a simple event of the experiment. However, the number of simple events is infinite and uncountable. It corresponds to the set of all points on the floor.

Building a probability theory for the case of finite experiments is relatively easy, the generalization to the countably infinite case is straightforward. However, the uncountably infinite case is different. We will point out these differences and technicalities but we will not dwell on the complex mathematical aspects.

1.2.2 Event

We consider the experiment of a dice toss. We want to study the "even face" event. This event happens when the face shown is even, that is, one of 2, 4, or 6.

Thus, we can say that this event "even face" contains three simple events $\{2, 4, 6\}$. This brings us to the definition:

Definition 2.4 *Let Ω be the set of simple events of a given random experiment. Ω is called the sample space or the universe. An event is simply a sub-set of Ω.*

Is any subset of Ω an event? This question will be answered below. We must not forget that an event occurs if the realized simple event belongs to this event.

1.2.3 Algebra of Events

We saw that an event is a subset of Ω. We would like to construct events from Ω. Let Ω be the universe and let ξ be the set of events we are interested in. We consider the set of all events. ξ is an algebra of events if the following axioms are satisfied:

A1: $\Omega \in \xi$,
A2: $\forall A \in \xi, A^c = \Omega \backslash A \in \xi$ (where $\Omega \backslash A$, called the complementary of A, is the set of all elements of Ω which do not belong to A),
A3: $\forall A_1, A_2, \ldots, A_n \in \xi, A_1 \cup A_2 \cup \ldots \cup A_n \in \xi$.

Axiom A1 says that the universe is an event. This event is certain since it happens each time that we undertake the experiment. Axiom A1 and axiom A2 imply that the empty set, denoted by $\emptyset$, is also an event but it is impossible since it never happens. Axiom A3 says that the union of a finite number of events is also an event. To be able to build an algebra of events associated with a random experiment encompassing a countable infinity of simple events, axiom A3 will be replaced by:

A3': $\cup_{n=1}^{\infty} A_n = A_1 \cup A_2 \cup \ldots \cup A_n \cup \ldots \in \xi$.

This algebra of events plays a very important role in the construction of the probability of events. The probabilities that we derive should follow the intuition developed previously.

1.2.4 Probability Axioms

Let Ω be the universe associated with a given random experiment on which we build the algebra of events ξ. We associate to each event $A \in \xi$ a probability noted Prob(A), representing the probability of event A occurring when we realize the experiment. From our intuitive setup, this probability must satisfy the following axioms:

P1: $\text{Prob}(\Omega) = 1$,
P2: $\forall A \in \xi, 0 \leq \text{Prob}(A) \leq 1$,
P3: if $A_1, A_2, \ldots, A_n, \ldots$ is a series of mutually exclusive events, that is: $\forall i \neq j, A_i \cap A_j = \emptyset$, then

$$\text{Prob}(\cup_{n=1}^{\infty} A_n) = \sum_{n=1}^{\infty} \text{Prob}(A_n). \quad (1.1)$$

Axiom P3 is called $\sigma-$additivity of probabilities. This axiom allows us to consider random experiments with an infinity of possible outcomes. From these axioms, we can see that

$$\text{Prob}(\emptyset) = 0 \quad \text{and} \quad \text{Prob}(A^c) = 1 - \text{Prob}(A) \tag{1.2}$$

which are intuitively true.

A very important property easy to derive is presented below.

Property 2.5 *Consider two events A and B, then*

$$\text{Prob}(A \cup B) = \text{Prob}(A) + \text{Prob}(B) - \text{Prob}(A \cap B). \tag{1.3}$$

The mathematical proof is immediate.

Proof: Let $A \setminus C$ be the event built from elements of A that do not belong to C.

$$A = (A \setminus C) \cup C \quad \text{where} \quad C = A \cap B. \tag{1.4}$$

Since $A \setminus C$ and C are disjoint, from axiom P3,

$$\text{Prob}(A) = \text{Prob}(A \setminus C) + \text{Prob}(C). \tag{1.5}$$

Similarly

$$\text{Prob}(B) = \text{Prob}(B \setminus C) + \text{Prob}(C). \tag{1.6}$$

Adding these two equations yields:

$$\text{Prob}(A \setminus C) + \text{Prob}(B \setminus C) + \text{Prob}(C) = \text{Prob}(A) + \text{Prob}(B) - \text{Prob}(C). \tag{1.7}$$

Moreover,

$$A \cup B = (A \setminus C) \cup (B \setminus C) \cup C, \tag{1.8}$$

and since $A \setminus C$, $B \setminus C$ and C are disjoint, we have

$$\text{Prob}(A \cup B) = \text{Prob}(A \setminus C) + \text{Prob}(B \setminus C) + \text{Prob}(C), \tag{1.9}$$

thus,

$$\text{Prob}(A \cup B) = \text{Prob}(A) + \text{Prob}(B) - \text{Prob}(C). \tag{1.10}$$

Example 2.6 Let's go back to the dice toss experiment with

$$\Omega = \{1, 2, 3, 4, 5, 6\}$$

and consider the events:

(a) $A = \{\text{“face smaller than 5”}\} = \{1, 2, 3, 4\}$.

Since events $\{1\}$, $\{2\}$, $\{3\}$, and $\{4\}$ are mutually exclusive, we know from axiom P3 that:

$$\text{Prob}(A) = \text{Prob}(\{1\}) + \text{Prob}(\{2\}) + \text{Prob}(\{3\}) + \text{Prob}(\{4\}) = \frac{4}{6}.$$

(b) $B = \{\text{"even faces"}\} = \{2, 4, 6\}$.

Thus, $A \cup B = \{1, 2, 3, 4, 6\}$ and $A \cap B = \{2, 4\}$. We also have, $\text{Prob}(A) = \frac{4}{6}$, $\text{Prob}(B) = \frac{3}{6}$, $\text{Prob}(A \cap B) = \text{Prob}(\{2, 4\}) = \frac{2}{6}$, which implies

$$\text{Prob}(A \cup B) = \text{Prob}(A) + \text{Prob}(B) - \text{Prob}(A \cap B) = \frac{4}{6} + \frac{3}{6} - \frac{2}{6} = \frac{5}{6}.$$

Next, we discuss events that may be considered as independent. To present this, we must first discuss the concept of conditional probability, i.e., the probability of an event occurring given that another event already happened.

1.2.5 Conditional Probabilities

Let A and B be any two events belonging to the same algebra of events. We suppose that B has occurred. We are interested in the probability of getting event A. To define it, we must look back to the construction of the algebras of events.

Within the universe Ω in which A and B are two well-defined events, if B has already happened, the elementary event associated with the result of this random experiment must be an element belonging to event B. This means that given B has already happened, the result of the experiment is an element of event B.

Intuitively, the probability of A occurring is simply the probability that this result is also an event of B. If B has already happened, the probability of getting A knowing B is the probability of $A \cap B$ divided by the probability of B. Therefore, we obtain

$$\text{Prob}(A|B) = \frac{\text{Prob}(A \cap B)}{\text{Prob}(B)}. \tag{1.11}$$

This definition of the conditional probability is called Bayes' rule.

This probability satisfies the set of axioms for probabilities introduced at the beginning of the section:

$$\text{Prob}(\Omega|B) = 1, \tag{1.12}$$

$$0 \leq \text{Prob}(A|B) \leq 1, \tag{1.13}$$

$$\text{Prob}(A^c|B) = 1 - \text{Prob}(A|B), \tag{1.14}$$

and

$$\text{Prob}(\cup_{n=1}^{\infty} A_n|B) = \sum_{n=1}^{\infty} \text{Prob}(A_n|B), \quad \forall i \neq j, \quad A_i \cap A_j = \emptyset. \tag{1.15}$$

This definition is illustrated next by way of examples.

Example 2.7 Consider the dice toss experiment with event

$$A = \{\text{“face smaller than 5"}\} = \{1, 2, 3, 4\}$$

and event

$$B = \{\text{“even face"}\} = \{2, 4, 6\}.$$

We know that

$$\text{Prob}(B) = \text{Prob}(\{2, 4, 6\}) = \frac{3}{6}$$

and

$$\text{Prob}(A) = \text{Prob}(\{1, 2, 3, 4\}) = \frac{4}{6}.$$

However, we want to know what is the probability of obtaining an even face knowing that the face is smaller than 5 (in other words, A has already happened). From Bayes' rule:

$$\begin{aligned}\text{Prob}(B|A) &= \frac{\text{Prob}(A \cap B)}{\text{Prob}(A)}\\ &= \frac{\text{Prob}(\{2, 4\})}{\text{Prob}(\{1, 2, 3, 4\})}\\ &= \frac{2/6}{4/6}\\ &= \frac{1}{2}.\end{aligned}$$

Example 2.8 From a population of N persons, we observe n_s smokers and n_c people with cancer. From these n_s smokers we observe $n_{s,c}$ individuals suffering from cancer. For this population, we can say that the probability that a person is a smoker is $\frac{n_s}{N}$ and the probability that a person has cancer is $\frac{n_c}{N}$. The probability that a person has cancer given that he is already a smoker is:

$$\text{Prob}(\text{cancer}|\text{smoker}) = \frac{\text{Prob}(\text{smoker and cancer})}{\text{Prob}(\text{smoker})} = \frac{n_{s,c}}{n_s}.$$

From this experiment, we note that the conditional probability can be smaller or greater than the probability considered *a priori*. Following this definition of the conditional probability, we examine next the independence of two events.

1.2.6 Independent Events

Two events are said to be statistically independent when the occurrence of one of them doesn't affect the probability of getting the other. A and B are said to be statistically independent if

$$\text{Prob}(A|B) = \text{Prob}(A). \tag{1.16}$$

From Bayes' rule, if A and B are two independent events then

$$\text{Prob}(A \cap B) = \text{Prob}(A)\text{Prob}(B). \tag{1.17}$$

Example 2.9 Consider the experiment of tossing a dice twice. Intuitively, we hope that the result of the first toss would be independent of the second one. From our preceding exposition, we can establish this independence as follows. Indeed, the universe of this experiment contains 36 simple events denoted by $(R1, R2)$ where $R1$ and $R2$ are respectively the results of the first and second tosses, with $(R1, R2)$ taking values (n, m) in

$$\Omega = \{1, 2, 3, 4, 5, 6\} \times \{1, 2, 3, 4, 5, 6\}.$$

The probability the first element $R1$ equals n is

$$\text{Prob}(R1 = n) = \frac{1}{6}, \quad \forall n \in \{1, 2, 3, 4, 5, 6\}$$

and the probability the second element $R2$ equals m is

$$\text{Prob}(R2 = m) = \frac{1}{6}, \quad \forall m \in \{1, 2, 3, 4, 5, 6\}.$$

Since $\text{Prob}(R1 = n, R2 = m) = \frac{1}{36}$, then the conditional probability

$$\begin{aligned} \text{Prob}(R2 = m | R1 = n) &= \frac{\text{Prob}(R1 = n, R2 = m)}{\text{Prob}(R1 = n)} \\ &= \frac{\frac{1}{36}}{\frac{1}{6}} = \frac{1}{6}, \end{aligned}$$

which gives us $\text{Prob}(R2 = m | R1 = n) = \text{Prob}(R2 = m) = \frac{1}{6}$. Hence, we conclude that $R2$ and $R1$ are independent.

Notes and Complementary Readings

The concepts presented in this chapter are fundamentals of the theory of probabilities. The reader could refer to the books written by Ross (2002 a and b) for example.

2
Introduction to Random Variables

In the previous chapter, we introduced some concepts of events and defined probabilities on sets of events. In this chapter, we will focus on the representation of realized events on the real axis and probability space in order to provide a quantification to be used in financial problems.

A random variable is a function mapping the sample space Ω to the real axis. Afterwards, a complete characterization of such random variables will be given by introducing the probability density function, the cumulative distribution function and the characteristic function. We will show examples of the most frequently-encountered random variables in finance. The characteristic function will be presented in order to give the reader a better understanding of random variables. We will not use it extensively later in the book, but it is useful to be familiar with it to enable us to follow some proofs.

We will also introduce the concept of transformation of random variables. This concept is the basis of random variables simulation under known distributions and will be used in subsequent chapters.

2.1 RANDOM VARIABLES

We have defined random events and the probabilities associated with these events. In finance, as in the sciences, random events are always associated with quantities such as indices, costs and interest rates which vary in a random way. This means that we could link these experiments' random effects to the real axis. In other words, we associate a real number with the result given by the experiment.

Before realizing the experiment, this number is not known – it behaves as a random result from a random experiment. This approach means that we are looking to create a random experiment on the real axis the results of which are what we will call a random variable.

Mathematically, the random experiment on the real axis is created by using a function (denoted by X) from the universe of events Ω on the real axis. The random results observed on the axis under this function are used as the basis to define the random events on the real axis. This representation on the real axis obeys the same rules or is subject to the same constraints as the original events.

This function, or transformation X, must satisfy the following condition: let x be any real value, the set of all elementary events ω such that $\{X(\omega) \leq x\}$ is an event associated with the original random experiment

$$A = \{\omega \text{ such that } X(\omega) \leq x\}. \tag{2.1}$$

In mathematical terms, this function is said to be measurable.

Now, using this random variable, we only need to look at the universe of events as the real axis and the events as a subset of the real line. The most simple events are open or closed intervals and open or closed half axes. The constructed algebra of events based on these natural events is known as the Borel Algebra of the real axis. One simple way to describe the Borel Algebra of the real axis is to construct events by combining the simple open and closed intervals and open and closed half axis of the real axis. Since Borel Algebra is not really necessary to follow the text, we will not dwell on it further.

2.1.1 Cumulative Distribution Function

Let X be a real-valued random variable, by definition its cumulative distribution function, noted $F_X(x)$, is:

$$F_X(x) = \text{Prob}(A) \quad \text{where} \quad A = \{\omega \text{ such that } X(\omega) \leq x\}. \tag{2.2}$$

Based on the previous definition of probability, we deduce the following properties:

(a) $0 \leq F_X(x) \leq 1$,
(b) $F_X(x)$ is monotone, non decreasing, i.e., if $x_1 < x_2$ then we have $F_X(x_1) \leq F_X(x_2)$,
(c) $F_X(-\infty) = 0$ and $F_X(+\infty) = 1$.

Properties (a), (b) and (c) follow from the probability axioms. When $F_X(x)$ is continuous, X is said to be a continuous random variable. When it is the case, it can take any value on the real axis as the result of the experiment. However, when $F_X(x)$ is a step function, X is said to be a discrete random variable. X may be a combination of continuous and discrete segments.

2.1.2 Probability Density Function

To keep it simple, consider X to be a continuous random variable. By analogy with the physical world, we can define its probability density function such that the integral of such a function on the event defined on the real axis gives the probability of this event.

This density function can be obtained from the cumulative distribution function when looking at an infinitely small event. To see that, consider the event

$$A = \{x < X \leq x + \Delta x\}. \tag{2.3}$$

On the one hand, the cumulative function gives

$$\text{Prob}(A) = F_X(x + \Delta x) - F_X(x), \tag{2.4}$$

and on the other hand we have

$$\text{Prob}(A) = \int_x^{x+\Delta x} f_X(\alpha) d\alpha, \tag{2.5}$$

where f_X is the probability density function of the random variable X.

On the infinitesimal interval $[x, x + \Delta x]$, since $f_X(.)$ is continuous, it remains constant so that we have:

$$f_X(x)\Delta x \approx \text{Prob}(A) = F_X(x + \Delta x) - F_X(x), \tag{2.6}$$

where

$$f_X(x) \approx \frac{F_X(x+\Delta x) - F_X(x)}{\Delta x}. \tag{2.7}$$

When Δx becomes infinitesimal, we see that the probability density function is the derivative of the cumulative distribution function:

$$f_X(x) = \frac{dF_X(x)}{dx}. \tag{2.8}$$

Property 1.1 *Function $f_X(x)$ is non negative. Since integrating the density function on an event gives us the probability of the event, if it were negative on a particular interval, integrating on this interval would give us a negative probability. This would violate our probability axioms. This property can be proved easily since the probability density function is the derivative of the cumulative distribution function. This cumulative function being a non decreasing function, its derivative can never be negative.*

Property 1.2

$$F_X(x) = \int_{-\infty}^{x} f_X(\alpha)d\alpha \leq 1, \tag{2.9}$$

$$F_X(-\infty) = 0 \quad \textit{and} \quad F_X(+\infty) = 1, \tag{2.10}$$

which leads to

$$f_X(x) \underset{|x|\to\infty}{\longrightarrow} 0 \tag{2.11}$$

and

$$\int_{-\infty}^{+\infty} f_X(\alpha)d\alpha = 1. \tag{2.12}$$

For a discrete random variable X, since X takes values in a finite (or countably-infinite) set, we prefer to use the term probability mass function. The probability mass is the probability that X takes a precise value in this finite or countably-infinite set:

$$\text{Prob}(X = k). \tag{2.13}$$

We present below examples of widely used random variables.

Example 1.3 We toss a dice and the random variable is defined by the face which is shown on the dice. We define the random variable X taking the values 1, 2, 3, 4, 5, and 6. We have

$$\text{Prob}(X = k) = \frac{1}{6}, \quad \forall k \in \{1, 2, 3, 4, 5, 6\}. \tag{2.14}$$

Example 1.4 We discussed above the number of calls received at a telephone exchange. Let X be this random variable. Then X can be 0, 1, 2, . . ., ∞. This phenomenon follows a distribution known as the Poisson distribution and its probability density function is defined by

$$\text{Prob}(X = k) = e^{-\lambda}\frac{\lambda^k}{k!}, \tag{2.15}$$

with $k = 0, 1, 2, \ldots, \infty$, where λ is a positive constant depicting the average number of calls observed.

This distribution is often used in finance in credit risk modeling, especially to describe credit default. In that case X can be the number of defaults in a given period and λ is the average number of defaults.

Example 1.5 The most common probability density functions are

(i) The Gaussian normal distribution having the probability density function

$$f_X(x) = \frac{1}{\sqrt{2\pi}\sigma}\exp\left(-\frac{(x-\mu)^2}{2\sigma^2}\right), \tag{2.16}$$

where μ and σ are constants, σ being positive. We show in the next section that μ and σ are respectively the mean and standard deviation of the random variable X. This distribution is often used in finance to represent asset returns. It is also a key distribution in statistical inference. Figure 2.1 plots the probability density function for a variable following a normal distribution.

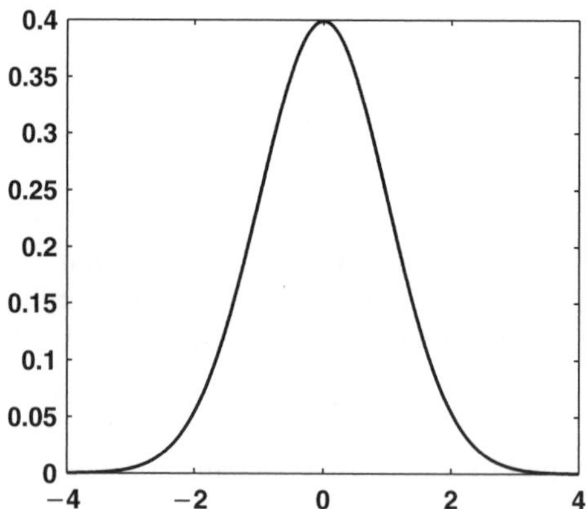

Figure 2.1 Gaussian density function

(ii) The exponential density:

$$f_X(x) = \alpha e^{-\alpha x}, \quad \forall x \in [0, +\infty], \tag{2.17}$$

where α is a positive constant. Figure 2.2 plots the probability density function for a variable following an exponential distribution.

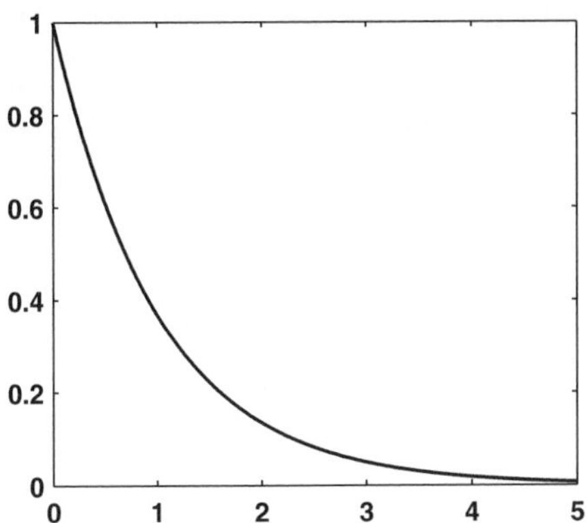

Figure 2.2 Exponential density function

(iii) The uniform density:

$$f_X(x) = \begin{cases} \dfrac{1}{b-a} & \text{for } a \leq x \leq b \\ 0 & \text{elsewhere} \end{cases}, \tag{2.18}$$

where a and b are constants with $b > a$. Figure 2.3 plots the probability density function for a variable following a uniform distribution.

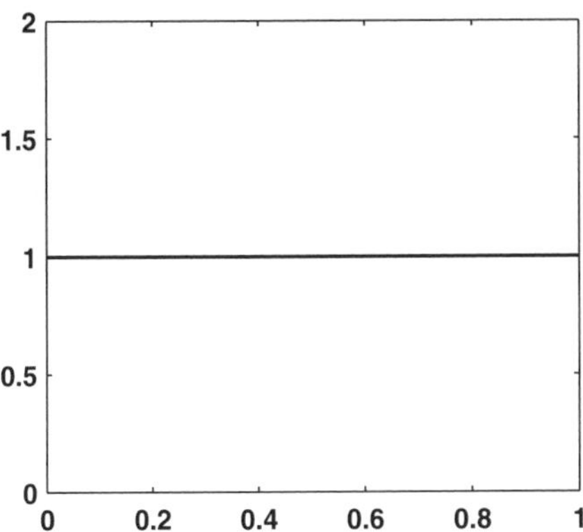

Figure 2.3 Uniform density function

Remark 1.6 Using the Dirac function δ defined by

$$\begin{aligned} &\delta(x) = 0 && x \neq 0; \\ &\int_{-\infty}^{+\infty} \delta(x)dx = 1 && \text{otherwise,} \end{aligned} \tag{2.19}$$

we can introduce the density function. For the purpose of this book, we prefer to straightforwardly introduce the probability masses fdx denoted by dF.

2.1.3 Mean, Variance and Higher Moments of a Random Variable

Physically, when we want to determine the average value of a random experiment, we repeat the experiment N times and we note the results x_i, $i \in \{1, 2, \ldots, N\}$.

Suppose that among the N experiments, x_i appears n_i times. The average value of the results is:

$$\overline{X} = \sum_{i=1}^{N} \left(\frac{n_i}{N}\right) x_i. \tag{2.20}$$

Intuitively, the quantity $\frac{n_i}{N}$ measures the probability of obtaining the result x_i. In this case, the experimental or empirical average is

$$\overline{X} = \sum_{i=1}^{N} x_i \text{Prob}\,(X = x_i)\,. \tag{2.21}$$

When N grows indefinitely, if X is a continuous random variable, the ratio $\frac{n_i}{N}$ goes to an infinitesimal quantity represented by $f_X(x_i)dx$ at point x_i.

This quantity with its physical interpretation is called statistical average and will be denoted

$$m_X = E\left[X\right] = \int_{-\infty}^{+\infty} x f_X(x) dx. \tag{2.22}$$

The notation $E[.]$ stands for the average value operator, commonly called mathematical expectation. This operator associated to an integral is linear, i.e.,

$$E\left[aX + bY\right] = aE\left[X\right] + bE\left[Y\right], \tag{2.23}$$

where a and b are two deterministic constants and X and Y are any two random variables.

If we now look at another random variable Y linked to the random variable X by the transformation $y = g(x)$, the average value of this new random variable Y is computed in making a large number N of experiments and denoting the results by x_i. Hence, the average value for Y is

$$\overline{Y} = \sum_{i=1}^{N} \frac{n_i}{N} y_i = \sum_{i=1}^{N} \frac{n_i}{N} g(x_i). \tag{2.24}$$

The relative frequency $\frac{n_i}{N}$, when N goes to infinity, corresponds to the probability of getting the result x_i. Thus we have:

$$m_Y = E\left[Y\right] = \int_{-\infty}^{+\infty} g(x) f_X(x) dx, \tag{2.25}$$

in particular when $Y = X^2$,

$$E\left[Y\right] = E\left[X^2\right] = \int_{-\infty}^{+\infty} x^2 f_X(x) dx \tag{2.26}$$

is by definition the second order moment of the random variable X.

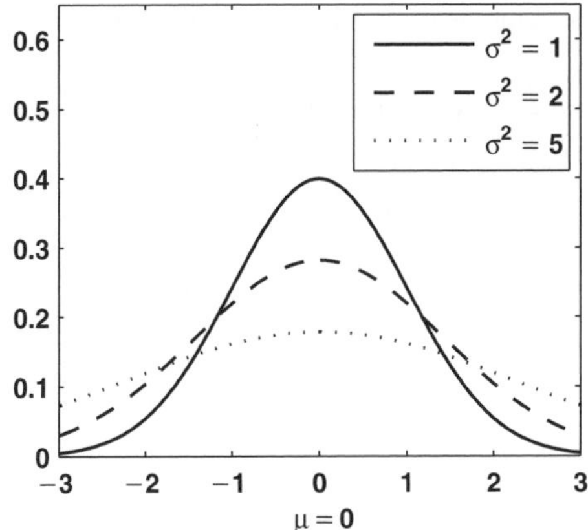

Figure 2.4 Three curves for the normal distribution with mean $\mu = 0$ and different σ

We can center the variable X around its average value by:

$$Y = X - E[X], \tag{2.27}$$

in this case $E[Y] = 0$ and

$$E\left[Y^2\right] = E\left[(X - E\left[X\right])^2\right] = E\left[X^2\right] - E\left[X\right]^2. \tag{2.28}$$

The second order moment of the centered variable Y is by definition the variance of the random variable X, frequently referred to as σ_X^2. Meanwhile, $\sigma_X = \sqrt{\sigma_X^2}$ is called the standard deviation of X.

Physically, σ_X measures the dispersion of the experiment's results around its average value. Figure 2.4 plots the probability density function of the Gaussian distribution for three different values of σ_X. When σ_X is small, the graph of the probability density function of X is a curve concentrated around its mean. When σ_X is large, this curve flattens and gets wider.

By the same means, we can introduce the moments of any order n:

$$\mathcal{M}_X^n = E\left[X^n\right] = \int_{-\infty}^{+\infty} x^n f_X(x)dx \tag{2.29}$$

and the order n centered moments

$$\mathcal{C}_X^n = E\left[(X - m_X)^n\right] = \int_{-\infty}^{+\infty} (x - m_X)^n f_X(x)dx. \tag{2.30}$$

Example 1.7 Let X be a Gaussian random variable with probability density function

$$f_X(x) = \frac{1}{\sqrt{2\pi}\sigma} e^{-\frac{(x-\mu)^2}{2\sigma^2}}, \quad \text{with} \quad \sigma > 0. \tag{2.31}$$

The mean value for X is:

$$m_X = E\left[X\right] = \int_{-\infty}^{+\infty} x f_X(x)dx = \frac{1}{\sqrt{2\pi}\sigma} \int_{-\infty}^{+\infty} x e^{-\frac{(x-\mu)^2}{2\sigma^2}} dx. \tag{2.32}$$

To compute this value, we change our variable such that: $u = x - \mu$, which implies

$$\begin{aligned}
E[X] &= \frac{1}{\sqrt{2\pi}\sigma}\int_{-\infty}^{+\infty}(u+\mu)e^{-\frac{u^2}{2\sigma^2}}du \\
&= \frac{1}{\sqrt{2\pi}\sigma}\int_{-\infty}^{+\infty}ue^{-\frac{u^2}{2\sigma^2}}du + \frac{1}{\sqrt{2\pi}\sigma}\int_{-\infty}^{+\infty}\mu e^{-\frac{u^2}{2\sigma^2}}du.
\end{aligned} \tag{2.33}$$

To evaluate these integrals, we define the Gamma function:

$$\Gamma(x) = \int_0^{+\infty} z^{x-1}e^{-z}dz, \quad \forall x > 0. \tag{2.34}$$

We can easily show that

$$\Gamma(x+1) = x\Gamma(x),$$

$$\Gamma(k+1) = k!,$$

and

$$\Gamma\left(\frac{1}{2}\right) = \sqrt{\pi}.$$

The Gamma function is widely used in statistics. With the properties of the Gamma function, the previous integrals can be computed by letting: $\frac{u^2}{2\sigma^2} = v$, $udu = \sigma^2 dv$, $du = \frac{\sigma dv}{\sqrt{2v}}$. This way, the first integral is zero and the second is equal to:

$$\frac{2\mu}{\sqrt{2\pi}\sigma}\int_0^{+\infty} e^{-\frac{u^2}{2\sigma^2}}du = \mu. \tag{2.35}$$

It follows $m_X = E[X] = \mu$.

Now we want to evaluate

$$\sigma_X^2 = E\left[(X - m_X)^2\right] = \int_{-\infty}^{+\infty}(x-\mu)^2 e^{-\frac{(x-\mu)^2}{2\sigma^2}}\frac{dx}{\sqrt{2\pi}\sigma}. \tag{2.36}$$

By the same changes of variables, we get

$$\begin{aligned}
\sigma_X^2 &= E\left[(X - m_X)^2\right] \\
&= \frac{2}{\sqrt{2\pi}\sigma}\int_0^{+\infty} u^2 e^{-\frac{u^2}{2\sigma^2}}du \\
&= \frac{2\sigma}{\sqrt{2\pi}\sigma\sqrt{2}}2\sigma^2\int_0^{+\infty} v^{\frac{3}{2}-1}e^{-v}dv \\
&= \frac{2\sigma^2}{\sqrt{\pi}}\int_0^{+\infty} v^{\frac{3}{2}-1}e^{-v}dv \\
&= \frac{2\sigma^2}{\sqrt{\pi}}\Gamma\left(\frac{3}{2}\right) \\
&= \frac{2\sigma^2}{\sqrt{\pi}}\frac{1}{2}\Gamma\left(\frac{1}{2}\right) \\
&= \sigma^2.
\end{aligned} \tag{2.37}$$

The Gaussian random variable is completely characterized by its mean m_X and its variance σ_X^2 since the higher moments can be expressed as a function of these first two moments. This is shown in the next section. Thus, the probability density function of a Gaussian variable is

$$f_X(x) = \frac{1}{\sqrt{2\pi}\sigma_X} e^{-\frac{(x-m_X)^2}{2\sigma_X^2}}. \tag{2.38}$$

Example 1.8 Let X be a Poisson random variable with parameter λ. It means that X takes non negative integer values with probability:

$$\text{Prob}(X = k) = e^{-\lambda}\frac{\lambda^k}{k!}, \quad \forall k = 0, 1, 2, \ldots, \infty. \tag{2.39}$$

Using the physical definition already introduced, the mean value of X is defined by the expression:

$$E[X] \equiv \sum_{k=0}^{\infty} k\text{Prob}(X = k) = \sum_{k=0}^{\infty} ke^{-\lambda}\frac{\lambda^k}{k!}. \tag{2.40}$$

To compute this value, we use the following simple and useful technique. Let

$$h(x) = \sum_{k=0}^{\infty} a_k x^k, \tag{2.41}$$

in their convergence domain, we get:

$$h'(x) = \frac{dh(x)}{dx} = \sum_{k=0}^{\infty} ka_k x^{k-1} = \frac{1}{x}\sum_{k=0}^{\infty} ka_k x^k, \tag{2.42}$$

thus

$$\sum_{k=0}^{\infty}(ka_k)x^k = xh'(x). \tag{2.43}$$

Using the same calculations we obtain:

$$\sum_{k=0}^{\infty} k^2 a_k x^k = x\frac{d}{dx}(xh'(x)). \tag{2.44}$$

Now we apply this technique to the Poisson distribution. From

$$\sum_{k=0}^{\infty}\frac{\lambda^k}{k!} = e^{\lambda}, \tag{2.45}$$

one gets

$$\sum_{k=0}^{\infty} k\frac{\lambda^k}{k!} = \lambda\frac{d}{d\lambda}(e^{\lambda}) = \lambda e^{\lambda}. \tag{2.46}$$

Then

$$m_X = E[X] = e^{-\lambda}\lambda e^{\lambda} = \lambda. \tag{2.47}$$

The second order moment becomes:

$$\begin{aligned} E\left[X^2\right] &= \sum_{k=0}^{\infty} k^2 \text{Prob}(X = k) \\ &= \sum_{k=0}^{\infty} k^2 e^{-\lambda} \frac{\lambda^k}{k!} \\ &= e^{-\lambda}\lambda \frac{d}{d\lambda}(\lambda e^{\lambda}) \\ &= e^{-\lambda}\lambda\left[\lambda e^{\lambda} + e^{\lambda}\right] \\ &= \lambda(\lambda + 1). \end{aligned} \tag{2.48}$$

Which implies

$$\begin{aligned} \sigma_X^2 &= E\left[X^2\right] - m_X^2 \\ &= \lambda(\lambda + 1) - \lambda^2 \\ &= \lambda. \end{aligned} \tag{2.49}$$

It is interesting to note that the mean and the variance of a Poisson variable are equal.

In the following two examples, we will study the binomial variable derived from an intuitive approach.

Example 1.9 Let X be a binary variable such that:

$$\text{Prob}(X = 1) = p \quad \text{and} \quad \text{Prob}(X = 0) = 1 - p. \tag{2.50}$$

Then its mean is

$$m_X = p \times 1 + (1 - p) \times 0 = p \tag{2.51}$$

and its second order moment is

$$\mathcal{M}_X^2 = p \times 1^2 + (1 - p) \times 0^2 = p. \tag{2.52}$$

Its variance becomes:

$$\begin{aligned} \sigma_X^2 &= \mathcal{M}_X^2 - (m_X)^2 \\ &= p - p^2 \\ &= p(1 - p). \end{aligned} \tag{2.53}$$

Example 1.10 Y is a binomial random variable defined by

$$Y = \sum_{i=1}^{N} X_i, \tag{2.54}$$

where X_i are independent binary variables. It follows that Y takes its values in the finite set $\{0, 1, \ldots, N\}$ with probability:

$$\text{Prob}(Y = k) = \binom{N}{k} p^k (1-p)^{N-k}. \tag{2.55}$$

Its mean is:

$$\begin{aligned} m_Y &= E[Y] \\ &= \sum_{k=0}^{N} k\text{Prob}(Y = k) \\ &= \sum_{k=0}^{N} k \binom{N}{k} p^k (1-p)^{N-k} \\ &= Np. \end{aligned} \tag{2.56}$$

Similarly, its second order moment is:

$$\begin{aligned} \mathcal{M}_Y^2 &= E[Y^2] \\ &= \sum_{k=0}^{N} k^2\text{Prob}(Y = k) \\ &= \sum_{k=0}^{N} k^2 \binom{N}{k} p^k (1-p)^{N-k} \\ &= Np(1 + (N-1)p). \end{aligned} \tag{2.57}$$

Hence, its variance is:

$$\begin{aligned} \sigma_Y^2 &= E\left[Y^2\right] - m_Y^2 \\ &= \mathcal{M}_Y^2 - m_Y^2 \\ &= Np(1-p). \end{aligned} \tag{2.58}$$

2.1.4 Characteristic Function of a Random Variable

Let X be a random variable with density function $f_X(x)$. The characteristic function of X is, by definition, the Fourier transform of its probability density function, i.e.:

$$\phi_X(w) = E\left[e^{iwX}\right] = \int_{-\infty}^{+\infty} e^{iwx} f_X(x)dx. \tag{2.59}$$

The characteristic function is an important analytical tool which enables us to analyze the sum of independent random variables. Moreover, this function contains all information specific to the random variable X.

Taking the Taylor series of the characteristic function, we get:

$$\phi_X(w) = \int_{-\infty}^{+\infty} \left[\sum_{k=0}^{\infty} \frac{(iw)^k}{k!} x^k f_X(x) dx \right] \tag{2.60}$$

and switching the integral with the summation, we have:

$$\phi_X(w) = \sum_{k=0}^{+\infty} \frac{(iw)^k}{k!} \int_{-\infty}^{+\infty} x^k f_X(x) dx = \sum_{k=0}^{+\infty} \frac{(iw)^k}{k!} \mathcal{M}_X^k. \tag{2.61}$$

This characteristic function contains all the moments of X, so we can easily deduce that:

$$\mathcal{M}_X^k = E\left[X^k\right] = \left[\frac{1}{i^k} \frac{d^k \phi_X(w)}{dw^k} \right]_{w=0}. \tag{2.62}$$

Example 2.11 From a Gaussian random variable with the probability density function

$$f_X(x) = \frac{1}{\sqrt{2\pi}\sigma} e^{-\frac{x^2}{2\sigma^2}}, \tag{2.63}$$

we can prove that its characteristic function is:

$$\phi_X(w) = e^{-\frac{\sigma^2}{2} w^2}. \tag{2.64}$$

Developing in power series the characteristic function, we obtain:

$$\phi_X(w) = \sum_{k=0}^{\infty} \left(\frac{\sigma^2}{2} \right)^k \frac{(-w^2)^k}{k!} = \sum_{k=0}^{\infty} \left(\frac{\sigma}{\sqrt{2}} \right)^{2k} \frac{(2k)!}{k!} \frac{(iw)^{2k}}{(2k)!}. \tag{2.65}$$

By doing a term by term identification, we observe that the odd order moments are all equal to zero and the even order moments are given by:

$$\mathcal{M}_X^{2k} = \frac{(2k)!}{k!} \left(\frac{\sigma^2}{2} \right)^k. \tag{2.66}$$

Example 2.12 For the case of a Poisson random variable with parameter λ, the probability mass is:

$$\text{Prob}(X = k) = e^{-\lambda} \frac{\lambda^k}{k!}, \quad k = 0, 1, 2, \ldots. \tag{2.67}$$

Its characteristic function is:

$$\begin{aligned}\phi_X(w) &= E\left[e^{iwX}\right] \\ &= \sum_{k=0}^{+\infty} e^{iwk}\text{Prob}(X = k) \\ &= e^{-\lambda}\sum_{k=0}^{+\infty}(e^{iw})^k \frac{\lambda^k}{k!} \\ &= e^{-\lambda}e^{\lambda e^{iw}}. \end{aligned} \tag{2.68}$$

Using the Taylor series of the first and second order, we find the mean and the variance as follows. From the expression,

$$\frac{d\phi_X(w)}{dw} = e^{-\lambda}e^{\lambda e^{iw}}\frac{d}{dw}(\lambda e^{iw}) = i\lambda e^{iw}e^{-\lambda}e^{\lambda e^{iw}}, \tag{2.69}$$

we obtain

$$m_X = \mathcal{M}_X^1 = \left[\frac{1}{i}\frac{d\phi_X(w)}{dw}\right]_{w=0} = \lambda. \tag{2.70}$$

And from the expression

$$\begin{aligned}\frac{d^2\phi_X(w)}{dw^2} &= e^{-\lambda}e^{\lambda e^{iw}}\frac{d}{dw}(\lambda e^{iw})\frac{d}{dw}(\lambda e^{iw}) + e^{-\lambda}e^{\lambda e^{iw}}\frac{d^2}{dw^2}(\lambda e^{iw}) \\ &= e^{-\lambda}e^{\lambda e^{iw}}\left\{\left[i\lambda e^{iw}\right]^2 + i^2\lambda e^{iw}\right\},\end{aligned}$$

we find

$$\mathcal{M}_X^2 = \left[\frac{1}{i^2}\frac{d^2\phi_X(w)}{dw^2}\right]_{w=0} = \lambda^2 + \lambda. \tag{2.71}$$

This result is identical to the one we have already obtained.

2.2 RANDOM VECTORS

So far, the concepts we introduced on random variables can be generalized to the multi-dimensional case. For simplicity, we focus on random vectors of two dimensions; formulas for the case of n dimensions can be obtained using a similar procedure.

We built a random variable by making an application of the random experiment to the real axis using a mapping from universe Ω (set of all possible events) on the real axis. This mapping defines a random variable if it is measurable. This allows us to construct the algebra of all possible events on the real axis.

Now, if we look at a mapping of universe Ω into the Euclidian space $\mathbb{R}^n$, and if this mapping is measurable, we will be able to define a random vector of dimension n.

This measurable mapping enables us to transform events in Ω into events in $\mathbb{R}^n$. That way, instead of studying probabilities in Ω, we study the probabilities of events defined in $\mathbb{R}^n$. As we have already discussed in the one dimension case, events in $\mathbb{R}^n$ are simply the Borel events of the $\mathbb{R}^n$ space.

2.2.1 Cumulative Distribution Function of a Random Vector

Let X be a two-dimensional random vector: $X = (X_1, X_2)$. The joint cumulative distribution function of the random variables X_1 and X_2, also called the cumulative distribution function of the random vector X, is given by:

$$F_{X_1,X_2}(x_1, x_2) = \text{Prob}(\{X_1 \leq x_1 \quad \text{and} \quad X_2 \leq x_2\}). \tag{2.72}$$

This probability is equal to the probability of event A with

$$A = \{w \quad \text{such that} \quad X_1(w) \leq x_1 \quad \text{and} \quad X_2(w) \leq x_2\}. \tag{2.73}$$

To simplify the notation, we often use $F_{\underline{X}}(\underline{x})$ instead of

$$F_{X_1,X_2}(x_1, x_2). \tag{2.74}$$

Directly from the probability axioms, we find that this joint cumulative distribution function has the following properties:

1. $0 \leq F_{X_1,X_2}(x_1, x_2) \leq 1$,
2. $F_{X_1,X_2}(+\infty, +\infty) = 1$,
3. $F_{X_1,X_2}(x_1, -\infty) = 0$ and $F_{X_1,X_2}(-\infty, x_2) = 0$,
4. if $x_1 \leq x_1'$ and $x_2 \leq x_2'$ then

$$F_{X_1,X_2}(x_1', x_2') + F_{X_1,X_2}(x_1, x_2)$$
$$-F_{X_1,X_2}(x_1, x_2') - F_{X_1,X_2}(x_1', x_2) \geq 0.$$

2.2.2 Probability Density Function of a Random Vector

As with the case of a single random variable, in the vector case, we can build a function called the joint probability density function of the variables X_1 and X_2 such that when integrated on an event E of $\mathbb{R}^2$ we obtain the probability of this event:

$$\text{Prob}(E) = \int\int_E f_{X_1,X_2}(x_1, x_2) dx_1 dx_2. \tag{2.75}$$

The function $f_{X_1,X_2}(x_1, x_2)$ is called probability density function because when integrated on an infinitesimal interval $E = \{x_1 < X_1 \leq x_1 + dx_1$ and $x_2 < X_2 \leq x_2 + dx_2\}$, we have:

$$\begin{aligned} \int\int_E f_{X_1,X_2}(x_1, x_2) dx_1 dx_2 &= F_{X_1,X_2}(x_1, x_2) dx_1 dx_2 \\ &= \text{Prob}(\{x_1 < X_1 \leq x_1 + dx_1 \\ &\qquad \text{and}\, x_2 < X_2 \leq x_2 + dx_2\}). \end{aligned} \tag{2.76}$$

This construction allows us to say that:

$$f_{X_1,X_2}(x_1, x_2) = \frac{\partial^2 F_{X_1,X_2}(x_1, x_2)}{\partial x_1 \partial x_2}. \tag{2.77}$$

The simplest way to obtain this relation is to consider the repartition function defined by:

$$F_{X_1,X_2}(x_1, x_2) = \int_{-\infty}^{x_2} \int_{-\infty}^{x_1} f_{X_1,X_2}(u, v)dudv. \tag{2.78}$$

Computing the derivative of this expression on both sides, we find the required result.

When the random variables X_1 and X_2 are discrete, we prefer to use the term probability mass:

$$\text{Prob}(X_1 = x_1 \quad \text{and} \quad X_2 = x_2), \tag{2.79}$$

where x_1 and x_2 are discrete values taken by X_1 and X_2.

2.2.3 Marginal Distribution of a Random Vector

Let (X, Y) be a random vector having the joint cumulative distribution function $F_{X,Y}(x, y)$. If we are only interested in one of the two variables, for example X, we can define its cumulative distribution function $F_X(x)$. This function is the marginal cumulative distribution function of X. We can deduce it from the joint cumulative distribution function $F_{X,Y}(x, y)$. In fact

$$\text{Prob}(X \leq x) = \text{Prob}(X \leq x \quad \text{and} \quad Y \leq +\infty). \tag{2.80}$$

This gives

$$F_X(x) = F_{X,Y}(x, +\infty). \tag{2.81}$$

The marginal probability density function of X is given by the derivative of the marginal cumulative distribution function:

$$f_X(x) = \frac{d}{dx} F_X(x). \tag{2.82}$$

Since

$$F_{X,Y}(x, y) = \int_{-\infty}^{x} \int_{-\infty}^{y} f_{X,Y}(u, v)dudv, \tag{2.83}$$

then

$$F_X(x) = F_{X,Y}(x, +\infty) = \int_{-\infty}^{x} \int_{-\infty}^{+\infty} f_{X,Y}(u, v)dudv. \tag{2.84}$$

Implying

$$f_X(x) = \frac{d}{dx} F_{X,Y}(x, +\infty), \tag{2.85}$$

from which

$$f_X(x) = \int_{-\infty}^{+\infty} f_{X,Y}(x, v)dv. \tag{2.86}$$

For practical purposes, in order to eliminate a variable, all we need is to integrate the function from $-\infty$ to $+\infty$ with respect to the variable in question to obtain the marginal density.

Example 2.1 Consider a Gaussian random vector with probability density function:

$$f_{X,Y}(x,y) = \frac{1}{2\pi\sqrt{1-\rho^2}\sigma_X\sigma_Y} \times e^{\frac{-1}{2(1-\rho^2)}\left\{\frac{(x-m_X)^2}{\sigma_X^2}+\frac{(y-m_Y)^2}{\sigma_Y^2}-\frac{2\rho}{\sigma_X\sigma_Y}(x-m_X)(y-m_Y)\right\}}. \tag{2.87}$$

This function represents the joint probability density function of two Gaussian random variables X, Y. The parameters m_X, m_Y, σ_X^2 and σ_Y^2 represent the means and variances of the two random variables X and Y respectively. ρ is known as the linear correlation between them; we will come back to this concept of dependence later.

The marginal probability density function of X is obtained as follows:

$$f_X(x) = \int_{-\infty}^{+\infty} f_{X,Y}(x,y)dy. \tag{2.88}$$

All we need is to integrate the joint probability density function from $-\infty$ to $+\infty$ with respect to Y. After integrating, we get the marginal density of X:

$$f_X(x) = \frac{1}{\sqrt{2\pi}\sigma_X} e^{-\frac{(x-m_X)^2}{2\sigma_X^2}}. \tag{2.89}$$

This means that the marginal density of X is Gaussian with mean m_X and variance σ_X^2.

2.2.4 Conditional Distribution of a Random Vector

For this section, we need to remember that the conditional probability of events is:

$$\text{Prob}(A|B) = \frac{\text{Prob}(A \cap B)}{\text{Prob}(B)}. \tag{2.90}$$

More generally, if A represents the event $A = \{X \leq x\}$, then

$$\text{Prob}(A|B) = \text{Prob}(\{X \leq x\}|B) = F_X(x|B). \tag{2.91}$$

Hence, the cumulative distribution function of a random vector X conditional to event B is by definition the probability:

$$\frac{\text{Prob}(\{X \leq x\} \cap B)}{\text{Prob}(B)}. \tag{2.92}$$

This general definition allows us to construct the following distributions. For the case where $B = \{Y = y\}$, we will get an indetermination since if Y is continuous, we have $\text{Prob}(Y = y) = 0$. However, this indetermination can be removed when considering the following event B:

$$B = \{y < Y \leq y + dy\}. \tag{2.93}$$

With this definition, the probability of B is infinitesimal. When dy tends toward 0, we find the result we were looking for. It means that

$$F_X(x|B) = \frac{\text{Prob}(\{X \leq x\} \cap \{y < Y \leq y + dy\})}{\text{Prob}(\{y < Y \leq y + dy\})}. \tag{2.94}$$

Under the hypothesis that Y is continuous, the probability of the infinitesimal event is proportional to the infinitesimal interval:

$$\begin{aligned} F_X(x|B) &= \frac{\text{Prob}(\{X \leq x\} \cap \{Y \leq y + dy\}) - \text{Prob}(\{X \leq x\} \cap \{Y \leq y\})}{f_Y(y)dy} \\ &= \frac{F_{X,Y}(x, y + dy) - F_{X,Y}(x, y)}{f_Y(y)dy}. \end{aligned} \tag{2.95}$$

This gives us

$$F_X(x|B) = \frac{\left[\frac{\partial}{\partial y} F_{X,Y}(x, y)\right] dy}{f_Y(y)dy} = \frac{\frac{\partial}{\partial y} F_{X,Y}(x, y)}{f_Y(y)}. \tag{2.96}$$

The conditional probability density function becomes

$$f_X(x|y) = \frac{\partial}{\partial x} F(x|y) = \frac{\partial}{\partial x}\left[\frac{\frac{\partial}{\partial y} F_{X,Y}(x, y)}{f_Y(y)}\right], \tag{2.97}$$

so

$$f_X(x|y) = \frac{\frac{\partial}{\partial x}\frac{\partial}{\partial y} F_{X,Y}(x, y)}{f_Y(y)} = \frac{f_{X,Y}(x, y)}{f_Y(y)}. \tag{2.98}$$

Thus, the law governing the conditional probabilities is similar to Bayes' rule.

For the case where the conditional probability density function $f_X(x|y)$ is equal to X's marginal density, $f_X(x)$, it means that Y's realization doesn't affect X's statistics. Then we say that X and Y are two independent random variables. Thus, for two independent random variables, their joint probability density function is given by the product of their respective marginal densities:

$$f_{X,Y}(x, y) = f_X(x) f_Y(y). \tag{2.99}$$

Example 2.2 (a) Taking the Gaussian vector example (X, Y). The joint density is

$$\begin{aligned} f_{X,Y}(x, y) = &\frac{1}{2\pi\sqrt{1-\rho^2}\sigma_X\sigma_Y} \\ &\times e^{\frac{-1}{2(1-\rho^2)}\left\{\frac{(x-m_X)^2}{\sigma_X^2} + \frac{(y-m_Y)^2}{\sigma_Y^2} - \frac{2\rho}{\sigma_X\sigma_Y}(x-m_X)(y-m_Y)\right\}}. \end{aligned} \tag{2.100}$$

The marginal density of Y is

$$f_Y(y) = \frac{1}{\sqrt{2\pi}\sigma_Y} e^{-\frac{(y-m_Y)^2}{2\sigma_Y^2}}. \tag{2.101}$$

It follows that X's conditional density with respect to Y is

$$f_X(x|y) = \frac{f_{X,Y}(x,y)}{f_Y(y)} = \frac{1}{\sqrt{2\pi}\sqrt{1-\rho^2}\sigma_X} e^{\frac{-1}{2(1-\rho^2)\sigma_X^2}\left\{x-m_X-\frac{2\rho\sigma_X}{\sigma_Y}(y-m_Y)\right\}^2}. \tag{2.102}$$

It is interesting to note that this conditional density corresponds to a Gaussian random variable's probability density function with mean given by

$$m_X + \frac{2\rho\sigma_X}{\sigma_Y}(y - m_Y) \tag{2.103}$$

and variance

$$\left(1-\rho^2\right)\sigma_X^2. \tag{2.104}$$

This means the average value of X conditional to Y depends on the value of Y.

(b) Let's now consider two independent random Gaussian variables X and Y with means m_X and m_Y respectively and variances σ_X^2 and σ_Y^2 respectively, then the joint density is

$$f_{X,Y}(x,y) = \frac{1}{2\pi\sigma_X\sigma_Y} e^{-\frac{1}{2}\left\{\frac{(x-m_X)^2}{\sigma_X^2}+\frac{(y-m_Y)^2}{\sigma_Y^2}\right\}} = f_X(x)f_Y(y). \tag{2.105}$$

As we can note from this joint density function, the independence of the two random Gaussian variables corresponds to $\rho = 0$.

2.2.5 Mean, Variance and Higher Moments of a Random Vector

As in the case of the scalar random variable, we can define the mean and the variance of joint random vectors and the moments of higher order as:

$$E[X] = m_X = \int_{-\infty}^{+\infty} x f_X(x)dx = \int_{-\infty}^{+\infty}\int_{-\infty}^{+\infty} x f_{X,Y}(x,y)dxdy. \tag{2.106}$$

$$E\left[X^2\right] = \int_{-\infty}^{+\infty} x^2 f_X(x)dx = \int_{-\infty}^{+\infty}\int_{-\infty}^{+\infty} x^2 f_{X,Y}(x,y)dxdy. \tag{2.107}$$

$$\sigma_X^2 = E\left[X^2\right] - m_X^2$$
$$= \int_{-\infty}^{+\infty}\int_{-\infty}^{+\infty} (x - m_X)^2 f_{X,Y}(x, y)dxdy. \tag{2.108}$$

We can also define the same quantities for Y.

In a general fashion we define X's nth order moment noted $\mathcal{M}_X^n$ by:

$$E\left[X^n\right] = \int_{-\infty}^{+\infty} x^n f_X(x)dx$$
$$= \int_{-\infty}^{+\infty}\int_{-\infty}^{+\infty} x^n f_{X,Y}(x, y)dxdy. \tag{2.109}$$

Similarly, the joint moments of order n, m of X and Y are:

$$\mathcal{M}_{X,Y}^{n,m} \triangleq E\left[X^n Y^m\right]$$
$$= \int_{-\infty}^{+\infty}\int_{-\infty}^{+\infty} x^n y^m f_{X,Y}(x, y)dxdy; \tag{2.110}$$

and the centered order n, m moments

$$\mathcal{C}_{X,Y}^{n,m} \triangleq E\left[(X - m_X)^n (Y - m_Y)^m\right]$$
$$= \int_{-\infty}^{+\infty}\int_{-\infty}^{+\infty} (x - m_X)^n (y - m_Y)^m f_{X,Y}(x, y)dxdy. \tag{2.111}$$

Among the centered moments, the most important one is $\mathcal{C}_{X,Y}^{1,1}$ called the covariance between X and Y. The matrix

$$\Lambda = \begin{bmatrix} \mathcal{C}_{X,X}^{1,1} & \mathcal{C}_{X,Y}^{1,1} \\ \mathcal{C}_{Y,X}^{1,1} & \mathcal{C}_{Y,Y}^{1,1} \end{bmatrix} \tag{2.112}$$

is called the variance-covariance matrix of the (X, Y) vector. This matrix can be explicitly expressed by:

$$\Lambda = E\left[\begin{pmatrix} X - m_X \\ Y - m_Y \end{pmatrix} \begin{pmatrix} X - m_X & Y - m_Y \end{pmatrix}\right]. \tag{2.113}$$

Appendix A provides an introduction to matrix algebra for those unfamiliar with it. The correlation coefficient between two variables X and Y is by definition:

$$\rho \triangleq \frac{E\left[(X - m_X)(Y - m_Y)\right]}{\sigma_X \sigma_Y} = \frac{\mathcal{C}_{X,Y}^{1,1}}{\sigma_X \sigma_Y}. \tag{2.114}$$

We write $\underline{X} = (X_1, \ldots, X_n)^\top$ to be the n dimension random vector. Since the random vector $\underline{X}$'s dimension is n, the covariance matrix's dimension is (n, n) and is defined:

$$\Lambda = E\left[(\underline{X} - \underline{m}_{\underline{X}})(\underline{X} - \underline{m}_{\underline{X}})^\top\right], \tag{2.115}$$

with $\underline{m}_{\underline{X}} = E\left[\underline{X}\right] = \left(m_{X_1}, \ldots, m_{X_n}\right)^\top$ the mean of vector $\underline{X}$.

Example 2.3 For the Gaussian vector having as density function

$$f_{X,Y}(x,y) = \frac{1}{2\pi\sqrt{1-\rho^2}\sigma_X\sigma_Y} \times e^{\frac{-1}{2(1-\rho^2)}\left\{\frac{(x-m_X)^2}{\sigma_X^2}+\frac{(y-m_Y)^2}{\sigma_Y^2}-\frac{2\rho}{\sigma_X\sigma_Y}(x-m_X)(y-m_Y)\right\}}, \tag{2.116}$$

the covariance between X and Y, $E[(X-m_X)(Y-m_Y)]$, is defined by:

$$\frac{1}{2\pi\sqrt{1-\rho^2}\sigma_X\sigma_Y}\int_{-\infty}^{+\infty}\int_{-\infty}^{+\infty}(x-m_X)(y-m_Y) \times e^{\frac{-1}{2(1-\rho^2)}\left\{\frac{(x-m_X)^2}{\sigma_X^2}+\frac{(y-m_Y)^2}{\sigma_Y^2}-\frac{2\rho}{\sigma_X\sigma_Y}(x-m_X)(y-m_Y)\right\}}dxdy. \tag{2.117}$$

The evaluation of this expression gives:

$$E\left[(X-m_X)(Y-m_Y)\right] = \rho\sigma_X\sigma_Y. \tag{2.118}$$

Thus, (X, Y)'s joint probability density parameter ρ is the correlation coefficient of X and Y.

The Gaussian vector (X, Y)'s variance-covariance matrix is:

$$\Lambda = \begin{bmatrix} \sigma_X^2 & \rho\sigma_X\sigma_Y \\ \rho\sigma_X\sigma_Y & \sigma_Y^2 \end{bmatrix}, \tag{2.119}$$

its determinant is:

$$|\Lambda| = \sigma_X^2\sigma_Y^2(1-\rho^2), \tag{2.120}$$

and its inverse is:

$$\Lambda^{-1} = \frac{1}{(1-\rho^2)\sigma_X^2\sigma_Y^2}\begin{bmatrix} \sigma_Y^2 & -\rho\sigma_X\sigma_Y \\ -\rho\sigma_X\sigma_Y & \sigma_X^2 \end{bmatrix}. \tag{2.121}$$

The joint density of variables X and Y can be written more compactly as:

$$f_{X,Y}(x,y) = \frac{1}{2\pi\,|\Lambda|^{\frac{1}{2}}}e^{-\frac{1}{2}\left[(X-m_X,Y-m_Y)\Lambda^{-1}\begin{pmatrix}X-m_X\\Y-m_Y\end{pmatrix}\right]}. \tag{2.122}$$

Generally, a n dimension random vector is said to be Gaussian if its joint probability density function takes the form:

$$f_{\underline{X}}(\underline{x}) = \frac{1}{(2\pi)^{\frac{n}{2}}\,|\Lambda|^{\frac{1}{2}}}e^{\frac{-1}{2}\left[\left(\underline{x}-\underline{m}_X\right)^{\top}\Lambda^{-1}(\underline{x}-\underline{m}_X)\right]}, \tag{2.123}$$

where $\underline{X} = (X_1,\ldots,X_n)^{\top}$, $\underline{m}_X = E\left[\underline{X}\right] = \left(m_{X_1},\ldots,m_{X_n}\right)^{\top}$ and Λ is the variance-covariance matrix of $\underline{X}$.

This density contains the inverse of Λ, and is only defined if Λ is a matrix of full rank. If Λ is singular, it means that at least one component of $\underline{X}$ is a linear combination of the other components.

2.2.6 Characteristic Function of a Random Vector

Let (X, Y) be a 2 dimensional random vector with probability density function $f_{X,Y}$. The joint characteristic function of vector (X, Y) denoted by $\phi_{X,Y}(w_1, w_2)$ is defined by the Fourier transform in 2 dimensions of the vector (X, Y) and can be written as:

$$\phi_{X,Y}(w_1, w_2) = \int_{-\infty}^{+\infty}\int_{-\infty}^{+\infty} e^{i(xw_1+yw_2)} f_{X,Y}(x, y)dxdy. \tag{2.124}$$

It is very important to note that when X and Y are two independent random variables, we have

$$f_{X,Y}(x, y) = f_X(x)f_Y(y). \tag{2.125}$$

Which implies:

$$\phi_{X,Y}(w_1, w_2) = \phi_X(w_1)\phi_Y(w_2). \tag{2.126}$$

This relation can be generalized for the case of random vectors with dimension greater than 2 as we show below.

As in the case of a scalar, we can use the characteristic function to obtain all moments of all order of variables X and Y as follows

$$E\left[X^nY^m\right] = \frac{1}{i^{n+m}}\frac{\partial^{n+m}\phi_{X,Y}(w_1, w_2)}{\partial w_1^n \partial w_2^m}\Big|_{w_1=w_2=0}. \tag{2.127}$$

In the more general case of a n dimensional random vector $\underline{X}$ having probability density function $f_{\underline{X}}(\underline{x})$, its characteristic function $\phi_{\underline{X}}$ is:

$$\begin{aligned}\phi_{\underline{X}}(\underline{w}) &= E\left[e^{i\underline{w}^{\top}\underline{X}}\right]\\ &\triangleq \int\int\cdots\int_{\mathbb{R}^n} f_{X_1X_2\ldots X_n}(x_1x_2\ldots x_n)\\ &\quad\times e^{i(w_1x_1+w_2x_2+\ldots+w_nx_n)}dx_1dx_2\ldots dx_n.\end{aligned} \tag{2.128}$$

In the case of independent vectors, we have:

$$\begin{aligned}\phi_{\underline{X}}(\underline{w}) &= \int\int\cdots\int_{\mathbb{R}^n} f_{X_1}(x_1)f_{X_2}(x_2)\ldots f_{X_n}(x_n)\\ &\quad\times e^{i(w_1x_1+w_2x_2+\ldots+w_nx_n)}dx_1dx_2\ldots dx_n\\ &= \int_{\mathbb{R}} f_{X_1}(x_1)e^{iw_1x_1}dx_1 \int_{\mathbb{R}} f_{X_2}(x_2)e^{iw_2x_2}dx_2\ldots\\ &\quad\times \int_{\mathbb{R}} f_{X_n}(x_n)e^{iw_nx_n}dx_n\\ &= \prod_{k=1}^{n}\int_{\mathbb{R}} f_{X_k}(x_k)e^{iw_kx_k}dx_k.\end{aligned} \tag{2.129}$$

Then, for all independent n dimensional random vector $\underline{X}$, one has:

$$\phi_{\underline{X}}(\underline{w}) = \prod_{k=1}^{n}\phi_{X_k}(w_k).$$

Example 2.4 Let $\underline{X}$ be a Gaussian random vector with density:

$$f_{\underline{X}}(\underline{x}) = \frac{1}{(2\pi)^{\frac{n}{2}}|\Lambda|^{\frac{1}{2}}} e^{-\frac{1}{2}(\underline{x}-\underline{m})^{\top}\Lambda^{-1}(\underline{x}-\underline{m})}, \tag{2.130}$$

where Λ is the variance-covariance matrix of $\underline{X}$, with

$$\Lambda = (\lambda_{kj})_{k,j} \tag{2.131}$$

and

$$\lambda_{kj} = E[(X_k - m_k)(X_j - m_j)]. \tag{2.132}$$

Thus the joint characteristic function of $\underline{X}$ is:

$$\phi_{\underline{X}}(\underline{w}) = e^{i\underline{m}^{\top}\underline{w}} e^{-\frac{1}{2}\underline{w}^{\top}\Lambda\underline{w}}. \tag{2.133}$$

2.3 TRANSFORMATION OF RANDOM VARIABLES

Let X be a random variable with probability density function $f_X(x)$. Let's consider the random variable Y obtained from the transformation $Y = g(X)$. We would like to find the probability density function of $f_Y(y)$ in terms of $f_X(x)$ and $g(X)$. In order to achieve this, we look at the event

$$A = \{y < Y \leq y + dy\}. \tag{2.134}$$

If Y is a continuous random variable, one has:

$$\text{Prob}(A) = f_Y(y)dy. \tag{2.135}$$

Let B be the inverse image of A, defined as $B = g^{-1}(A)$. It is given by:

$$\begin{aligned} B = \{&(x_1 < X \leq x_1 + |dx_1|) \cup (x_2 < X \leq x_2 + |dx_2|) \cup \ldots \\ &\cup (x_n < X \leq x_n + |dx_n|)\}. \end{aligned} \tag{2.136}$$

Thus we have

$$\text{Prob}(B) = \sum_{k=1}^{n} f_X(x_k)\,|dx_k|. \tag{2.137}$$

Since A and B must have the same probability, Prob(A) = Prob(B), one finds:

$$f_Y(y)dy = \sum_{k=1}^{n} f_X(x_k)\,|dx_k|, \tag{2.138}$$

which implies

$$\begin{aligned} f_Y(y) &= \sum_{k=1}^{n} f_X(x_k) \left|\frac{dx_k}{dy}\right| \\ &= \sum_{k=1}^{n} \frac{f_X(x_k)}{\left|\frac{dy}{dx}\right|_{x=x_k}}, \end{aligned} \tag{2.139}$$

x_k's being the solutions of $y = g(x)$, $x_k = g^{-1}(y)$, $k = 1, 2, \ldots, n$. This simple relation is very useful for the simulation of random variables on a computer.

Example 3.1 Affine transformation of a uniform variable.

Let

$$f_X(x) = \begin{cases} \frac{1}{b-a} & a \leq x \leq b \\ 0 & \text{elsewhere} \end{cases} \tag{2.140}$$

be the density function of a uniform random variable X. If we set $y = \alpha x + \beta$, then $x = \frac{y-\beta}{\alpha}$. For this transformation, only one solution to the equation $y = g(x)$ obtains or $x = g^{-1}(y)$ exists. The probability density function of variable Y is

$$\begin{aligned} f_Y(y) &= \frac{f_X(x)}{\left|\frac{dy}{dx}\right|} \\ &= \frac{f_X(\frac{y-\beta}{\alpha})}{|\alpha|} \\ &= \begin{cases} \frac{1}{|\alpha|(b-a)} & \alpha a + \beta \leq y \leq \alpha b + \beta \\ 0 & \text{elsewhere.} \end{cases} \end{aligned} \tag{2.141}$$

One can see that an affine transformation of a uniform random variable gives rise to another uniform random variable.

Example 3.2 Affine transformation of a Gaussian variable

Let X be a Gaussian random variable with probability density function

$$f_X(x) = \frac{1}{\sqrt{2\pi}\sigma_X} e^{-\frac{(x-m_X)^2}{2\sigma_X^2}}. \tag{2.142}$$

Let $y = \alpha x + \beta$, then $x = \frac{y-\beta}{\alpha}$. The probability density function of Y is

$$\begin{aligned} f_Y(y) &= \frac{f_X(x)}{\left|\frac{dy}{dx}\right|} \\ &= \frac{f_X(\frac{y-\beta}{\alpha})}{|\alpha|} \\ &= \frac{1}{\sqrt{2\pi}\,|\alpha|\,\sigma_X} e^{-\frac{(y-\beta-\alpha m_X)^2}{2\alpha^2\sigma_X^2}}. \end{aligned} \tag{2.143}$$

The affine transformation transforms a Gaussian random variable into a new Gaussian random variable whose mean and variance can be easily computed:

$$E[Y] = m_Y = \alpha m_X + \beta \quad \text{and} \quad \sigma_Y^2 = \alpha^2 \sigma_X^2. \tag{2.144}$$

Example 3.3 Log-normal distribution

Let a Gaussian random variable X have the probability density function

$$f_X(x) = \frac{1}{\sqrt{2\pi}\sigma} e^{-\frac{(x-m)^2}{2\sigma^2}}. \tag{2.145}$$

The transformed variable Y from X given by the equation $y = e^x = g(x)$ has a unique solution $x = \log(y)$. The probability density function of Y is given by

$$\begin{aligned} f_Y(y) &= \frac{f_X(x)}{\left|\frac{dy}{dx}\right|} \\ &= \frac{f_X(x)}{e^x} = \frac{f_X(\log(y))}{y} \\ &= \frac{1}{y}\frac{1}{\sqrt{2\pi}\sigma} e^{-\frac{(\log(y)-m)^2}{2\sigma^2}}. \end{aligned} \tag{2.146}$$

This probability density function of the log-normal law is very useful in finance and we will explore it later.

Example 3.4 Let X be a random variable of uniform density:

$$f_X(x) = \begin{cases} \frac{1}{2\pi} & 0 \le x \le 2\pi \\ 0 & \text{elsewhere.} \end{cases} \tag{2.147}$$

Consider the modified variable Y from the variable X: $y = \sin(x)$. This transformation forces $|y| \le 1$, which means that $f_Y(y) = 0$ for $|y| > 1$. The equation $y = \sin(x)$ has two solutions for $0 \le y \le 1$:

$$x_1 = \arcsin(y) \quad \text{and} \quad x_2 = \pi - \arcsin(y), \tag{2.148}$$

and for negative y, $(-1 \le y \le 0)$,

$$x_1 = \pi - \arcsin(y) \quad \text{and} \quad x_2 = 2\pi + \arcsin(y). \tag{2.149}$$

The $\arcsin(y)$ function is a function taking values only in the interval $\left[-\frac{\pi}{2}, \frac{\pi}{2}\right]$. Thus for $0 \le y \le 1$,

$$f_Y(y) = \frac{f_X(x_1)}{\left|\frac{dy}{dx}\right|_{x=x_1}} + \frac{f_X(x_2)}{\left|\frac{dy}{dx}\right|_{x=x_2}}, \tag{2.150}$$

with

$$\left|\frac{dy}{dx}\right| = |\cos(x)| = \sqrt{1-\sin(x)^2} = \sqrt{1-y^2}. \tag{2.151}$$

Since this derivative is independent of the points x_1 and x_2, then

$$\begin{aligned} f_Y(y) &= \frac{\frac{1}{2\pi}}{\sqrt{1-y^2}} + \frac{\frac{1}{2\pi}}{\sqrt{1-y^2}} \\ &= \frac{1}{\pi\sqrt{1-y^2}}. \end{aligned} \tag{2.152}$$

Example 3.5 Let X be a continuous random variable having probability density function $f_X(x)$ and cumulative distribution function $F_X(x)$. Then

$$f_X(x) = \frac{d}{dx} F_X(x). \tag{2.153}$$

Let's consider a new random variable Y defined by the transformation $y = F_X(x)$. This transformation restricts y to the interval [0, 1]. Then the probability density function for Y is given by:

$$f_Y(y) = \frac{f_X(x)}{\left|\frac{dy}{dx}\right|} \tag{2.154}$$

and since

$$\frac{dy}{dx} = \frac{dF_X(x)}{dx} = f_X(x), \tag{2.155}$$

it follows:

$$f_Y(y) = \begin{cases} 1 & 0 \le y \le 1 \\ 0 & \text{elsewhere.} \end{cases} \tag{2.156}$$

This formula is interesting since it can be used to generate random variables.

Example 3.6

(i) Let X be a random variable uniformly distributed between 0 and 1. We seek to determine the transformation $Y = g(X)$, i.e.,

$$x = g^{-1}(y) \tag{2.157}$$

such that the new random variable Y has the probability density function $f_Y(y)$. From the last example's result, we will study the mapping $y = F_y^{-1}(x)$ where $F_Y(y)$ is the distribution function of Y and $F_y^{-1}(x)$ is the inverse function of F_Y. Thus, the probability density function of Y is given by:

$$f_Y(y) = \frac{f_X(x)}{\left|\frac{dy}{dx}\right|}. \tag{2.158}$$

Then we have

$$y = F_Y^{-1}(x) \Longrightarrow \frac{dy}{dx} = \frac{dF_Y^{-1}(x)}{dx}. \tag{2.159}$$

Finally, this density is equal to $\left|\frac{dx}{dy}\right|$ with $x = F_Y(y)$ where

$$\frac{dx}{dy} = f_Y(y). \tag{2.160}$$

(ii) Application: Let X be a random variable uniformly distributed on the interval [0, 1]. Find $y = g(x)$ such that Y has probability density function $\alpha e^{-\alpha y} 1_{\{y \ge 0\}}$. The cumulative distribution function of Y is

$$F_Y(y) = \int_0^y \alpha e^{-\alpha x} dx = (1 - e^{-\alpha y})1_{\{y \geq 0\}}. \tag{2.161}$$

Then, $y = F_Y^{-1}(x)$ with $x = F_Y(y) = (1 - e^{-\alpha y})1_{\{y \geq 0\}}$. Finally, we have

$$y = -\frac{1}{\alpha}\log(1 - x). \tag{2.162}$$

2.4 TRANSFORMATION OF RANDOM VECTORS

Let (X, Y) be a random vector with density $f_{X,Y}(x, y)$. Consider the mappings $V = g(x, y)$ and $W = h(x, y)$. Let's define the event

$$A = \{(v < V \leq v + dv) \cap (w < W \leq w + dw)\} \tag{2.163}$$

and B be the inverse image of A defined by:

$$B = \left\{ \begin{array}{c} \{(x_1 < X \leq x_1 + |dx_1|) \cap (y_1 < Y \leq y_1 + |dy_1|)\} \ldots \\ \cup \ldots \cup \{(x_n < X \leq x_n + |dx_n|) \cap (y_n < Y \leq y_n + |dy_n|)\} \end{array} \right\}. \tag{2.164}$$

Since A and B have the same probability of occurring, we conclude:

$$f_{V,W}(v, w)dvdw = \sum_k f_{X,Y}(x_k, y_k)\,|dx_k dy_k|\,. \tag{2.165}$$

This implies:

$$f_{V,W}(v, w) = \sum_k f_{X,Y}(x_k, y_k)\frac{1}{\left|\frac{dvdw}{dxdy}\right|_{x=x_k, y=y_k}}, \tag{2.166}$$

where $\frac{dvdw}{dxdy}$ is the Jacobian of the coordinates' mapping defined by:

$$\mathcal{J} = \begin{bmatrix} \frac{\partial v}{\partial x} & \frac{\partial v}{\partial y} \\ \frac{\partial w}{\partial x} & \frac{\partial w}{\partial y} \end{bmatrix} = \begin{bmatrix} \frac{\partial g}{\partial x} & \frac{\partial g}{\partial y} \\ \frac{\partial h}{\partial x} & \frac{\partial h}{\partial y} \end{bmatrix}. \tag{2.167}$$

Let the n dimensional random vector $\underline{X} = (X_1, \ldots, X_n)^\top$ have the density function $f_{\underline{X}}(\underline{x})$. Denote $\underline{Y}$ as the new random vector obtained from $\underline{X}$ by the transformation

$$\underline{Y} = \underline{g}(\underline{X}), \tag{2.168}$$

with

$$Y_k = g_k(\underline{X}) = g_k(X_1, X_2, \ldots, X_n), \quad k = 1, 2, \ldots, n. \tag{2.169}$$

Suppose that $\underline{Y} = \underline{g}(\underline{X})$ has an inverse image composed of m vectors $\underline{x}^1, \underline{x}^2, \ldots, \underline{x}^m$, that is

$$\underline{y} = \underline{g}(\underline{x}^i), \quad i = 1, 2, \ldots, m, \tag{2.170}$$

where the m vectors $\underline{x}^i$, $\quad i = 1, 2, \ldots, m$, transform into the same vector $\underline{y}$.

Let $\mathcal{J}$ be the Jacobian of the transformation defined by

$$\mathcal{J}(\underline{x}) = \begin{bmatrix} \frac{\partial y_1}{\partial x_1} & \cdots & \frac{\partial y_1}{\partial x_n} \\ \vdots & . & \vdots \\ \frac{\partial y_n}{\partial x_1} & \cdots & \frac{\partial y_n}{\partial x_n} \end{bmatrix}. \tag{2.171}$$

The joint density function of $\underline{Y}$ is given by:

$$f_{\underline{Y}}(\underline{y}) = \sum_{i=1}^{m} \frac{f_{\underline{X}}(\underline{x}^i)}{|\mathcal{J}(\underline{x}^i)|}. \tag{2.172}$$

Example 4.1 Affine transformation of a Gaussian vector

Consider the Gaussian random vector $\underline{X}$ with mean $m_{\underline{X}}$ and covariance matrix $\Lambda_{\underline{X}}$, denoted by $N(m_{\underline{X}}, \Lambda_{\underline{X}})$. Set $\underline{Y} = \Sigma \underline{X} + \mu$, where Σ is a matrix with appropriate dimensions. Then the affine transformation changes the Gaussian vector $\underline{X}$ into a new Gaussian random vector $\underline{Y}$ with mean and variance-covariance matrix given by

$$E\left[\underline{Y}\right] = m_{\underline{Y}} = \Sigma m_{\underline{X}} + \mu \tag{2.173}$$

and

$$\Lambda_{\underline{Y}} = \Sigma \Lambda_{\underline{X}} \Sigma^{\top}. \tag{2.174}$$

Example 4.2

(i) Let (X, Y) be an independent Gaussian random vector with the probability density function:

$$f_{X,Y}(x, y) = \frac{1}{2\pi\sigma^2} e^{-\frac{x^2+y^2}{2\sigma^2}}. \tag{2.175}$$

Set $V = \sqrt{X^2 + Y^2}$ and $W = \arctan(\frac{Y}{X})$. If we restrict W to $[0, 2\pi]$, this transformation forces V to be non negative and the inverse image consists only of one element:

$$X = V\cos(W) \quad \text{and} \quad Y = V\sin(W). \tag{2.176}$$

Then the density is

$$f_{V,W}(v, w) = f_{X,Y}(x, y)\,|\mathcal{J}| \quad \text{where} \quad \mathcal{J} = \begin{bmatrix} \frac{\partial x}{\partial v} & \frac{\partial x}{\partial w} \\ \frac{\partial y}{\partial v} & \frac{\partial y}{\partial w} \end{bmatrix}. \tag{2.177}$$

The determinant of $\mathcal{J}$ is

$$|\mathcal{J}| = \begin{vmatrix} \cos(w) & -v\sin(w) \\ \sin(w) & v\cos(w) \end{vmatrix} = v. \tag{2.178}$$

Which implies

$$f_{V,W}(v, w) = \frac{1}{2\pi\sigma^2} e^{-\frac{v^2}{2\sigma^2}} v 1_{\{v \geq 0\}}. \tag{2.179}$$

This joint density of V and W is interesting since we recognize that:

$$f_V(v) = \int_0^{2\pi} f_{V,W}(v, w) dw = \frac{v}{\sigma^2} e^{-\frac{v^2}{2\sigma^2}} 1_{\{v \geq 0\}}. \tag{2.180}$$

Which allows us to write:

$$f_{V,W}(v, w) = f_V(v) f_W(w), \tag{2.181}$$

where

$$f_W(w) = \begin{cases} \frac{1}{2\pi} & 0 < w < 2\pi \\ 0 & \text{elsewhere} \end{cases}. \tag{2.182}$$

This implies that V and W are two independent random variables. The random variable V is called a Rayleigh variable.

(ii) Also from the random variables V and W, we could reconstruct the independent Gaussian random vector (X, Y) as follows:

$$X = V \cos(W) \text{ and}$$
$$Y = V \sin(W). \tag{2.183}$$

2.5 APPROXIMATION OF THE STANDARD NORMAL CUMULATIVE DISTRIBUTION FUNCTION

In the rest of the book, we frequently use the Gaussian cumulative distribution function. This function is usually denoted by $N(.)$. There is no exact formula to compute the Gaussian normal cumulative distribution function $N(.)$. Tables of values of $N(x)$ are available in most statistical or mathematical books.

However, it is important to be able to compute values of $N(x)$ in algorithms without having to refer to a statistics table. For this, we will give an approximation of the exact value of $N(x)$ which is accurate up to six decimals.

$$N(x) \approx 1 - n(x)(a_1 k + a_2 k^2 + a_3 k^3 + a_4 k^4 + a_5 k^5) \quad \text{if } x \geq 0, \tag{2.184}$$

and

$$N(x) = 1 - N(-x) \quad \text{if } x \leq 0, \tag{2.185}$$

where

$$k = \frac{1}{1 + \gamma x},$$
$$\gamma = 0.2316419,$$
$$a_1 = 0.319381530,$$
$$a_2 = -0.356563782,$$
$$a_3 = 1.781477937,$$
$$a_4 = -1.821255978,$$
$$a_5 = 1.330274429,$$

and the probability density function is

$$\begin{aligned} n(x) &= N'(x) \\ &= \frac{\partial N(x)}{\partial x} \\ &= \frac{1}{\sqrt{2\pi}} e^{-x^2/2}. \end{aligned} \tag{2.186}$$

For example, with the MATLAB® software, $N(x)$ can be computed using the function: *normcdf*.

```
DistNormCum=normcdf(x);
```

Appendix B contains a list of commonly used functions in MATLAB.

Notes and Complementary Readings

For further readings on the topics covered in this chapter, the reader can consult the following books: Ross (2002 a and b), Hogg and Craig (1995), Wackerly, Mendenhall and Scheaffer (1996) among others.

3

Random Sequences

The preceding chapter has enabled us to describe and characterize random variables. However, many real phenomena, and particularly those encountered in finance, can be modeled by a sequence of random variables. This means that we need an asymptotic characterization of these random sequences in order to deduce their properties. These properties will be useful in many cases as we shall see.

Convergence and limit concepts studied in this chapter will be useful when we have to characterize the precision, convergence and control of simulation techniques presented later.

To construct the probability of events, we resort to the notion of relative frequency obtained by realizing a large number of random experiments and counting the number of outcomes. This repetition of experiments implies the use of a large number of random variables. We will study a very important property in statistics theory that will be useful later.

3.1 SUM OF INDEPENDENT RANDOM VARIABLES

Definition 1.1 $\{X_k\}_{k=1,2,\ldots,\infty}$ *is called a sequence of independent and identically distributed random variables if all the variables X_k have the same probability density function and any arbitrary number of these variables form an independent random vector.*

Let $\{X_k\}_{k=1,\ldots,\infty}$ be a sequence of independent and identically distributed random variables. One can construct the following series:

$$S_n = \sum_{k=1}^{n} X_k \tag{3.1}$$

and

$$M_n = \frac{1}{n} \sum_{k=1}^{n} X_k. \tag{3.2}$$

M_n is the normalized sum of the X_k's and is often called the arithmetic mean of these n variables. Their means are easy to calculate:

$$\begin{aligned} E\left[S_n\right] &= E\left[\sum_{k=1}^{n} X_k\right] \\ &= \sum_{k=1}^{n} E\left[X_k\right] \\ &= n m_X \end{aligned} \tag{3.3}$$

and

$$E[M_n] = \frac{1}{n}E[S_n]$$
$$= m_X, \tag{3.4}$$

where m_X is the shared mean of all the X_k variables.

The variance of S_n is

$$\text{Var}[S_n] = E\left[S_n^2\right] - E[S_n]^2 \tag{3.5}$$

where

$$E[S_n]^2 = n^2 m_X^2. \tag{3.6}$$

Then we need to compute $E[S_n^2]$ as follows:

$$\begin{aligned} E\left[S_n^2\right] &= E\left[\sum_{k=1}^{n}\sum_{j=1}^{n} X_k X_j\right] \\ &= E\left[\sum_{k=1}^{n} X_k^2\right] + E\left[\sum_{k\neq j} X_k X_j\right] \\ &= \sum_{k=1}^{n} E\left[X_k^2\right] + \sum_{k\neq j} E\left[X_k X_j\right]. \end{aligned} \tag{3.7}$$

Since X_k and X_j are independent when $k \neq j$, we have:

$$E[X_k X_j] = E[X_k]E[X_j], \tag{3.8}$$

thus

$$\begin{aligned} E\left[S_n^2\right] &= \sum_{k=1}^{n} E\left[X_k^2\right] + \sum_{k\neq j} m_X^2 \\ &= nE\left[X^2\right] + (n^2 - n)m_X^2. \end{aligned} \tag{3.9}$$

Which implies

$$\begin{aligned} \text{Var}[S_n] &= nE\left[X^2\right] + (n^2 - n)m_X^2 - n^2 m_X^2 \\ &= n\left[E\left[X^2\right] - m_X^2\right] \\ &= n\sigma_X^2, \end{aligned} \tag{3.10}$$

where σ_X^2 is the variance of the random variables X_k. This result is well known since the variance of a sum of independent random variables is equal to the sum of their variances.

To obtain the variance of M_n, we note that $M_n = \frac{1}{n}S_n$, then

$$\begin{aligned} \text{Var}[M_n] &= \frac{1}{n^2}\text{Var}[S_n] \\ &= \frac{\sigma_X^2}{n}. \end{aligned} \tag{3.11}$$

3.2 LAW OF LARGE NUMBERS

Previously, we have intuitively studied the relative frequency that a given event occurs. We expect that when the number of experiments becomes very large, this relative frequency should converge to the event's probability. In reality, this relation is obtained from the law of large numbers regardless of the studied distribution. In fact, we have the weak and strong law of large numbers. The weak one is as follows.

Let $\{X_k\}_{k=1,\ldots,\infty}$ be a sequence of independent and identically distributed random variables and $M_n = \frac{1}{n}\sum_{k=1}^{n} X_k$ the arithmetic mean having finite mean and variance. We already found the mean and variance of M_n: $E[M_n] = m_X$ and $\text{Var}\,[M_n] = \frac{\sigma_X^2}{n}$.

Definition 2.1 ***Chebychev inequality****: Let X be a random variable with expected value μ and finite variance σ^2, then for any positive number k, we have*

$$\text{Prob}\,(|X-\mu| \geq k) \leq \frac{\sigma^2}{k^2} \tag{3.12}$$

or equivalently

$$\text{Prob}\,(|X-\mu| \geq k\sigma) \leq \frac{1}{k^2}. \tag{3.13}$$

On the one hand, applying this above Chebychev's inequality, we have:

$$\text{Prob}\,(|M_n - m_X| \geq \varepsilon) \leq \frac{\sigma_X^2}{n\varepsilon^2} \tag{3.14}$$

or more precisely

$$\text{Prob}\,(|M_n - m_X| \leq \varepsilon) \geq 1 - \frac{\sigma_X^2}{n\varepsilon^2}. \tag{3.15}$$

This inequality means that, for any ε, we have:

$$\lim_{n \longrightarrow \infty} \text{Prob}\,(|M_n - m_X| \leq \varepsilon) = 1. \tag{3.16}$$

This is exactly the formulation of the *weak law of large numbers*. It tells us that when the number of experiments tends toward infinity, the empirical mean converges in probability to the mathematical expectation.

The fact that this empirical mean converges to its expected value regardless of the distribution law of the X_k's shows us that our intuition about the relative frequency was right. This result allows us to compute the expected value of the mathematical expectation using the empirical mean estimated on a very large number of experiments.

On the other hand, the second formulation of the law of large numbers is more complicated to prove but confirms that it is proper to use the mean in more complex situations. The *strong law of large numbers* states that

$$\text{Prob}\left(\lim_{n \longrightarrow \infty} M_n = m_X\right) = 1. \tag{3.17}$$

We refer to the Chebychev's inequality to gauge the mathematical expectation estimate precision when using the arithmetic mean. Effectively, we can rewrite this relation as:

$$\text{Prob}\left(|M_n - m_X| \leq \varepsilon\sigma_X\right) \geq 1 - \frac{1}{n\varepsilon^2}, \tag{3.18}$$

ε is called the relative precision and $1 - \frac{1}{n\varepsilon^2}$ is called the confidence interval.

Then, to get a precision of 1% with a 95% confidence, we must choose n such that:

$$1 - \frac{1}{n\varepsilon^2} = 1 - \frac{1}{n(0.01)^2} \simeq 0.95 \tag{3.19}$$

or

$$n = \frac{1}{0.05(0.01)^2} = 200000. \tag{3.20}$$

This number seems relatively high with respect to the desired precision. This phenomenon is caused by the fact that the Chebychev's inequality has been established for all laws of probability, which means that the bound is relatively large.

In the following section, we will look at an approach that allows us to decrease the required number of simulations.

3.3 CENTRAL LIMIT THEOREM

The physical observations due to the superposition of a large number of effects can be characterized as having a distribution with a bell shape (Gaussian). This theorem has been well established since the beginning of the 20th century.

Let $\{X_k\}_{k=1,\ldots,\infty}$ be a sequence of independent and identically distributed random variables, with finite mean m_X and variance σ_X^2. Consider the variable:

$$\begin{aligned} Z_n &= \frac{1}{\sqrt{n}\sigma_X}\left[\sum_{k=1}^{n}(X_k - m_X)\right] \\ &= \frac{1}{\sqrt{n}\sigma_X}\left[\left(\sum_{k=1}^{n} X_k\right) - nm_X\right], \end{aligned} \tag{3.21}$$

it immediately follows that the mean of Z_n is zero and its variance is one:

$$E[Z_n] = 0 \quad \text{and} \quad \text{Var}[Z_n] = 1. \tag{3.22}$$

Theorem 3.1 *The central limit theorem states that when n approaches infinity, this random variable Z_n converges towards a Gaussian distribution with zero mean and unit variance.*

Proof: The proof of this theorem uses the characteristic function. An heuristic approach of the proof is as follows.

Let

$$\phi_X(w) = E\left[e^{iwX}\right] \tag{3.23}$$

and

$$\phi_{Z_n}(w) = E\left[e^{iwZ_n}\right]$$
$$= E\left[e^{iw\sum_{k=1}^{n}\left(\frac{X_k - m_X}{\sqrt{n}\sigma_X}\right)}\right]. \tag{3.24}$$

Since the random variables X_k are independent, it follows:

$$\phi_{Z_n}(w) = E\left[e^{iw\left(\frac{X_1 - m_X}{\sqrt{n}\sigma_X}\right)}\right] \times \ldots \times E\left[e^{iw\left(\frac{X_n - m_X}{\sqrt{n}\sigma_X}\right)}\right]$$
$$= \left\{E\left[e^{iw\left(\frac{X - m_X}{\sqrt{n}\sigma_X}\right)}\right]\right\}^n. \tag{3.25}$$

The Taylor series development gives:

$$E\left[e^{iw\left(\frac{X - m_X}{\sqrt{n}\sigma_X}\right)}\right] = E\Big[1 + i\frac{w}{\sqrt{n}\sigma_X}(X - m_X) - \frac{w^2}{2n\sigma_X^2}(X - m_X)^2$$
$$+ o\left(\frac{1}{n\sqrt{n}}\right)\Big]. \tag{3.26}$$

Finally,

$$\phi_{Z_n}(w) = \left(1 - \frac{w^2}{2n} + o\left(\frac{1}{n\sqrt{n}}\right)\right)^n. \tag{3.27}$$

When n approaches infinity,

$$\phi_{Z_n}(w) \simeq \left(1 - \frac{w^2}{2n}\right)^n \simeq e^{-\frac{w^2}{2}}. \tag{3.28}$$

This result allows us to deduce that Z_n is a Gaussian random variable with zero mean and unit variance.

This theorem allows us to improve the number of experiments n in the estimation of the mathematical expectation by the arithmetic mean. To achieve this, we use the probabilistic inequality:

$$\text{Prob}\,(a < Z_n < b) \simeq \frac{1}{\sqrt{2\pi}} \int_a^b e^{-\frac{z^2}{2}}\,dz. \tag{3.29}$$

In practice when n gets larger than 30, we could consider Z_n to be Gaussian.

Indeed, we want to compute the necessary number of experiments to obtain $\varepsilon = 1\%$ as relatively precise with a $1 - \alpha = 95\%$ confidence level. We know that

$$M_n - m_X = \frac{1}{n}\sum_{k=1}^{n}(X_k - m_X)$$
$$= \frac{\sigma_X}{\sqrt{n}}\frac{1}{\sqrt{n}\sigma_X}\sum_{k=1}^{n}(X_k - m_X), \tag{3.30}$$

thus

$$M_n - m_X = \frac{\sigma_X}{\sqrt{n}} Z_n. \tag{3.31}$$

From Chebychev's inequality, we have

$$\text{Prob}\left(|M_n - m_X| < \varepsilon\sigma_X\right) \geq 1 - \frac{1}{n\varepsilon^2} = 1 - \alpha, \tag{3.32}$$

and

$$\begin{aligned}\text{Prob}\left(-\varepsilon\sigma_X < \frac{\sigma_X}{\sqrt{n}} Z_n < \varepsilon\sigma_X\right) &= \text{Prob}\left(-\varepsilon\sqrt{n} < Z_n < \varepsilon\sqrt{n}\right)\\ &\simeq \frac{1}{\sqrt{2\pi}} \int_{-\varepsilon\sqrt{n}}^{\varepsilon\sqrt{n}} e^{-\frac{z^2}{2}} dz\\ &= \frac{2\sqrt{2}}{\sqrt{2\pi}} \int_0^{\varepsilon\sqrt{\frac{n}{2}}} e^{-\frac{u^2}{2}} du.\end{aligned} \tag{3.33}$$

Thus

$$\begin{aligned}\text{Prob}\left(-\varepsilon\sqrt{n} < Z_n < -\varepsilon\sqrt{n}\right) &= \text{erf}\left(\varepsilon\sqrt{\frac{n}{2}}\right)\\ &= 1 - \alpha,\end{aligned} \tag{3.34}$$

where

$$\text{erf}(x) = \frac{2\sqrt{2}}{\sqrt{2\pi}} \int_0^x e^{-\frac{u^2}{2}} du = \frac{2}{\sqrt{\pi}} \int_0^x e^{-\frac{u^2}{2}} du, \tag{3.35}$$

which implies

$$n = \frac{2}{\varepsilon^2}\left[\text{erf}^{-1}(1-\alpha)\right]^2. \tag{3.36}$$

3.4 CONVERGENCE OF SEQUENCES OF RANDOM VARIABLES

Until now we have studied a sequence of independent random variables having exactly the same distribution. In this context, we looked at a particular variable corresponding to M_n. If we study the sequence of these random variables M_n, we see that they are no longer independent and do not have the same distribution. However, we see that they converge in a particular direction given by the laws of large numbers and the central limit theorem. It is therefore important to introduce other convergence concepts pertaining to random variables.

3.4.1 Sure Convergence

Remember that a random variable is a function resulting from an application of the set of events (universe Ω) into a set of the real axis. Consider the sequence of random variables defined on the same space of events Ω.

For an elementary event w of Ω, $X_n(w)$ is a deterministic numerical sequence. Suppose that this sequence converges to a value $X(w)$ when n goes to infinity,

$$\lim_{n \longrightarrow \infty} X_n(w) = X(w), \tag{3.37}$$

X can be random or not.

The sequence X_n is said to *surely converge* if the sequence $X_n(w)$ converges for all w in Ω. We can verify this convergence using the Cauchy criterion for all elements w in Ω. Intuitively, the Cauchy criterion states that when an infinite sequence converges, it converges to a finite limit.

3.4.2 Almost Sure Convergence

Generally, sure convergence is hard to obtain. It is possible that the sequence $X_n(w)$ converges only for certain values w belonging to a subset A; this means that for all w belonging to subset A, $X_n(w)$ converges to $X(w)$.

We say that the sequence of random variables X_n almost surely converges to X if Prob$(A) = 1$. In this situation, there exists a subset for which the sequence X_n does not converge. However, the probability of this event is zero, and thus physically not interesting. We can verify an almost sure convergence with the Cauchy criterion for all sequences $X_n(w)$ with w belonging to A.

3.4.3 Convergence in Probability

As we saw in the case of the weak law of large numbers, we say that a sequence of random variables converges in probability, if there exists a random variable X such that:

$$\lim_{n \longrightarrow \infty} \text{Prob}\left(|X_n - X| > \varepsilon\right) = 0, \quad \forall \varepsilon > 0. \tag{3.38}$$

3.4.4 Convergence in Quadratic Mean

This mode of convergence concerns only the second order moments. We say that a sequence of random variables converges to X in quadratic mean or in mean square if there exists a random variable X of finite second order moment such that:

$$\lim_{n \longrightarrow \infty} E[|X_n - X|^2] = 0. \tag{3.39}$$

This concept of convergence in mean square can be generalized to any order. In the case of the first order moment, we say that the sequence of random variables X_n *strongly* converges or converges in mean to X if:

$$\lim_{n \longrightarrow \infty} E[|X_n - X|] = 0. \tag{3.40}$$

However, sometimes we are only interested by the distribution of the random variables X_n. In this case we say that the sequence X_n converges in *distribution* to a random variable X when:

$$\lim_{n \longrightarrow \infty} F_{X_n}(x) = F_X(x). \tag{3.41}$$

In this case the moments of X_n converge to the moments of X.

If we are interested in a function of X_n, the sequence of random variables X_n *weakly* converges to X if

$$\lim_{n \longrightarrow \infty} E\left[g(X_n)\right] = E\left[g(X)\right]. \tag{3.42}$$

These two modes of convergence, strong and weak, are very important in Monte Carlo simulations. Indeed, we can use the strong or weak mode following the objective of the financial problem studied. For example, if we are interested in the average value of a financial asset at a given date, we could replace a complex distribution f_n by another distribution f providing that X converges to the desired value with respect to $g(X)$.

Notes and Complementary Readings

Further readings can be found in the following books: Ross (2002 a and b), Hogg and Craig (1995), Wackerly, Mendenhall and Scheaffer (1996).

4

Introduction to Computer Simulation of Random Variables

In finance, as in many other areas of social and human sciences, it is often very difficult or even impossible to find an analytical solution for most of the problems we have to solve. This is the case with the evaluation of complex and interdependent financial products. However, there are many numerical techniques available to evaluate these products. One of the techniques that we present in this book is the computer based simulation method. From its inherent nature, this method offers a wide flexibility, especially when evaluating financial products dependent on many state variables.

How can a computer generate random events, since if it executes a given algorithm knowing the initial result, we should be able to guess the results at the outset? In fact, results generated on a computer are not conceptually random but, from the point of view of an observer, behave like random ones.

These results occur with a statistical regularity as discussed in the previous chapters. The regularity associated with the results generated by a computer can be explained as follows: if the algorithm generated by a computer is chaotic then it will produce unpredictable results for an observer. Thus, to build a dynamically chaotic algorithm is sufficient to generate random events.

The previous chapters showed how to obtain random variables for which we know the distribution function from a uniform random variable. The problem of generating random variables on computer is the same as generating a uniform random variable.

In order to generate a uniform random variable without resorting to a complex chaotic dynamic, all we need to do is to build an algorithm such that the generated result has the statistical regularity of a uniform random variable.

If the generated number is expressed with a binary representation, the number of 0 and 1 should be approximately equal, the number of two following 0 and two following 1 should be approximately equal, etc.

In the last 50 years, we have seen researchers focussing on building algorithms that yield this statistical regularity. Because a computer has a finite precision, the generator can't generate an infinite number of different outcomes but only a finite number of results. This means that the series of generated results is periodic. Generally, we choose the algorithm that gives us the longest possible period.

In this chapter, we define basic concepts regarding the generation of random variables on computers and we present the techniques used to generate some widely used random variables in finance. After that, we present the simulation of random vectors using variance-covariance matrix decomposition techniques such as the Cholesky decomposition and the eigenvalue decomposition. The financial assets variance-covariance matrix decomposition is important in the study of risk factors, and more precisely in the pricing of financial instruments and risk management. Finally, we introduce the acceptance-rejection and Monte Carlo Markov Chain (MCMC) generation methods that could both be used in many simulation cases in finance.

In this chapter, as well as in the followings, we include MATLAB® programs in order to illustrate the theory presented. A list of most frequently used functions in MATLAB is given in Appendix B.

4.1 UNIFORM RANDOM VARIABLE GENERATOR

As discussed above, the series of numbers generated by the computer must have the longest possible period. The most frequently used algorithm is of the form:

$$x_{n+1} = ax_n + b \quad (\bmod m). \tag{4.1}$$

The series of results obtained from an initial value corresponds to the realization of a sequence of uniform random variables on the set

$$\{0, 1, 2, \ldots, m-1\}. \tag{4.2}$$

In reality, in order for the period of the series generated with this algorithm to be m, we must choose integer a, b and m in an appropriate way, because this period is equal to m if and only if

(i) b is relatively prime with m,
(ii) $a-1$ is a multiple of any prime number that divides m, for example a multiple of 3 if m is a multiple of 3.

The parameters used by MATLAB's generator are described in Moler (1995) and given by:

$$\begin{aligned} m &= 2^{31} - 1 = 2147483647, \\ b &= 0, \quad \text{and} \\ a &= 7^5 = 16807. \end{aligned}$$

This algorithm generates a series of integer numbers between 0 and $m-1$. If we divide the result by m, we get results in the interval [0, 1]. Since m is very large, the difference between 2 successive numbers is relatively small and thus we can consider this discrete variable to be a continuous variable in [0, 1].

In MATLAB, to generate a uniform random variable between 0 and 1, often denoted by $U(0, 1)$, we use the command *rand*. The command *rand* generates one random variable uniformly distributed on the interval [0, 1]. The command *rand* (m, n) generates $m \times n$ random variables uniformly distributed on [0, 1] and stocked in a matrix of m rows and n columns.

From the examples presented in previous chapters, a uniformly distributed random variable on the set $[a, b]$ called $U(a, b)$ can be generated from the variable $U(0, 1)$ using the relation

$$U(a, b) = (b-a)U(0, 1) + a. \tag{4.3}$$

4.2 GENERATING DISCRETE RANDOM VARIABLES

4.2.1 Finite Discrete Random Variables

Let the random variable X on the finite space of events $\{x_1, x_2, \ldots, x_n\}$ have the respective probabilities $p_1, p_2, \ldots, p_n$. We can simulate X with a uniform random variable $U(0, 1)$ in setting:

$$X = x_1 \quad \text{if} \quad U \leq p_1, \tag{4.4}$$
$$X = x_2 \quad \text{if} \quad p_1 < U \leq p_1 + p_2, \tag{4.5}$$
$$\vdots$$
$$X = x_n \quad \text{if} \quad p_1 + p_2 + \cdots + p_{n-1} < U \leq p_1 + p_2 + \cdots + p_n. \tag{4.6}$$

This method simply means that we divide the interval [0, 1] in n sub-intervals with lengths corresponding to $p_1, p_2, \ldots, p_n$. In generating a uniform random variable, this subdivision uniquely defines X.

Example 2.1 We want to generate the daily price fluctuation of a financial asset that can have an increase of Δ_1 with probability p_1, decrease of $-\Delta_2$ with probability p_2, or stays the same with probability $p_3 = 1 - p_1 - p_2$ (each p_i should be positive and $p_1 + p_2 + p_3$ must equal 1). That is,

$$X \in \{-\Delta_2, 0, \Delta_1\} \text{ with } \begin{cases} \text{Prob}(X = \Delta_1) = p_1, \\ \text{Prob}(X = 0) = 1 - p_1 - p_2 = p_3, \\ \text{Prob}(X = -\Delta_2) = p_2. \end{cases} \tag{4.7}$$

To obtain the realization of X, we generate a uniform random variable $U(0, 1)$ and X is given by:

$$\begin{array}{lll} U \leq p_1 & \Longrightarrow & X = \Delta_1, \\ p_1 < U \leq p_1 + p_2 & \Longrightarrow & X = -\Delta_2, \\ p_1 + p_2 < U & \Longrightarrow & X = 0. \end{array} \tag{4.8}$$

In MATLAB, the program is:

```
function X=GenerateVariable(p1, p2, Delta1, Delta2)
%X takes value Delta1 with probability p1
%X takes value -Delta2 with probability p2
%X takes value 0 with probability 1-p1-p2

U = rand; %Uniform random variable
X=Delta1 * (U<=p1)-Delta2 * (p1<U) * (p1+p2 >= U);

end
```

Example 2.2 Let a binomial variable $X = B(N, p)$ that is a variable taking value in $\{0, 1, 2, \ldots, N\}$ with respective probabilities:

$$p_k = \text{Prob}(X = k) = \binom{N}{k} p^k (1 - p)^{N-k}, \quad k = 0, 1, \ldots, N. \tag{4.9}$$

This variable is the sum of N independent binary random variables B_i such that

$$X = B_1 + B_2 + \cdots + B_N, \tag{4.10}$$

with Prob($B_i = 0$) $= 1 - p$ and Prob($B_i = 1$) $= p$. When N is relatively small, for example smaller than 30, we can generate $B(N, p)$ by generating N binary variables B_i, each one being generated from a uniform random variable $U(0, 1)$ as follows in MATLAB:

```
function B=Binary(p)
%B takes value 1 with probability p
%B takes value 0 with probability 1-p

U = rand;
B=(U<=p);

end
```

To generate the random variable X, we can use the recursive form:

```
function X=Binomial(NbBinary, p)
%Function that simulates the Binomial variable X

X=0;
for n=1:NbBinary
    X=X+(rand<=p);
end

end
```

In MATLAB, using the loop command *for ... end* means that the calculations are performed many times, that is, it generates the random variables one after another and sums them as they are generated.

When the number of random variables N is small, the computation time of the loop is not a big problem. On the other hand, when N is large, computation time of the loop is very large and not so efficient with MATLAB. In such situations, we can increase the speed of the program using vectors in the algorithm. In doing so, the previous program can be written:

```
function X=Binomial2(NbBinary, p)
%Function that simulates the Binomial variable X

X=sum(rand(1, NbBinary)<=p);

end
```

4.2.2 Infinite Discrete Random Variables: Poisson Distribution

Define a Poisson random variable X with parameter λ as follows:

$$\text{Prob}(X = k) = \frac{e^{-\lambda}\lambda^k}{k!}, \quad k = 0, 1, 2, \ldots, \infty. \tag{4.11}$$

To generate this random variable we can use the previous technique and discard the events corresponding to high k, or in generating a series of independent random variables U_i uniformly distributed on [0, 1], we can prove that:

$$\begin{aligned} &\text{Prob}(U_1 \geq p, U_1U_2 \geq p, \ldots, U_1U_2\ldots U_k \geq p, U_1U_2\ldots U_{k+1} < p) \\ &= \frac{p}{k!}(-1)^k(\log(p))^k, \quad 0 < p < 1. \end{aligned} \tag{4.12}$$

In choosing $p = e^{-\lambda}$, we get:

$$\begin{aligned} &U_1 < e^{-\lambda}\} && \Longrightarrow X = 0, \\ &\left.\begin{array}{l} U_1 \geq e^{-\lambda} \text{ and} \\ U_1U_2 < e^{-\lambda} \end{array}\right\} && \Longrightarrow X = 1, \\ & && \vdots \\ &\left.\begin{array}{l} U_1 \geq e^{-\lambda}, \\ U_1U_2 \geq e^{-\lambda}, \\ \ldots, \\ U_1U_2\ldots U_k \geq e^{-\lambda} \text{ and} \\ U_1U_2\ldots U_{k+1} < e^{-\lambda} \end{array}\right\} && \Longrightarrow X = k. \end{aligned} \tag{4.13}$$

This algorithm gives us

$$\text{Prob}(X = k) = e^{-\lambda}\frac{\lambda^k}{k!}. \tag{4.14}$$

With MATLAB, we can generate such a random variable in the following manner:

```
function X=Poisson(lambda)
%Function that generates a Poisson variable X

X=0;
U=rand;
while (U>exp(-lambda))
    X=X+1;
    U=U*rand;
end

end
```

4.3 SIMULATION OF CONTINUOUS RANDOM VARIABLES

Let F be a given continuous cumulative distribution function and U a uniform random variable on [0, 1], then the cumulative distribution function of the random variable

$$X = F^{-1}(U) \tag{4.15}$$

is F (this was shown in Chapter 2). Now this result helps us to generate variables with known distribution functions.

4.3.1 Cauchy Distribution

The probability density function of the Cauchy distribution is:

$$f_X(x) = \frac{1}{\pi(x^2+1)}, \tag{4.16}$$

and its cumulative distribution function is:

$$F_X(x) = \frac{1}{\pi}\int_{-\infty}^{x} \frac{du}{u^2+1} = \frac{1}{\pi}\left[\arctan(x) - \frac{\pi}{2}\right] = u. \tag{4.17}$$

Thus

$$U = F_X(X) \Longrightarrow X = F_X^{-1}(U) = \tan\left(\pi U + \frac{\pi}{2}\right). \tag{4.18}$$

Hence, to generate X, we use the relation:

$$X = \tan\left(\pi\left(U + \frac{1}{2}\right)\right), \tag{4.19}$$

or

$$X = \tan\left(\pi\left(U - \frac{1}{2}\right)\right), \tag{4.20}$$

since the tangent function is periodic with period π. Such a variable can be generated with the following MATLAB program:

```
function X=Cauchy
%Function that generates the Cauchy variable X

X=tan(pi*(rand+1/2));

end
```

4.3.2 Exponential Law

A random variable X is called exponential if its probability density function is:

$$f_X(x) = \alpha e^{-\alpha x} 1_{\{x\geq 0\}}, \quad \alpha > 0. \tag{4.21}$$

Its cumulative distribution function is:

$$F_X(x) = \left(1 - \alpha e^{-\alpha x}\right) 1_{\{x\geq 0\}}. \tag{4.22}$$

Let

$$1 - \alpha e^{-\alpha x} = u \Longrightarrow x = -\frac{1}{\alpha}\log(1-u), \tag{4.23}$$

hence

$$X = -\frac{1}{\alpha}\log(1-U). \tag{4.24}$$

Since U is uniformly distributed on [0, 1], then $1 - U$ is also uniformly distributed on [0, 1]. It follows that X can be generated by:

$$X = -\frac{1}{\alpha}\log(U), \tag{4.25}$$

where U is a uniform random variable on [0, 1]. In MATLAB, this procedure gives:

```
function X=Exp(alpha)
%Function that generates the Exponential variable X

X = -log(rand)/alpha;

end
```

4.3.3 Rayleigh Random Variable

X is a Rayleigh random variable if its density function is equal to

$$f_X(x) = xe^{-\frac{x^2}{2}}1_{\{x\geq 0\}}. \tag{4.26}$$

Its cumulative distribution function is then:

$$F_X(x) = \int_0^x ve^{-\frac{v^2}{2}}dv = 1 - e^{-\frac{x^2}{2}} = u \Longrightarrow x = \sqrt{-2\log(1-u)}. \tag{4.27}$$

X can therefore be generated from a uniform random variable $U(0, 1)$ by the relation:

$$X = \sqrt{-2\log(1-U)}. \tag{4.28}$$

Since $1 - U$ also follows a uniform law on [0, 1], we can directly generate X by:

$$X = \sqrt{-2\log(U)}. \tag{4.29}$$

The MATLAB program is

```
function X=Rayleigh
%Function that generates the Rayleigh variable X

X = sqrt(-2*log(rand));

end
```

4.3.4 Gaussian Distribution

Consider a standard Gaussian random variable X with zero mean and unit variance, denoted by $N(0, 1)$. X can be generated following three different approaches.

Method 1

Let 12 random variables $\{U_i\}_{i=1,\ldots,12}$ uniformly distributed on [0, 1], we study their sum:

$$X = U_1 + U_2 + \ldots + U_{12} - 6. \tag{4.30}$$

Since

$$E[U_i] = \frac{1}{2} \quad \text{and} \quad \text{Var}[U_i] = \frac{1}{12}, \tag{4.31}$$

it follows:

$$E[X] = 0 \quad \text{and} \quad \text{Var}[X] = 1. \tag{4.32}$$

X is thus of zero mean and unit variance. Since X is the sum of 12 independent random variables having the same probability law, by virtue of the central limit theorem, we can consider X as a Gaussian variable. This way of generating a Gaussian random variable is interesting but not very precise since it is not possible to obtain rare events at the tail of the distribution. In fact, with this simulation Prob($X > 6$) $= 0$ but for a standard Gaussian random variable Prob($X >$ $6) \simeq 10^{-7}$.

The program in MATLAB is:

```
function X=Gaussian1
%Generation of a Gaussian variable with method 1

X = sum(rand(1,12))-6;

end
```

Method 2

We saw in Chapter 2 that two Gaussian random variables X and Y with mean of 0 and variance of 1 can be generated from a Rayleigh variable with density

$$f_\rho(\rho) = \rho e^{-\frac{\rho^2}{2}} 1_{\{\rho \geq 0\}} \tag{4.33}$$

and a uniform random variable on $[0, 2\pi]$ of density

$$f_\theta(\theta) = \frac{1}{2\pi}, \quad 0 \leq \theta \leq 2\pi. \tag{4.34}$$

For the simulation, we set

$$X = \rho \cos(\theta) \tag{4.35}$$

and

$$Y = \rho \sin(\theta). \tag{4.36}$$

We saw that ρ and θ can be generated from two uniformly distributed random variables on $[0, 1]$:

$$\rho = \sqrt{-2 \log(U_1)} \tag{4.37}$$

and

$$\theta = 2\pi U_2. \tag{4.38}$$

Then we can generate two Gaussian random variables from two uniform random variables on [0, 1] with the following formulas known as the Box-Muller method:

$$X = \sqrt{-2\log(U_1)}\cos(2\pi U_2) \tag{4.39}$$

and

$$Y = \sqrt{-2\log(U_1)}\sin(2\pi U_2). \tag{4.40}$$

The program in MATLAB language is:

```
function [X,Y]=Gaussian2
%Function that generates two Gaussian random variables with method 2

U1=rand;
U2=rand;
X=sqrt(-2*log(U1))*cos(2*pi*U2);
Y=sqrt(-2*log(U1))*sin(2*pi*U2);

end
```

Method 3

In MATLAB, the command *randn* directly generates a Gaussian random variable with mean of 0 and variance of 1. If we want to generate a matrix $n \times m$ with elements being Gaussian with zero mean and unit variance, the command is *randn(n, m).*

Thus, in MATLAB, in order to generate a Gaussian random variable X with mean μ and variance σ^2, the command is:

```
function X=Gaussian3(mu,sigma)
%Function that generates a Gaussian variable X
%with mean mu and standard deviation sigma with method 3

X = sigma * randn + mu;

end
```

We now compare all three methods of generating Gaussian random variables. We present a small program generating N Gaussian random variables following each of the three methods. We also compute their means and standard deviations.

```
function Gaussian(N)
%Function that compares the different methods of generating
% a Gaussian random variable
%N must be an even number

%Method 1
A = sum(rand(N,12),2) - 6;
MeanA = mean(A,1);
```

Table 4.1 Mean and standard deviation using the three methods for generating a Gaussian random variable

	Method 1		Method 2		Method 3	
N	Mean	Std.	Mean	Std.	Mean	Std.
10	0.1066	1.4399	0.0007	1.0938	0.3265	0.1817
10^2	−0.1719	0.9127	−0.1286	0.9488	0.0188	1.0673
10^3	0.0517	0.9755	−0.0296	0.9886	0.0253	0.9677
10^4	0.0044	1.0155	−0.0023	1.0194	−0.0035	0.9967
10^5	−0.0062	1.0009	−0.0048	1.0024	0.0015	1.0044
10^6	0.0019	0.9991	−0.0015	1.0005	0.0002	1.0009

```
StdA = std(A);
sprintf('Method 1 \n Mean: %g, Standard deviation: %g', MeanA, StdA)

%Method 2
U1 = rand(1,N/2);
U2 = rand(1,N/2);
B1 = sqrt(-2*log(U1)).*cos(2*pi*U2);
B2 = sqrt(-2*log(U1)).*sin(2*pi*U2);
B = [B1,B2]';
MeanB = mean(B);
StdB = std(B);
sprintf('Method 2 \n Mean: %g, Standard deviation: %g', MeanB, StdB)

%Method 3
C = randn(N,1);
MeanC = mean(C);
StdC = std(C);
sprintf('Method 3 \n Mean: %g, Standard deviation: %g', MeanC, StdC)
end
```

We call the program with different values for N. Table 4.1 simply shows the simulated mean and standard deviation of a standardized normal random variable (mean zero and standard deviation one) using each of the three methods.

4.4 SIMULATION OF RANDOM VECTORS

In this section, we would like to generate a Gaussian random vector $\underline{X}$ having a known variance-covariance matrix $\Lambda_{\underline{X}} = \text{cov}(\underline{X}, \underline{X}^\top)$. Let $\underline{Z} = (Z_1, \ldots, Z_n)^\top$ be an independent Gaussian random vector of zero mean and unit variance: $\underline{Z} \sim N(\underline{0}, I)$, that is

$$E[\underline{Z}] = \underline{0} \quad \text{and} \quad \text{Var}(\underline{Z}) = I, \tag{4.41}$$

where I is the identity matrix with 1 on the diagonal and 0 elsewhere. We want to use such a vector to create the random vector $\underline{X}$. We include a review on matrix algebra in Appendix A.

4.4.1 Case of a Two-Dimensional Random Vector

We want to generate the vector $\underline{X}$ with the following properties:

$$\underline{X} = \begin{pmatrix} X_1 \\ X_2 \end{pmatrix} \sim N\left(\underline{0}, \begin{pmatrix} \sigma_1^2 & \rho\sigma_1\sigma_2 \\ \rho\sigma_1\sigma_2 & \sigma_2^2 \end{pmatrix}\right). \tag{4.42}$$

Then

$$E[X_i] = 0, \quad E[X_i^2] = \sigma_i^2, \quad E[X_1 X_2] = \rho\sigma_1\sigma_2. \tag{4.43}$$

Let the Gaussian random vector

$$Z = \begin{pmatrix} Z_1 \\ Z_2 \end{pmatrix} \sim N\left(\underline{0}, \begin{pmatrix} 1 & 0 \\ 0 & 1 \end{pmatrix}\right). \tag{4.44}$$

Then setting

$$\begin{aligned} X_1 &= \sigma_1 Z_1 \\ X_2 &= \alpha Z_1 + \beta Z_2 \text{'} \end{aligned} \tag{4.45}$$

we obtain

$$E[X_1 X_2] = \alpha\sigma_1 E[Z_1^2] = \alpha\sigma_1. \tag{4.46}$$

However, we want to have $E[X_1X_2] = \rho\sigma_1\sigma_2$, hence $\alpha = \rho\sigma_2$. Moreover

$$\mathrm{Var}(X_2) = \alpha^2 + \beta^2 = \sigma_2^2 \quad \Rightarrow \beta = \pm\sqrt{\sigma_2^2(1-\rho^2)}. \tag{4.47}$$

We choose $\beta = \sqrt{\sigma_2^2(1-\rho^2)}$. Hence

$$\begin{pmatrix} X_1 \\ X_2 \end{pmatrix} = \begin{pmatrix} \sigma_1 & 0 \\ \rho\sigma_2 & \sqrt{1-\rho^2}\sigma_2 \end{pmatrix} \begin{pmatrix} Z_1 \\ Z_2 \end{pmatrix}. \tag{4.48}$$

Thus, we can generate such variables in MATLAB using the following program:

```
function rep=RandomVector(sigma1, sigma2, rho)
%Generation of a random vector of dimension 2 and correlation rho

MatrixL = [sigma1, 0;rho*sigma2, sigma2*sqrt(1-rho^2)];
rep = MatriceL*randn(2, 1);

end
```

4.4.2 Cholesky Decomposition of the Variance-Covariance Matrix

In the more general case of any n-dimensional random vector, if we take

$$\underline{X} = L\underline{Z} \quad \Longrightarrow \quad \mathrm{cov}(\underline{X}, \underline{X}^\top) = E[L\underline{Z}\,\underline{Z}^\top L^\top], \tag{4.49}$$

where L is a matrix with the appropriate dimensions. Since $E[\underline{Z}] = \underline{0}$ and $\text{cov}(\underline{Z}, \underline{Z}^\top) = I$, then

$$E[\underline{X}] = \underline{0}, \tag{4.50}$$

$$\text{cov}(\underline{X}, \underline{X}^\top) = LE[\underline{Z}\,\underline{Z}^\top]L^\top = LIL^\top = LL^\top. \tag{4.51}$$

But we would like to have

$$\text{cov}(\underline{X}, \underline{X}^\top) = \Lambda_X, \tag{4.52}$$

thus

$$LL^\top = \Lambda_X, \tag{4.53}$$

and L can consequently be obtained with the decomposition $LL^\top$ (Cholesky decomposition) of Λ_X. Thus, knowing the decomposition $LL^\top$ of matrix Λ_X, in order to generate a random vector $\underline{X}$ with covariance matrix Λ_X, we generate a Gaussian random vector $\underline{Z}$ with zero mean and identity covariance matrix, $N(\underline{0}, I)$, and compute the matrix multiplication $\underline{X} = L\underline{Z}$.

We only need to determine the decomposition $LL^\top$ of Λ_X. Therefore, we note that if Λ_X is positive definite, that is

$$\underline{Y}^\top \Lambda_X \underline{Y} > 0 \quad \forall \underline{Y} \neq 0, \tag{4.54}$$

then the matrix L exists and is unique. The function *chol*(Λ_X) of MATLAB allows us to obtain the matrix L.

In the case where the matrix Λ_X is not positive definite, we can reduce it into a matrix of a smaller dimension that is positive definite and on which we can use the Cholesky decomposition.

Determination of L in dimension 2 and 3

Let's go back to the case of a vector of 2 random variables. Its variance-covariance matrix A is of dimension 2, and we want to determine its Cholesky decomposition, or its decomposition of the form $LL^\top$:

$$\begin{aligned} A &= \begin{pmatrix} \sigma_1^2 & \rho_{12}\sigma_1\sigma_2 \\ \rho_{12}\sigma_2\sigma_1 & \sigma_2^2 \end{pmatrix} \\ &= \begin{pmatrix} a_{11} & 0 \\ a_{21} & a_{22} \end{pmatrix} \begin{pmatrix} a_{11} & a_{12} \\ 0 & a_{22} \end{pmatrix} \\ &= \begin{pmatrix} a_{11}^2 & a_{11}a_{12} \\ a_{21}a_{11} & a_{21}^2 + a_{22}^2 \end{pmatrix}. \end{aligned} \tag{4.55}$$

We identify the parameters appearing in the previous expression.

$$\begin{aligned} a_{11}^2 = \sigma_1^2 &\Rightarrow a_{11} = \sigma_1, \\ a_{11}a_{12} = \rho_{12}\sigma_1\sigma_2 &\Rightarrow a_{12} = \rho_{12}\sigma_2, \\ a_{12}^2 + a_{22}^2 = \sigma_2^2 &\Rightarrow \rho_{12}^2\sigma_2^2 + a_{22}^2 = \sigma_2^2, \\ &\Rightarrow a_{22} = \sigma_2\sqrt{1 - \rho_{12}^2}, \end{aligned}$$

thus

$$L = \begin{pmatrix} \sigma_1 & 0 \\ \rho_{12}\sigma_2 & \sqrt{1-\rho_{12}^2\sigma_2} \end{pmatrix}. \tag{4.56}$$

Now we complicate the problem and see what happens in the case of a vector with 3 random variables or a three-dimension covariance matrix.

$$\begin{aligned} A &= \begin{pmatrix} \sigma_1^2 & \rho_{12}\sigma_1\sigma_2 & \rho_{13}\sigma_1\sigma_3 \\ \rho_{12}\sigma_2\sigma_1 & \sigma_2^2 & \rho_{23}\sigma_2\sigma_3 \\ \rho_{13}\sigma_3\sigma_1 & \rho_{23}\sigma_3\sigma_2 & \sigma_3^2 \end{pmatrix} \\ &= \begin{pmatrix} a_{11} & 0 & 0 \\ a_{21} & a_{22} & 0 \\ a_{31} & a_{32} & a_{33} \end{pmatrix} \begin{pmatrix} a_{11} & a_{12} & a_{13} \\ 0 & a_{22} & a_{23} \\ 0 & 0 & a_{33} \end{pmatrix} \\ &= \begin{pmatrix} a_{11}^2 & a_{11}a_{21} & a_{11}a_{31} \\ a_{11}a_{21} & a_{21}^2 + a_{22}^2 & a_{31}a_{21} + a_{22}a_{23} \\ a_{31}a_{11} & a_{31}a_{21} + a_{32}a_{22} & a_{31}^2 + a_{32}^2 + a_{33}^2 \end{pmatrix}. \end{aligned} \tag{4.57}$$

As in the case of 2 variables, we get:

$$\begin{aligned} a_{11} &= \sigma_1, \\ a_{21} &= \rho_{12}\sigma_2, \\ a_{22} &= \sigma_2\sqrt{1-\rho_{12}^2}, \end{aligned}$$

and for the other parameters, we have

$$\begin{aligned} a_{31}a_{11} = \rho_{13}\sigma_3\sigma_1 &\Rightarrow a_{31} = \rho_{13}\sigma_3, \\ a_{31}a_{21} + a_{32}a_{22} = \rho_{23}\sigma_2\sigma_3 &\Rightarrow a_{32} = \frac{\rho_{32}\sigma_2\sigma_3 - a_{31}a_{21}}{a_{22}} \\ &\qquad = \sigma_3\frac{\rho_{23} - \rho_{13}\rho_{12}}{\sqrt{1-\rho_{12}^2}} \end{aligned}$$

and

$$\begin{aligned} a_{31}^2 + a_{32}^2 + a_{33}^2 = \sigma_3^2 \Rightarrow a_{33} &= \sqrt{\sigma_3^2 - a_{31}^2 - a_{32}^2} \\ &= \sigma_3\sqrt{1-\rho_{13}^2 - \frac{(\rho_{23}-\rho_{13}\rho_{12})^2}{1-\rho_{12}^2}}. \end{aligned}$$

Hence

$$L = \begin{pmatrix} \sigma_1 & 0 & 0 \\ \rho_{12}\sigma_2 & \sqrt{1-\rho_{12}^2}\sigma_2 & 0 \\ \rho_{13}\sigma_3 & \dfrac{\rho_{23}-\rho_{13}\rho_{12}}{\sqrt{1-\rho_{12}^2}}\sigma_3 & \sqrt{1-\rho_{13}^2 - \dfrac{(\rho_{23}-\rho_{13}\rho_{12})^2}{1-\rho_{12}^2}}\sigma_3 \end{pmatrix}. \tag{4.58}$$

Example 4.1 Consider matrix A given by the following values

$$\sigma_1 = 0.10,$$
$$\sigma_2 = 0.20,$$
$$\sigma_3 = 0.25,$$
$$\rho_{12} = 0.75,$$
$$\rho_{13} = -0.50,$$
$$\rho_{23} = -0.35.$$

Hence matrix A is

$$A = \begin{pmatrix} \sigma_1^2 & \rho_{12}\sigma_1\sigma_2 & \rho_{13}\sigma_1\sigma_3 \\ \rho_{12}\sigma_2\sigma_1 & \sigma_2^2 & \rho_{23}\sigma_2\sigma_3 \\ \rho_{13}\sigma_3\sigma_1 & \rho_{23}\sigma_3\sigma_3 & \sigma_3^2 \end{pmatrix} = \begin{pmatrix} 0.01 & 0.015 & -0.0125 \\ 0.015 & 0.04 & -0.0175 \\ -0.0125 & -0.0175 & 0.0625 \end{pmatrix}. \tag{4.59}$$

The MATLAB command to get L is

```
%Command to get the Cholesky decomposition

chol(A); %This gives the upper triangular matrix
L=chol(A)'; %To get the lower triangular matrix
```

The result is

$$L = \begin{pmatrix} 0.1000 & 0 & 0 \\ 0.1500 & 0.1323 & 0 \\ -0.1250 & 0.0094 & 0.2163 \end{pmatrix}. \tag{4.60}$$

4.4.3 Eigenvalue Decomposition of the Variance-Covariance Matrix

The alternative to the Cholesky decomposition is the eigenvalue decomposition, also known as principal components analysis. It is slightly more difficult to program than the Cholesky method, but it works even for matrices that are not positive definite. This means that the method works for variance-covariance matrices with many risky factors (even hundreds).

The eigenvalue decomposition also has the advantage that it can give intuition on the risks' random structure, which can help reduce the number of necessary simulations.

However, the eigenvalue decomposition can be difficult to obtain if different parts of the matrix have been generated from data spanning different time periods, since the inconsistency in data can produce negative variances for some principal components.

The eigenvalue decomposition works in the following way. Find two matrices D and P satisfying equation:

$$\mathrm{Var}(\underline{X}) = \Lambda_X = PDP^\top, \tag{4.61}$$

where Λ_X is the variance-covariance matrix, D is a matrix such that the only non zero elements are the ones on the diagonal, and P is an orthogonal matrix, that is:

$$I = PP^\top. \tag{4.62}$$

This method rests on the eigenvectors forming a basis, which is guaranteed in this case since the matrix Λ_X is symmetric. The elements on the diagonal of matrix D are the eigenvalues of matrix Λ_X. Knowing that D is a diagonal matrix with all positive elements

$$D = \begin{pmatrix} d_1 & 0 & 0 \\ 0 & \ddots & 0 \\ 0 & 0 & d_n \end{pmatrix}, \tag{4.63}$$

the matrix Λ_X can be partitioned in two, such that

$$\Lambda_X = LL^\top, \quad \text{with} \quad L = P\sqrt{D}, \tag{4.64}$$

and

$$\sqrt{D} = \begin{pmatrix} \sqrt{d_1} & 0 & 0 \\ 0 & \ddots & 0 \\ 0 & 0 & \sqrt{d_n} \end{pmatrix}. \tag{4.65}$$

From this decomposition of matrix Λ_X, the vector $\underline{X}$ can be obtained exactly as in the case of the Cholesky decomposition in setting

$$\underline{X} = L\underline{Z}, \tag{4.66}$$

with the vector $\underline{Z}$ being composed of n independent random variables with unit variance, that is, $\text{Var}(\underline{Z}) = I$.

Example 4.2 If we take the matrix A given previously, that is

$$A = \begin{pmatrix} 0.01 & 0.015 & -0.0125 \\ 0.015 & 0.04 & -0.0175 \\ -0.0125 & -0.0175 & 0.0625 \end{pmatrix}. \tag{4.67}$$

We obtain the following matrices P and D

$$P = \begin{pmatrix} 0.9367 & 0.2285 & -0.2652 \\ -0.3359 & 0.7998 & -0.4975 \\ 0.0985 & 0.5551 & 0.8259 \end{pmatrix} \tag{4.68}$$

$$D = \begin{pmatrix} 0.0033 & 0 & 0 \\ 0 & 0.0321 & 0 \\ 0 & 0 & 0.0771 \end{pmatrix}. \tag{4.69}$$

These matrices can be computed in MATLAB with the command

```
%Command giving the eigenvalues and eigenvectors
%of matrix A

[P,D] = eig(A); %P->eigenvectors' matrix
        %D->corresponding eigenvalues' matrix
```

Matrix L is obtained with the command

```
%Computation of L with matrices P and D

L=P*D.^(0.5);
```

and thus

$$L = \begin{pmatrix} 0.0539 & 0.0410 & -0.0736 \\ -0.0193 & 0.1434 & -0.1381 \\ 0.0057 & 0.0995 & 0.2293 \end{pmatrix} \tag{4.70}$$

with the decomposition

$$A = LL^{\top}. \tag{4.71}$$

4.4.4 Simulation of a Gaussian Random Vector with MATLAB

To simulate an independent Gaussian random vector of dimension n with mean 0 and variance-covariance matrix I (denoted by $N(0, I)$) in MATLAB, we use the command *randn(n, 1)*. To simulate the vector $\underline{Y} = h(\underline{X})$, we simulate $\underline{X}$ and we apply the function h to it.

Hence, to simulate the Gaussian random vector $\underline{Y}$ with mean μ and the positive definite matrix Λ as its variance-covariance matrix, we express $\underline{Y}$ as a function of an independent Gaussian random vector $N(0, I)$ as follows.

We express $\Lambda = \sqrt{\Lambda}\sqrt{\Lambda}^{\top}$, then $\underline{Y} = \sqrt{\Lambda}\underline{X} + \mu$ is the Gaussian random vector $N(\mu, \Lambda)$. In MATLAB, we will use *chol*(Λ) to get $\sqrt{\Lambda}$. Hence in MATLAB, the command for simulating a Gaussian random vector $N(\mu, \Lambda)$ with dimension n is

```
function Y=GaussianVector(n,Lambda,mu)
%Function that generates a Gaussian random vector
%n: Vector's dimension
%Lambda: Covariance matrix
%mu: Vector of means

Y = chol(Lambda)'*randn(n,1) + mu;

end
```

4.5 ACCEPTANCE-REJECTION METHOD

We want to simulate a random vector $\underline{X}$ having probability density function $f(\underline{x})$. We suppose that there is already a program on the computer allowing us to generate a random vector $\underline{Y}$ of same dimension of $\underline{X}$, with a probability density function $g(\underline{y})$ satisfying the following inequality:

$$f(\underline{x}) \leq kg(\underline{x}), \tag{4.72}$$

where k is a given positive constant. We set

$$\alpha(\underline{x}) = \frac{f(\underline{x})}{kg(\underline{x})}. \tag{4.73}$$

Generation algorithm

1- We generate the vector $\underline{Y}_1$ with probability density function $g(\underline{y})$ and a random variable U_1 independent of $\underline{Y}_1$, uniformly distributed between 0 and 1.

2- If $U_1 \leq \alpha(\underline{Y}_1)$, we choose $\underline{X} = \underline{Y}_1$, otherwise we reject $\underline{Y}_1$ and re-generate new $\underline{Y}$ and U until $U_m \leq \alpha(\underline{Y}_m)$, then we will choose $\underline{X} = \underline{Y}_m$. This way, the generated random vector $\underline{X}$ follows the probability law $f(\underline{x})$.

In order to illustrate this result, we consider the event $\{\underline{X} \in E\}$, where E is a subset of the real axis. Because $\underline{Y}_m$ and U_m are all independent, we immediately note that the events

$$\{\underline{X} = \underline{Y}_1\}, \{\underline{X} = \underline{Y}_2\}, \ldots, \{\underline{X} = \underline{Y}_m\} \tag{4.74}$$

are mutually exclusive, which gives

$$\begin{aligned}\text{Prob}(\underline{X} \in E) &= \text{Prob}(\{\underline{X} = \underline{Y}_1, \underline{X} \in E\} \text{ or } \ldots \\ &\quad \text{or } \{\underline{X} = \underline{Y}_m, \underline{X} \in E\} \text{ or } \ldots) \\ &= \sum_{m=1}^{\infty} \text{Prob}(\{\underline{X} = \underline{Y}_m, \underline{X} \in E\}).\end{aligned} \tag{4.75}$$

We know that

$$\begin{aligned}\text{Prob}(\{\underline{X} = \underline{Y}_m, X \in E\}) &= \text{Prob}(\{U_1 > \alpha(\underline{Y}_1)\} \cap \{U_2 > \alpha(\underline{Y}_2)\} \cap \ldots \\ &\quad \cap \{U_{m-1} > \alpha(\underline{Y}_{m-1})\} \cap \{U_m \leq \alpha(\underline{Y}_m)\} \\ &\quad \cap \{\underline{Y}_m \in E\}) \\ &= \text{Prob}(\{U_1 > \alpha(\underline{Y}_1)\}) \times \\ &\quad \text{Prob}(\{U_2 > \alpha(\underline{Y}_2)\}) \times \ldots \\ &\quad \times \text{Prob}(\{U_{m-1} > \alpha(\underline{Y}_{m-1})\}) \\ &\quad \times \text{Prob}(\{U_m \leq \alpha(\underline{Y}_m), \underline{Y}_m \in E\}) \\ &= (1-p)^{m-1}\text{Prob}(\underline{Y}_m \in E \mid U_m \leq \alpha(\underline{Y}_m)) \\ &\quad \times \text{Prob}(U_m \leq \alpha(\underline{Y}_m)),\end{aligned} \tag{4.76}$$

where $p = \text{Prob}(U \leq \alpha(\underline{Y}))$.

Since

$$\text{Prob}(\underline{Y}_m \in E \mid U_m \leq \alpha(\underline{Y}_m)) \tag{4.77}$$

is identical to

$$\text{Prob}(\underline{Y} \in E \mid U \leq \alpha(\underline{Y})), \tag{4.78}$$

we have

$$\text{Prob}(\{\underline{X} = \underline{Y}_m, \underline{X} \in E\}) = p(1-p)^{m-1}\text{Prob}(\underline{Y} \in E \mid U \leq \alpha(\underline{Y})). \tag{4.79}$$

Finally,

$$\begin{aligned}
\text{Prob}(\underline{X} \in E) &= \sum_{m=1}^{\infty} p(1-p)^{m-1}\text{Prob}(\underline{Y} \in E \mid U \leq \alpha(\underline{Y})) \\
&= p\text{Prob}(\underline{Y} \in E \mid U \leq \alpha(\underline{Y}))\sum_{m=1}^{\infty}(1-p)^{m-1} \\
&= \text{Prob}(\underline{Y} \in E \mid U \leq \alpha(\underline{Y})) \\
&= \frac{\text{Prob}(\underline{Y} \in E, U \leq \alpha(\underline{Y}))}{\text{Prob}(U \leq \alpha(\underline{Y}))}.
\end{aligned} \tag{4.80}$$

To determine $\text{Prob}(\underline{X} \in E)$, we must compute $\text{Prob}(\underline{Y} \in E, U \leq \alpha(\underline{Y}))$ and $\text{Prob}(U \leq \alpha(\underline{Y}))$. We have

$$\begin{aligned}
\text{Prob}(U \leq \alpha(\underline{Y})) &= \int \text{Prob}(U \leq \alpha(\underline{y}))g(\underline{y})dy \\
&= \int \alpha(\underline{Y})g(\underline{y})dy \\
&= \int \frac{f(\underline{y})}{kg(\underline{y})}g(\underline{y})dy \\
&= \frac{1}{k},
\end{aligned} \tag{4.81}$$

and

$$\begin{aligned}
\text{Prob}(\underline{Y} \in E, U \leq \alpha(\underline{Y})) &= \int_E g(\underline{y})dy \int_0^{\alpha(\underline{y})} du \\
&= \int_E \alpha(\underline{y})g(\underline{y})dy \\
&= \int_E \frac{f(\underline{y})}{kg(\underline{y})}g(\underline{y})dy \\
&= \frac{1}{k}\int_E f(\underline{y})dy.
\end{aligned} \tag{4.82}$$

Which gives

$$\text{Prob}(\underline{X} \in E) = \int_E f(\underline{x})dx. \tag{4.83}$$

This relation shows that the probability density function of $\underline{X}$ is effectively $f(\underline{x})$.

Remark 5.1 We have shown that $\text{Prob}(U \leq \alpha(\underline{Y})) = \frac{1}{k}$, which means that the rate of rejection is very high when k is large. When k approaches 1, the rate of rejection decreases rapidly. Thus, in practice, we should choose a function $g(\underline{y})$ with values of similar size to $f(\underline{x})$.

4.6 MARKOV CHAIN MONTE CARLO METHOD (MCMC)

4.6.1 Definition of a Markov Process

Let a random process $\{X_n, n = 0, 1, 2, \ldots\}$ be given. Refer to Chapter 7 for a more detailed analysis of random processes.

We suppose that X_n take their values in the states' set Ω. We say that the process $\{X_n, n = 0, 1, 2, \ldots\}$ is a Markov chain if

$$\text{Prob}(X_{n+1} = x_{n+1} \mid X_n = x_n, X_{n-1} = x_{n-1}, \ldots, X_0 = x_0) \tag{4.84}$$

is equal to

$$\text{Prob}(X_{n+1} = x_{n+1} \mid X_n = x_n). \tag{4.85}$$

It means that the probability that the process is in state x_{n+1} at $n + 1$, knowing that is was in state x_n at n, is independent of everything that happened before n. All that matters are the successive moments n and $n + 1$.

Moreover, the Markov chain will be called homogeneous if

$$\text{Prob}(X_{n+1} = y \mid X_n = x) = p_{x,y}. \tag{4.86}$$

That is, the probability of being in state y knowing that the process was in state x previously, $p_{x,y}$, is totally independent of n. All that matters is the evolution between two successive dates.

4.6.2 Description of the MCMC Technique

We will show in Chapter 5 that the so-called Monte Carlo method can be used to estimate the mathematical expectation of a random quantity $q(X)$, where X is a random variable with probability density function $f_X(x)$:

$$E[q(X)] \approx \frac{1}{N}\sum_{n=1}^{N} q(X_n), \tag{4.87}$$

where the samples X_n are independently generated by computer.

It is not always easy to directly generate X_n if $f_X(x)$ is complicated. Because the estimator (6.4) doesn't require the independence hypothesis for the X_n, we can use any method to generate them, provided that X_n has $f_X(x)$ as its density function. This explains the idea of using a Markov chain.

Suppose that we have a homogeneous Markov chain such that the successive states $\{X_0, X_1, X_2, \ldots\}$ are characterized by the transition probability

$$\text{Prob}(X_{n+1} \mid X_n). \tag{4.88}$$

The homogeneity ensures that $\text{Prob}(X_{n+1} \mid X_n)$ doesn't depend on n.

How does the choice of X_0 affect X_n? Expressed differently, what is the form of $f_{X_n}(x|x_0)$? It is known that, under very general regularity conditions, $f_{X_n}(x|x_0)$ becomes independent of x_0 when n is very large, that is, when the chain is in a stationary regime.

We denote by $\varphi_X(x)$ the density function of X in the state when the chain reaches the permanent regime assuming that we can construct the chain such that $\varphi_X(x)$ is identical to the desired $f_X(x)$. We let the chain evolve until it reaches the stationary regime (i.e., large M) and then use the following simulated states to estimate $E[q(X)]$:

$$E[q(X)] \approx \frac{1}{N-M} \sum_{n=M+1}^{N} q(X_n). \tag{4.89}$$

This result of using part of the simulated states to estimate the expected value is known under the name "ergodic mean".

The most widely known method of generating a Markov chain with $\varphi_X(x)$ identical to $f_X(x)$ is the Metropolis-Hastings algorithm. Let $g(x|y)$ be any conditional density function.

Let's define

$$\alpha(x, y) = \min\left(1, \frac{f_X(y)g(x|y)}{f_X(x)g(y|x)}\right). \tag{4.90}$$

Assuming that at any time n, the chain is in state $X_n = x_n$, in order to construct the desired Markov chain we generate two random variables. The first, Y, is characterized by the density function $g(y|x_n)$ and the second one, U_n, is independent of the first and is uniformly distributed between 0 and 1. X_{n+1} is then defined by

$$X_{n+1} = \begin{cases} Y, & \text{if } U \leq \alpha(x_n, y); \\ X_n, & \text{if } U > \alpha(x_n, y). \end{cases} \tag{4.91}$$

As seen in Section 4.5, this is precisely the rejection method.

It is important to note that since there is no predefined form for $g(y|x)$, we will choose a particular formulation in order to suit the model under study.

Notes and Complementary Readings

For further readings, readers can eventually refer to the following publications on Monte Carlo simulations and numerical methods: Kloeden, Platen and Schurz (1997), Press, Teukolsky, Vetterling and Flannery (1992), Rubinstein (1981) and Seydel (2002).

For a quick learning of MATLAB, the reader can refer to Etter and Kuncicky (2002) and Pratap (2002), and for complementary references on random variables generation with MATLAB, we suggest Martinez and Martinez (2002).

Useful references on Markov chains and random processes are the books of Ross (2002 a and b) and Kloeden and Platen (1992).

5

Foundations of Monte Carlo Simulations

In finance, asset pricing generally consists of computing the mathematical expectation of the payoffs. In this chapter, we describe how simulation techniques can be used to perform approximatively these mathematical expectations. This involves the notion of approximation precision.

Several techniques exist that enhance the precision of the approximations and reduce the computation time. We introduce the Barraquand (1995) quadratic resampling technique used to improve the estimation precision for the variance-covariance matrix pervasive in financial modeling. We also introduce techniques that reduce the computation time and the variance reduction techniques such as the antithetic variables technique, the control variates technique and the importance sampling technique.

We end the chapter with application examples which constitute exercises for the reader. The MATLAB® programs are provided as solutions for the application cases.

5.1 BASIC IDEA

The Monte Carlo (MC) method is a numerical calculation method used to perform numerical computations of functions of random variables. Its origin can be traced back to when Laplace and Bouffon computed the numerical value of π using a random experiment. Later, during the building of the atomic bomb in Los Alamos, Newman and Ulam developed this technique extensively to calculate complex integrals.

The approach consists of performing a sequence of experiments and taking their average value. To clarify the concept, let us examine the following example:

Example 1.1 Consider the following integral:

$$\mathcal{I} = \int_0^1 \cos(2\pi x)dx. \tag{5.1}$$

In general, we can calculate the expectation using the Monte Carlo method. To do that, we define $\mathcal{I}$ as the mathematical expectation $E[\ .\ ]$ of a random variable as follows:

$$\mathcal{I} = E\left[\cos(2\pi X)\right], \tag{5.2}$$

where the random variable X follows a uniform distribution $U(0, 1)$.

We generate N independent values of a uniform random variable over the interval [0, 1]. The strong law of large numbers allows us to estimate $\mathcal{I}$ by taking the arithmetic average of the realized results:

$$\widehat{\mathcal{I}}_N = \frac{1}{N}\sum_{i=1}^{N} \cos(2\pi x_i), \tag{5.3}$$

where x_i are the realizations of uniform random variables. A computer program to perform this task can be the following:

```
function I=IntegralMC(N)
%Function to calculate the integral I by the Monte Carlo method
%N: Number of simulated points to approximate the integral

X = rand(N, 1);
I = mean(cos(2*pi*X));

end
```

When N goes to infinity, the estimator $\widehat{\mathcal{I}}_N$ converges to the exact value of $\mathcal{I}$. Table 5.1 gives an illustration of that convergence to the theoretical value of zero.

Table 5.1 Estimation of an integral using Monte Carlo simulations

Number of experiments: N	$\hat{\mathcal{I}}_N$
10	−0.1005
100	0.0289
1000	0.0317
10 000	0.0110
100 000	-3.5618×10^{-8}
1 000 000	-7.5336×10^{-8}

In the above example, we can clearly see that in the computation process, we made two fundamentally important assumptions:

(i) We succeed in generating by computer a uniform random variable $U(0, 1)$, and
(ii) The realizations $x_1, x_2, \ldots, x_N$ are obtained from random variables $X_1, X_2, \ldots, X_N$ which are statistically independent and identically distributed.

To check whether these random variables $X_1, X_2, \ldots, X_N$ are uniformly distributed, we only need to examine their histogram. It consists of dividing the interval formed by the simulated values into sub-intervals, called bins. The histogram is the graph of the step function with values equal to the number of values in each bin.

Depending on the length of the bins, we obtain different histograms. If the histogram remains roughly constant, we can conclude experimentally that the random variables are uniform over the interval [0, 1].

To verify the statistical independence of the generated samples, we plot the points (U_n, U_{n+1}). If the points appear to be widely spread in the unit square, we can assume the samples generated to be statistically independent.

If the data are not appropriately distributed over the square, we can use correction techniques such as the shuffling technique (see for example Knuth (1981) and Rubinstein (1981)). However, since the MATLAB generator *rand* is sufficiently satisfactory for most of our financial applications, we do not resort to these techniques.

5.2 INTRODUCTION TO THE CONCEPT OF PRECISION

Let X be a random variable with probability density function $f_X(x)$. We would like to calculate $E[g(X)]$ where $g(.)$ is a given function. The numerical value of $E[g(X)]$ is often difficult to obtain. One then needs to estimate this value using the Monte Carlo simulation technique, which consists of generating N independent samples X_i of the random variable X, and use them to evaluate the estimator.

The expectation $h = E[g(X)]$ is approximated by the arithmetic average

$$\widehat{h} = \frac{1}{N}\sum_{i=1}^{N} g(X_i). \tag{5.4}$$

From the law of large numbers, we have:

$$\text{Prob}\left(\left|h - \widehat{h}\right| < \varepsilon\sigma_h\right) \geq 1 - \frac{1}{N\varepsilon^2}. \tag{5.5}$$

It means that h lies in the interval

$$\widehat{h} - \varepsilon\sigma_h \leq h \leq \widehat{h} + \varepsilon\sigma_h \tag{5.6}$$

with probability at least $1 - \frac{1}{N\varepsilon^2}$. We choose a confidence level α, between 0 and 1, so that the probability that h is in the interval

$$\left[\widehat{h} - \varepsilon\sigma_h, \widehat{h} + \varepsilon\sigma_h\right] \tag{5.7}$$

is greater or equal to $1 - \alpha$, which requires a minimum number of simulations

$$N > \frac{1}{\alpha\varepsilon^2}. \tag{5.8}$$

In statistical terminology, it means the hypothesis that h is in the interval for $N > \frac{1}{\alpha\varepsilon^2}$ is acceptable with a confidence level α and the interval

$$\left[\widehat{h} - \varepsilon\sigma_h, \widehat{h} + \varepsilon\sigma_h\right] \tag{5.9}$$

is called confidence interval at $100(1 - \alpha)\%$.

Note that σ_h is not known. We can, however, estimate its value the same way as we did for the mean. In other words, in practice, one has to replace σ_h by its estimator:

$$\widehat{\sigma}_h^2 = \frac{1}{N-1}\sum_{i=1}^{N}\left(g(X_i) - \widehat{h}\right)^2. \tag{5.10}$$

Example 2.1 Let X be a log-normal random variable with probability density function:

$$f_X(x) = \frac{1}{x\sqrt{2\pi}\sigma} e^{-\frac{1}{2\sigma^2}(\log(x)-m)^2} \quad \text{for} \quad x > 0, \tag{5.11}$$

with $\sigma^2 = 0.1$ and $m = 5$. We would like to calculate the following quantity:

$$c = E\left[\max(0, X - 110)\right]. \tag{5.12}$$

This example is an illustration of a European call option value calculation, which we discuss in more detail later when we introduce the applications in finance.

To generate X, we first generate a Gaussian random variable $Z \sim N(0, 1)$ and next $Y = \sigma Z + m$, where Y is a Gaussian random variable with mean m and variance σ^2. The random variable $X = e^Y$ is exactly the variable with the log-normal distribution.

In MATLAB, we have:

```
%Generation of the random variable X

X = exp(sqrt(0.1) * randn + 5);
```

We generate N values of this type and then calculate the call price defined by (5.12). Here is the MATLAB program for that exercise:

```
function Call=CalculateCall(NbTraj)
%Function to price a call option
%NbTraj: Number of generated points to compute the expectation

c = 0;
for i=1:NbTraj
    x = exp(sqrt(0.1) * randn + 5);
    c = c + max(0,x - 110);
end
Call = c/NbTraj;

end
```

This subroutine is not efficient because of the "do-loop"; we can write it in a vector format as follows:

```
function Call=CalculateCall2(NbTraj)
%Function to price a call option
%NbTraj: Number of generated points to compute the expectation

x = exp(sqrt(0.1) * randn(1,NbTraj) + 5);
Call = mean( max(x - 110,0));

end
```

The number of simulations required under the strong law of large numbers can be improved by using the central limit theorem presented in Chapter 3. Let

$$Z = \frac{1}{\sigma_h \sqrt{N}} \sum_{i=1}^{N} (g(X_i) - h), \tag{5.13}$$

with $h = E[g(X)]$. Z is a random variable with zero mean and unit variance. Since

$$\begin{aligned} Z &= \frac{\sqrt{N}}{\sigma_h} \frac{1}{N} \sum_{i=1}^{N} (g(X_i) - h) \\ &= \frac{\sqrt{N}}{\sigma_h} \left(\widehat{h} - h\right), \end{aligned} \tag{5.14}$$

it implies that

$$\text{Prob}\left(\left|\widehat{h}-h\right|<\varepsilon\sigma_h\right)=\text{Prob}\left(\frac{\sqrt{N}}{\sigma_h}\left|\widehat{h}-h\right|<\frac{\sqrt{N}}{\sigma_h}\varepsilon\sigma_h\right)$$
$$=\text{Prob}\left(|Z|<\varepsilon\sqrt{N}\right). \tag{5.15}$$

When N is relatively large, Z can be approximated by a Gaussian random variable with zero mean and unit variance. Hence

$$\text{Prob}\left(|Z|<\varepsilon\sqrt{N}\right)\simeq\frac{1}{\sqrt{2\pi}}\int_{-\varepsilon\sqrt{N}}^{\varepsilon\sqrt{N}}e^{-\frac{x^2}{2}}dx$$
$$=\frac{2}{\sqrt{\pi}}\int_0^{\varepsilon\sqrt{\frac{N}{2}}}e^{-u^2}du$$
$$=\text{erf}\left(\varepsilon\sqrt{\frac{N}{2}}\right). \tag{5.16}$$

We can obtain the number of simulations from the confidence interval as follows

$$\text{Prob}\left(|Z|<\varepsilon\sqrt{N}\right)>1-\alpha=\text{erf}(\beta), \tag{5.17}$$

where

$$\beta=\text{erf}^{-1}(1-\alpha). \tag{5.18}$$

It implies

$$\text{erf}\left(\varepsilon\sqrt{\frac{N}{2}}\right)\geq\text{erf}(\beta). \tag{5.19}$$

Since erf is an increasing function, it yields:

$$\varepsilon\sqrt{\frac{N}{2}}\geq\beta, \tag{5.20}$$

thus

$$N\geq2\left(\frac{\beta}{\varepsilon}\right)^2. \tag{5.21}$$

Hence, if $\alpha=0.05$, we have $\beta=\text{erf}^{-1}(0.95)=1.96$. For $\varepsilon=0.01$, we have

$$N=\frac{2(1.96)^2}{10^{-4}}=76{,}832. \tag{5.22}$$

This is an improvement compared to 200 0000 obtained using equation (5.8).

5.3 QUALITY OF MONTE CARLO SIMULATIONS RESULTS

In the previous section, we have shown how Monte Carlo simulations can be used to estimate the mathematical expectation of functions of random variables by computing the average of large samples obtained from the simulations. Therefore, if $Y = g(X)$, the following expectation

$$h = E[Y] = E[g(X)] \tag{5.23}$$

can be approximated by

$$\frac{1}{N}\sum_{i=1}^{N} g(X_i) = \widehat{h}. \tag{5.24}$$

Hence, when the number of simulations is large, it is possible to replace the precision results,

$$\text{Prob}\left(\left|\widehat{h} - h\right| < \varepsilon\sigma_h\right) > 1 - \frac{1}{N\varepsilon^2}, \tag{5.25}$$

by the relation

$$\text{Prob}\left(\left|\widehat{h} - h\right| < \varepsilon\sigma_h\right) > \text{erf}\left(\varepsilon\sqrt{\frac{N}{2}}\right). \tag{5.26}$$

However, if σ_h^2 is generally not known, we then use its empirical value:

$$\widehat{\sigma}_h^2 = \frac{1}{N-1}\sum_{i=1}^{N}\left(g(X_i) - \widehat{h}\right)^2. \tag{5.27}$$

In general, the precision on $\widehat{\sigma}_h^2$ is relatively complex; however, if $g(X_i)$ is Gaussian, $\widehat{\sigma}_h^2$ tends toward σ_h^2 for very large N. In practice, the Gaussian assumption on $g(X_i)$ is hardly acceptable, and we therefore need to find a way to approximate this Gaussian case.

This consists of performing M calculations, each corresponding to N Monte Carlo simulations. Hence, we obtain

$$\widehat{h}_k = \frac{1}{N}\sum_{i=1}^{N} g(X_{k,i}), \tag{5.28}$$

where $X_{k,i}$ is the ith simulation result of the kth calculation. This means that $(\widehat{h}_1, \ldots, \widehat{h}_M)$ are estimators of h. From the central limit theorem, when N is relatively large, $\widehat{h}_k$ can be considered as Gaussian.

We can apply the precision concept discussed above to each $\widehat{h}_k$. Exact σ_h being unknown, we use instead $\widehat{\sigma}_h$.

With M realized experiments, all the results $\widehat{h}_k$ can be considered as independent Gaussian random variables with the same statistics. The estimator $\widehat{h}$ can be estimated as:

$$\widehat{h} = \frac{1}{M}\sum_{k=1}^{M}\widehat{h}_k \tag{5.29}$$

and the variance of $\widehat{h}$ is:

$$\widehat{\sigma}_{\widehat{h}}^2 = \frac{1}{M-1}\sum_{k=1}^{M}\left(\widehat{h}_k - \widehat{h}\right)^2. \tag{5.30}$$

Hence, when M is fairly large, to obtain the Gaussian characteristic of $\widehat{h}_k$, the variable

$$T_M = \frac{\widehat{h} - h}{\sqrt{\frac{\widehat{\sigma}_{\widehat{h}}^2}{M}}} \tag{5.31}$$

follows a Student's t-distribution with $M-1$ degrees of freedom. The Student's t-distribution is used to cope with uncertainty resulting from estimating the standard deviation from a sample. This distribution is often used for confidence intervals and hypothesis tests.

The precision on $\widehat{h}$ is now defined by:

$$\text{Prob}\left(\left|\widehat{h}-h\right|<a\right)=\text{Prob}\left(|T_M|<t\right), \tag{5.32}$$

where

$$t=\frac{a}{\sqrt{\frac{\widehat{\sigma}^2_{\widehat{h}}}{M}}}. \tag{5.33}$$

For a confidence level $100\alpha\%$, we need to verify if the test variable

$$T^0_M=\frac{\widehat{h}-h_0}{\sqrt{\frac{\widehat{\sigma}^2_{\widehat{h}}}{M}}}, \tag{5.34}$$

with the mean h_0 satisfies the inequality:

$$\left|T^0_M\right|<t_{1-\alpha,M-1}, \tag{5.35}$$

where the values of the parameter t are presented in statistical tables. If the inequality is violated, h_0 has to be rejected, unless we accept it on the base of the test. Thus, the confidence interval at the level α is defined by: $\left(\widehat{h}-a,\widehat{h}+a\right)$, where

$$a=t_{1-\alpha,M-1}\sqrt{\frac{\widehat{\sigma}^2_{\widehat{h}}}{M}}. \tag{5.36}$$

All the values h_0 in this interval can be considered as the estimator.

Example 3.1 We would like to estimate

$$E\left[\max(0,X-K)\right]. \tag{5.37}$$

To achieve that, we run 30 times 100 variables (NbTraj $=100$, NbSeries $=30$). We then calculate

$$h_k=\frac{1}{100}\sum_{i=1}^{100}g(X_{k,i}) \tag{5.38}$$

with

$$g(X_{k,i})=\max\left(0,X_{k,i}-K\right). \tag{5.39}$$

Hence

$$\widehat{h}=\frac{1}{30}\sum_{k=1}^{30}h_k. \tag{5.40}$$

We then proceed with the Student test. Let's start by generating the variables $X_{k,i}$ with $\sigma^2 = 0.1$ and $m = 5$. The MATLAB program is the following:

```
function X=GenerateVariables(NbSeries,NbTraj)
%Function generating log-normal variables Xk,i
%NbSeries: Number of batches of variables
%NbTraj: Number of variables per batch

X = exp(sqrt(0.1) * randn(NbSeries,NbTraj) + 5);

end
```

Next, after calculating $g(X_{i,k}) = \max(0, X_{i,k} - 150)$ and summing, we obtain h_k and $\widehat{h}$. We then calculate $\widehat{\sigma}^2_{\widehat{h}}$. The complete MATLAB program is

```
function [hHat,sigmaHat]=CalculateParameters(NbSeries,NbTraj,alpha)
%Function calculating the values of hHat and sigmaHat
%NbSeries: Number of batches of variables
%NbTraj: Number of variables per batch
%alpha: The confidence level of the confidence interval

X = exp(sqrt(0.1) * randn(NbSeries,NbTraj) + 5);

%The mean of hk is taken with respect to the 2nd dimension
(columns)
hk = mean(max(0,X - 150),2);
hHat = mean(hk,1);
sigmaHat = std(hk);

Interval=[hHat - tinv(1-alpha,NbTraj-1)*sigmaHat/sqrt(NbTraj),...
          hHat + tinv(1-alpha,NbTraj-1)*sigmaHat/sqrt(NbTraj)];

end
```

As we can see, to find $t_{1-\alpha,M-1}$, MATLAB provides the following function

```
%MATLAB function for the inverse function of the Student
distribution

t = tinv(1-alpha,M-1);
```

The results obtained with different values of α are presented in Table 5.2.

Table 5.2 Confidence intervals of the Monte Carlo simulations

$\widehat{h}$	$\widehat{\sigma}^2_{\widehat{h}}$	α	$t_{1-\alpha,M-1}$	Interval
21.7806	12.9871	0.1000	1.3114	[20.9177, 22.6434]
21.7806	12.9871	0.0500	1.6991	[20.6626, 22.8985]
21.7806	12.9871	0.0100	2.4620	[20.1607, 23.4005]

5.4 IMPROVEMENT OF THE QUALITY OF MONTE CARLO SIMULATIONS OR VARIANCE REDUCTION TECHNIQUES

As we have discussed above, to obtain adequate precision we need to significantly increase the number of Monte Carlo simulations. With the modern computing power available nowadays, the number of simulations is no longer a major concern.

However, in some complex situations, where the whole process (instead of a single variable) needs to be simulated dynamically, the computation time can become an important issue. Then ways must be found to reduce the required number of simulations.

We examine four commonly used techniques: the first is used to improve precision and the remaining three to reduce the computation time.

5.4.1 Quadratic Resampling

When we generate random variables, we obtain sample statistics which do not in general coincide with the model statistics. To exploit the properties of the theoretical formulas containing these statistics, we need to transform the data in order to establish the equality between the sample parameters and the theoretical parameters. The parameter invariably encountered in the calculations is the covariance matrix of a given random vector.

The quadratic resampling technique introduced by Barraquand in 1995 is very useful for probabilistic multidimensional integration. The technique is built as follows.

Let $\underline{X} = (X_1, \ldots, X_n)^\top$ be a n-dimensional random vector with mean

$$\underline{m_{\underline{X}}} = E\left[\underline{X}\right] = \left(E\left[X_1\right], \ldots, E\left[X_n\right]\right)^\top \tag{5.41}$$

and covariance matrix

$$\begin{aligned}\Lambda_{\underline{X}} &= E\left[\left(\underline{X} - \underline{m_{\underline{X}}}\right)\left(\underline{X} - \underline{m_{\underline{X}}}\right)^\top\right] \\ &= E\left[\underline{X}\underline{X}^\top\right] - \underline{m_{\underline{X}}}\,\underline{m_{\underline{X}}}^\top.\end{aligned} \tag{5.42}$$

To estimate $\underline{m_{\underline{X}}}$ and $\Lambda_{\underline{X}}$, we can run M simulations and the sample statistics obtained are

$$\widehat{\underline{m_{\underline{X}}}} = \frac{1}{M}\sum_{k=1}^{M} \underline{X}^k \tag{5.43}$$

and

$$\widehat{\Lambda_{\underline{X}}} = \frac{1}{M}\sum_{k=1}^{M}\left(\underline{X}^k - \widehat{\underline{m_{\underline{X}}}}\right)\left(\underline{X}^k - \widehat{\underline{m_{\underline{X}}}}\right)^\top, \tag{5.44}$$

where $\underline{X}^k$ is the vector obtained from the kth simulation. Developing the expression of the sample variance, we obtain:

$$\widehat{\Lambda_{\underline{X}}} = \frac{1}{M}\sum_{k=1}^{M}\underline{X}^k\left(\underline{X}^k\right)^\top - \widehat{\underline{m_{\underline{X}}}}\,\widehat{\underline{m_{\underline{X}}}}^\top. \tag{5.45}$$

From the law of large numbers when M is very large, $\widehat{\underline{m_{\underline{X}}}}$ and $\widehat{\Lambda_{\underline{X}}}$ become close to $\underline{m_{\underline{X}}}$ and $\Lambda_{\underline{X}}$ with a greater precision.

When M is small, this precision can be very poor. However, we can modify the data $\underline{X}$ such that the sample mean and covariance matrix coincide with the statistical mean and covariance matrix. In practice, $\widehat{\Lambda}_{\underline{X}}$ is a symmetric and positive definite square matrix. The square root of the matrix $\widehat{\Lambda}_{\underline{X}}$ exists and is regular.

Let's define the matrix

$$H = \sqrt{\Lambda_{\underline{X}}}\left(\sqrt{\widehat{\Lambda}_{\underline{X}}}\right)^{-1} \tag{5.46}$$

and the following vector

$$\underline{Y} = H\left(\underline{X} - \widehat{\underline{m}}_{\underline{X}}\right) + \underline{m}_{\underline{X}}. \tag{5.47}$$

For M simulations, the new sample vector is:

$$\underline{Y}^k = H\left(\underline{X}^k - \widehat{\underline{m}}_{\underline{X}}\right) + \underline{m}_{\underline{X}} \tag{5.48}$$

and the sample mean of $\underline{Y}^k$ becomes:

$$\widehat{\underline{m}}_{\underline{Y}} = \frac{1}{M}\sum_{k=1}^{M}\underline{Y}^k. \tag{5.49}$$

Developing this sum, we obtain the equality between the sample mean of $\underline{Y}$ and the statistical mean of $\underline{X}$:

$$\widehat{\underline{m}}_{\underline{Y}} = \frac{1}{M}\sum_{k=1}^{M}\underline{Y}^k = \underline{m}_{\underline{X}}. \tag{5.50}$$

Similarly, we can calculate the sample covariance matrix of $\underline{Y}$ as follows:

$$\begin{aligned}
\widehat{\Lambda}_{\underline{Y}} &= \frac{1}{M}\sum_{k=1}^{M}\left(\underline{Y}^k - \widehat{\underline{m}}_{\underline{Y}}\right)\left(\underline{Y}^k - \widehat{\underline{m}}_{\underline{Y}}\right)^{\top} \\
&= \frac{1}{M}\sum_{k=1}^{M}\left(H\left(\underline{X}^k - \widehat{\underline{m}}_{\underline{X}}\right) + \underline{m}_{\underline{X}} - \widehat{\underline{m}}_{\underline{Y}}\right) \\
&\quad \times \left(H\left(\underline{X}^k - \widehat{\underline{m}}_{\underline{X}}\right) + \underline{m}_{\underline{X}} - \widehat{\underline{m}}_{\underline{Y}}\right)^{\top} \\
&= \frac{1}{M}\sum_{k=1}^{M} H\left(\underline{X}^k - \widehat{\underline{m}}_{\underline{X}}\right)\left(\underline{X}^k - \widehat{\underline{m}}_{\underline{X}}\right)^{\top} H^{\top} \\
&= H\widehat{\Lambda}_{\underline{X}}H^{\top} \\
&= \sqrt{\Lambda_{\underline{X}}}\left(\sqrt{\widehat{\Lambda}_{\underline{X}}}\right)^{-1}\left(\sqrt{\widehat{\Lambda}_{\underline{X}}}\sqrt{\widehat{\Lambda}_{\underline{X}}}\right)\left(\sqrt{\widehat{\Lambda}_{\underline{X}}}\right)^{-1}\sqrt{\Lambda_{\underline{X}}} \\
&= \Lambda_{\underline{X}}.
\end{aligned} \tag{5.51}$$

This transformation implies that the sample mean of $\underline{Y}^k$ is identical to the statistical mean of $\underline{X}$ and the sample covariance matrix of $\underline{Y}^k$ is identical to the statistical covariance matrix of $\underline{X}$.

To perform this transformation, we need to know the statistical covariance matrix of $\underline{X}$. Under such situations, this transformation improves the precision of the calculations obtained by Monte Carlo simulations.

5.4.2 Reduction of the Number of Simulations Using Antithetic Variables

To obtain the mean of a random variable with larger variance, one needs to run a very large number of simulations to attain the desired precision. In contrast, when the variance is small, the number of simulations needed is low. Therefore, it is imperative to find transformations in order to reduce the variance of the obtained variable.

The simplest variance reduction technique is the use of antithetic variables. This consists of generating N random variables X_i and building N other variables from these with the same distribution but negatively correlated with the generated variables.

It is easy to show that the variance of the sample mean obtained from the $2N$ variables is lower than the variance obtained from $2N$ independent variables. Indeed, consider

$$\widehat{m}_a = \frac{1}{2N}\sum_{k=1}^{N}\left(X_k + X_k^a\right), \tag{5.52}$$

where

$$\begin{aligned} E\left[\left(X_k^a - m_X\right)\left(X_j - m_X\right)\right] &= -\delta_{k,j}\sigma_X^2 \\ &= \begin{cases} -\sigma_X^2 & k = j \\ 0 & k \neq j \end{cases}. \end{aligned} \tag{5.53}$$

The variance of the sample mean $\widehat{m}_a$ is equal to:

$$\begin{aligned} \mathrm{Var}(\widehat{m}_a) &= E\left[(\widehat{m}_a - m_X)^2\right] \\ &= E\left[\left(\frac{1}{2N}\sum_{k=1}^{N}\left(X_k + X_k^a\right) - m_X\right)^2\right] \\ &= E\left[\left(\frac{1}{2N}\sum_{k=1}^{N}X_k + \frac{1}{2N}\sum_{k=1}^{N}X_k^a - m_X\right)^2\right] \\ &= E\left[\left(\frac{1}{2N}\sum_{k=1}^{N}(X_k - m_X) + \frac{1}{2N}\sum_{k=1}^{N}\left(X_k^a - m_X\right)\right)^2\right]. \end{aligned} \tag{5.54}$$

Since X_k are independent as well as the X_k^a, all the $2N$ variables X_k and X_j^a are independent except for the pairs X_k and X_k^a. We can then develop the expression for the variance to obtain:

$$\begin{aligned} \mathrm{Var}(\widehat{m}_a) = {} & \frac{1}{4N^2}\sum_{k=1}^{N}\sigma_X^2 + \frac{1}{4N^2}\sum_{k=1}^{N}\sigma_X^2 \\ & + \frac{1}{4N^2}\sum_{k=1}^{N}\sum_{j=1}^{N}E\left[(X_k - m_X)\left(X_j^a - m_X\right)\right]. \end{aligned} \tag{5.55}$$

The expectation of the last term in brackets is zero except for $k = j$ where

$$E[(X_k - m_X)\left(X_k^a - m_X\right)] = -\sigma_X^2. \tag{5.56}$$

Hence,

$$\text{Var}(\widehat{m}_a) = \frac{1}{2N}\sigma_X^2 - \frac{1}{4N}\sigma_X^2 = \frac{1}{4N}\sigma_X^2. \tag{5.57}$$

Meanwhile, the sample variance of 2*N* independent random variables is equal to

$$\frac{1}{2N}\sigma_X^2. \tag{5.58}$$

We can therefore note that we have improved twofold the variance of the sample mean by only generating half random variables.

Remark 4.1 In some cases, we cannot obtain a perfect antithetic variable, i.e. 100% negatively correlated with the generated variables. In this kind of situation, we will choose variables with same distribution and partially negatively correlated with the generated variables.

Example 4.2 Let's consider a random variable X uniformly distributed over the interval $[a, b]$, i.e. $U(a, b)$. The variable $X^a = b + a - X$ is a perfect antithetic variable of X. Indeed, we can see that X^a is uniformly distributed over the interval $[a, b]$ and is perfectly negatively correlated with X.

Example 4.3 Let's consider a Gaussian random variable X with mean m and variance σ, i.e. $X = N(m, \sigma^2)$. The variable $X^a = 2m - X$ is an antithetic variable with the same distribution and perfectly negatively correlated with X.

Example 4.4 Let's consider an exponential random variable X with probability density function:

$$f_X(x) = e^{-x}\mathbf{1}_{\{x \geq 0\}}. \tag{5.59}$$

We observe that, for this distribution, we cannot obtain a perfect antithetic variable from X. However, we can generate X from a uniform random variable $U(0, 1)$ with the transformation $X = -\log(1 - U)$.

We then use the transformed variable $\widetilde{X} = -\log(U)$. This transformation gives a variable $\widetilde{X}$ with the same statistics as X but its correlation with X is not -1. Indeed, $m_X = 1$ and

$$\begin{aligned} E\left[(X - m_X)(\widetilde{X} - m_X)\right] &= E\left[(\log(U) + 1)(\log(1 - U) + 1)\right] \\ &= 2E[\log(U)] + E[\log(U)\log(1 - U)] + 1. \end{aligned} \tag{5.60}$$

5.4.3 Reduction of the Number of Simulations Using Control Variates

The objective of simulations is to reduce the variance of the estimator used. We have just shown how the use of antithetic variables can significantly reduce the variance and, in the best case, we have a variance reduction of 50%. The antithetic variables technique exploits the negative correlations properties of the variables. Hence, if one can use other variables, not necessarily antithetic but negatively correlated with the generated variables, it is possible to reduce the variance of the estimator.

Let's consider a random variable X and another random variable Y correlated with X. We call Y, control variate of X. Assuming the statistical mean of Y is known, let's construct the following new variable:

$$X^* = X + \alpha \left(Y - E\left[Y\right]\right). \tag{5.61}$$

We observe that the statistical mean of X^* is identical to that of X: $m_X = m_{X^*}$. Hence, instead of estimating the mean of X, it is equivalent to estimate the mean of X^*.

The objective is to choose α by reducing the following variance of X^*:

$$\begin{aligned}\text{Var}(X^*) &= E\left[\left(X^* - m_{X^*}\right)^2\right] = E\left[\left(X + \alpha\left(Y - E\left[Y\right]\right) - m_{X^*}\right)^2\right] \\ &= \text{Var}(X) + \alpha^2\text{Var}(Y) + 2\alpha\text{Cov}(X, Y),\end{aligned} \tag{5.62}$$

where

$$\text{Cov}(X, Y) = E\left[(X - m_X)(Y - m_Y)\right]. \tag{5.63}$$

The optimal choice α^* is such that:

$$\frac{d\text{Var}(X^*)}{d\alpha} = 0 \quad \Rightarrow \quad 2\alpha^*\text{Var}(Y) + 2\text{Cov}(X, Y) = 0. \tag{5.64}$$

It implies

$$\alpha^* = -\frac{\text{Cov}(X, Y)}{\text{Var}(Y)}. \tag{5.65}$$

With this choice, the variance of X^* becomes:

$$\text{Var}(X^*) = \text{Var}(X) - \frac{[\text{Cov}(X, Y)]^2}{\text{Var}(Y)}. \tag{5.66}$$

This shows that Var(X^*) is lower than Var(X) which is our objective.

This analysis can also be applied with multiple control variates $Y_1, Y_2, \ldots, Y_k$ of X. The new transformed variable is:

$$X^* = X + \alpha_1\left(Y_1 - E\left[Y_1\right]\right) + \cdots + \alpha_k\left(Y_k - E\left[Y_k\right]\right). \tag{5.67}$$

Using vectorial form, we can rewrite the equation as follows:

$$X^* = X + \underline{\alpha}^\top(\underline{Y} - \underline{m_Y}), \tag{5.68}$$

where $\underline{\alpha} = (\alpha_1, \ldots, \alpha_k)^\top$, $\underline{Y} = (Y_1, \ldots, Y_k)^\top$ and $\underline{m_Y} = (E\left[Y_1\right], \ldots, E\left[Y_k\right])^\top$.

The variance of X^* becomes:

$$\begin{aligned}\mathrm{Var}(X^*) &= E\left[\left(X^* - m_{X^*}\right)^2\right] \\ &= E\Big[\left(X - m_X + \underline{\alpha}^\top(\underline{Y} - \underline{m}_Y)\right) \\ &\quad \times \left(X - m_X + (\underline{Y} - \underline{m}_Y)^\top \underline{\alpha}\right)\Big].\end{aligned} \tag{5.69}$$

Developing the right-hand side product yields:

$$\mathrm{Var}(X^*) = \mathrm{Var}(X) + \underline{\alpha}^\top \Lambda_{\underline{Y}} \underline{\alpha} + 2\underline{\alpha}^\top \underline{P}, \tag{5.70}$$

where

$$\underline{P} = E\left[(\underline{Y} - \underline{m}_Y)(X - m_X)\right] = (\mathrm{Cov}(X, Y_1), \ldots, \mathrm{Cov}(X, Y_k))^\top. \tag{5.71}$$

Assuming the covariance matrix of vector $\underline{Y}$ to be positive definite, the optimal choice for the vector $\underline{\alpha}$ corresponds to the solution of the equation:

$$\frac{d\mathrm{Var}(X^*)}{d\underline{\alpha}} = \left(\frac{d\mathrm{Var}(X^*)}{d\alpha_1}, \ldots, \frac{d\mathrm{Var}(X^*)}{d\alpha_k}\right)^\top = 0. \tag{5.72}$$

Applying the differential rule of a function with respect to a vector, it yields:

$$\frac{d\mathrm{Var}(X^*)}{d\underline{\alpha}} = 2\underline{P} + 2\Lambda_{\underline{Y}}\underline{\alpha} = 0. \tag{5.73}$$

Since the matrix $\Lambda_{\underline{Y}}$ is positive definite, it is therefore invertible and regular, and the solution of $\underline{\alpha}$ becomes:

$$\underline{\alpha}^* = -\Lambda_{\underline{Y}}^{-1}\underline{P}. \tag{5.74}$$

With this optimum choice, the variance of $X*$ becomes:

$$\mathrm{Var}(X^*) = \mathrm{Var}(X) - \underline{P}^\top \Lambda_{\underline{Y}}^{-1} \underline{P}. \tag{5.75}$$

Since the matrix $\Lambda_{\underline{Y}}$ is positive definite, its inverse is also positive definite. Thus, under the quadratic form, $\underline{P}^\top \Lambda_{\underline{Y}}^{-1} \underline{P}$ is a positive quantity, which means that Var(X^*) is lower than Var(X). In the next section, we provide an illustrative example and the MATLAB program for the implementation of this technique.

5.4.4 Importance Sampling

The sample mean is the estimator commonly used in the Monte Carlo method. We have also seen that the statistical precision (measured by the variance of the estimator) is inversely proportional to the variance of the random variable where we wish to calculate the mean. For rare events, this variance is too low, which means that we will need a very large number of simulations to reach the desired precision. This number of simulations required for precision purposes becomes prohibitive. In these situations, the classical Monte Carlo method is impractical.

The importance sampling technique is a method used to overcome this problem. It simply consists of transforming the variables in order to reduce the variance of the simulated variables.

The Approach

The principle of the method is explained as follows. Let's consider a random variable X with probability density function $f_X(x)$ and Y a transformation of X:

$$Y = h(X). \tag{5.76}$$

The mathematical expectation of Y is given by

$$E[Y] = m_Y = \int h(x) f_X(x) dx, \tag{5.77}$$

and its sample mean obtained with N samples X_k is:

$$\widehat{E}[Y] = \widehat{m}_Y = \frac{1}{N} \sum_{k=1}^{N} h(X_k), \tag{5.78}$$

where the sample variables X_k are independent and have the same probability density function $f_X(x)$.

Let $g_Y(y)$ be a given probability density function. Analytically, equation (5.77) can be rewritten as follows

$$E[Y] = \int h(y) \frac{f_X(y)}{g_Y(y)} g_Y(y) dy. \tag{5.79}$$

The integral (5.79) can be interpreted as the mean value of the random variable Z obtained from the transformation of the random variable Y with the probability density function $g_Y(y)$, where

$$Z(Y) = h(Y) \frac{f_X(Y)}{g_Y(Y)}. \tag{5.80}$$

Hence

$$E[Y] = E[Z]. \tag{5.81}$$

The sample mean of Z is therefore

$$\widehat{E}[Z] = \widehat{m}_Z = \frac{1}{N*} \sum_{k=1}^{N^*} Z(Y_k), \tag{5.82}$$

where the N^* random variables Y_k are independent and have the same probability density function $g_Y(y)$.

It is interesting to note that

$$E[\widehat{E}[Y]] = E[\widehat{E}[Z]]. \tag{5.83}$$

This means that one can use $\widehat{E}[Z]$ to estimate $E[Y]$. In the particular case where

$$Y = X = h(X), \tag{5.84}$$

equation (5.82) becomes

$$\widehat{E}[Z] = \frac{1}{N*} \sum_{k=1}^{N^*} \frac{Y_k f_X(Y_k)}{g_Y(Y_k)}, \tag{5.85}$$

and the relative error of the estimation is

$$\text{Prob}\left(\left|\frac{\widehat{E}[Z] - E[Z]}{E[Z]}\right| > \varepsilon\right) \leq \eta, \tag{5.86}$$

where η is the degree of certainty (i.e. $1 - \eta$ is the confidence level of the estimator).

When N and N^* are large, the precision of the estimator $\widehat{E}[Z]$ (or $\widehat{E}[Y]$) is given by

$$N^* \geq \left[Q^{-1}\left(\frac{\eta}{2}\right)\right]^2 \frac{1}{\varepsilon^2} \frac{\text{Var}(Z)}{E[Z]^2}, \tag{5.87}$$

with

$$Q(x) = \frac{1}{\sqrt{2\pi}} \int_x^{\infty} e^{-\frac{u^2}{2}} du = \frac{1}{2}\text{erfc}\left(\frac{x}{\sqrt{2}}\right). \tag{5.88}$$

Thus, N^* depends on Var(Z). To reduce N^*, one needs to reduce Var(Z). The reduction ratio for this kind of precision is by definition

$$\frac{\text{Var}(Z)}{\text{Var}(X)}. \tag{5.89}$$

Solving the problem consists of determining $g_Y(y)$ to reduce Var(Z).

Illustration

To illustrate the procedure, let's consider the following example. Consider V a standard Gaussian random variable. We would like to compute the following quantity using the Monte Carlo method:

$$\text{Prob}(V > 6) = \frac{1}{\sqrt{2\pi}} \int_6^{\infty} e^{-\frac{v^2}{2}} dv = Q(6). \tag{5.90}$$

This quantity is relatively small, i.e., approximately 10^{-9}. The classic Monte Carlo technique consists of generating N independent samples V_k and to estimate Prob($V > 6$):

$$\widehat{\text{Prob}}(V > 6) = \frac{1}{N} \sum_{k=1}^{N} I_6(V_k), \tag{5.91}$$

where

$$I_6(x) = \begin{cases} 1, & x \geq 6; \\ 0, & x < 6. \end{cases} \tag{5.92}$$

To obtain $\eta = 0.05$ and $\varepsilon = 0.1$, we have $\frac{1}{\eta} = 20$ and $\left[Q^{-1}\left(\frac{0.05}{2}\right)\right]^2 = 3.84$, hence

$$N \geq 3.84 \frac{1}{0.01} \frac{\sigma_Z^2}{E[Z]^2}. \tag{5.93}$$

$$X = I_6(x) = \begin{cases} 0, & x < 6; \\ 1, & x \geq 6. \end{cases} \tag{5.94}$$

It yields

$$E[X] = \text{Prob}(V \geq 6) \tag{5.95}$$

and

$$\text{Var}(X) = E[X^2] - E[X]^2 = \text{Prob}(V \geq 6) - E[X]^2. \tag{5.96}$$

Since $E[X] = \text{Prob}(V \geq 6) \sim 10^{-9}$, $E[X]^2$ is negligible and (5.93) becomes

$$N \geq \frac{3.84}{0.01}\frac{E[X]}{E[X]^2} = \frac{384}{E[X]} = 3.84 \times 10^{11}. \tag{5.97}$$

We then observe that the number of simulations required to reach the desired quality is excessively prohibitive. To significantly reduce the number of simulations, we need to determine an appropriate probability density function $g_Y(y)$, i.e., with $g_Y(y)$, Y occurs relatively frequently over the zone where we need to have $X > 6$. One immediate possible choice (illustrated by Figure 5.1) is

$$g_Y(y) = \frac{1}{\sqrt{2\pi}} e^{-\frac{(y-6)^2}{2}}. \tag{5.98}$$

Hence, using equation (5.80) we obtain:

$$Z = X(v)\frac{f(v)}{g(v)}, \tag{5.99}$$

and since

$$\frac{f(v)}{g(v)} = e^{-\frac{v^2}{2} + \frac{(v-6)^2}{2}} = e^{\frac{36}{2}} e^{-6v}, \tag{5.100}$$

it implies

$$Z(V) = X(V)e^{-6v}e^{18}, \tag{5.101}$$

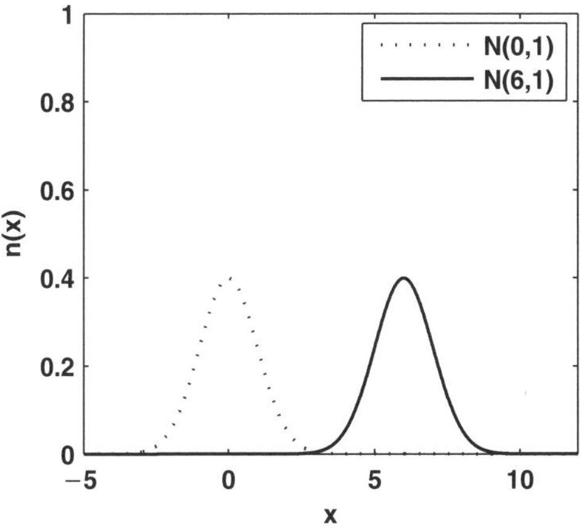

Figure 5.1 Probability density functions of the Normal distribution N(0, 1) and N(6, 1)

where

$$X(V) = \begin{cases} 0, & V < 6; \\ 1, & V \geq 6. \end{cases} \tag{5.102}$$

We have already shown that $E[Z] = E[X]$. We need to compute the variance of Z,

$$\text{Var}(Z) = E[Z^2] - E[Z]^2, \tag{5.103}$$

where

$$\begin{aligned} E[Z^2] &= \int z^2(v) f_V(v) dv \\ &= \int_6^\infty e^{-12v} e^{36} \frac{1}{\sqrt{2\pi}} e^{-\frac{v^2}{2}} dv \\ &= \frac{1}{\sqrt{2\pi}} e^{36} \int_6^\infty e^{-\frac{(v+12)^2}{2} + \frac{12^2}{2}} dv \\ &= e^{36+72} \frac{1}{\sqrt{2\pi}} \int_6^\infty e^{-\frac{(v+12)^2}{2}} dv. \end{aligned} \tag{5.104}$$

Applying the following transformation of variables: $v + 12 = u$, we obtain

$$\begin{aligned} E[Z^2] &= e^{108} \frac{1}{\sqrt{2\pi}} \int_{18}^\infty e^{-\frac{u^2}{2}} du \\ &= e^{108} Q(18). \end{aligned} \tag{5.105}$$

When α is large, we can approximate $Q(\alpha)$ by $\frac{1}{\sqrt{2\pi}\alpha} e^{-\frac{\alpha^2}{2}}$. Finally, we have:

$$\begin{aligned} E[Z^2] &= e^{108} \frac{1}{\sqrt{2\pi} 18} e^{-\frac{18^2}{2}} \\ &= \frac{e^{-162+108}}{\sqrt{2\pi} 18} \\ &= \frac{e^{-54}}{\sqrt{2\pi} 18}. \end{aligned} \tag{5.106}$$

From the previous calculations, we obtain $E[Z]^2$, which allows us to determine Var(Z).

Using (5.87) (with $\eta = 0.05$ and $\varepsilon = 0.1$), we observe that the reduction in the number of simulations is impressive. The number of simulations needed is around 1000.

5.5 APPLICATION CASES OF RANDOM VARIABLES SIMULATIONS

5.5.1 Application Case: Generation of Random Variables as a Function of the Number of Simulations

This application consists of writing a program to generate two Gaussian random variables (X_1, X_2) with the following moments: $E[X_1] = 0$, $E[X_2] = 0$, $E[X_1^2] = a^2$, $E[X_2^2] = b^2$ and $E[X_1 X_2] = c^2$.

Table 5.3 Impact of the number of simulations with simple simulations

N	$E[X_1]$	$E[X_1^2]$	$E[X_2]$	$E[X_2^2]$	$E[X_1X_2]$	ρ
10	−0.089	0.087	−0.322	0.726	0.191	0.760
100	0.054	0.176	0.042	0.671	0.284	0.826
1000	−0.023	0.155	−0.051	0.622	0.235	0.757
10000	0.004	0.158	0.011	0.637	0.247	0.779
100000	0.001	0.160	0.003	0.639	0.250	0.782
Exact values	0.000	0.160	0.000	0.640	0.250	0.781

Simple Simulations

Generate $N = 10$, 100, 1000, 10000 and 100000 pairs of variables with the following parameters: $a = 0.40$, $b = 0.80$, $c = 0.50$. Evaluate their first and second order sample moments, as well as the empirical correlation between the two variables. Compare the sample statistics with the theoretical statistics for different values of N. What do you observe?

The MATLAB program used to produce the simulation results given in Table 5.3 is the following:

```
function [Moy,Cov]=NumberSim(a,b,c,NbTraj)
%Function comparing the sample statistics as a function of
%the number of simulations
%a: Standard deviation of X1
%b: Standard deviation of X2
%c: Covariance of X1 and X2
%NbTraj: Number of simulations

MatrixCovariance = [a^2,c^2;c^2,b^2];
MatrixL = chol(MatrixCovariance)';

X = MatrixL*randn(2,NbTraj);
Moy=mean(X,2);
Cov=cov(X');

end
```

where the MATLAB functions *mean* and *cov* give the mean vector and the covariance matrix of X.

Table 5.3 shows that one needs a relatively large number of simulations to yield more accurate first and second order moments.

Simulations with Quadratic Resampling Technique

Use the quadratic resampling technique of Barraquand (1995) to generate $N = 10$, 100, 1000, 10000 and 100000 pairs of variables with the following parameters: $a = 0.40$, $b = 0.80$, $c = 0.50$. Evaluate their first and second order sample moments, as well as the sample correlation between the two random variables. Compare the sample statistics with the theoretical statistics for different values of N. What do you observe?

Here is the MATLAB program for the generation of samples using the quadratic resampling technique.

```
function Rep=ReQuadratic(X,MoyTheo,CovTheo)
%Function to perform the quadratic resampling
%X: Sample matrix of the variables where the number of columns
%  is equal to the number of simulations and the number of line is
%  the dimension of the vector
%MoyTheo: Theoretical mean vector of the random vector
%CovTheo: Theoretical covariance matrix of the random vector
%Rep: Sample matrix of the modified sample values

NbTraj = size(X,2);

%Determination of the sample parameters
MoyEmp = mean(X,2);
CovEmp = cov((X-repmat(MoyEmp,1,NbTraj))');
LEmp = chol(CovEmp)';

LTheo = chol(CovTheo)';

Rep = LTheo*inv(LEmp)*(X-repmat(MoyEmp,1,NbTraj)) ...
        + repmat(MoyTheo,1,NbTraj);

end
```

We can then use the quadratic resampling technique in the general program as follows

```
function [Moy,Cov]=SimulationsWithRQ(a,b,c,NbTraj)
%Function comparing the sample moments as a function of
%the number of simulations
%a: Standard deviation of X1
%b: Standard deviation of X2
%c: Covariance of X1 and X2
%NbTraj: Number of simulations

%Theoretical parameters of the variables
MoyTheo=[0;0];
CovTheo=[a^2,c^2;c^2,b^2];
L=chol(CovTheo)';

%Simulation of the random variables
Sample=randn(2,NbTraj);
SampleSimple=repmat(MoyTheo,1,NbTraj)+L*Sample;

%Calling the function ReQuadratic
XRQ=ReQuadratic(SampleSimple,MoyTheo,CovTheo);

Moy=mean(XRQ,2);
Cov=cov(XRQ');

end
```

Table 5.4 Impact of the number of simulations with the quadratic resampling

N	$E[X_1]$	$E[X_1^2]$	$E[X_2]$	$E[X_2^2]$	$E[X_1X_2]$	ρ
10	0.000	0.160	0.000	0.640	0.250	0.781
100	0.000	0.160	0.000	0.640	0.250	0.781
1000	0.000	0.160	0.000	0.640	0.250	0.781
10000	0.000	0.160	0.000	0.640	0.250	0.781
100000	0.000	0.160	0.000	0.640	0.250	0.781
Exact values	0.000	0.160	0.000	0.640	0.250	0.781

Results are presented in Table 5.4. Contrary to the simple simulation case, the quadratic resampling technique gives the exact first and second order moments, i.e., the sample moments are equal to the theoretical moments regardless of the number of simulations.

5.5.2 Application Case: Simulations and Improvement of the Simulations' Quality

Let's consider two Gaussian random variables X_1 and X_2 with means $m_1 = 10$ and $m_2 = 15$, and variances $\sigma_1^2 = 0.20^2$ and $\sigma_2^2 = 0.50^2$, respectively. We assume the correlation between the two Gaussian random variables to be $\rho = -0.30$.

Simulations with Antithetic Variables

Use antithetic variables in your simulations to calculate the sample first order moments of the random variables $Y_1 = e^{X_1}$ and $Y_2 = e^{X_2}$. Devoid of a variance reduction scheme, the MATLAB program used to simulate may be as follows

```
function Moy=SimulationsWithoutTechnique
%Function to calculate the mean of the variable Y1 without using
%a simulation improving quality technique

NbTraj=100; %Number of simulations
sigma1=0.2; %Standard deviation of X1
sigma2=0.5; %Standard deviation of X1
rho=-0.3;   %Correlation between X1 and X2

%Theoretical mean and covariance of the variables X1 and X2.
MoyTheo=[10;15];
CovTheo=[sigma1^2,rho*sigma1*sigma2;rho*sigma1*sigma2,sigma2^2];

Sample=randn(2,NbTraj); %Simulation of the Gaussian variables
L=chol(CovTheo)';       %Cholesky factorization

%Simulation of the variables X1 and X2
SampleSimple=repmat(MoyTheo,1,NbTraj)+L*Sample;

%Transformation of the variables X1 and X2 into Y1 and Y2
Y1Simple=exp(SampleSimple(1,:));
```

```
Y2Simple=exp(SampleSimple(2,:));

Moy=mean(Y1Simple,2);

end
```

The MATLAB simulation program with antithetic variables may be as follows:

```
function Rep=SimulationsAnti
%Function to calculate the mean of the variable Y1 using the
%antithetic variables technique.
%Rep: Mean of the variable Y1.

NbTraj=100;
sigma1=0.2;
sigma2=0.5;
rho=-0.3;

%Theoretical parameters
MoyTheo=[10;15];
CovTheo=[sigma1^2,rho*sigma1*sigma2;rho*sigma1*sigma2,sigma2^2];
L=chol(CovTheo)';

%Simulation of the random variables.
Sample=randn(2,NbTraj);
SampleSimple=repmat(MoyTheo,1,NbTraj)+L*Sample;

%Introduction of the antithetic variables
XAnti=cat(2,SampleSimple,2*repmat(MoyTheo,1,NbTraj)-...
                  SampleSimple);

%Transformation of Xi into Yi
Y1Anti=exp(XAnti(1,:));
Y2Anti=exp(XAnti(2,:));

Rep=mean(Y1Anti,2);

end
```

Simulation results are presented in Table 5.5.

Table 5.5 Simulations with antithetic variables

	Simple		Antithetic	
NbTraj	Estimation	Error	Estimation	Error
100	2.2097 E04	418	2.2424 E04	302
1000	2.2264 E04	141	2.2482 E04	103
10000	2.2450 E04	46	2.2482 E04	32
100000	2.2456 E04	14	2.2469 E04	10
1000000	2.2478 E04	5	2.2472 E04	3

We note that the antithetic variables not only improve the precision, but also considerably reduce the variance of the simulated values.

Simulations with Control Variates

Use the control variates in your simulations to obtain the sample first order moments of the random variables $Y_1 = e^{X_1}$ and $Y_2 = e^{X_2}$. The implementation of this method is as follows. We use X_i as a control variate for Y_i.

```
function Rep=SimulationsCont
%Function to calculate the mean of the variable Y1 using the
%control variates technique

NbTraj=100;
sigma1=0.2;
sigma2=0.5;
rho=-0.3;

% Theoretical parameters
MoyTheo=[10;15];
CovTheo=[sigma1^2,rho*sigma1*sigma2;rho*sigma1*sigma2,sigma2^2];
L=chol(CovTheo)';

%Simulation of random variables
Sample=randn(2,NbTraj);
SampleSimple=repmat(MoyTheo,1,NbTraj)+L*Sample;

%Transformation of Xi into Yi using the function Control given
below
% for the control variates
Y1Cont=Control(exp(SampleSimple(1,:)),...
                      SampleSimple(1,:),10);
Y2Cont=Control(exp(SampleSimple(2,:)),...
                      SampleSimple(2,:),15);

Rep=mean(Y1Cont,2);

end


function Rep=Control(A,B,MoyB)
%Function using the control variates technique
%to adjust the simulated variables.
%A: Simulated variables
%B: Control variables
%MoyB: Theoretical mean of the control variables
%Rep: Modified variables

%Covariance between A and B
MatrixCovEmp = cov(A,B);
```

Table 5.6 Simulations with control variates

	Simple		Control	
NbTraj	Estimation	Error	Estimation	Error
100	2.2097 E04	418	2.2414 E04	48
1000	2.2264 E04	141	2.2471 E04	20
10000	2.2450 E04	46	2.2482 E04	7
100000	2.2456 E04	14	2.2469 E04	2
1000000	2.2478 E04	5	2.2472 E04	1

```
%Calculation of the parameter alpha
alpha = - MatrixCovEmp(1,2)/MatrixCovEmp(2,2);

Rep = A + alpha*(B - MoyB);

end
```

With these control variates, we obtain more precise results as shown in Table 5.6.

An interesting exercise for the reader would be to combine the different variance reduction techniques with those that improve the precision (we may call this an hybrid approach).

Notes and Complementary Readings

For additional references, the reader can eventually consult the following classical books on Monte Carlo simulations and numerical methods: Press, Teukolsky, Vetterling and Flannery (1992), and Rubinstein (1981).

For complementary readings on variance reduction techniques and simulation quality improvement methods, see Dupire (1998), Glasserman (2003), Jäckel (2002), Kloeden, Platen and Schurz (1997), Lapeyre, Pardoux and Sentis (1998).

6

Fundamentals of Quasi Monte Carlo (QMC) Simulations

In the previous chapter, we introduced the Monte Carlo simulation techniques and presented variance reduction and precision improving schemes. We also saw that the Monte Carlo method allows us to estimate the mathematical expectation of a random quantity by generating a number of statistically independent and identically distributed variables.

Monte Carlo simulation is a reasonable choice when we can't analytically estimate this mathematical expectation. We shouldn't forget that the mathematical expectation is represented by a multi-dimensional integral (in the case of random vectors). Viewed in this perspective, the Monte Carlo method is an interesting alternative when we want to numerically evaluate complex integrals.

This method has a weakness stemming from the random nature of the results. Because of this, not long after the introduction of the Monte Carlo method at the end of the 1940s, researchers were interested in the possibility of replacing the random samples in the computations with deterministic series. This corresponds to the fundamental idea of the Quasi Monte Carlo method.

These sequences are known as low discrepancy sequences. As we saw previously, we can always find transformation of variables to transform the integration domain to a hypercube. Building a low discrepancy sequence consists of choosing the points (or sequences) inside the hypercube in order to assure good numerical results for the integration.

The concept of low discrepancy corresponds to the gap between the sample originating from a deterministic sequence and that obtained from a uniform random variable. The sequence has the property that, for all integers n, the first n elements of the sequence are almost uniformly distributed on $[0, 1]$. The definition of "almost uniformly distributed" may vary depending on the measure used to define the difference between two sequences.

In this chapter, we present different algorithms used to generate low discrepancy sequences (LDS). The Van Der Corput sequence is the simplest one and serves as a base in building other sequences used in finance. The best known sequences are those of Halton, Faure and Sobol. The building principle of these sequences consists of dividing the unit hypercube into smaller hypercubes whose faces are parallel to the faces of the unit hypercube. One point of the sequence is placed in each small hypercube. Once all the hypercubes contain one point, then the unit hypercube is subdivided into smaller ones as new points are distributed in the empty spaces.

The dimension of a sequence d is usually defined as the number of time steps $\frac{T}{\Delta t}$ or the number of underlying assets depending on the problem to be solved. The biggest challenge for having a good low discrepancy sequence is to avoid the clustering of points in a small region. This phenomenon of finding many points in a small region is often found in standard Monte Carlo simulations and is the result of correlations between the dimensions of a sequence, that is the correlation between two instants t and s or the one of two underlying asset values simulated. This correlation is described later in the chapter.

At the end of the chapter, we provide a comparative overview of the different sequences. Another application of the Quasi Monte Carlo method is presented in Chapter 15. However, it is important to note that the efficiency of this method is not always guaranteed; it depends on the problem we are studying.

6.1 VAN DER CORPUT SEQUENCE (BASIC SEQUENCE)

The Van Der Corput sequence is the basic sequence of many Quasi Monte Carlo simulations (QMC). We now present the method to follow in order to determine the nth element of the sequence. We begin by choosing a prime number b. To find the nth number, we simply have to perform the following operations:

1. Write n in base b; this allows us to find $a_j(n)$ such that:

$$n = \sum_{j=0}^{m} a_j(n) b^j, \tag{6.1}$$

   where m is the smallest integer such that $a_j(n) = 0$ for all $j > m$.
2. "Reverse" the number n to the decimal point (see example) to find the value of the nth element which we denote by b_n:

$$b_n = \Phi_b(n) = \sum_{j=0}^{m} \frac{a_j(n)}{b^{j+1}}. \tag{6.2}$$

   In reversing the number, we make sure that the value lies in the interval (0, 1). For example, if $n = 11_{10}$, or equivalently 102_3, then $3_n = 19/27$ which equals 0.201_3.

If the chosen base is 2, then we have the following sequence:

$$0, 1/2, 1/4, 3/4, 1/8, 5/8, 3/8, 7/8, 1/16, 9/16, 3/16, 11/16, 5/16, 13/16, \ldots \tag{6.3}$$

However, in the case of base 3, we have:

$$0, 1/3, 2/3, 1/9, 4/9, 7/9, 2/9, 5/9, 8/9, 1/27, 10/27, 19/27, 2/27, \ldots \tag{6.4}$$

The further we look into the sequence, the closer to 1 the points will be (without ever getting exactly 1). We present next a MATLAB program that allows us to find the nth element of the sequence in base b.

```
function rep=VanDerCorput(n,b)
%Function that computes the elements of the Van Der Corput sequence
%n: Beginning point to generate the sequence
%b: base of the sequence
%The n th element in base b
bn=0;
%j represents the powers of b in the decomposition of n
j=0;
```

```
while n~=0
    bn=bn + mod(n,b)/b^(j+1);
    n=floor(n/b);
    j=j+1;
end

rep=bn;
end
```

6.2 HALTON SEQUENCE

The Halton sequence is a multi-dimensional extension of the Van Der Corput sequence. This sequence is easily derived from the Van Der Corput method. To build the Halton sequence, we use the points in the sequence of the Van Der Corput but change the base for each dimension. We use base 2 for the first dimension, base 3 for the second dimension, base 5 for the third dimension, etc. In fact, the xth dimension will be the Van Der Corput sequence obtained from the xth prime number. In Table 6.1, we show the first elements of the Halton sequence in dimensions 1, 2, 3 and 4.

If we use MATLAB's random number generator to generate 1000 couples in the unit square, then we obtain Figure 6.1.

In the Halton sequence case, we get Figure 6.2 for dimensions 1 and 2 when we have 1000 points.

We can see from Figure 6.2 that the points are more evenly distributed and scattered in the unit square. With MATLAB's random generator, the sequence contains many points condensed and clustered in the same area. The problem with the Halton sequence occurs with higher dimensions. Too many points are needed to cover the entire unit hypercube. For example, the points for the 27th and 28th dimensions are represented in Figure 6.3.

To solve this problem, we will permute some Van Der Corput sequences in order to disperse our sample.

Table 6.1 First terms of Halton sequence

Term	Dimension 1	Dimension 2	Dimension 3	Dimension 4
	base 2	base 3	base 5	base 7
1	1/2	1/3	1/5	1/7
2	1/4	2/3	2/5	2/7
3	3/4	1/9	3/5	3/7
4	1/8	4/9	4/5	4/7
5	5/8	7/9	1/25	5/7
6	3/8	2/9	6/25	6/7
7	7/8	5/9	11/25	1/49
8	1/16	8/9	16/25	8/49
9	3/16	1/27	21/25	15/49

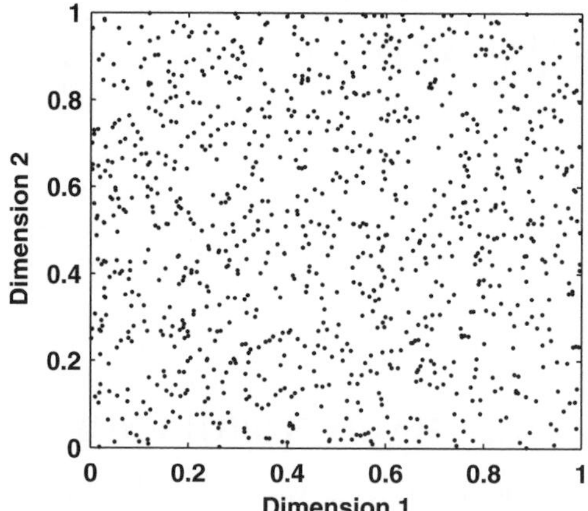

Figure 6.1 MATLAB's random generator

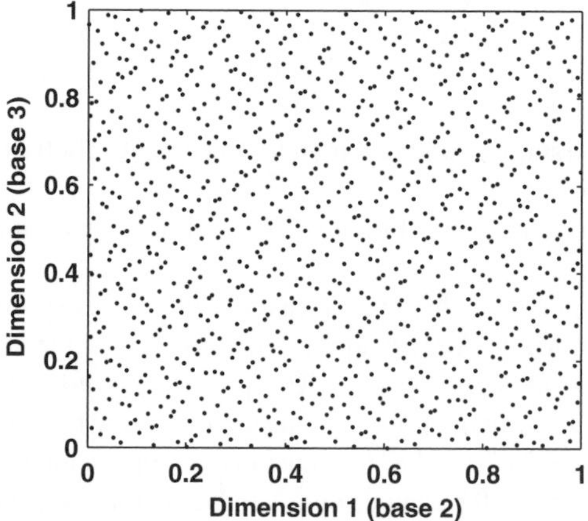

Figure 6.2 1000 elements of the Halton sequence in dimensions 1 and 2

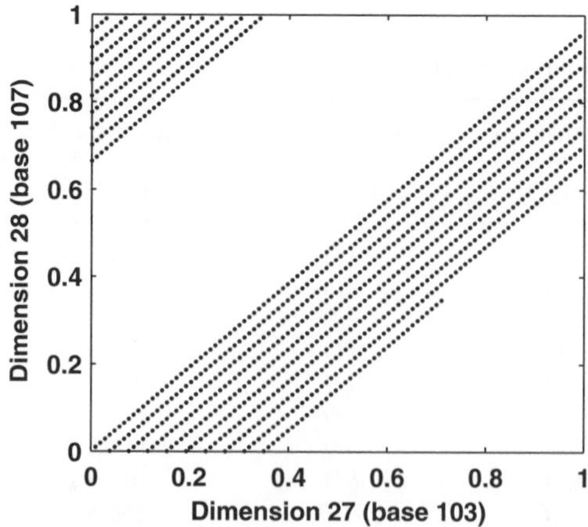

Figure 6.3 1000 terms of the Halton sequence for dimensions 27 and 28

6.3 FAURE SEQUENCE

The Faure sequence looks like the Halton one, with two major differences:

- We choose the same base for all of our problem's dimensions,
- We use a permutation of the vector composed of the elements for each dimension.

For a d-dimensional simulation, we take Van Der Corput sequence in base b, where b is the smallest prime number such that $b \geq d$ and we permute the terms. The algorithm is given by:

1. $n = \sum_{i=0}^{m} a_i^1(n) b^i$,
2. $b_n^1 = \sum_{i=0}^{m} \frac{a_i^1(n)}{p^{i+1}}$,
3. $a_i^k(n) = \sum_{j=0}^{m} \frac{j!}{i!(j-i)!} a_i^{k-1}(n) \quad \mathrm{mod}(b)$,
4. $b_n^k = \sum_{i=0}^{m} \frac{a_i^k(n)}{b^{i+1}}$.

We can further simplify the calculations by using matrix notation. The previously presented algorithm can be rewritten as:

$$\begin{pmatrix} a_0^k(n) \\ a_1^k(n) \\ a_2^k(n) \\ a_3^k(n) \\ \vdots \end{pmatrix} = \begin{pmatrix} \binom{0}{0} & \binom{1}{0} & \binom{2}{0} & \binom{3}{0} & \cdots \\ 0 & \binom{1}{1} & \binom{2}{1} & \binom{3}{1} & \cdots \\ 0 & 0 & \binom{2}{2} & \binom{3}{2} & \cdots \\ 0 & 0 & 0 & \binom{3}{3} & \cdots \\ \vdots & \vdots & \vdots & \vdots & \ddots \end{pmatrix} \begin{pmatrix} a_0^{k-1}(n) \\ a_1^{k-1}(n) \\ a_2^{k-1}(n) \\ a_3^{k-1}(n) \\ \vdots \end{pmatrix}. \tag{6.5}$$

In MATLAB this algorithm can be implemented as follows

```
function Faure(nb, Dim1, b)
%Function that generates Faure sequence elements
%nb: Number of elements to generate
%Dim1: First dimension of the random points
%b: base

bn=zeros(nb,2);

for l=1:nb
  %We decompose l in base b
  a=decompose(l,b);
  m=size(a,1);

  %Transition matrix between dimensions
  MatTrans=zeros(m,m);
  for j=1:m
    for i=j:m
      MatTrans(j,i)=nchoosek(i-1,j-1);
    end
  end

  %Computation of vector a and for next iteration
  a=mod(MatTrans^(Dim1-1)*a,b);
  aplus1=mod(MatTrans*a,b);
```

```
    %Computations of points bn
    for f=1:m
      bn(1,1)=bn(1,1)+a(f,1)/b^(f);
      bn(1,2)=bn(1,2)+aplus1(f,1)/b^(f);
    end
end

%We plot the points we got
figure
plot(bn(:,1),bn(:,2),'.')
end


%Function that decomposes a number in the given base
function rep=decompose(n,b)
%n: Number to decompose
%b: base of the decomposition

temp=1;
while n~=0
  rep(temp,1)=mod(n,b);
  n=floor(n/b);
  temp=temp+1;
end
end
```

Using this program, we obtain the random samples plotted in Figures 6.4 and 6.5.

Similar to the Halton case, Faure sequence's speed decreases when the dimension increases. However, this feature is less problematic than the Halton sequence since the prime numbers used are smaller. For example, when working in dimension 50 the Faure sequence uses the prime number 53, the smallest prime number greater than 50, while the Halton sequence uses

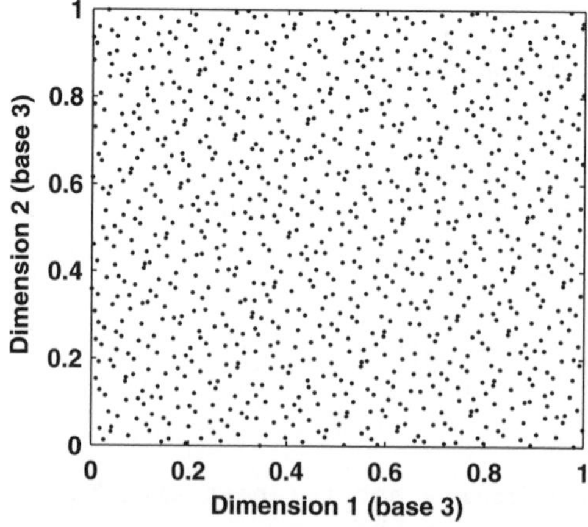

Figure 6.4 1000 terms of Faure sequence in dimensions 1 and 2

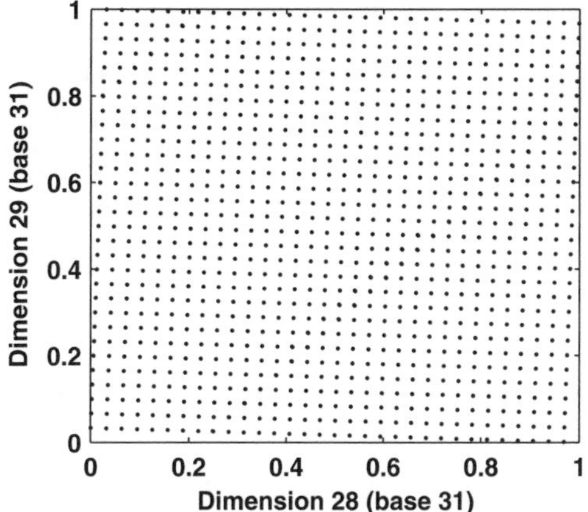

Figure 6.5 1000 terms of Faure sequence in dimensions 28 and 29

prime number 229 which is the 50th prime number. Faure's approach links the theory of low discrepancy sequence with the combinatorial theory of vector permutations. Faure sequence's speed decreases starting from the 25th dimension. Many people consider the Faure sequence to be significantly more time consuming than the Halton sequence, or the Sobol sequence which is described in the next section.

6.4 SOBOL SEQUENCE

The Sobol sequence is built from the Van Der Corput sequence by alternating the elements for each dimension. We still have the same elements but we permute the order. We present the algorithm and its implementation for obtaining the Sobol sequence. Suppose that we want to generate the $n+1^{th}$ term of the sequence for dimension j denoted by $x^j{}_{n+1}$. We begin the sequence with $x_1 = 0.5$ in base ten or equivalently 0.1 in binary. We begin by writing n in binary.

$$n = n_w 2^{w-1} + n_{w-1} 2^{w-2} + \ldots + n_2 2^1 + n_1. \tag{6.6}$$

We call k the subscript i of the first coefficient $n_i \neq 0$ in the binary representation of n. For example, if $n_1 = 1$ ($n_1 \neq 0$) then $k = 1$, if $n_1 = 0$ and $n_2 = 1$ ($n_2 \neq 0$) then we take $k = 2, \ldots$ Finally, we only need to compute element x_{n+1} in the following way:

$$x_{n+1} = x_n \oplus v_k, \tag{6.7}$$

where v_k is the kth direction for dimension j (keep in mind that all the calculations are only for dimension j). The v_k are deterministic numbers. The symbol $\oplus$ represents the exclusive binary operator "OR". The elements v_k are used to permute the Van Der Corput sequence terms. They are generated by recurrence:

$$v_i = a_1 v_{i-1} \oplus a_2 v_{i-2} \oplus \ldots \oplus a_{q-1} v_{i-q+1} \oplus v_{i-q} \oplus (v_{i-q}/2^q), \tag{6.8}$$

where this time, $i > q$ and a_l are the coefficients (0 or 1) of a degree q primitive polynomial of the form $P(x) = x^q + a_1 x^{q-1} + a_2 x^{q-2} + \ldots + a_{q-1} x^1 + 1$. We associate a primitive polynomial with each dimension in order to permute the sequence. Our aim with this book is

Table 6.2 Primitive polynomials for first dimensions

Degree	Primitive polynomials modulo 2
1	$x+1$
2	x^2+x+1
3	x^3+x+1 and x^3+x^2+1
4	x^4+x+1 and x^4+x^3+1
5	$x^5+x^2+1, x^5+x^3+1, x^5+x^3+x^2+x+1, x^5+x^4+x^2+x+1, x^5+x^4+x^3+x+1$ and $x^5+x^4+x^3+x^2$
6	$x^6+x+1, x^6+x^4+x^3+x+1, x^6+x^5+1, x^6+x^5+x^2+x+1, x^6+x^5+x^3+x^2+1$ and $x^6+x^5+x^4+x+1$

not to go over the theory of primitive polynomials or the algebraic theory so we are presenting only some of them here. We fill Table 6.2 with primitive polynomials up to degree 6.

Very often it is more convenient to modify the v_i and work with the values M_i. The values of M_i are defined by:

$$M_i = 2^i v_i \tag{6.9}$$

and thus satisfy the recurrence

$$M_i = 2a_1M_{i-1} \oplus 2^2a_2M_{i-2} \oplus \ldots \oplus 2^{q-1}a_{q-1}M_{i-q+1} \oplus 2^qM_{i-q} \oplus M_{i-q}. \tag{6.10}$$

It follows from the properties of v_i that M_i is an integer odd number between 0 and 2^i. In order to get the values of M_i by recurrence, we need the starting points for each dimension.

Table 6.3 presents some examples of the terms used for the implementation. We must remark that the number of initial values depends on the dimension of our problem since for higher dimensions M_i depends on $M_{i-1}, M_{i-2}, M_{i-3} \ldots$.

In order to simplify the algorithm, instead of generating values of x_i, we will re-scale the values to generate y_i which will be a multiple of x_i. Suppose we want to generate x_{n+1}. Set m_{n+1} to be the smallest power of 2 such that

$$2^{m_{n+1}} \geq n+1. \tag{6.11}$$

We can show that

$$m_{n+1} = [\log(n+1)/\log(2)]. \tag{6.12}$$

Table 6.3 M_i's initial values

Degree	Polynomial	Initial values			
1	0	1			
2	1	1	1		
3	1	1	3	7	
3	2	1	3	3	
4	1	1	1	3	13
4	4	1	1	5	9

By setting $y_{n+1} = 2^{m_{n+1}} x_{n+1}$, we can compute

$$\begin{aligned} y_{n+1} &= 2^{m_{n+1}} x_{n+1} \\ &= 2^{m_n}(x_n \oplus v_k) \\ &= 2^{m_n}(x_n \oplus M_k/2^k) \\ &= 2^{m_n} x_n \oplus 2^{m-k} M_k \\ &= \begin{cases} y_n \oplus 2^{m_{n+1}-k} M_k & \text{if } \mathrm{m_n} = \mathrm{m_{n+1}} \\ 2y_n \oplus 2^{m_{n+1}-k} M_k & \text{if not} \end{cases}. \end{aligned} \tag{6.13}$$

Let us now present an algorithm to generate the Sobol sequence. This algorithm borrowed from *Numerical Recipes in C* by Press et al. (1992) will be programmed in MATLAB. QMC techniques rely heavily on number theory, which can be too technical. For practical purposes, we provide here only a general description of the method.

1. Select a primitive polynomial for dimension j.
2. Randomly choose the starting values for the first terms M_i (those we need to begin the recurrence).
3. Determine position k of the rightmost zero in the decomposition of n in base 2.
4. Compute a new M_i by recurrence if needed with the chosen polynomial in step 1 and the starting values of M.
5. Compute the value of y_{n+1} with the formula shown above.
6. Compute x_{n+1} from y_{n+1} using $x_{n+1} = y_{n+1}/2^{m_{n+1}}$.
7. Return to step 3 to generate the following elements of the sequence.

Example 4.1 We begin with the polynomial

$$P(x) = x^2 + x + 1 \tag{6.14}$$

and with initial values $M_1 = 1$, $M_2 = 1$, $y_1 = 1$. It follows that $x_1 = 1/2$. For the second term, we have $k = 2$ since $1_{base10} = 1_{base2} = 1 * 2^0 + 0 * 2^1$ and $m_2 = 2$ since $2^2 \geq 3$ and $2^1 < 3$. Thus

$$\begin{aligned} y_2 &= 2y_1 \oplus M_2 \\ &= 10_2 \oplus 2^0 1_2 \\ &= 11_2 \\ &= 3_{10} \end{aligned}$$

and $x_2 = y_2/2^2 = 0.75$. For the third term, $k = 1$ since $2_{base10} = 01_{base2} = 0 * 2^0 + 1 * 2^1$, $m_3 = 2$ since $2^2 \geq 4$ and $2^1 < 4$,

$$\begin{aligned} y_3 &= y_2 \oplus 2^{2-1} M_1 \\ &= 11_2 \oplus 10_2 \\ &= 01_2 \\ &= 1_{10} \end{aligned}$$

and $x_3 = y_3/2^2 = 0.25$. For the fourth term, $k = 3$ since $3_{base10} = 110_{base2} = 1 * 2^0 + 1 * 2^1 + 0 * 2^2$, $m_4 = 3$ since $2^3 \geq 8$ and $2^2 < 8$. We find $M_3 = 7$ and

$$\begin{aligned} y_4 &= 2y_3 \oplus 2^0 M_3 \\ &= 10_2 \oplus 111_2 \\ &= 101_2 \\ &= 5_{10} \end{aligned}$$

and $x_4 = y_4/2^3 = 0.6250$.

Here is a MATLAB program to generate the Sobol sequence.

```
function rep=SobolShuffle(Nb)
%Function that generates points of Sobol sequence
%Nb: Number of points to simulate
Polynomial=1; %Choice of a polynomial
Degree=2; %Degree of chosen polynomial
M=[1;1]; %Initial values of the M_i's
%First step
m=1;
y(1)=1;
x(1)=y(1)/2^m;
%Principal loop for elements 2 and above
for n=2:Nb
    Position=Pos(n-1);
    %Add an element to vector M
    if Position>size(M)
        M=AddM(M,Polynomial,Degree);
    end
    m=ceil(log(n+1)/log(2));
    y(n)=bitxor(2^(m==Position)*y(n-1),...
                    2^(m-Position)*M(Position));
    x(n)=y(n)/2^m;
end
rep=x;
end

%Function determining position of rightmost
%zero in the decomposition in base 2 of k
function rep=Pos(k)
%k: Number to decompose
PosTemp=1;
while bitand(k,1)==1
    PosTemp=PosTemp+1;
    k=bitshift(k,-1);
end
rep=PosTemp;
end
```

```
%Function that computes a new value M
function rep=AddM(M,Polynomial,Degree)
%M: actual vector
%Polynomial: Primitive polynomial
%Degree: Degree of the chosen polynomial (from table)
Length=size(M,1);
Temp=bitxor(2^(Degree)*M(Length+1-Degree),...
               M(Length+1-Degree));
i=Degree-1;
while Polynomial~=0
   Temp=bitxor(Temp,2^(i)*mod(Polynomial,2)*M(Length+1-i));
   Polynomial=bitshift(Polynomial,-1);
   i=i-1;
end
rep=[M;Temp];
end
```

This sequence has been used as a benchmark for many efficiency tests for QMC deterministic methods.

6.5 LATIN HYPERCUBE SAMPLING

This method is different from the previous ones since it is no longer deterministic but random. In fact, we proceed as follows:

1. Divide each dimension of our space in N sections.
2. Generate a uniform random variable and randomly distribute it anywhere in the first section.
3. We repeat the previous steps to distribute the values in all the sections of our problem.

We present here the MATLAB program that follows these steps. In this program, we set N to be the number of points to simulate while k is the dimension of the sample:

```
function rep = LHS(N,k)
%Function using the latin hypercube method
%N: Number of points to generate
%k: Dimension of the sample

%Generation of the random numbers matrix
Matrix = rand(N,k);
%Loop to generate the permutations and mixing the terms

for j=1:k
    per = randperm(N);
    Matrix(:,j) = (per'-1+Matrix(:,j))/N;
end

rep = Matrix;

end
```

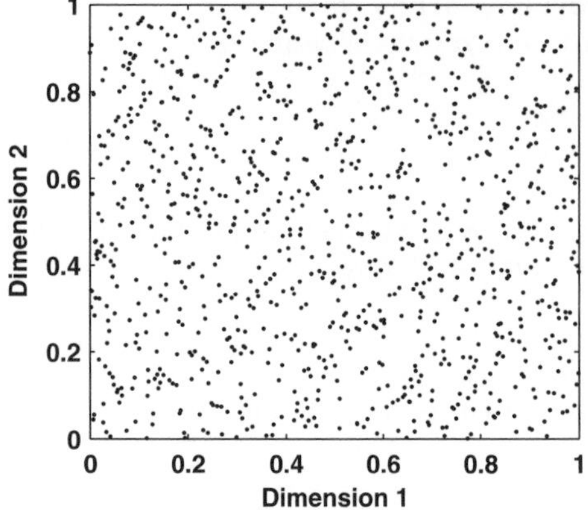

Figure 6.6 1000 points of the Latin Hypercube in dimensions 1 and 2

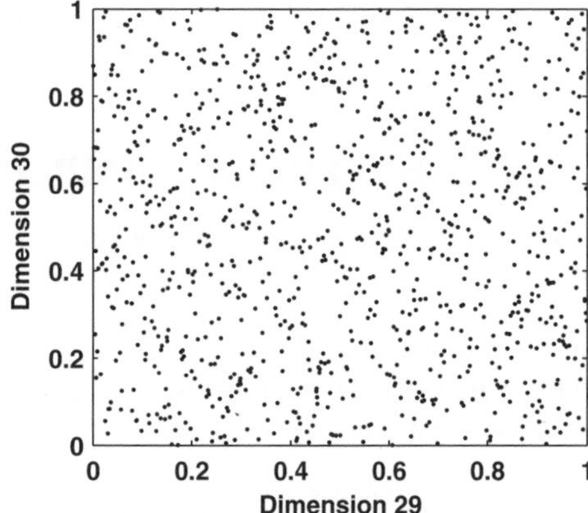

Figure 6.7 1000 points of the Latin Hypercube in dimensions 29 and 30

We can see from Figures 6.6 and 6.7 that the points are as well distributed in dimension 1 as in superior dimensions.

6.6 COMPARISON OF THE DIFFERENT SEQUENCES

In this section we use the Quasi Monte Carlo methods to solve an elementary problem.

Example 6.1 Suppose that we want to evaluate the volume defined below the surface $yz + x^2 = 1$ in the unit cube $[0, 1] \times [0, 1] \times [0, 1]$ in $\mathbb{R}^3$. In order to find this value, we need to generate triplets (a, b, c) in the unit cube and verify that relation $bc + a^2 < 1$ holds. Then we find the fraction of triplets that satisfy the relation. This will give us an approximative value of the volume, that is an integral. We used the different QMC methods to generate the triplets and present the results in Table 6.4. We compare the results with MATLAB's uniform random number generator.

Table 6.4 Comparison of QMC methods

N	MATLAB	Halton	Faure	Sobol	Hypercube
1000	0.8490	0.8610	0.8540	0.8550	0.8400
2000	0.8605	0.8600	0.8500	0.8540	0.8470
3000	0.8657	0.8587	0.8507	0.8537	0.8587
4000	0.8400	0.8570	0.8515	0.8538	0.8548
5000	0.8462	0.8568	0.8512	0.8556	0.8508
6000	0.8558	0.8567	0.8522	0.8547	0.8553
7000	0.8481	0.8564	0.8536	0.8540	0.8570
8000	0.8526	0.8560	0.8535	0.8538	0.8519
9000	0.8560	0.8549	0.8537	0.8543	0.8549
10000	0.8574	0.8546	0.8537	0.8541	0.8542

We present below the program allowing us to estimate the integral using the different sequences. Since the principal functions used to generate QMC sequences have been built in previous sections, we use them to generate the points.

```
function CompareQMC(NbTraj)
%Function that computes the volume under surface
%yz+x^2=1.
%NbTraj: Number of points to generate.
a=rand(NbTraj,1);
b=rand(NbTraj,1);
c=rand(NbTraj,1);
disp('Evaluation with MATLAB');
mean(b.*c+a.*a<1)
a=Halton(NbTraj,3);
b=Halton(NbTraj,5);
c=Halton(NbTraj,7);
disp('Evaluation with Halton sequence');
mean(b.*c+a.*a<1)
a=Faure(NbTraj,1,3);
b=Faure(NbTraj,2,3);
c=Faure(NbTraj,3,3);
disp('Evaluation with Faure sequence');
mean(b.*c+a.*a<1)
a=SobolShuffle(NbTraj,1,2,[1;1]);
b=SobolShuffle(NbTraj,1,3,[1;3;7]);
c=SobolShuffle(NbTraj,2,3,[1;3;3]);
disp('Evaluation with Sobol sequence');
mean(b.*c+a.*a<1)
Temp=LHS(NbTraj,3);
a=Temp(:,1);
b=Temp(:,2);
c=Temp(:,3);
disp('Evaluation with latin hypercube sequence');
mean(b.*c+a.*a<1)
end
```

```
%Functions that generates Halton sequence elements
function rep=Halton(nb, b1)
    rep=zeros(nb,1);
    for j=1:nb
        rep(j,1)=VanDerCorput(j,b1);
    end
end

%Function that generates elements of Faure sequence
function rep=Faure(nb, Dim1, b)
    bn=zeros(nb,1);
    for l=1:nb
        a=decompose(l,b);
        m=size(a,1);
        MatTrans=zeros(m,m);
        for j=1:m
              for i=j:m
                  MatTrans(j,i)=nchoosek(i-1,j-1);
              end
        end
        a=mod(MatTrans^(Dim1-1)*a,b);
        for f=1:m
            bn(l,1)=bn(l,1)+a(f,1)/b^(f);
        end
    end
    rep=bn;
    function rep=decompose(n,b)
        temp=1;
        while n~=0
            rep(temp,1)=mod(n,b);
            n=floor(n/b);
            temp=temp+1;
        end
    end
end

%Function that generates elements of Sobol sequence
function rep=SobolShuffle(Nb,Polynomial,Degree,M)
    %First step
    m=1;
    y(1)=1;
    x=zeros(Nb,1);
    x(1,1)=y(1)/2^m;
    %Principal loop
    for n=2:Nb
        Position=Pos(n-1);
        if Position>size(M)
            M=AddM(M,Polynomial,Degree);
        end
```

```
          m=ceil(log(n+1)/log(2));
          y(n)=bitxor(2^(m==Position)*y(n-1),2^(m-Position)*M
(Position));
          x(n,1)=y(n)/2^m;
      end
      rep=x;
      %Function that finds the position of the
      %rightmost zero in the decomposition
      %of k in base two
      function rep=Pos(k)
          PosTemp=1;
          while bitand(k,1)==1
              PosTemp=PosTemp+1;
              k=bitshift(k,-1);
          end
          rep=PosTemp;
      end
      %Function that computes a new value for M
      function rep=AddM(M,Polynomial,Degree)
          Length=size(M,1);
          Temp=bitxor(2^(Degree)*M(Length+1-Degree),
M(Length+1-Degree));
          i=Degree-1;
          while Polynomial~=0
              Temp=bitxor(Temp,2^(i)*mod(Polynomial,2)*M
(Length+1-i));
              Polynomial=bitshift(Polynomial,-1);
              i=i-1;
          end
          rep=[M;Temp];
      end
 end

 %Function that generates element of latin hypercube sequence
 function rep = LHS(N,k)
 Matrix = rand(N,k);
 for j=1:k
     per = randperm(N);
     Matrix(:,j) = (per'-1+Matrix(:,j))/N;
 end
 rep = Matrix;
 end
```

The volume estimated by MATLAB is close to 0.854. In this simple problem, the results using the Halton, Faure and Sobol methods converge faster than those with MATLAB's generator. However, we must remember that this problem is in dimension 3 only. With higher dimensions, the Halton and Faure sequences lose their effectiveness much faster than the Sobol sequence. For the Latin hypercube method, regardless of the dimension, we do not note any loss of efficiency. The hypercube method only redistributes "more uniformly" the values generated by MATLAB.

Example 6.2 We are still seeking to compare QMC sequences with MATLAB random number generator but this time we want to compute the expectation

$$E[\max(S_1 - 1.0, S_2 - 0.8, S_3 - 1.3, 0)], \tag{6.15}$$

where $S_i = e^{Z_i}$ with $Z_i \sim N(0, 1)$ (the dimension of this problem is still 3). For this simulation, we transform uniform random variables obtained from the sequences into normal random variables. We present the MATLAB code using Halton sequence in dimension 3 to generate the results. For the other sequences, the adaptations are similar.

```
function ComputeExpectation(NbTraj)
%Function that computes the expectation using Halton sequence
%in dimension 3
%NbTraj: Number of points to generate
%Transformation of the uniform variables into normal variables
S=norminv([Faure(NbTraj,2,3),Faure(NbTraj,3,5),...
                    Faure(NbTraj,4,5)]);
%Computation of cash flows given by the function maximum
Payoff=zeros(NbTraj,1);
for l=1:NbTraj
  temp=max(max(exp(S(l,1))-1,0),max(exp(S(l,2))-0.8,0));
  Payoff(l)=max(temp,max(exp(S(l,3))-1.3,0));
end
disp('Mean');
disp(mean(Payoff));
disp('Standard error');
disp(std(Payoff)/sqrt(NbTraj));
end

%Function that generates elements of Faure sequence
function rep=Faure(nb, Dim1, b)
bn=zeros(nb,1);
for l=1:nb
     a=decompose(l,b);
     m=size(a,1);
     MatTrans=zeros(m,m);
     for j=1:m
          for i=j:m
               MatTrans(j,i)=nchoosek(i-1,j-1);
          end
     end
     a=mod(MatTrans^Dim1*a,b);
     for f=1:m
          bn(l,1)=bn(l,1)+a(f,1)/b^(f);
     end
end
rep=bn(:,1);
end
%Decomposition of n in base b
function rep=decompose(n,b)
```

```
temp=1;
while n~=0
    rep(temp,1)=mod(n,b);
    n=floor(n/b);
    temp=temp+1;
end
end
```

We show the results in Table 6.5 where the numbers in parenthesis represent the standard error (standard deviation divided by the square root of the number of simulations). It is interesting to note a slightly smaller variation in the results when using Quasi Monte Carlo methods.

Table 6.5 Comparison of the sequences for an option-like problem

N	MATLAB	Halton	Faure	Sobol	Hypercube
200	2.10	1.87	2.01	1.94	2.15
	(0.19)	(0.14)	(0.16)	(0.16)	(0.20)
400	1.96	1.98	2.02	2.03	2.14
	(0.12)	(0.12)	(0.12)	(0.12)	(0.14)
600	2.05	2.00	2.09	2.07	2.12
	(0.13)	(0.10)	(0.11)	(0.11)	(0.12)
800	2.03	2.04	2.08	2.10	2.17
	(0.10)	(0.09)	(0.09)	(0.09)	(0.10)
1000	2.16	2.05	2.08	2.11	2.15
	(0.10)	(0.08)	(0.08)	(0.09)	(0.09)

As indicated in the introduction, a program using QMC simulations to compute the value at risk of a portfolio of bonds is presented later in Chapter 15.

Notes and Complementary Readings

For a complementary review of literature on Quasi Monte Carlo simulations, the reader can consult the books of Glasserman (2003) and Niederreiter (1992), and articles by Joy, Boyle and Tan (1996), Galanti and Jung (1997), Papageorgiou and Paskov (1999) and Tan and Boyle (2000).

7 Introduction to Random Processes

When we observe, for instance, the variations of stock prices, interest rates, currencies and commodities, we reckon that the fluctuations cannot be precisely predicted at a future date. These variables evolve in a random way. We qualify these processes as random processes.

A random process, which we denote by X, can be heuristically considered as a function of time such that at each moment the value $X(t)$ is a random variable.

From a mathematical standpoint, a random vector is a function of the space of events in a space containing the functions called realizations of the process. Conceptually, a process is composed of the set of all possible functions that can be observed. In order to characterize it, we will use probabilistic concepts already introduced previously in this book.

In this chapter, first we define and characterize random processes. Then we treat random processes that are widely used in finance, such as the Gaussian or Wiener processes as well as Brownian bridges. These processes are very useful to characterize those processes describing financial assets values. Numerical solutions of the stochastic differential equations constructed from Wiener processes are presented in a more detailed manner in the next chapter.

7.1 CHARACTERIZATION

7.1.1 Statistics

Since a random process is a function of time, the value X at time t is therefore a random variable. To characterize it statistically, we need to know its probability density function $f_X(x, t)$.

We write the argument t to point out that this function depends on the time t at which we examine the process X. This density known, we can deduce the mean of $X(t)$, $m_X(t)$, as follows:

$$m_X(t) = E\left[X(t)\right] = \int_{-\infty}^{+\infty} x f_X(x, t) dx. \tag{7.1}$$

If this mean is a function of time, then we can obtain the variance of $X(t)$ as:

$$\sigma_X^2(t) = E\left[(X(t) - m_X(t))^2\right] = \int_{-\infty}^{+\infty} \left(x - m_X(t)\right)^2 f_X(x, t) dx. \tag{7.2}$$

Physically, $m_X(t)$ represents the mean variation of the process and $\sigma_X^2(t)$ measures the fluctuation of the process around its mean trajectory $m_X(t)$.

If we are now interested in the value taken at two different times, $X(t_1)$ and $X(t_2)$, we have to analyze two random variables. In other words, we are dealing with a 2-dimensional random vector. We write $X_1 = X(t_1)$ and $X_2 = X(t_2)$.

This vector (X_1, X_2) is fully characterized if we know its joint probability density function

$$f_{X_1,X_2}(x_1, x_2, t_1, t_2). \tag{7.3}$$

It is natural to posit that this probability density function depends simultaneously on t_1 and t_2 for which we examine the values of the process. As we have seen in the previous chapter, this joint density contains all the information on the marginal densities

$$f_{X_i}(x_i, t_i) = \int_{-\infty}^{+\infty} f_{X_i,X_j}(x_i, x_j, t_i, t_j)dx_j, \quad \text{with} \quad i, j \in \{1, 2\}. \tag{7.4}$$

Thus, this joint density allows us to compute the mean and variance of the process. Moreover, we can compute the joint moment:

$$E[X_1X_2] = \int_{-\infty}^{+\infty}\int_{-\infty}^{+\infty} x_1x_2 f_{X_1,X_2}(x_1, x_2, t_1, t_2)dx_1dx_2. \tag{7.5}$$

This joint moment denoted by $\mathcal{R}_{XX}(t_1, t_2)$ is called the autocorrelation function of the process:

$$\mathcal{R}_{XX}(t_1, t_2) \triangleq E[X(t_1)X(t_2)]. \tag{7.6}$$

It simultaneously depends on the 2 time values t_1 and t_2. Centered joint moments are defined as follows:

$$\mathcal{C}_{XX}(t_1, t_2) \triangleq E[(X(t_1) - m_X(t_1))(X(t_2) - m_X(t_2))]. \tag{7.7}$$

We call it the auto-covariance function of the process.

Now, by considering any n points in time $t_1, t_2, \ldots, t_n$, we can define the joint probability density function

$$f_{X_1,X_2,\ldots,X_n}(x_1, x_2, \ldots, x_n, t_1, t_2, \ldots, t_n). \tag{7.8}$$

The process is said to be perfectly characterized if, for any n and for any set $(t_1, t_2, \ldots, t_n)$, the joint density of order n is completely defined.

Note that it is generally impossible to characterize a random process. Fortunately, problems of interest in finance do not require this perfect characterization. Instead, we only need to characterize the first and second order moments. Another way to avoid this problem is to describe how the process is going to be generated.

7.1.2 Stationarity

In many cases, when we look at a random process's variations, we note that the process fluctuates in a jagged way as illustrated in Figure 7.1.

Intuitively, we recognize a certain invariant character with respect to time. In fact, this random process belongs to the stationary processes (strict stationarity). This class of processes is characterized by the fact that the probability density functions of any order

$$f_{X_1,X_2,\ldots,X_n}(x_1, x_2, \ldots, x_n, t_1, t_2, \ldots, t_n) \tag{7.9}$$

are independent of time origin. In practice, such a constraint seems strong. Moreover, in the following chapters we will usually only use the first order density $f_{X_1}(x_1, t_1)$ and the second order density $f_{X_1,X_2}(x_1, x_2, t_1, t_2)$.

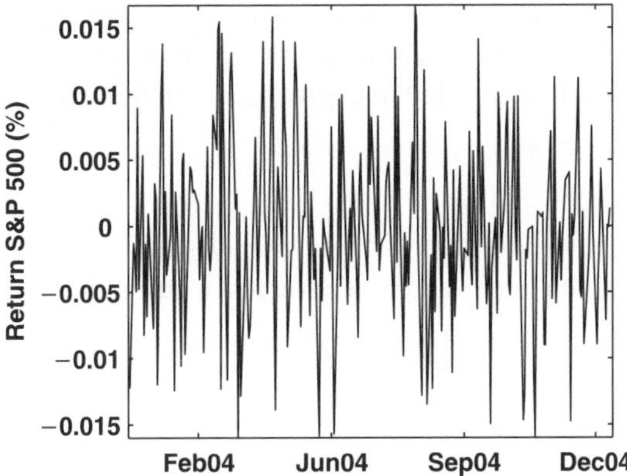

Figure 7.1 S&P 500 daily returns for year 2004

This brings us to the definition of a second order stationary processes class. It is defined as the set of all processes such that their first order density function $f_{X_1}(x_1, t_1)$ and their second order one $f_{X_1,X_2}(x_1, x_2, t_1, t_2)$ don't depend on the time origin.

Hence, for a stationary process, we have:

$$f_X(x, t) = f_X(x) \tag{7.10}$$

and

$$f_{X_1,X_2}(x_1, x_2, t_1, t_2) = f_{X_1,X_2}(x_1, x_2, t_2 - t_1). \tag{7.11}$$

Which implies that $m_X(t)$ is a constant and

$$\mathcal{R}_{XX}(t_1, t_2) = \mathcal{R}_{XX}(t_2 - t_1). \tag{7.12}$$

Therefore, for the second order stationary processes, the mean is constant and the autocorrelation function depends only on the differences in the instants for which it is defined.

7.1.3 Ergodicity

To compile these statistics in a perfect way in practice, we need to have an infinity of process realizations. Instead, we only have one realization of the process as a function of time. Based on the statistics of the process, if we imagine that this function evolves from $-\infty$ to $+\infty$, this is tantamount to saying that, using these variations from $-\infty$ to $+\infty$, we can compile all of our process's statistics. Processes having this property are said to be ergodic.

Since the ergodicity concept is not used often in this book, we do not dwell on it.

7.2 NOTION OF CONTINUITY, DIFFERENTIABILITY AND INTEGRABILITY

Since a random process is an infinite set of trajectories (abstract representation), concepts of continuity, differentiability and integrability for a process must be defined in terms of convergence criteria.

Obviously, as seen in the previous chapters, many convergence criteria can be used. Since our focus is on Monte Carlo simulations, we adopt the quadratic mean convergence criterion. This criterion will be used to define the continuity, differentiability and integrability of random processes.

7.2.1 Continuity

A random process $X(t)$ with finite variance converges in quadratic mean to time point t_0 if

$$E\left[(X(t)-X(t_0))^2\right] \underset{t \to t_0}{\longrightarrow} 0. \tag{7.13}$$

If $X(t)$ is continuous in quadratic mean for all $t_0 \in [a, b]$, we say that $X(t)$ is continuous in quadratic mean on this interval. Continuity in quadratic mean is characterized by the following theorem.

Theorem 2.1 *$X(t)$ is said to be continuous in quadratic mean on interval $[a, b]$ if and only if $\mathcal{R}_{XX}(t_1, t_2)$ is continuous on the diagonal $a \le t_1 = t_2 \le b$.*

Proof: That is:

$$E\left[(X(t)-X(t_0))^2\right] = E\left[X(t)^2\right] + E\left[X(t_0)^2\right] - 2\mathcal{R}_{XX}(t, t_0). \tag{7.14}$$

If $X(t)$ is continuous in quadratic mean at t_0, then

$$\lim_{t \to t_0} \mathcal{R}_{XX}(t, t_0) = E\left[X(t_0)^2\right]. \tag{7.15}$$

Conversely, if $\mathcal{R}_{XX}(t, t_0)$ is continuous on the diagonal $t = t_0$ then

$$\lim_{t \to t_0} \mathcal{R}_{XX}(t, t_0) = \mathcal{R}_{XX}(t_0, t_0) = E\left[X(t_0)^2\right]. \tag{7.16}$$

7.2.2 Differentiability

The concept of differentiability in quadratic mean is defined in a similar manner as for the continuity. Let $X(t)$ be a random process, we say that $X(t)$ is differentiable in quadratic mean at time t_0 if there exists a process $Y(t)$ such that:

$$\lim_{t \to t_0} E\left[\left(\frac{X(t)-X(t_0)}{t-t_0} - Y(t_0)\right)^2\right] = 0. \tag{7.17}$$

Since $Y(t_0)$ is not known, we can use the Cauchy criterion as follows:

$$\lim_{t_n \to 0, t_m \to 0} E\left[\left(\frac{X(t_0+t_n)-X(t_0)}{t_n} - \frac{X(t_0+t_m)-X(t_0)}{t_m}\right)^2\right] = 0. \tag{7.18}$$

If $X(t)$ can be differentiated in quadratic mean for all $t \in [a, b]$, we say that $X(t)$ is differentiable in quadratic mean and this differentiability in quadratic mean is characterized by the following theorem.

Theorem 2.2 *A process $X(t)$ is differentiable in quadratic mean on the interval $[a, b]$ if and only if*

$$\frac{\partial^2}{\partial t_1 \partial t_2} \mathcal{R}_{XX}(t_1, t_2) \tag{7.19}$$

exists and is continuous on the diagonal $a \leq t_1 = t_2 \leq b$.

Proof: The proof is similar to the proof of Theorem 2.1.

7.2.3 Integrability

Let $X(t)$ be a random process, we subdivide the interval $[a, b]$ into n sub-intervals of length

$$\Delta t = \frac{b-a}{n}. \tag{7.20}$$

We say that $X(t)$ is integrable in quadratic mean if there exists a random variable Y such that:

$$\lim_{n \to \infty} E\left[\left(\sum_{k=0}^{n-1} X(k\Delta t + a) \times \Delta t - Y\right)^2\right] = 0. \tag{7.21}$$

And we note

$$\int_a^b X(t)dt = Y, \tag{7.22}$$

the integral of X on the interval $[a, b]$. The integrability in quadratic mean is characterized by the following theorem.

Theorem 2.3 *A random process $X(t)$ is integrable in quadratic mean on the interval $[a, b]$ if and only if*

$$\int_a^b \int_a^b \mathcal{R}_{XX}(t_1, t_2) dt_1 dt_2 \tag{7.23}$$

converges.

7.3 EXAMPLES OF RANDOM PROCESSES

7.3.1 Gaussian Process

A process $X(t)$ is said to be Gaussian if its order n probability density function is Gaussian. The density function

$$f_{X_1, X_2, \ldots, X_n}(x_1, x_2, \ldots, x_n, t_1, t_2, \ldots, t_n) \tag{7.24}$$

is given by the formula

$$\frac{1}{(2\pi)^{\frac{n}{2}} |\Lambda|^{\frac{1}{2}}} \exp\left(-\frac{1}{2}\left(\underline{x}-\underline{m}\right)^\top \Lambda^{-1}\left(\underline{x}-\underline{m}\right)\right), \tag{7.25}$$

where

$$\underline{x} = (x_1, \ldots, x_n)^\top, \quad \underline{m} = (m_X(t_1), \ldots, m_X(t_n))^\top \tag{7.26}$$

and

$$\Lambda = \left(\Lambda_{ij}\right)_{i,j=1,\ldots,n} \tag{7.27}$$

with

$$\Lambda_{ij} = \mathcal{C}_{XX}(t_i, t_j) = E\left[(X_i - m_X(t_i))\left(X_j - m_X(t_j)\right)\right]. \tag{7.28}$$

For a Gaussian process, if we know its mean trajectory $m_X(t)$ and its autocorrelation function $\mathcal{R}_{XX}(t, t')$, we can obtain its density of order n for any n. Indeed, we have:

$$\Lambda_{ij} = \mathcal{R}_{XX}(t_i, t_j) - m_X(t_i)m_X(t_j). \tag{7.29}$$

In summary, a Gaussian process is perfectly characterized by its mean and its autocorrelation function.

7.3.2 Random Walk

We subdivide the half-line $[0, \infty]$ into sub-intervals of equal duration Δt. Over the sub-interval $[k\Delta t, (k+1)\Delta t]$, $X(t)$ stays constant, that is

$$X(t) = X(k\Delta t), \quad \forall t \in [k\Delta t, (k+1)\Delta t[\quad \text{and} \quad X(0) = 0. \tag{7.30}$$

Then

$$X((k+1)\Delta t) = X(k\Delta t) + B_k, \tag{7.31}$$

where the B_k's are independent binary random variables with density function:

$$\text{Prob}(B_k = \delta) = \frac{1}{2} \quad \text{and} \quad \text{Prob}(B_k = -\delta) = \frac{1}{2}. \tag{7.32}$$

The so defined process $X(t)$ is called a random walk.

We can compute $g(t)$ as follows:

$$\forall t > 0, \quad g(t) = \text{Int}\left(\frac{t}{\Delta t}\right), \tag{7.33}$$

where $\text{Int}(x)$ stands for the integer value of x. $g(t)$ is the highest positive integer less or equal to t divided by Δt.

Thus,

$$X(t) = X(g(t)\Delta t) = \sum_{k=1}^{g(t)} B_k, \tag{7.34}$$

therefore,

$$m_X(t) = E[X(t)] = E\left[\sum_{k=1}^{g(t)} B_k\right]. \tag{7.35}$$

Since the B_k's are independent with zero mean, we have $m_X(t) = 0$. The variance of $X(t)$ becomes

$$\begin{aligned}\sigma_X^2(t) &= \text{Var}(X(t)) \\ &= \text{Var}\left(\sum_{k=1}^{g(t)} B_k\right) \\ &= \sum_{k=1}^{g(t)} \text{Var}(B_k).\end{aligned} \tag{7.36}$$

Since

$$\text{Var}(B_k) = \delta^2, \tag{7.37}$$

then

$$\sigma_X^2(t) = g(t)\delta^2. \tag{7.38}$$

It is interesting to note that the variance of a random walk increases with t while the mean remains at 0. Physically, this means that the trajectory of the random process wanders around the horizontal axis. Moreover

$$X(t_2) - X(t_1) = \sum_{k=g(t_1)+1}^{g(t_2)} B_k, \tag{7.39}$$

$$X(t_3) - X(t_2) = \sum_{k=g(t_2)+1}^{g(t_3)} B_k. \tag{7.40}$$

If $t_1 \le t_2 \le t_3$ then $g(t_1) \le g(t_2) \le g(t_3)$. Since B_k's are statistically independent, then $X(t_3) - X(t_2)$ is independent of $X(t_2) - X(t_1)$.

Random processes exhibiting this property are qualified as *independent increment* processes. On the other hand, we observe that:

$$X(t_m) = X(t_n) + \sum_{k=g(t_n)+1}^{g(t_m)} B_k, \tag{7.41}$$

where

$$g(t_m) = \text{Int}\left(\frac{t_m}{\Delta t}\right) \quad \text{and} \quad g(t_n) = \text{Int}\left(\frac{t_n}{\Delta t}\right). \tag{7.42}$$

It is clear that

$$\text{Prob}(X(t_m) \le x | X(t_n), X(t_{n-1}), \ldots, X(t_1)) = \text{Prob}(X(t_m) \le x | X(t_n)), \tag{7.43}$$

for $t_1 < \ldots < t_{n-1} < t_n < t_m$. Processes with this property are called *Markovian processes.*

7.3.3 Wiener Process

Let us examine the limit case of a random walk

$$X(t) = \sum_{k=1}^{g(t)} B_k, \quad \text{where} \quad g(t) = \text{Int}\left(\frac{t}{\Delta t}\right). \tag{7.44}$$

We have seen that $m_X(t) = 0$ and $\sigma_X^2(t) = g(t)\delta^2$. Suppose that the jump δ is proportional to the duration of the interval Δt, $\delta = \sqrt{\Delta t}$, then $\sigma_X^2(t) = g(t)\Delta t$. When Δt goes to 0, $g(t)\Delta t$ tends to t. Thus, taking the limit,

$$\sigma_X^2(t) = t. \tag{7.45}$$

On the other hand, when Δt goes to 0, $X(t)$ is the sum of a large number of independent binary random variables. By virtue of the central limit theorem, it converges to a Gaussian random variable.

Taken to the limit, the random walk tends toward a Gaussian random process with zero mean, variance $\sigma_X^2(t) = t$ and independent increments. Such a process is by definition a standard Wiener process.

Definition 3.1 *$W(t)$ is a standard Wiener process if*

(i) $W(0) = 0$,
(ii) $W(t)$ has independent increments, which means that

$$\forall \;\; t_1 < t_2 < t_3 < t_4, \quad W(t_4) - W(t_3) \quad \textit{and} \quad W(t_2) - W(t_1)$$

are independent,
(iii) $Z(t) = W(t) - W(t_0)$ is Gaussian with zero mean and variance

$$\sigma_Z^2 = t - t_0, \quad t_0 \le t.$$

From this definition we can deduce the following basic properties for a standard Wiener process.

Property 3.2 $\text{Var}(W(t)) = t$ *and* $m_W(t) = E[W(t)] = 0$. *Since its variance increases with time t, the trajectory of this process moves away from the horizontal axis when t increases.*

Property 3.3 *From the law of large numbers, we can prove that:*

$$\frac{W(t)}{t} \underset{t\to\infty}{\longrightarrow} 0. \tag{7.46}$$

Property 3.4 *W's trajectory, even if it is continuous, varies in a very irregular way that makes it non differentiable. Heuristically, this result comes from* $\Delta W(t) = W(t + \Delta t) - W(t)$ *being proportional to* $\sqrt{\Delta t}$. *This property is often called Levy's oscillatory property.*

Property 3.5 *The autocorrelation function of* $W(t)$ *is given by:*

$$\mathcal{R}_{WW}(t_1, t_2) = \min(t_1, t_2). \tag{7.47}$$

Proof: Indeed,

$$\mathcal{R}_{WW}(t_1, t_2) = E\left[W(t_1)W(t_2)\right]. \tag{7.48}$$

Without loss of generality, we suppose $t_1 < t_2$ then

$$\mathcal{R}_{WW}(t_1, t_2) = E\left[(W(t_2) - W(t_1))\, W(t_1) + W(t_1)^2\right]. \tag{7.49}$$

Since $W(t)$ has independent increments,

$$E\left[(W(t_2) - W(t_1))\, W(t_1)\right] = E\left[W(t_1)\right] E\left[W(t_2) - W(t_1)\right] = 0. \tag{7.50}$$

Which implies that

$$\mathcal{R}_{WW}(t_1, t_2) = E\left[W(t_1)^2\right] = \mathrm{Var}(W(t_1)) = t_1 = \min(t_1, t_2). \tag{7.51}$$

Property 3.6 *The standard Wiener process exhibits a very important property called the martingale property, that is:*

$$E\left[W(t_n)|W(t_{n-1}), W(t_{n-2}), \ldots, W(t_1)\right] = W(t_{n-1}), \quad t_1 < t_2 < \ldots < t_n. \tag{7.52}$$

Proof: Since $W(t)$ has independent increments, we have:

$$E\left[W(t_n)|W(t_{n-1}), \ldots, W(t_1)\right] \tag{7.53}$$

or

$$E\left[W(t_n) - W(t_{n-1}) + W(t_{n-1})|W(t_{n-1}), \ldots, W(t_1)\right]. \tag{7.54}$$

Moreover, the expression

$$E\left[W(t_n) - W(t_{n-1})|W(t_{n-1}), \ldots, W(t_1)\right] \tag{7.55}$$

can be rewritten as

$$\begin{aligned} E\left[W(t_n) - W(t_{n-1})|W(t_{n-1})\right] = E\left[W(t_n)|W(t_{n-1})\right] \\ -E\left[W(t_{n-1})|W(t_{n-1})\right]. \end{aligned} \tag{7.56}$$

Since $W(t_n) - W(t_{n-1})$ and $W(t_{n-1})$ are independent,

$$\begin{aligned} E\left[W(t_n)|W(t_{n-1})\right] - E\left[W(t_{n-1})|W(t_{n-1})\right] &= E\left[W(t_n) - W(t_{n-1})\right] \\ &= 0. \end{aligned} \tag{7.57}$$

Given that

$$E\left[W(t_{n-1})|W(t_{n-1})\right] = W(t_{n-1}), \tag{7.58}$$

we have

$$E\left[W(t_n)|W(t_{n-1})\right] = W(t_{n-1}). \tag{7.59}$$

7.3.4 Brownian Bridge

A very useful process obtained from the standard Wiener process that passes through predetermined points at $t = 0$ and $t = T$ is called a Brownian bridge and is denoted by $\mathcal{B}_{0,x}^{T,y}(t)$. All realizations of this bridge satisfy:

$$\forall x, y, \quad \mathcal{B}_{0,x}^{T,y}(0) = x \quad \text{and} \quad \mathcal{B}_{0,x}^{T,y}(T) = y. \tag{7.60}$$

This bridge can be expressed as follows:

$$\mathcal{B}_{0,x}^{T,y}(t) = x + W(t) - \frac{t}{T}\left(W(T) - y + x\right). \tag{7.61}$$

This is equivalent to applying the Thales theorem (interpolation) in the random processes case. From this definition, we can deduce the mean of the Brownian bridge to be:

$$m_{\mathcal{B}}(t) = x - \frac{t}{T}(x - y) \tag{7.62}$$

and its covariance

$$\begin{aligned} C_{\mathcal{B},\mathcal{B}}(t_1, t_2) &= E\left[\left(\mathcal{B}_{0,x}^{T,y}(t_1) - m_{\mathcal{B}}(t_1)\right)\left(\mathcal{B}_{0,x}^{T,y}(t_2) - m_{\mathcal{B}}(t_2)\right)\right] \\ &= \min(t_1, t_2) - \frac{t_1 t_2}{T}. \end{aligned} \tag{7.63}$$

By means of MATLAB, many Brownian bridges can be generated quickly. Set $x = 100$, $y = 105$, $T = 1$. We generate 40 trajectories with 100 steps each.

```
function rep=BBridge(NbTraj,NbPas,T,x,y)
%Function that generates many Brownian bridges
%NbTraj: Number of bridges to generate
%NbPas: Number of steps in each bridge
%T: Period on which the bridge is generated
%x: Starting point of the bridge
%y: Final point of the bridge

DeltaT=T/NbPas;

%Generation of the increments and bridges
```

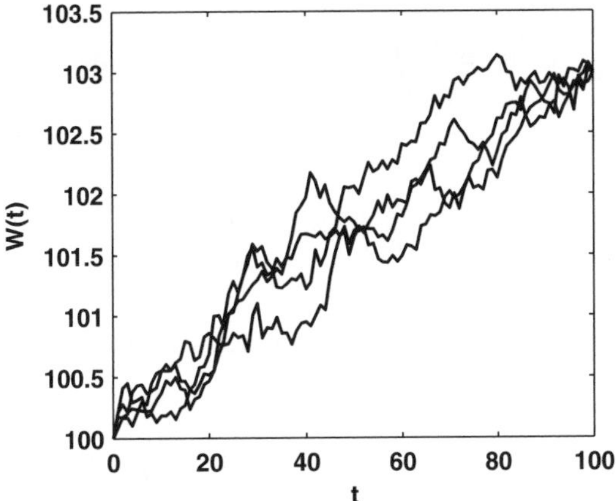

Figure 7.2 Brownian bridge examples

```
dW=[zeros(NbTraj,1), sqrt(DeltaT)*randn(NbTraj, NbPas)];
W=cumsum(dW,2);
Inc=[zeros(NbTraj,1), ...
          repmat(DeltaT/T*(y-x-W(:, NbPas+1)),1,NbPas)];
rep=W+x+cumsum(Inc,2);

%Graphs of the bridges
figure
plot([0:DeltaT:1],rep)

end
```

An example of possible results obtained from this program is given in Figure 7.2.

7.3.5 Fourier Transform of a Brownian Bridge

We take the Brownian bridge

$$\mathcal{B}(t) = W(t) - \frac{t}{T}W(T), \tag{7.64}$$

that is $x = 0$ and $y = 0$. On the interval $[0, T]$, we can expand $\mathcal{B}(t)$ and obtain the Fourier series expansion, that is

$$\mathcal{B}(t) = a_0 + \sum_{k=1}^{\infty} \left(a_k \cos(kw_0 t) + b_k \sin(kw_0 t)\right), \tag{7.65}$$

with

$$a_0 = \frac{1}{T}\int_0^T \mathcal{B}(t)dt, \tag{7.66}$$

$$a_k = \frac{2}{T}\int_0^T \mathcal{B}(t)\cos(kw_0 t)dt \quad \text{and} \tag{7.67}$$

$$b_k = \frac{2}{T}\int_0^T \mathcal{B}(t)\sin(kw_0 t)dt. \tag{7.68}$$

It is important to note that $\mathcal{B}(t)$ is a Gaussian process with zero mean and auto-covariance function

$$\mathcal{C}_{\mathcal{B},\mathcal{B}}(t_1, t_2) = \min(t_1, t_2) - \frac{t_1 t_2}{T}. \tag{7.69}$$

This allows us to conclude that a_k and b_k are Gaussian random variables with mean of zero.

7.3.6 Example of a Brownian Bridge

In this section, we present a possible application of the Brownian bridges' method. In finance, often the price of a product does not depend only on the final value of the asset. This price could be a function of the asset's price at several dates prior to maturity of a derivative security. In this case, to increase the simulation's speed, we can use Brownian bridges to simulate the asset's price only at the required dates in question.

For example, suppose that we have a product with price depending on the arithmetic mean of the Wiener process on days 75, 80 and 85. We suppose that the process has an initial value of 100 today and that its maturity is 90 days. The paid price will be the difference between the average price and the strike price of 100. Here are the steps that we have to execute:

1. Generate a terminal value for W, which we denote by WT.
2. Generate 20 trajectories $W_i(t)$ that will be used to compute the value of the asset for days 75, 80, 85 and 90.
3. From these trajectories $W_i(t)$, build $\mathcal{B}_i(t)$ that correspond to the values of the asset on days 75, 80, 85 and 90 as follows:

$$\mathcal{B}_{0,x}^{T,y}(t) = x + W(t) - \frac{t}{T}(W(T) - y + x), \tag{7.70}$$

   where x represents the initial asset value 100 and y the terminal value WT.
4. Compute the mean of $\mathcal{B}_i(t)$ for each trajectory.
5. Compute the final payoff. This payoff is thus associated with the terminal value WT.
6. Repeat steps 1 to 5, 10 000 times.
7. Compute the mean of the 10 000 payoffs.

We present below the MATLAB program that executes these steps. Note that we only generate values for the points we are interested in, i.e., the values of $W(t)$ for $t = 75$, 80, 85 and 90.

```
function rep=MeanArith3Days
%Function that computes the price of an option written on
  the mean of
%the price of an asset. The mean is computed on days
```

```
%75, 80 and 85 and we use Brownian bridges to decrease
%the number of necessary simulations

%Initial parameters
NbTraj=10000;
NbPas=90;
T=90/360;
x=100;
Strike=100;
Traj=20;
DeltaT=T/NbPas;

%Generation of final values of the process
WT=sqrt(T)*randn(NbTraj,1)+100;

%Vector to save the arithmetic means
A=zeros(NbTraj,1);

for i=1:NbTraj

    %Generation of the increments to build the bridge for WT(i)
    dW=[sqrt((75-0)*DeltaT)*randn(Traj,1), ...
              sqrt((80-75)*DeltaT)*randn(Traj,1),...
              sqrt((85-80)*DeltaT)*randn(Traj,1),...
              sqrt((90-85)*DeltaT)*randn(Traj,1)];
    W=cumsum(dW,2);

    %Building of the Brownian bridge for all the simulations
    %between x and WT(i)
    B(:,1)=x+W(:,1)-(75*DeltaT)/T*(W(:,4)-WT(i)+x);
    B(:,2)=x+W(:,2)-(80*DeltaT)/T*(W(:,4)-WT(i)+x);
    B(:,3)=x+W(:,3)-(85*DeltaT)/T*(W(:,4)-WT(i)+x);

    %Compute the means for each of the simulations
    TheMean=mean(B,2);

    %Compute the cash flows for each of the simulations
    Payoff=max(0,TheMean-Strike);

    %Compute the mean of the simulation for
    %final value WT(i)
    A(i)=mean(Payoff,1);
end

%Return the mean of each scenarios
rep=mean(A,1);

end
```

Executing this program, we find that the price should be about 0.30$. We have been able to compute the price without having to simulate the intermediate trajectories between the dates we were interested in. In many applications, this allows programmers to save computation time and memory. As a matter of fact, when dealing with bigger simulations, we will be able to compute the price of a derivative product faster because we only need to generate the trajectories on some specific dates.

Notes and Complementary Readings

For a complementary review of literature about concepts covered in this chapter, refer to the following books of different levels of sophistication: Baxter and Rennie (1996), Bjork (1999), Cvitanic and Zapatero (2004), Demange and Rochet (2005), Duffie (2001), Lamberton and Lapeyre (1992), Malliaris and Brock (1982), Merton (1992), Neftci (2000).

8
Solution of Stochastic Differential Equations

As mentioned in the previous chapter, most phenomena in finance are random. For example, Figure 8.1 shows the daily prices of the American index S&P 500 for year 2004.

These random phenomena can be analyzed with the statistical tools from stochastic calculus.

From the heuristic construction of the Wiener process, we introduce the stochastic differential equations. However, it is important to note that our objective is not to present an extensive treatment of stochastic calculus in this chapter. We rather provide intuitions linked to the Ito-Taylor's lemma and its applications in numerical methods.

We also present numerical discretization schemes that will be used in simulations. Practical application cases in the form of exercises are proposed and MATLAB programs are provided as solutions to these exercises. Note that, in all these programs, variance reduction and precision improvement techniques covered in Chapter 5 are used. Finally, we introduce processes with jumps.

As we will see in the following chapter on contingent claims valuation, two equivalent approaches are used in the valuation of derivative securities in finance: the state variables approach which consists of solving partial differential equations and the probabilistic approach or equivalent martingale. The equivalence between the two approaches is established by the Feynman-Kac formula. Since our approach is based principally on numerical solutions of stochastic differential equations using Monte Carlo simulations, this chapter is one of the cornerstones of this book.

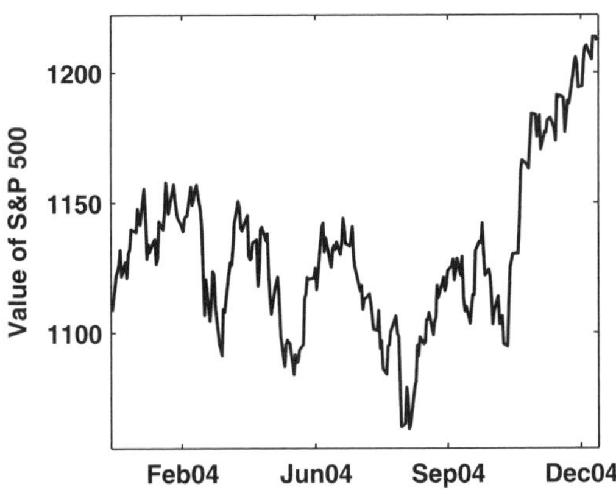

Figure 8.1 Daily S&P 500 index prices for 2004

8.1 INTRODUCTION TO STOCHASTIC CALCULUS

Let X be a random process. We consider the probability space

$$\{\Omega, \mathbf{F}, \mathcal{P}, t \in [0, T]\}$$

generated by the process X, where Ω is the sample space, $\mathbf{F}$ is the set of all possible events, $\mathcal{P}$ is the set of probability measures and $[0, T]$ is the time axis.

Definition 1.1 ***Filtration***:

The set of all events generated by the random variables

$$\{X(\tau), \tau \in [0, t]\} \tag{8.1}$$

denoted by $\mathcal{F}_t$ is called a filtration. This filtration $\mathcal{F}_t$ contains all the available information until time t. Thus, we have

$$\mathcal{F}_{t_1} \subset \mathcal{F}_{t_2} \subset \mathbf{F} \quad \forall t_1 < t_2. \tag{8.2}$$

The set $\{\mathcal{F}_{t_i}, t_i \in [0, T]\}$ refers to the concept of sigma-field or sigma-algebra generated by the random process X. Generally, in finance, $\mathcal{F}_t$ constitutes the information available up to time t. A rigorous treatment of sigma-algebra or sigma-field or measurable space will push us far into the probability measure theory, which is not the purpose of this chapter. (The interested reader can start with Williams (1991), for instance.)

Definition 1.2 ***Adapted***:

The process X is said to be adapted to the filtration $\{\mathcal{F}_{t_i}, t_i \in [0, T]\}$ if X is a measurable function under $(\mathcal{F}_{t_i}, \Omega)$ for all i. In other words, a stochastic process is an adapted process if it cannot be anticipated into the future.

Definition 1.3 ***Martingale***:

A random process X is a martingale if:

$$E\left[X(t) \middle| \mathcal{F}_\tau, \tau < t\right] = X(\tau). \tag{8.3}$$

In this definition, the conditional event is the information set available up to time τ, $\mathcal{F}_\tau$, which contains all past realizations of X up to date τ, so the conditional expectation of X with respect to $\mathcal{F}_\tau$ is equal to $X(\tau)$. This definition of the conditional expectation is the one used so far.

We study the random process X on the interval $[t_0, t]$. We subdivide the time interval into sub-intervals Δt and look at the increment:

$$X(t + \Delta t) - X(t) = \Delta X(t). \tag{8.4}$$

We study the process from t_0 to t, that is $X(\tau)$ with $t_0 \leq \tau \leq t$. The conditional means

$$E[\Delta X(t)|X(\tau), t_0 \leq \tau \leq t] \tag{8.5}$$

correspond to what we call the increment prediction $\Delta X(t)$ using the knowledge of the process until time t. We denote this prediction by $\Delta Y(t)$, then:

$$E[\Delta X(t)|X(\tau), t_0 \le \tau \le t] = \Delta Y(t). \tag{8.6}$$

We can thus write $\Delta X(t) = \Delta Y(t) + \Delta Z(t)$ where ΔZ is the prediction error. Therefore, physically, ΔZ is purely random. Summing the increment predictions from t_0 until t, we get:

$$X(t) - X(t_0) = \sum_{k=0}^{n-1} \Delta Y(t_k) + \sum_{k=0}^{n-1} \Delta Z(t_k), \tag{8.7}$$

with $t_0 \le t_1 \le \ldots \le t_k \le ... \le t_n = t$ and $\Delta Y(t_k) = E[\Delta X(t_k)|X(\tau), t_0 \le \tau \le t_k]$.

Note that any process $X(t)$ has two components: $Y(t)$ and $Z(t)$. $Y(t)$ is the conditional expectation of $X(t)$ with respect to the information up to time t and $Z(t)$ is the residual part of the process, i.e. $X(t) - Y(t)$. The process Y exhibits less variation since it is the conditional expectation with respect to the observed trajectory of the process. The process Z is a purely random component that can vary widely since it is residual.

To summarize, any random process is the sum of two processes: one from the prediction being less erratic than the other one which represents the prediction error.

Let's come back to equation $\Delta X(t) = \Delta Y(t) + \Delta Z(t)$, where $\Delta Y(t)$ is the prediction of the increment of X at instant t. We expect it to vary slowly as a function of time, that is:

$$\Delta Y(t_k) = A(t_k)\Delta t. \tag{8.8}$$

When Δt goes to 0 then:

$$Y(t) = \sum_{k=0}^{n} A(t_k)\Delta t \underset{\Delta t \to 0}{\longrightarrow} \int_{t_0}^{t} A(\tau)d\tau. \tag{8.9}$$

On the other hand, $E[\Delta Z] = 0$ and $Z(t_0) = 0$. Moreover,

$$E\left[Z(t + \Delta t)|Z(\tau),\ t_0 \le \tau \le t\right] = Z(t). \tag{8.10}$$

This means that $Z(t)$ is a martingale. This implies

$$E\left[\Delta Z(t)|Z(\tau),\ t_0 \le \tau \le t\right] = 0. \tag{8.11}$$

Remark 1.4 It is interesting to note that martingales can be obtained from a transformation of the standard Wiener process. This transformation is characterized by the following theorem.

Theorem 1.5 ***Lévy-Doob Theorem****:*

Let $W(t)$, $0 \le t$ be a finite variance martingale such that:

(a) $W(0) = 0$,

(b) $E\left[dW(t)|W(\tau), 0 \le \tau \le t\right] = 0$ *where* $dW(t) = W(t + dt) - W(t)$,

(c) $E\left[(dW(t))^2|W(\tau), 0 \le \tau \le t\right] = dt$.

Then $W(t)$ is a standard Wiener process.

8.2 INTRODUCTION TO STOCHASTIC DIFFERENTIAL EQUATIONS

8.2.1 Ito's Integral

We saw in a heuristic way that a random process can be described by the following equation:

$$X(t) = X(0) + \int_0^t a(X(\tau), \tau)\, d\tau + \int_0^t b(X(\tau), \tau)\, dW(\tau). \tag{8.12}$$

In this model, the first integral can be interpreted as being the quadratic mean integral described in the previous chapter. On the other hand, the second integral is of a new type, involving the standard Wiener process. This type of integral was first introduced by Ito in 1949.

On an infinitesimal interval, we can write it in a differential form:

$$dX(t) = a(X(t), t)\, dt + b(X(t), t)\, dW(t), \tag{8.13}$$

where $a(X(t), t)$ and $b(X(t), t)$ are respectively the instantaneous mean and instantaneous standard deviation. These parameters generally depend on the past and on the process's trajectory.

Generally,

$$X(t) = X(0) + \int_0^t A(\tau)\, d\tau + \int_0^t B(\tau)\, dW(\tau), \tag{8.14}$$

where $A(t)$ and $B(t)$ are functionals of $X(\tau)$ for $0 \le \tau \le t$. We are interested in the case:

$$\int_0^t E\left[|A(\tau)|\right] d\tau + \int_0^t E\left[|B(\tau)|^2\right] d\tau < \infty. \tag{8.15}$$

Processes that are solutions to this equation are called Ito processes. We already studied the integral $\int_0^t A(\tau)\, d\tau$ in the quadratic mean sense. For the second integral $\int_0^t B(\tau)\, dW(\tau)$, Ito provided mathematical construct and related calculus rules. Ito's integral is defined as follows:

$$\int_0^t B(\tau)\, dW(\tau) = \lim_{n\to\infty} \sum_{k=0}^{n-1} B(t_k)\left[W(t_{k+1}) - W(t_k)\right], \quad \text{where} \quad t_k = k\frac{t}{n}. \tag{8.16}$$

Remark 2.1 In the particular case where $B(t)$ is a deterministic function, this integral is called a Wiener integral.

8.2.2 Ito's Lemma

Let X be a uni-dimensional process defined as:

$$dX(t) = a(X(t), t)\, dt + b(X(t), t)\, dW(t). \tag{8.17}$$

Let $Y(t) = g(t, X(t))$ where g is twice continuously differentiable, that is, $\frac{\partial g}{\partial t}$, $\frac{\partial g}{\partial x}$, $\frac{\partial^2 g}{\partial t^2}$, $\frac{\partial^2 g}{\partial t \partial x}$ and $\frac{\partial^2 g}{\partial x^2}$ exist and are continuous. We suppose that a, b and g are memoryless transformations, i.e. they contain no information (memory) of earlier realizations of the random variable X.

Since g is twice differentiable with respect to t and X, we can use the Taylor series expansion to have:

$$
\begin{aligned}
g(t, X(t)) = g(0, X(0)) &+ \sum_j \frac{\partial g}{\partial t_j}\Delta t_j + \sum_j \frac{\partial g}{\partial x_j}\Delta X_j \\
&+ \frac{1}{2}\sum_j \frac{\partial^2 g}{\partial t_j^2}(\Delta t_j)^2 + \frac{1}{2}\sum_j \frac{\partial^2 g}{\partial t_j \partial x_j}(\Delta t_j)(\Delta X_j) \\
&+ \frac{1}{2}\sum_j \frac{\partial^2 g}{\partial x_j^2}(\Delta X_j)^2 + o((\Delta t_j)^3, (\Delta X_j)^3). \qquad (8.18)
\end{aligned}
$$

Moreover

$$(\Delta X_j)^2 = (a_j \Delta t_j + b_j \Delta W_j)^2 = a_j^2(\Delta t)^2 + b_j^2(\Delta W)^2 + 2a_j b_j \Delta t \Delta W. \qquad (8.19)$$

Heuristically, when Δt_j goes to 0, then

$$(\Delta t)^2, \Delta t \Delta W, \Delta W \Delta t \longrightarrow 0, \quad (\Delta W(t))^2 = \Delta t \longrightarrow dt \qquad (8.20)$$

and

$$(\Delta X(t))^2 = b^2 \Delta t \longrightarrow b^2 dt, \qquad (8.21)$$

since $(\Delta W)^2 = O(\Delta t)$ as Δt goes to zero, because $\Delta W = \sqrt{\Delta t}\xi$ where $\xi \sim N(0, 1)$. Then

$$\sum_j \frac{\partial g}{\partial t_j}\Delta t_j \longrightarrow \int_0^t \frac{\partial g}{\partial \tau} d\tau, \qquad (8.22)$$

$$\sum_j \frac{\partial g}{\partial x_j}\Delta X_j \longrightarrow \int_0^t \frac{\partial g}{\partial x} dX(\tau), \qquad (8.23)$$

$$\sum_j \frac{\partial^2 g}{\partial X_j^2}(\Delta X_j)^2 \longrightarrow \int_0^t \frac{\partial^2 g}{\partial x^2} b^2 d\tau. \qquad (8.24)$$

Which implies

$$g(t, X(t)) = g(0, X(0)) + \int_0^t \frac{\partial g}{\partial \tau} d\tau + \int_0^t \frac{\partial g}{\partial x} dX(\tau) + \frac{1}{2}\int_0^t \frac{\partial^2 g}{\partial x^2} b^2 d\tau. \qquad (8.25)$$

So

$$
\begin{aligned}
dY(t) &= \frac{\partial g}{\partial t} dt + \frac{\partial g}{\partial x} dX + \frac{1}{2}\frac{\partial^2 g}{\partial x^2} b^2 dt \\
&= \left(\frac{\partial g}{\partial t} + a\frac{\partial g}{\partial x} + \frac{1}{2} b^2 \frac{\partial^2 g}{\partial x^2}\right) dt + b\frac{\partial g}{\partial x} dW, \qquad (8.26)
\end{aligned}
$$

which constitutes Ito's lemma. So Ito's lemma is

$$dY = \left(\frac{\partial g}{\partial t} + a(X(t),t)\frac{\partial g}{\partial x} + \frac{1}{2}b^2(X(t),t)\frac{\partial^2 g}{\partial x^2}\right)dt + b(X(t),t)\frac{\partial g}{\partial x}dW. \tag{8.27}$$

Now, we examine some application examples of Ito's lemma.

Example 2.2 In this example, we want to compute the integral

$$\int_0^t W(\tau)dW(\tau). \tag{8.28}$$

To do the computation, we set $X(t) = W(t)$ and choose

$$\begin{aligned} Y(t) &= g(t, X(t)) \\ &= \frac{1}{2}W^2(t). \end{aligned} \tag{8.29}$$

We apply Ito's lemma and obtain

$$dY(t) = W(t)dW(t) + \frac{1}{2}dt. \tag{8.30}$$

So we have

$$\begin{aligned} \int_0^t W(\tau)dW(\tau) &= Y(t) - Y(0) - \frac{1}{2}t \\ &= \frac{1}{2}W^2(t) - \frac{1}{2}t. \end{aligned} \tag{8.31}$$

We clearly see that when working with stochastic integrals, we must be careful because the calculus rules are not the same as the "regular" differential calculus rules that we are used to.

The results from this computation can be directly obtained from the Ito's integral definition. Indeed, the integral:

$$\begin{aligned} \int_0^t W(\tau)dW(\tau) &= \lim_{\Delta t \to 0} \sum_{k=0}^{n-1} W(t_k)\left[W(t_{k+1}) - W(t_k)\right] \\ &= \lim_{\Delta t \to 0} \sum_{k=0}^{n-1} \frac{1}{2}\left[W^2(t_{k+1}) - W^2(t_k)\right] \\ &\quad - \frac{1}{2}\left[W(t_{k+1}) - W(t_k)\right]^2 \\ &= \lim_{\Delta t \to 0} \left[\frac{1}{2}W^2(t_n) - \frac{1}{2}\sum_{k=0}^{n-1}\left[\Delta W(t_k)\right]^2\right]. \end{aligned} \tag{8.32}$$

We show that

$$\lim_{\Delta t \to 0} \left[\sum_{k=0}^{n-1}\left[\Delta W(t_k)\right]^2 - t\right] = 0 \tag{8.33}$$

in quadratic mean. That is, we prove

$$E\left[\left(\sum_{k=0}^{n-1}[\Delta W(t_k)]^2 - t\right)^2\right] \underset{\Delta t \to 0}{\longrightarrow} 0. \tag{8.34}$$

In fact,

$$E\left[\left(\sum_{k=0}^{n-1}\left([\Delta W(t_k)]^2 - \Delta t\right)\right)^2\right], \tag{8.35}$$

once developed gives

$$E\left[\sum_{k=0}^{n-1}\sum_{j=0}^{n-1}\left(\Delta W^2(t_k) - \Delta t\right)\left(\Delta W^2(t_j) - \Delta t\right)\right] \tag{8.36}$$

which can also be expanded to

$$E\left[\sum_{k=0}^{n-1}\sum_{j=0}^{n-1}\Delta W^2(t_k)\Delta W^2(t_j) - \Delta t\left(\Delta W^2(t_k) + \Delta W^2(t_j)\right) + (\Delta t)^2\right]. \tag{8.37}$$

For this equation, as the number of steps n is inversely proportional to Δt, roughly, the expression is of order $(\Delta t)^2$, hence in the limit as Δt tends to zero, this expectation vanishes and yields 0. Thus we conclude that

$$\int_0^t W(\tau)dW(\tau) = \frac{1}{2}W^2(t) - \frac{1}{2}t. \tag{8.38}$$

Example 2.3 In this example, we want to compute the integral

$$\int_0^t \tau dW(\tau). \tag{8.39}$$

We set $Y(t) = tX(t)$ where $X(t) = W(t)$. Ito's lemma implies

$$dY(t) = X(t)dt + tdX(t) = d(tX(t)) \tag{8.40}$$

or

$$tX(t) = \int_0^t X(\tau)d\tau + \int_0^t \tau dX(\tau). \tag{8.41}$$

Thus

$$\int_0^t \tau dW(\tau) = tW(t) - \int_0^t W(\tau)d\tau. \tag{8.42}$$

Generally, we have the following integration by part rule:

$$\int_0^t g(\tau)dW(\tau) = g(t)W(t) - \int_0^t W(\tau)dg(\tau). \tag{8.43}$$

8.2.3 Ito's Lemma in the Multi-Dimensional Case

Similarly to the one-dimensional case, the same rule applies to the multi-dimensional case. Let $\underline{X} \in \mathbb{R}^n$ be a random vector with process

$$d\underline{X}(t) = A(\underline{X}(t), t)dt + B(\underline{X}(t), t)d\underline{W}(t), \tag{8.44}$$

where $A(\underline{X}(t), t) \in \mathbb{R}^n$, $\underline{W}(t) \in \mathbb{R}^m$ and $B(\underline{X}(t), t) \in \mathbb{R}^{n\times m}$.

Set

$$\begin{aligned}\underline{Y}(t) &= \underline{g}(t, \underline{X}(t)) \\ &= (Y_1(t), ..., Y_d(t))^\top,\end{aligned} \tag{8.45}$$

with $\underline{g} : \mathbb{R} \times \mathbb{R}^n \longrightarrow \mathbb{R}^d$, then the generalized Ito's lemma is

$$dY_k(t) = \frac{\partial g_k}{\partial t}dt + \sum_i \frac{\partial g_k}{\partial x_i}dX_i(t) + \frac{1}{2}\sum_{i,j} \frac{\partial^2 g_k}{\partial x_i \partial x_j}dX_i(t)dX_j(t). \tag{8.46}$$

Using Ito's lemma, many stochastic differential equations can be analytically solved. However, Ito's lemma was not derived with the objective of finding analytical solutions to differential equations.

8.2.4 Solutions of Some Stochastic Differential Equations

Although the objective of this chapter is not to provide an advanced treatise of stochastic calculus, we will study some stochastic differential equations commonly used in finance. Indeed, some relatively simple processes with closed form solutions are often employed in finance, such as the Ornstein-Uhlenbeck process and the geometric Brownian process. The Ornstein-Uhlenbeck process is used to describe mean reverting processes. An example of its use can be found in models of interest rate movements. The geometric Brownian motion is frequently used to model movements of an asset in the Black-Scholes-Merton model. We describe these processes in the following examples.

Example 2.4 Ornstein-Uhlenbeck process

Let X be a random process represented by

$$\frac{dX(t)}{dt} = -aX(t) + b\xi(t), \tag{8.47}$$

where ξ follows a normal distribution. If we set $\xi(t) = \dfrac{dW(t)}{dt}$ with W the Wiener process, then

$$dX(t) = -aX(t)dt + bdW(t). \tag{8.48}$$

The computation of this differential equation implies

$$X(t) = X(0)e^{-at} + \int_0^t e^{-a(t-s)} b dW(s). \tag{8.49}$$

In finance, this mean-reverting process is often used to describe the dynamics of interest rates and stochastic volatilities of asset returns.

Example 2.5 Log-normal process

Consider the process

$$dX(t) = aX(t)dt + bX(t)dW(t) \tag{8.50}$$

or

$$X(t) = X(0) + \int_0^t aX(s)ds + \int_0^t bX(s)dW(s). \tag{8.51}$$

Set

$$Y(t) = g(Z(t)) = e^{Z(t)} \tag{8.52}$$

with

$$dZ(t) = \alpha dt + \beta dW(t). \tag{8.53}$$

Ito's lemma implies

$$\begin{aligned} dY(t) &= \frac{\partial g}{\partial Z} dZ(t) + \frac{1}{2}\frac{\partial^2 g}{\partial Z^2}(dZ(t))^2 \\ &= Y(t)(\alpha dt + \beta dW(t)) + \frac{1}{2}Y(t)\beta^2 dt \\ &= Y(t)\left(\alpha + \frac{1}{2}\beta^2\right)dt + \beta Y(t)dW(t). \end{aligned} \tag{8.54}$$

If we choose α and β such that:

$$dZ(t) = \left(a - \frac{1}{2}b^2\right)dt + b dW(t), \tag{8.55}$$

then we note that $X(t) = e^{Z(t)}$. Since Z can be written as

$$Z(t) = Z(0) + \left(a - \frac{1}{2}b^2\right)t + bW(t), \tag{8.56}$$

this brings us to the exact solution

$$X(t) = X(0)e^{(a-\frac{1}{2}b^2)t + bW(t)}, \quad \text{with} \quad X(0) = X(t)|_{t=0} = e^{Z(0)}. \tag{8.57}$$

This process is regularly used to describe financial assets dynamics.

In practice, it is often very hard, if not impossible, to obtain an explicit solution of a stochastic differential equation. In such situations, we need to find a numerical solution using Monte Carlo simulation techniques introduced in this book.

8.3 INTRODUCTION TO STOCHASTIC PROCESSES WITH JUMPS

We saw that the classical model to represent the variation in financial asset values is of the form:

$$dX(t) = \mu(t, X(t))dt + \sigma(t, X(t))dW(t), \tag{8.58}$$

where $X(t)$, μ and σ are respectively the value of process X at time t, the drift and diffusion coefficient. $W(t)$ is a standard Wiener process.

In reality, sharp and large variations for $X(t)$ do occur. These sharp and large variations are linked to market-microstructure mechanisms and information arrivals and most of the time represent sudden events. Merton (1976) proposed to account for these jumps in the model shown in (3.1). We have a diffusion process with jumps under the form

$$dX(t) = \mu(t, X(t))dt + \sigma(t, X(t))dW(t) + J(t, X(t_-))dN(t), \tag{8.59}$$

where $N(t)$ is a Poisson process. In the simplest case, $N(t)$ is a Poisson process with parameter λ, that is if $N(t)$ represents the number of jumps on interval $[0, t]$, it follows

$$\text{Prob}(N(t) = n) = e^{-\lambda t}\frac{(\lambda t)^n}{n!}, \quad n = 0, 1, 2, ... \tag{8.60}$$

In this case,

$$\text{Prob}(dN(t) = 1) = \lambda dt \tag{8.61}$$

and $J(t, X(t_-))$ corresponds to the jump's amplitude.

Equation (3.2) can be written:

$$X(t) = X(t_0) + \int_{t_0}^{t} \mu(s, X(s))ds + \int_{t_0}^{t} \sigma(s, X(s))dW(s) + \int_{t_0}^{t} J(s, X(s_-))dN(s). \tag{8.62}$$

Before the jump, that is at time t, equation (3.5) is of the form

$$X(t) = X(t_0) + \int_{t_0}^{t} \mu(s, X(s))ds + \int_{t_0}^{t} \sigma(s, X(s))dW(s), \tag{8.63}$$

and the jump adds its effect to (3.6) to yield

$$X(t) = X(t_-) + J(t, X(t_-))dN(t), \tag{8.64}$$

where $dN(t)$ is the number of jumps that occurred between t_- and $t_- + dt$.

Example 3.1 We consider the simple following case:

$$dX(t) = \mu X(t)dt + \sigma X(t)dW(t) + X(t_-)dJ(t), \tag{8.65}$$

where μ and σ are constant drift and diffusion coefficients and dJ represents the relative amplitude of the jump at time t.

$dX(t)$ has two components: one coming from the log-normal process and the other originating from jump $dJ(t)$. The term $dJ(t)$ represents the relative amplitude of the jump at time t. We see that $dJ(t)$ gives us information about the jump: the probability of the jump happening at time t and the relative amplitude of the jump. We can represent it by $\gamma_n dN(t_n)$, where γ_n is the relative amplitude of the jump and

$$\text{Prob}(dN(t_n) = 1) = \lambda dt, \qquad \text{Prob}(dN(t_n) = 0) = 1 - \lambda dt. \tag{8.66}$$

Without the jump, we have

$$X(t_n^+) = X(t_n^-)e^{(\mu - \frac{\sigma^2}{2})dt + \sigma dW(t)}, \tag{8.67}$$

and if a jump occurs at time t_n, equation (3.10) becomes

$$X(t_n^+) = X(t_n^-)e^{(\mu - \frac{\sigma^2}{2})dt + \sigma dW(t)}(1 + \gamma_n). \tag{8.68}$$

We assume that γ_n are independent, identically distributed random log-normal variables, i.e., $G_n = \ln(1 + \gamma_n)$ is a Gaussian random variable. Given these characterizations, the solution of the simple model (3.8) is:

$$X(t + h) = X(t)e^{(\mu - \frac{\sigma^2}{2})h + \sigma\sqrt{h}Z + \sum_{n=1}^{m} G_n}, \tag{8.69}$$

where m is the total number of jumps happening between t and $t + h$. G_n are independent identically distributed Gaussian random variables and Z is a standard Gaussian random variable independent of G_n.

8.4 NUMERICAL SOLUTIONS OF SOME STOCHASTIC DIFFERENTIAL EQUATIONS (SDE)

Let a vector of stochastic differential equations be

$$\underline{X}(t) = \underline{X}(t_0) + \int_{t_0}^{t} \underline{a}(\underline{X}(s), s)ds + \int_{t_0}^{t} \underline{b}(\underline{X}(s), s)d\underline{W}(s), \tag{8.70}$$

with $\underline{X} \in \mathbb{R}^d$, $\underline{a} \in \mathbb{R}^d$, $\underline{W} \in \mathbb{R}^m$, and $\underline{b} \in \mathbb{R}^{d\times m}$. This vectorial equation can be decomposed into d differential equations as follows:

$$X_k(t) = X_k(t_0) + \int_{t_0}^{t} a_k(X(s), s)ds + \sum_{i=1}^{m} \int_{t_0}^{t} b_k^i(X(s), s)dW^i(s), \tag{8.71}$$

for $k = 1, \ldots, d$.

So, let us consider the following representative one-dimensional differential equation

$$dX(t) = a(X(t), t)dt + b(X(t), t)dW(t) \tag{8.72}$$

or equivalently

$$X(t) = X(t_0) + \int_{t_0}^{t} a(X(s), s)ds + \int_{t_0}^{t} b(X(s), s)dW(s), \tag{8.73}$$

with a representing the drift or trend and b the diffusion coefficient or the volatility. To solve this equation numerically, we have to: (i) discretize the time and space, and (ii) use an iterative technique that will allow us to arrive at the results.

8.4.1 Ordinary Differential Equations

To get a grasp on the solution of stochastic differential equations, we need to recall the schemes for numerical discretization of ordinary differential equations. This enables us to understand Euler and Milstein discretization schemes that will be covered later. We present some classical schemes that are most often used in ordinary differential equations discretization.

Set the ordinary differential equation

$$dx = a(x, t)dt, \quad \text{with initial condition} \quad x(t_0) = x_0. \tag{8.74}$$

We define

$$t_{n+1} = t_n + \Delta t, \quad x(t_{n+1}) = x_n + \Delta x = x_{n+1} \tag{8.75}$$

and $y_{n+1} = y(t_{n+1})$ the linear approximation of x_{n+1}, i.e.

$$y(t_n + \Delta t) \approx y(t_n) + \frac{dy}{dt}\Delta t. \tag{8.76}$$

Figure 8.2 provides an illustration of the approximation using the Euler method we discussed below.

The local error is obtained by

$$\epsilon_l(n+1) = |x_{n+1} - y_{n+1}| \tag{8.77}$$

and the global error is

$$\epsilon_g(n+1) = |x_{n+1} - y_{(n+1,x_0)}|, \tag{8.78}$$

where $y_{(n+1,x_0)}$ is the approximation value at t_{n+1} with the starting value x_0 using equation (4.7). We say that the approximation is stable if, for $\Delta t \to 0$, the error goes to zero.

Many approximation techniques exist to numerically estimate this differential equation. We list some of these below.

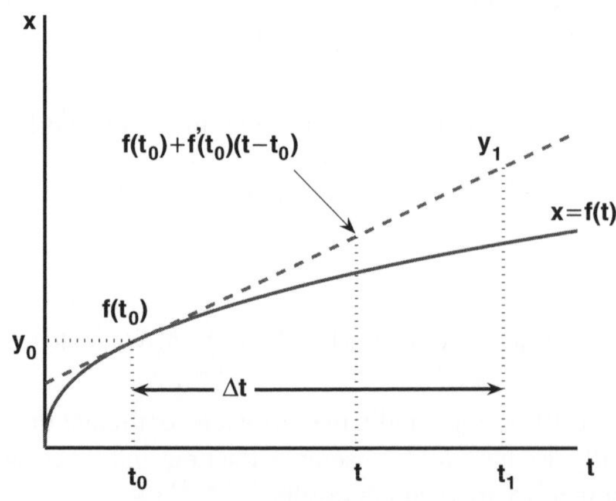

Figure 8.2 Approximation using the Euler method

Euler method

We consider the approximation

$$y_{n+1} = y_n + a(y_n, t_n)\Delta t, \tag{8.79}$$

that corresponds to the 1st order Taylor series expansion. If $\epsilon_g < K(\Delta t)^\gamma$, we say that γ is the speed or convergence degree of the algorithm. For deterministic equations, Euler method gives us unitary speed $\gamma = 1$.

Runge-Kutta method

This method is based on the following approximation scheme

$$y_{n+1} = y_n + \frac{1}{6}\left(k_n^1 + 2k_n^2 + 2k_n^3 + k_n^4\right)\Delta t, \tag{8.80}$$

where

$$\begin{aligned}
k_n^1 &= a(y_n, t_n), \\
k_n^2 &= a\left(y_n + \frac{1}{2}k_n^1 \Delta t, t_n + \frac{1}{2}\Delta t\right), \\
k_n^3 &= a\left(y_n + \frac{1}{2}k_n^2 \Delta t, t_n + \frac{1}{2}\Delta t\right), \\
k_n^4 &= a\left(y_n + k_n^3 \Delta t, t_{n+1}\right).
\end{aligned}$$

This is the fourth-order Runge-Kutta algorithm that has an accumulated error proportional to $(\Delta t)^4$.

Implicit method

We take the slope $\dfrac{a(y_n, t_n) + a(y_{n+1}, t_{n+1})}{2}$, which brings us to the numerical approximation

$$y_{n+1} = y_n + \frac{1}{2}(a(y_n, t_n) + a(y_{n+1}, t_{n+1}))\Delta t. \tag{8.81}$$

While Euler and Runge-Kutta are explicit approximation methods, this method is implicit because the solution is obtained iteratively.

8.4.2 Stochastic Differential Equations

Ito-Taylor expansion

From equation

$$X_t = X_{t_0} + \int_{t_0}^{t} a ds + \int_{t_0}^{t} b dW_s, \tag{8.82}$$

if we set $f(X_t) = Y_t$, by way of Ito's lemma we obtain

$$\begin{aligned}
dY_t &= \frac{\partial f}{\partial t}dt + \frac{\partial f}{\partial x}dX_t + \frac{1}{2}\frac{\partial^2 f}{\partial x^2}(dX_t)^2 \\
&= \left(\frac{\partial f}{\partial t} + a\frac{\partial f}{\partial x} + \frac{1}{2}b^2\frac{\partial^2 f}{\partial x^2}\right)dt + b\frac{\partial f}{\partial x}dW_t.
\end{aligned} \tag{8.83}$$

From this,

$$f(X_t) = f(X_{t_0}) + \int_{t_0}^{t} \left(\frac{\partial f}{\partial s} + a\frac{\partial f}{\partial x} + \frac{1}{2}b^2\frac{\partial^2 f}{\partial x^2} \right) ds + \int_{t_0}^{t} b\frac{\partial f}{\partial x} dW_s. \tag{8.84}$$

Function f doesn't explicitly depend on time then:

$$dY_t = \left(a\frac{\partial f}{\partial x} + \frac{1}{2}b^2\frac{\partial^2 f}{\partial x^2} \right) dt + b\frac{\partial f}{\partial x} dW_t. \tag{8.85}$$

We can rewrite it as

$$dY_t = L^0 f dt + L^1 f dW_t, \tag{8.86}$$

with

$$L^0 f = a\frac{\partial f}{\partial x} + \frac{1}{2}b^2\frac{\partial^2 f}{\partial x^2}, \tag{8.87}$$

$$L^1 f = b\frac{\partial f}{\partial x}. \tag{8.88}$$

To ease the algebra, we will use the two operators L^0 and L^1. Thus

$$f(X_t) = f(X_{t_0}) + \int_{t_0}^{t} L^0 f(X_s) ds + \int_{t_0}^{t} L^1 f(X_s) dW_s. \tag{8.89}$$

If we apply equation (4.20) (i.e. apply operators L^0 and L^1) to functions a and b, we get

$$\begin{aligned} X_t = X_{t_0} &+ \int_{t_0}^{t} \left(a(X_{t_0}) + \int_{t_0}^{s} L^0 a(X_z) dz + \int_{t_0}^{s} L^1 a(X_z) dW_z \right) ds \\ &+ \int_{t_0}^{t} \left(b(X_{t_0}) + \int_{t_0}^{s} L^0 b(X_z) dz + \int_{t_0}^{s} L^1 b(X_z) dW_z \right) dW_s. \end{aligned} \tag{8.90}$$

This implies

$$X_t = X_{t_0} + a(X_{t_0})(t - t_0) + b(X_{t_0})(W_t - W_{t_0}) + \int_{t_0}^{t} \int_{t_0}^{s} L^1 b(X_z) dW_z dW_s + \mathcal{O}, \tag{8.91}$$

with $\mathcal{O}$ containing terms of higher order or equal to $t^{3/2}$. And since

$$\begin{aligned} \int_{t_0}^{t} \int_{t_0}^{s} L^1 b(X_z) dW_z dW_s = \int_{t_0}^{t} \int_{t_0}^{s} \Big(L^1 b(X_{t_0}) &+ \int_{t_0}^{z} L^0 L^1 b(X_v) dv \\ &+ \int_{t_0}^{z} L^1 L^1 b(X_v) dW_v \Big) dW_z dW_s, \end{aligned} \tag{8.92}$$

we finally have

$$X_t = X_{t_0} + a(X_{t_0})(t - t_0) + b(X_{t_0})(W_t - W_{t_0}) + b\frac{\partial b}{\partial x} \int_{t_0}^{t} \int_{t_0}^{s} dW_z dW_s + \mathcal{O}', \tag{8.93}$$

with $\mathcal{O}'$ containing terms of higher order or equal to $t^{3/2}$.

Although the above equations involve tedious algebra, X can be approximated by Y as follows:

$$Y_{k+1} = Y_k + a(Y_k)\Delta t + b(Y_k)\Delta W_k + b(Y_k)\frac{\partial b}{\partial x}(Y_k) \int_{t_k}^{t_{k+1}} \int_{t_k}^{s} dW_z dW_s. \tag{8.94}$$

The solution which satisfies this equation can be weak or strong depending on the type of convergence used. Note that the convergence in quadratic mean of sequence of random variables has been discussed in Chapter 3. The strong solution is preferred to study options which depend on the asset value paths (for example American and Exotic options). However, for European options, we only require that X converges weakly to Y since we only need the final expected values to be equal at maturity.

Strong solutions take more computer time to obtain since they need the path of the solution to be close to the trajectory of the exact value. The weak solution needs only the moments at terminal points to be the same for any trajectory. In this case, we can use the Euler scheme which is an algorithm of degree 0.5.

Euler scheme

We retain only the terms of order 1 in the Taylor expansion. In this case, we have the Euler scheme

$$Y_{k+1} = Y_k + a(Y_k)\Delta t + b(Y_k)\Delta W_k. \tag{8.95}$$

As we said above, this algorithm is of degree 0.5. To obtain a higher degree approximation, we can use the Milstein scheme.

Milstein scheme

From the approximation of X,

$$Y_{k+1} = Y_k + a(Y_k)\Delta t + b(Y_k)\Delta W_k + b(Y_k)\frac{\partial b}{\partial x}(Y_k)\int_{t_k}^{t_{k+1}}\int_{t_k}^{s} dW_z dW_s, \tag{8.96}$$

we compute the last term

$$\begin{aligned}
\int_{t_k}^{t_{k+1}}\left(\int_{t_k}^{s} dW_z\right)dW_s &= \int_{t_k}^{t_{k+1}}(W_s - W_k)dW_s \\
&= \frac{1}{2}(W_{k+1}^2 - W_k^2 - (t_{k+1} - t_k)) \\
&\quad - W_k(W_{k+1} - W_k) \\
&= -\frac{1}{2}\Delta t + \frac{1}{2}(W_{k+1} - W_k)(W_{k+1} + W_k - 2W_k) \\
&= \frac{1}{2}(\Delta W_k)^2 - \frac{1}{2}\Delta t,
\end{aligned} \tag{8.97}$$

then

$$Y_{k+1} = Y_k + a(Y_k)\Delta t + b(Y_k)\Delta W_k + \frac{1}{2}b(Y_k)\frac{\partial b}{\partial x}(Y_k)((\Delta W_k)^2 - \Delta t). \tag{8.98}$$

This approximation is called the Milstein scheme. This scheme gives us a precision of order 1.

Note that these approximation schemes have been developed for one-dimensional cases. For higher than one dimension stochastic differential equations, the interested reader can read Kloeden and Platen (1992). However, using the simple Milstein scheme in (4.29) combined with the Cholesky decomposition in the multi-dimensional case can lead to satisfactory results relative to Euler ones.

8.5 APPLICATION CASE: GENERATION OF A STOCHASTIC DIFFERENTIAL EQUATION USING THE EULER AND MILSTEIN SCHEMES

In this section, we present an application case using the different discretization schemes that we previously presented. The aim of this exercise is to simulate a stochastic process using the discretization schemes of Euler and Milstein.

Consider the following stochastic differential equation:

$$dX(t) = aX(t)dt + bX(t)dW(t), \tag{8.99}$$

with $X(0) = 100$, $a = 0.05$ and $b = 0.20$. This equation can be solved as

$$\log(X(t)) = \log(X(0)) + \left(a - \frac{b^2}{2}\right)t + bW(t), \tag{8.100}$$

which yields

$$X(t) = X(0)e^{(a-\frac{b^2}{2})t+bW(t)}. \tag{8.101}$$

Based on this expression, in MATLAB, the simulation of trajectories can be performed in the following way.

```
%Steps to simulate trajectories.
%NbTraj: Number of trajectories.

%Computation of gaussian variables
WT = sqrt(T)*randn(NbTraj, 1);

%Computation of trajectories
Traj = X0*exp((a-b*b/2)*T+b*WT);
```

Using a discretization step of Δ, the Euler scheme is described by

$$X_{n+1} = X_n + aX_n\Delta t + bX_n\Delta W_n, \tag{8.102}$$

and the Milstein scheme is given by

$$X_{n+1} = X_n + aX_n\Delta t + bX_n\Delta W_n + \frac{1}{2}b^2X_n((\Delta W_n)^2 - \Delta t), \tag{8.103}$$

where ΔW_n is a Gaussian random variable with zero mean and variance of Δt.

For Euler's approximations, the trajectories can be simulated with MATLAB in the following way:

```
%Steps to compute Euler approximations
%NbTraj: Number of trajectories
%NbStep: Number of step to simulate

%Computation of Gaussian variables
DeltaW = sqrt(DeltaT)*randn(NbTraj,NbStep);

%Matrices used to store the approximations
Traj=zeros(NbTraj,NbStep+1);
Traj(:,1) = X0*ones(NbTraj,1);
```

```
%Loop that simulates all the time steps
for i=1:NbStep
    Traj(:,i+1) = Traj(:,i).*(1+a*DeltaT+b*DeltaW(:,i));
end
```

For Milstein's scheme, we need to add the term $\frac{1}{2}b^2((\Delta W_n)^2 - \Delta t)$ just at time $i+1$.

```
%Steps to compute Milstein approximations
%NbTraj: Number of trajectories
%NbStep: Number of steps to simulate

%Computations of the Gaussian variables
DeltaW = sqrt(DeltaT)*randn(NbTraj,NbStep);

%Addition for Milstein approximation
DeltaW2 = DeltaW.*DeltaW;

%Matrices used to store the approximations
Traj=zeros(NbTraj,NbStep+1);
Traj(:,1) = X0*ones(NbTraj,1);

%Loop that simulates all the time steps
for i=1:NbStep
    Traj(:,i+1) = Traj(:,i).*(1+a*DeltaT+b*DeltaW(:,i) + ...
                       b^2/2*(DeltaW2(:,i) - ...
                       DeltaT*ones(NbTraj,1)));
end
```

When we perform Monte Carlo simulations, it is important to provide a measure for the quality of the obtained results. Sensitivity studies allow us to observe the variation in the quality of the simulations when we change the number of simulations, the confidence interval or the discretization step.

8.5.1 Sensitivity with Respect to the Number of Simulated Series

For each of the schemes, simulate 10, 100, 1000, 10 000 and 100 000 series (*NbSeries*) of *NbTraj* = 1000 simulations of this process on 365 days and considering a weekly discretization step $\Delta t = 1/52$. Then compute the absolute approximation error ϵ with a confidence interval of $\alpha = 95\%$ for each scheme.

We use Euler and Milstein methods already coded with the parameters given above. Below is a program for the Euler method case. We employ a method using the logarithm of X to optimize the program with matrix functions in MATLAB. In fact, we simulate the value of the logarithm of X_{n+1}. For Euler's approximation, we have

$$\begin{aligned}\log(X_{n+1}) &= \log(X_n(1 + a\Delta t + b\Delta W_n)) \\ &= \log(X_n) + \log(1 + a\Delta t + b\Delta W_n) \\ &= \log(X_0) + \sum_{i=0}^{n} \log(1 + a\Delta t + b\Delta W_i). \end{aligned} \tag{8.104}$$

To get the exact solutions, we can also use a similar method. Computing the value of the logarithm of $X(t)$, we have

$$\begin{aligned}\log(X(t)) &= \log(X(0)e^{(a-\frac{1}{2}b^2)t+bW(t)}) \\ &= \log(X(0)) + \left(a - \frac{1}{2}b^2\right)t + bW(t).\end{aligned} \tag{8.105}$$

The exact solutions at point $t = (n+1)\Delta t$ is given by

$$\begin{aligned}\log(X((n+1)\Delta t)) &= \log(X(0)) + \left(a - \frac{1}{2}b^2\right)(n+1)\Delta t + bW((n+1)\Delta t) \\ &= \log(X(0)) \\ &\quad + \sum_{i=0}^{n}\left(\left(a - \frac{1}{2}b^2\right)\Delta t + b(W((i+1)\Delta t) - W(i\Delta t))\right).\end{aligned} \tag{8.106}$$

```
function rep=Euler(NbSeries,NbTraj,NbStep,alpha)
%Function that computes the approximations error when we use
%the Euler discretization and presents the confidence interval
%NbSeries: Number of series to simulate
%NbTraj: Number of trajectories by series
%NbStep: Number of steps to simulate
%alpha: Confidence level for the error

%Initial parameters
 X0=100;
 a=0.05;
 b=0.20;
 T=1;
 DeltaT = 1/NbStep;
 SqDeltaT = sqrt(DeltaT);

%Vector of average epsilons for each series
EpsilonSeries = zeros(NbSeries,1);

%For each series we simulate the analytical solutions and
%the approximations
for i=1:NbSeries

  %Simulation of the Gaussian variables
  DeltaW = SqDeltaT*randn(NbTraj,NbStep);

  %Construction of exact solutions
  Increments = (a-b*b/2)*DeltaT + b*DeltaW;
  LogPaths=cumsum([log(X0)*ones(NbTraj,1),Increments],2);
  SPaths = exp(LogPaths);

  %Construction of Euler approximations
  EulerInc = log([X0*ones(NbTraj,1),ones(NbTraj,NbStep) +...
                  a*DeltaT*ones(NbTraj,NbStep)+b*DeltaW]);
```

Table 8.1 Sensitivity of the results to the number of series

	Euler		Milstein	
NbSeries	ϵ	Interval	ϵ	Interval
10	0.3287	[0.3257, 0.3316]	0.0170	[0.0167, 0.0173]
100	0.3277	[0.3265, 0.3290]	0.0169	[0.0168, 0.0170]
1000	0.3281	[0.3277, 0.3286]	0.0170	[0.0170, 0.0170]
10000	0.3278	[0.3277, 0.3280]	0.0170	[0.0170, 0.0170]
100000	0.3279	[0.3279, 0.3280]	0.0170	[0.0170, 0.0170]

```
    EulerIncCum = cumsum(EulerInc,2);
    Euler = exp(EulerIncCum);

    %Temporary variable to store the approximation errors
    temp=0;
    for j=1:NbTraj
        temp=temp+abs(Euler(j,NbStep+1) - SPaths(j,NbStep+1));
    end;

    %Computation of the average of the errors for series
    EpsilonSeries(i,1)=temp/NbTraj;
end;

%Computation of the average and variance of errors for all series
Epsilon = mean(EpsilonSeries,1);
Var = var(EpsilonSeries);

%Computation of the confidence interval
DeltaEpsilon = tinv(alpha,NbSeries-1)*sqrt((Var/NbSeries));

%Confidence interval at level alpha%
rep=[Epsilon-DeltaEpsilon, Epsilon, Epsilon+DeltaEpsilon];
```

We obtain the results presented in Table 8.1. Note that the confidence interval decreases with the number of simulated series.

8.5.2 Sensitivity with Respect to the Confidence Interval

We repeat the preceding simulations with $NbSeries = 1000$, but this time we compute the approximation error as a function of $\alpha = 90\%, 95\%, 99\%$.

The results are presented in Table 8.2. We see that, based on the desired level of confidence, we come up with slightly different intervals. In other cases, the effect of the parameter α can be much more important.

8.5.3 Sensitivity with Respect to the Number of Simulations

We repeat the simulations with $NbSeries = 1000$ and $\alpha = 95\%$, but this time we compute the approximation error as a function of the number of simulations $NbTraj = 10, 100, 1000, 10\,000$. The results are presented in Table 8.3.

Table 8.2 Sensitivity of the results to the confidence interval

	Euler		Milstein	
α	ϵ	Interval	ϵ	Interval
0.90	0.3283	[0.3279, 0.3286]	0.01697	[0.01695, 0.01699]
0.95	0.3274	[0.3269, 0.3278]	0.01699	[0.01696, 0.01701]
0.99	0.3286	[0.3279, 0.3292]	0.01696	[0.01692, 0.01699]

Table 8.3 Sensitivity of the results to the number of simulations

	Euler		Milstein	
NbTraj	ϵ	Interval	ϵ	Interval
10	0.3305	[0.32615, 0.32805]	0.01688	[0.016632, 0.017135]
100	0.3267	[0.32538, 0.32805]	0.01703	[0.016944, 0.017109]
1000	0.3279	[0.32745, 0.32832]	0.01699	[0.016968, 0.017017]
10000	0.3279	[0.32778, 0.32804]	0.01698	[0.016968, 0.016983]

Table 8.4 Sensitivity of the results to the discretization step

	Euler		Milstein	
Δt	ϵ	Interval	ϵ	Interval
1/12	0.67480	[0.67386, 0.67574]	0.07201	[0.07190, 0.07212]
1/52	0.32784	[0.32740, 0.32827]	0.01698	[0.01695, 0.01700]
1/365	0.12427	[0.12411, 0.12444]	0.002431	[0.002427, 0.002434]

8.5.4 Sensitivity with Respect to the Time Step

Using parameters *NbSeries* = 1000, *NbTraj* = 1000, $\alpha = 95\%$, compute the approximation error as a function of $\Delta t = 1/365$ (days), 1/52 (weeks) and 1/12 (months).

The results are presented in Table 8.4. The discretization step can significantly affect the results precision.

8.6 APPLICATION CASE: SIMULATION OF A STOCHASTIC DIFFERENTIAL EQUATION WITH CONTROL AND ANTITHETIC VARIABLES

In this section, we present an application case to illustrate the use of simulation quality improvement concepts described in previous chapters.

We take the same stochastic differential equation:

$$dX(t) = aX(t)dt + bX(t)dW(t) \tag{8.107}$$

with $X(0) = 100$, $a = 0.05$ and $b = 0.20$.

In the following section we use Euler's scheme with discretization step $\Delta t = 1/100$ on one period $T = 1$.

Table 8.5 Simulations without variance reduction technique

	Mean		Variance	
NbTraj	Estimate	Interval	Estimate	Interval
10	105.18	[104.82, 105.54]	406.88	[395.76, 418.00]
100	105.25	[105.13, 105.37]	445.84	[441.95, 449.73]
1000	105.12	[105.08, 105.15]	451.34	[450.05, 452.63]
10000	105.13	[105.12, 105.14]	450.67	[450.29, 451.06]

8.6.1 Simple Simulations

Perform $NbSeries = 1000$ series with $NbTraj = 10, 100, 1000, 10\,000$ simulations to come up with the mean and the variance of the process X at $T = 1$, denoted by $E[X(1)]$ and $\text{Var}(X(1))$. Then compute the confidence interval.

Table 8.5 presents the simulations results.

8.6.2 Simulations with Control Variables

We use the same program but introduce here a control variable. We proceed in the following way. For each generated value of $X(1)$, we use the control variate

$$\sum_{n=0}^{100} \Delta W_n \tag{8.108}$$

to readjust the value of $X(1)$. This can be done quickly in MATLAB by:

```
function EulerCont(NbSeries, NbTraj, NbStep, alpha)
%Function that computes the mean and variance of variable X
%using the control variables method
%NbSeries: Number of series to simulate
%NbTraj: Number of trajectories for each series
%NbStep: Number of steps to generate
%alpha: Level of confidence for the error

%Initial parameters
 X0=100;
 a=0.05;
 b=0.20;
 DeltaT = 1/NbStep;
 T=1;

SqDeltaT = sqrt(DeltaT);

%Averages and variances vector
AverageSeries = zeros(NbSeries,1);
VarSeries=zeros(NbSeries,1);

for i=1:NbSeries
```

```
   %Simulation of Gaussian variables
   DeltaW = SqDeltaT*randn(NbTraj,NbStep);

   %Euler approximations with logarithms method
   EulerInc = log([X0*ones(NbTraj,1), ones(NbTraj,NbStep) + ...
              a*DeltaT*ones(NbTraj,NbStep)+b*DeltaW]);
   EulerIncCum = cumsum(EulerInc,2);
   Euler = exp(EulerIncCum);

   %Control variable
   A=Euler(:,NbStep+1);
   B=sum(DeltaW,2);
   MatrixCovariance=cov(A,B);
   correction=-MatrixCovariance(1,2)/var(B);
   A=A+correction*(B-mean(B));

   AverageSeries(i,1)=mean(A,1);
   VarSeries(i,1)=var(A,1);
end

%Computation of the average of averages and variances of the series
Average = mean(AverageSeries,1);
Variance=mean(VarSeries,1);

%Computation of the variance of the averages and variances of series
VarAverage = var(AverageSeries,1);
VarVariance=var(VarSeries,1);

%Computation of the confidence interval for the mean and variance
DeltaAverage=tinv(alpha,NbSeries-1)*sqrt(VarAverage/NbSeries);
DeltaVariance=tinv(alpha,NbSeries-1)*sqrt(VarVariance/NbSeries);

IntervalAverage = [Average-DeltaAverage, Average, Average+
                            DeltaAverage]
IntervalVariance = [Variance-DeltaVariance, Variance, ...
                        Variance+DeltaVariance]
end
```

Simulation results are shown in Table 8.6. After running the preceding program 1000 times we obtain the confidence interval for the mean and the variance.

Table 8.6 Simulations with control variables

	Mean		Variance	
NbTraj	Estimate	Interval	Estimate	Interval
10	105.30	[104.82, 105.52]	5.52	[5.12, 5.92]
100	105.17	[105.06, 105.27]	8.33	[8.13, 8.53]
1000	105.12	[105.09, 105.16]	8.83	[8.76, 8.90]
10000	105.12	[105.11, 105.13]	8.86	[8.84, 8.89]

8.6.3 Simulations with Antithetic Variables

We use antithetic variables to increase the precision of each series. We proceed as follows to generate the variables ΔW.

```
function EulerAnti(NbSeries,NbTraj,NbStep,alpha)
%Function that computes the mean and variance of variable X
%using the antithetic variables technique
%NbSeries: Number of series to generate
%NbTraj: Number of trajectories for each series
%NbStep: Number of steps to generate
%alpha: Confidence level for the error

%Initial parameters
X0=100;
a=0.05;
b=0.20;
DeltaT = 1/NbStep;
T=1;
SqDeltaT = sqrt(DeltaT);

%Averages and variances vector
AverageSeries = zeros(NbSeries,1);
VarSeries=zeros(NbSeries,1);

for i=1:NbSeries

   %Generation of random variables and antithetic variables
   DeltaW = SqDeltaT*randn(NbTraj,NbStep);
   DeltaW=[DeltaW;-DeltaW];

   %Euler approximations with logarithms method
   EulerInc = log([X0*ones(2*NbTraj,1), ones(2*NbTraj,
              NbStep) + ...
            a*DeltaT*ones(2*NbTraj,NbStep)+b*DeltaW]);
   EulerIncCum = cumsum(EulerInc,2);
   Euler = exp(EulerIncCum);

   AverageSeries(i,1)=mean(Euler(:,NbStep+1),1);
   VarSeries(i,1)=var(Euler(:,NbStep+1),1);

end

%Computation of the average of averages and variances of series
Average = mean(AverageSeries,1);
Variance=mean(VarSeries,1);

%Computation of the variance of averages and variances of series
VarAverage = var(AverageSeries,1);
VarVariance=var(VarSeries,1);
```

Table 8.7 Simulations with antithetic variables

	Mean ($)		Variance (^{2})	
NbTraj	Estimate	Interval	Estimate	Interval
10	105.09	[105.05, 105.14]	441.40	[430.96, 451.84]
100	105.11	[105.10, 105.13]	447.11	[443.63, 450.58]
1000	105.13	[105.12, 105.13]	450.87	[449.77, 451.97]
10000	105.12	[105.12, 105.13]	450.22	[449.87, 450.57]

```
%Computation of the confidence interval for the mean and the
variance
DeltaAverage=tinv(alpha,NbSeries-1)*sqrt(VarAverage/NbSeries);
DeltaVariance=tinv(alpha,NbSeries-1)*sqrt(VarVariance/NbSeries);

IntervalAverage = [Average-DeltaAverage, Average, Average+
                   DeltaAverage]
IntervalVariance = [Variance-DeltaVariance, Variance, ...
                    Variance+DeltaVariance]

end
```

Simulation results are presented in Table 8.7.

The reader is invited to study simulation cases combining several different techniques of variance reduction and precision enhancement as practice exercises.

8.7 APPLICATION CASE: GENERATION OF A STOCHASTIC DIFFERENTIAL EQUATION WITH JUMPS

For this application case, we consider an alternative version of equation (3.12) from Merton's (1976) work:

$$S(t+h) = S(t)e^{(\mu-\delta-\lambda k-0.5\sigma^2)h+\sigma\sqrt{h}Z}e^{m(\mu_J-0.5\sigma_J^2)+\sigma_J\sum_{i=0}^{m}G_i}, \tag{8.109}$$

where μ_J and σ_J are the average and standard deviation of the jump's magnitude, and Z and G_i are Gaussian random variables. μ represents the instantaneous expected rate of return of the asset, δ is the dividend rate, σ is the instantaneous volatility of the asset's return, λ is the yearly average of the number of jumps, m is a Poisson random variable with mean λ and h is the time step. The case without jump can be obtained with $m = 0$, $\mu_J = \sigma_J = \lambda = 0$.

This stochastic differential equation with jumps represents a financial asset's price process. Merton (1976) assumes the jumps to be independent and idiosyncratic, meaning that jumps are diversifiable. Diversification means that by holding a portfolio of several financial assets, one is more likely to cancel the effect of jumps all together.

Parameter k is given by:

$$k = e^{-\mu_J} - 1, \tag{8.110}$$

with $\mu_J \geq 0$. k representing the negative value of the expected percentage jump.

Using the following values for the parameters, $S(0) = \$\ 100$, $\mu_J = 0.02$, $\sigma_J = 0.10$, $\mu = 0.05$, $\delta = 0$, $\sigma = 0.30$, $\lambda = 3$ and $T = 1$ year, perform the simulations of the processes with and without jumps and plot their graphical representations.

In MATLAB, a program simulating these trajectories with jumps might look like the following one (where we directly generate $\log(S(t))$). We use 250 steps per year and the variable *NbDays* represents the number of days for the simulation. In our case, we also have 250 because the simulation covers a whole year. A MATLAB program is written as follows:

```
function Jump
%Function that simulates a stochastic process with jumps

%Initial parameters
X0=100;
mu=0.05;
Div=0.00;
Lambda= 3;
sigma=0.3;
muJ=0.02;
sigmaJ=0.10;
T=1;
NbStep=250; %Number of steps per year
DeltaT=1/NbStep;
NbDays=T*NbStep;
k=exp(-muJ)-1;

%Simulation of Poisson and Gaussian random variables
 PoissonG=poissrnd(Lambda/NbPas,1,NbDays);
 DeltaZ=randn(1,NbDays);
 PoissonJumps=zeros(1,NbDays);

%Determination of jumps for the Poisson process
for i=1:NbDays
   PoissonJumpss(1,i)=sum(randn(PoissonG(1,i),1));
end

%Constructing the increments
IncrementsJumps=(mu-Div-Lambda*k-0.5*sigma^2)*DeltaT*...
               ones(1,NbDays)+sigma*sqrt(DeltaT)*DeltaZ+...
               (muJ-0.5*sigmaJ^2)*PoissonG+sigmaJ*...
               PoissonJumps;
Increments=(mu-Div-0.5*sigma^2)*DeltaT*ones(1,NbDays)+...
               sigma*sqrt(DeltaT)*DeltaZ;
SolJumps=exp(cumsum([log(X0),IncrementsJumps],2));
Sol=exp(cumsum([log(X0),Increments],2));

%Graph of the trajectories with and without jumps
figure
hold on
plot(0:1:NbDays,SolJumps,0:1:NbDays,Sol);
legend('With jumps','Without jump');
hold off

end
```

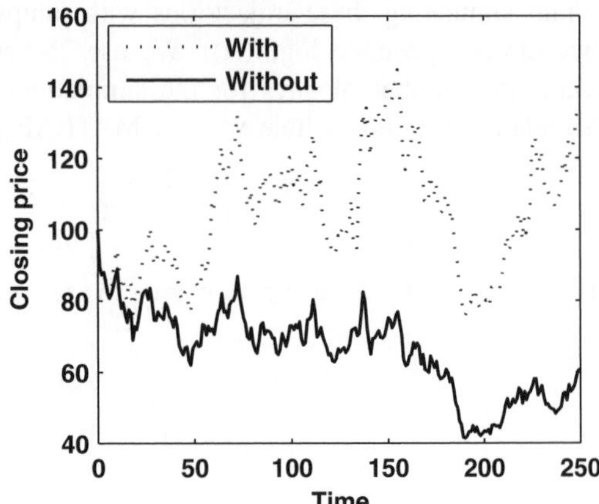

Figure 8.3 Simulations with and without jumps

Thus, we can draw a graph showing two trajectories resulting from the same variables Z, one with jumps and the other without jump. Figure 8.3 illustrates this process with and without jumps.

Notes and Complementary Readings

For a complementary review of literature on stochastic calculus, the reader can consult the following references: Bjork (1999), Choe (1983), Demange and Rochet (2005), Lamberton and Lapeyre (1992), Merton (1992), Neftci (2000), Kloeden and Platen (1992), Kloeden, Platen and Schurz (1997) and Oksendal (2003).

For a complementary reference on numerical schemes using MATLAB, one can read Borse (1997).

9

General Approach to the Valuation of Contingent Claims

This chapter presents the basis for valuing contingent claims such as financial options. We begin with a brief definition of simple options, the most widely known contingent claims.

Definition *An option is a financial security or a real asset that gives the right to its owner/holder to buy or to sell another asset (called the underlying asset) at a specific date (maturity date or exercise date) or for a given period, and at a predetermined price (called strike price or exercise price).*

Many types of options, explicit or implicit, exist. A call option allows its owner to buy the underlying asset at the strike price before or at maturity date and a put option allows its owner to sell the underlying asset at the exercise price before or at the maturity date. Figures 9.1 and 9.2 depict the payoffs of an option at maturity date as a function of the price of the underlying asset.

The option is called European if it can be exercised only at the maturity date. An option is said to be American if it can be exercised at any time before or at the maturity date.

In addition to these relatively simple options, there are more complex options which depend on the complexity of the choice of the underlying assets and the payoff structure. One popular complex option are the so-called Asian options whose payoffs depend on all the underlying asset price trajectories. Options whose payoffs depend on the trajectories of their underlying assets prices are called path-dependent options.

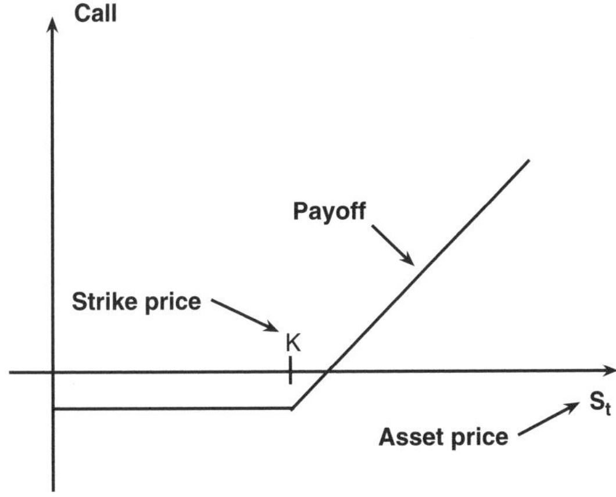

Figure 9.1 Call option

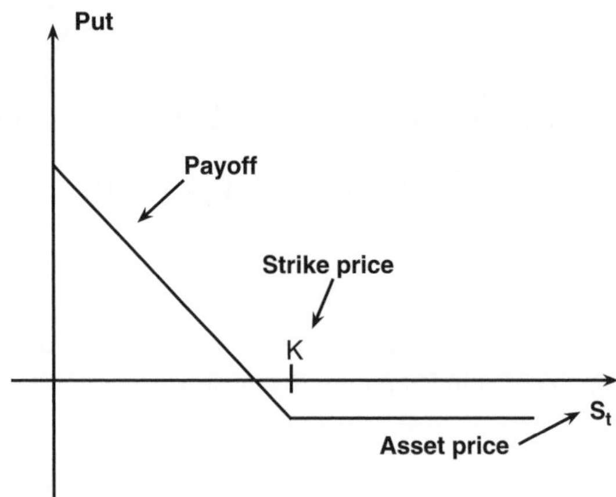

Figure 9.2 Put option

We begin with the simple binomial pricing model to present the intuition of a hedge portfolio and the "risk-neutralized" principle (term used in Ingersoll (1987)) or risk-neutral pricing. Then we continue with the Black-Scholes-Merton partial differential equation. We also introduce the sensitivity coefficients called Greeks. Afterwards, we present the probabilistic approach of contingent claims valuation or the equivalent martingale approach using stochastic differential equations. The latter approach will form the backbone of the next chapter, which is on the pricing of complex options with no known analytical closed form solutions.

9.1 THE COX, ROSS AND RUBINSTEIN (1979) BINOMIAL MODEL OF OPTION PRICING

To grasp the intuition in the famous Black and Scholes formula to value European options, we first present the binomial model for option valuation that was developed by Cox, Ross and Rubinstein in 1979. This model will allow the reader to understand the risk-neutralized or risk neutral concept.

Consider a government zero-coupon bond that yields a risk-free rate r; this represents a risk-free investment for its owner since it generates a sure return (same payments regardless of the state of the economy). We also assume the existence of a risky asset that follows a multiplicative binomial process in discrete time. This entails only two states to complete the economy (good or bad), with the asset price increasing if the good state occurs and decreasing if the bad state happens. The other assumptions of the model are:

9.1.1 Assumptions

1. In the good state, the asset price increases at a rate u with probability p_r and in the bad state, it decreases at a rate d with probability $1 - p_r$.
2. The asset price today is S.
3. The asset doesn't pay dividend.
4. The risk-free rate r is positive and constant with $d < r < u$.

Schematically, the asset price's process over one period can be represented as follows:

$$S \begin{array}{l} \nearrow \quad S_u = (1+u)S \quad \text{prob. } p_r \\ \\ \searrow \quad S_d = (1+d)S \quad \text{prob. } 1 - p_r. \end{array} \tag{9.1}$$

9.1.2 Price of a Call Option

We consider a call option on asset S (underlying asset) described above. The case of a put option can be developed in a similar way. The option's strike price is K and the option's price is Call. This means that at the end of the period the payoffs of the option are

$$C_u = \max(0, S_u - K) = \max(0, (1+u)S - K) \tag{9.2}$$

in the good state and

$$C_d = \max(0, S_d - K) = \max(0, (1+d)S - K) \tag{9.3}$$

in the bad state. Schematically, we can represent the evolution of the option's value the following way:

$$\text{Call} \begin{array}{l} \nearrow \quad C_u \equiv \max(0, (1+u)S - K) \quad \text{prob. } p_r \\ \\ \searrow \quad C_d \equiv \max(0, (1+d)S - K) \quad \text{prob. } 1 - p_r. \end{array} \tag{9.4}$$

We will show that it is possible to reproduce future payments of the option with the right combination of risk-free bonds and the underlying asset. In order to do that, we consider the following portfolio consisting of Δ asset and an amount B of debt (risk-free bond). The portfolio's process is the following:

$$\Delta S + B \begin{array}{l} \nearrow \quad \Delta(1+u)S + (1+r)B \quad \text{prob.} p_r \\ \\ \searrow \quad \Delta(1+d)S + (1+r)B \quad \text{prob.} 1 - p_r. \end{array} \tag{9.5}$$

In order to reproduce the call, we require that

$$\begin{aligned} \Delta(1+u)S + (1+r)B &= C_u, \\ \Delta(1+d)S + (1+r)B &= C_d. \end{aligned} \tag{9.6}$$

Which is equivalent to solving the following system of equations:

$$\begin{pmatrix} (1+u)S & 1+r \\ (1+d)S & 1+r \end{pmatrix} \begin{pmatrix} \Delta \\ B \end{pmatrix} = \begin{pmatrix} C_u \\ C_d \end{pmatrix}. \tag{9.7}$$

The solution is

$$\Delta = \frac{C_u - C_d}{(u-d)S} \quad \text{and} \quad B = \frac{(1+u)C_d - (1+d)C_u}{(u-d)(1+r)}. \tag{9.8}$$

To rule out arbitrage possibilities, the portfolio's value must be the same as the call's value (law of one price). No arbitrage means no free lunch, i.e., if two assets offer the same future payments, they must have the same price today, otherwise one can buy the cheaper one and sell the expensive one. In other words, we rule out the possibility of being able to have positive gains out of zero investment. Thus

$$\text{Call} = \Delta S + B = \frac{C_u - C_d}{(u-d)S} S + \frac{(1+u)C_d - (1+d)C_u}{(u-d)(1+r)}, \tag{9.9}$$

which implies

$$\text{Call} = \frac{\frac{r-d}{u-d} C_u + \frac{u-r}{u-d} C_d}{1+r}. \tag{9.10}$$

This expression can be written as

$$\text{Call} = \frac{p_n C_u + (1-p_n) C_d}{1+r}, \quad \text{where} \quad p_n \equiv \frac{r-d}{u-d}. \tag{9.11}$$

p_n and $1 - p_n$ are the risk-neutral probabilities. Note that these probabilities don't depend on the initial physical and real probabilities p_r and $1 - p_r$. In fact, these risk-neutral probabilities are obtained as a transformation of the real probability space into a new probability space, called the risk-neutral measure. We will come back later to this point.

Example 1.1 Consider the case where $1 + u = 1.2$, $1 + d = 0.80$, $1 + r = 1.05$, $S = \$\,45$ and $K = \$\,40$. With these values, we compute

$$C_u = \max(0, 1.2 \times 45 - 40) = 54 - 40 = \$\,14,$$

$$C_d = \max(0, 0.8 \times 45 - 40) = \$\,0,$$

and

$$p_n = \frac{1.05 - 0.80}{1.2 - 0.80} = 0.625, \qquad 1 - p_n = 1 - 0.625 = 0.375.$$

Which implies

$$\text{Call} = \frac{p_n C_u + (1-p_n) C_d}{1+r} = \frac{0.625 \times 14 + 0.375 \times 0}{1.05} = \$\,8.33.$$

Remark 1.2 Probability p_r doesn't appear in these formulas. Thus, even if investors have different subjective probabilities for the up and down movements, they do agree on the relation between Call, S and r. So the option's value doesn't depend on the investors' attitude toward risk.

Remark 1.3 The value of the option depends only on the underlying asset's value, and doesn't explicitly depend on other factors like the market portfolio, for example.

Remark 1.4 The quantity

$$p_n = \frac{r-d}{u-d} \tag{9.12}$$

can be considered as a probability. It is the value that p_r must have at equilibrium **as if** investors are risk neutral, no where, we make the assumption that agents are risk neutral. The risk-neutral pricing implies a probability measure transformation using the concept of market price of risk discussed in the next section. Indeed, the market price of risk allows us to transform the return in the real world into a risk-free return under the risk-neutral probability. In other words, the expected return in a risk-neutralized economy is r. To see this, let us perform the following computation

$$1+r = \frac{p_r(1+u)S + (1-p_r)(1+d)S}{S} = p_r(1+u) + (1-p_r)(1+d). \tag{9.13}$$

Which implies

$$p_r = \frac{r-d}{u-d} = p_n, \tag{9.14}$$

from which we deduce the risk-neutralized principle also called risk-neutral.

9.1.3 Extension To *N* Periods

For the case of a binomial tree with two periods, the computation of the call price is carried out as follows. We first specify the process of the underlying asset's price:

$$\begin{array}{ccccc} & & & & S_{uu} = (1+u)^2 S \\ & & & \nearrow & \\ & & S_u = (1+u)S & & \\ & \nearrow & & \searrow & \\ S & & & & S_{ud} = (1+u)(1+d)S \\ & \searrow & & \nearrow & \\ & & S_d = (1+d)S & & \\ & & & \searrow & \\ & & & & S_{dd} = (1+d)^2 S \end{array} \tag{9.15}$$

The call option price process will be

$$\begin{array}{ccccc} & & & & C_{uu} = \max(0, (1+u)^2 S - K) \\ & & & \nearrow & \\ & & C_u & & \\ & \nearrow & & \searrow & \\ \text{Call} & & & & C_{ud} = \max(0, (1+u)(1+d)S - K) \\ & \searrow & & \nearrow & \\ & & C_d & & \\ & & & \searrow & \\ & & & & C_{dd} = \max(0, (1+d)^2 S - K) \end{array} \tag{9.16}$$

From the preceding analysis we have

$$C_u = \frac{p_n C_{uu} + (1-p_n)C_{ud}}{1+r}, \tag{9.17}$$

$$C_d = \frac{p_n C_{ud} + (1-p_n)C_{dd}}{1+r}. \tag{9.18}$$

Substituting these two expressions in

$$\text{Call} = \frac{p_n C_u + (1 - p_n) C_d}{1 + r}, \tag{9.19}$$

we get

$$\begin{aligned}
\text{Call} &= \frac{(p_n)^2 C_{uu} + 2p_n(1 - p_n)C_{ud} + (1 - p_n)^2 C_{dd}}{(1 + r)^2} \\
&= \frac{\left\{\begin{array}{l} (p_n)^2 \max(0, (1 + u)^2 S - K) \\ \quad +2p_n(1 - p_n) \max(0, (1 + u)(1 + d)S - K) \\ \quad +(1 - p_n)^2 \max(0, (1 + d)^2 S - K) \end{array}\right\}}{(1 + r)^2} \\
&= \frac{\sum_{j=0}^{2} \binom{2}{j} (p_n)^j (1 - p_n)^{2-j} \max(0, (1 + u)^j (1 + d)^{2-j} S - K)}{(1 + r)^2}.
\end{aligned} \tag{9.20}$$

By induction, we can generalize to N periods

$$\text{Call} = \frac{\sum_{j=0}^{N} \binom{N}{j} (p_n)^j (1 - p_n)^{N-j} \max(0, (1 + u)^j (1 + d)^{N-j} S - K)}{(1 + r)^N}. \tag{9.21}$$

Moreover, expression max(.) can be eliminated by finding the smallest integer value a such that:

$$(1 + u)^a (1 + d)^{N-a} S \geq K, \tag{9.22}$$

that is

$$a \geq \ln(K/(S(1 + d)^N))/\ln((1 + u)/(1 + d)), \tag{9.23}$$

in this case

$$\text{Call} = \frac{\sum_{j=a}^{N} \binom{N}{j} (p_n)^j (1 - p_n)^{N-j} ((1 + u)^j (1 + d)^{N-j} S - K)}{(1 + r)^N}. \tag{9.24}$$

For a big value of N, the formula converges to the Black-Scholes formula that we study later in this chapter. Now, in order to code these formulas in MATLAB, we use MATLAB's functions *ceil*() and *nchoosek*().

```
function Rep=Binomial(N,u,d,r,S0,Strike,T)
%Function using binomial trees in order to compute
%a call option's value.
%N: Number of periods
%u: Increasing rate
%d: Decreasing rate
%r: Risk free interest rate
%S0: Stock's initial value
%Strike: Option's strike price
%T: Maturity

%Computation of the interest rate per period
 InterestRate=(1+r)^(T/N)-1;
```

```
%Probability of a up movement
p=(InterestRate-d)/(u-d);

a=ceil(log(Strike/(S0*(1+d)^N))/(log((1+u)/(1+d))));

%Computation of expected payoffs at maturity
ExpectedPayoffs=0;
for j=a:N
    inc=nchoosek(N,j)*p^(j)*(1-p)^(N-j)*((1+u)^(j)*...
                          (1+d)^(N-j)*S0-Strike);
    ExpectedPayoffs=ExpectedPayoffs+inc;
end

Rep=ExpectedPayoffs/(1+InterestRate)^N;

end
```

For a put option, Put, we find the largest integer a such that

$$(1+u)^a(1+d)^{N-a}S \leq K, \text{ that is, } a \leq \ln(K/(S(1+d)^N))/\ln((1+u)/(1+d)), \tag{9.25}$$

which gives:

$$\text{Put} = \frac{\sum_{j=0}^{a}\binom{N}{j}(p_n)^j(1-p_n)^{N-j}(K-(1+u)^j(1+d)^{N-j}S)}{(1+r)^N}. \tag{9.26}$$

Example 1.5 We consider a call option with strike price $K = \$\ 50$ on an asset whose price today is $S = \$\ 48$. The maturity of the option is $\tau = 55$ days which corresponds to $\frac{55}{365} = 0.151$ year. The risk-free interest rate is $r = 3\%$ per year. To value this option, we consider a two-period binomial tree, $N = 2$, with $1 + u = 1.25$ and $1 + d = 0.80$ per period.

We first compute the one period interest rate as follows:

$$1 + \widehat{r} \equiv (1.03)^{\tau/n} = (1.03)^{0.151/2} = 1.0022. \tag{9.27}$$

The option price process is therefore

$$\begin{array}{ccccl} & & & \nearrow & C_{uu} = \max(0,\ 1.25^2 \times 48 - 50) = 25 \\ & \nearrow & C_u & & \\ \text{Call} & & & \searrow\nearrow & C_{ud} = \max(0,\ 1.25 \times 0.8 \times 48 - 50) = 0 \\ & \searrow & C_d & & \\ & & & \searrow & C_{dd} = \max(0,\ 0.8^2 \times 48 - 50) = 0 \end{array} \tag{9.28}$$

and

$$p_n = \frac{\widehat{r} - d}{u - d} = \frac{1.0022 - 0.80}{1.25 - 0.80} = 0.4493. \tag{9.29}$$

Thus

$$C_u = (p_n C_{uu} + (1 - p_n)C_{ud})/(1 + \widehat{r}) = \$\ 11.21 \quad (9.30)$$
$$C_d = (p_n C_{ud} + (1 - p_n)C_{dd})/(1 + \widehat{r}) = \$\ 0 \quad (9.31)$$

and

$$\text{Call} = (p_n C_u + (1 - p_n)C_d)/(1 + \widehat{r}) = \$\ 5.02. \quad (9.32)$$

9.2 BLACK AND SCHOLES (1973) AND MERTON (1973) OPTION PRICING MODEL

In this section, we derive the fundamental equation to value contingent claims also known as the Black-Scholes-Merton partial differential equation which represents the state variables approach.

9.2.1 Fundamental Equation for the Valuation of Contingent Claims

Consider an asset S whose price follows a geometric Brownian motion process as follows:

$$dS(t) = \mu S(t)dt + \sigma S(t)dW(t). \quad (9.33)$$

In this stochastic differential equation, μ represents the expected instantaneous rate of return of the asset, σ the instantaneous volatility of its returns, and W is a standard Wiener process.

We consider a contingent claim on asset S, which means that the asset S is the underlying asset. The price of the contingent claim on underlying S at date t is denoted by $P(S(t), t)$. We also suppose that the maturity of this contract is T, thus the terminal value of the contingent claim is $P(S(T), T)$.

If the contingent claim is a European call option with maturity T and strike price K, then its terminal value is

$$P(S(T), T) = \max(0, S(T) - K), \quad (9.34)$$

however, if it is a European put option with same maturity and strike price, its value will be

$$P(S(T), T) = \max(0, K - S(T)). \quad (9.35)$$

From Ito's lemma, the contingent claim price's process, $P(S(t), t)$, can be expressed as:

$$\begin{aligned} dP(S(t), t) &= \frac{\partial P(S(t), t)}{\partial S} dS(t) + \frac{\partial P(S(t), t)}{\partial t} dt \\ &\quad + \frac{1}{2}\frac{\partial^2 P(S(t), t)}{\partial S^2}\sigma^2 S(t)^2 dt \\ &= \left[\frac{\partial P(S(t), t)}{\partial t} + \mu S(t)\frac{\partial P(S(t), t)}{\partial S} \right. \\ &\quad \left. + \frac{1}{2}\sigma^2 S(t)^2 \frac{\partial^2 P(S(t), t)}{\partial S^2}\right] dt \\ &\quad + \frac{\partial P(S(t), t)}{\partial S}\sigma S(t)dW(t). \end{aligned} \quad (9.36)$$

From this stochastic differential equation, the expected instantaneous rate of return and the instantaneous volatility of the returns of the contingent claim are:

$$\mu_P = \frac{E\left[\frac{dP}{dt}\right]}{P}$$
$$= \frac{\frac{\partial P(S(t),t)}{\partial t} + \mu S(t)\frac{\partial P(S(t),t)}{\partial S} + \frac{1}{2}\sigma^2 S(t)^2 \frac{\partial^2 P(S(t),t)}{\partial S^2}}{P}, \tag{9.37}$$

$$\sigma_P = \frac{\frac{\partial P(S(t),t)}{\partial S}\sigma S(t)}{P}. \tag{9.38}$$

Which allows us to rewrite the process of $P(S(t), t)$ as

$$dP(S(t),t) = \mu_P P(S(t),t)dt + \sigma_P P(S(t),t)dW(t). \tag{9.39}$$

We now form a portfolio with ω fraction of the contingent claim and $(1-\omega)$ in asset S. Let us call V the value of this portfolio. The return of this specific portfolio is:

$$\frac{dV(t)}{V(t)} = \omega\frac{dP(S(t),t)}{P(S(t),t)} + (1-\omega)\frac{dS(t)}{S(t)}$$
$$= [\omega\mu_P + (1-\omega)\mu]dt + [\omega\sigma_P + (1-\omega)\sigma]dW(t). \tag{9.40}$$

The return of the portfolio would be instantaneously risk-free if the diffusion term was zero, that is, if the coefficient of dW was equal to zero. This implies

$$\omega\sigma_P + (1-\omega)\sigma = 0 \tag{9.41}$$

or also

$$\omega = \frac{\sigma}{\sigma - \sigma_P}. \tag{9.42}$$

Since the portfolio is risk free, its expected return must be equal to the risk-free interest rate r, so

$$\frac{dV(t)}{V(t)} = r\,dt. \tag{9.43}$$

Comparing this expression to equation (9.40), and using the expression for ω given by equation (9.42) above, we get

$$r = \omega\mu_P + (1-\omega)\mu$$
$$= \frac{\sigma}{\sigma-\sigma_P}\mu_P - \frac{\sigma_P}{\sigma-\sigma_P}\mu$$
$$= \frac{\sigma\mu_P - \sigma_P\mu}{\sigma - \sigma_P} \tag{9.44}$$

or also

$$r(\sigma - \sigma_P) = \sigma\mu_P - \sigma_P\mu \quad \Rightarrow \quad \sigma(\mu_P - r) = \sigma_P(\mu - r). \tag{9.45}$$

Thus

$$\frac{\mu - r}{\sigma} = \frac{\mu_P - r}{\sigma_P}. \tag{9.46}$$

This is the market price of risk. It means that the risk premiums divided by their risk levels, known as Sharpe ratios, for the underlying asset and the contingent claim are equal. Note that

$$\mu - \left(\frac{\mu - r}{\sigma}\right)\sigma = r, \tag{9.47}$$

which means that the market price of risk allows us to adjust the real return to obtain the risk-free return in the risk-neutral world.

Substituting equations (9.37) and (9.38) into equation (9.46), we get

$$\frac{\frac{1}{2}\sigma^2 S^2 \frac{\partial^2 P}{\partial S^2} + \mu S \frac{\partial P}{\partial S} + \frac{\partial P}{\partial t} - rP}{\frac{\partial P}{\partial S} S\sigma} = \frac{\mu - r}{\sigma}. \tag{9.48}$$

Rewriting the equation and simplifying gives

$$\frac{1}{2}\sigma^2 S^2 \frac{\partial^2 P}{\partial S^2} + rS\frac{\partial P}{\partial S} + \frac{\partial P}{\partial t} - rP = 0. \tag{9.49}$$

This last equation (9.49) is the celebrated Black-Scholes-Merton partial differential equation and represents the fundamental equation for the valuation of contingent claims with terminal condition $P(S(T), T)$.

This is an example of a heat equation well known in physical sciences. Under specific boundary conditions, it is possible to solve it yielding a solution in exact analytical form. This is the case, for example, for the European call and put options.

9.2.2 Exact Analytical Value of European Call and Put Options

For a call option on the underlying asset S with strike price K and maturity T, the solution to equation (9.49) with boundary condition

$$P(S(T), T) = \max(0, S(T) - K), \tag{9.50}$$

gives the following formula for the price of the call option

$$\text{Call} = S(0)N(d_1) - Ke^{-rT}N(d_2), \tag{9.51}$$

with

$$d_1 = \frac{\ln(S(0)/K) + rT}{\sigma\sqrt{T}} + \frac{1}{2}\sigma\sqrt{T}, \qquad d_2 = d_1 - \sigma\sqrt{T}, \tag{9.52}$$

where $N(.)$ is the normal cumulative distribution function, σ the instantaneous volatility of the underlying asset returns and r is the risk-free interest rate.

Although MATLAB's Financial Toolbox contains valuation functions for options and sensitivity coefficients in the Black-Scholes world, for pedagogical purposes, the MATLAB program used to compute the price of an European call option using the Black-Scholes formula is:

```
function rep=CallBS(S0,K,T)
%Function computing the price of a call option using
%Black-Scholes analytical formula
%S0: Initial price of the underlying asset
%K: Strike price of the option
%T: Maturity of the option
```

```
%Parameters initial values
 sigma=0.1;
 r=0.06;
 div=0.00; %Dividend rate

%Computation of di's
d1=(log(S0/K)+(r-div)*T)/(sigma*sqrt(T))+sigma*sqrt(T)/2;
d2=d1-sigma*sqrt(T);

rep=S0*exp(-div*T)*normcdf(d1)-K*exp(-r*T)*normcdf(d2);

end
```

For a put option on the underlying asset S with strike price K and maturity T, the boundary condition is

$$P(S(T), T) = \max(0, K - S(T)). \tag{9.53}$$

The solution to equation (9.49) gives rise to the analytical formula for the put option price

$$\text{Put} = Ke^{-rT}N(-d_2) - S(0)N(-d_1), \tag{9.54}$$

with d_1 and d_2 defined above.

The MATLAB program to compute the price of a European put option using the Black and Scholes formula is:

```
function rep=PutBS(S0,K,T)
%Function computing the price of a put option using
%Black-Scholes analytical formula
%S0: Underlying asset initial price
%K: Option's strike price
%T: Option's maturity

%Parameters initial values
 sigma=0.2;
 r=0.05;
 div=0.00; %Dividend rate

%Computation of di's
d1=(log(S0/K)+(r-div)*T)/(sigma*sqrt(T))+sigma*sqrt(T)/2;
d2=d1-sigma*sqrt(T);

rep=K*exp(-r*T)*normcdf(-d2)-S0*exp(-div*T)*normcdf(-d1);

end
```

Example 2.1 Let a European call on the underlying asset S have a strike price $K = \$\ 50$ and a maturity of 4 months. Thus, in years, $T = 4/12$ year. Today's price of the underlying asset is $S(0) = \$\ 60$ and its volatility is $\sigma = 0.375$. The risk-free interest rate is $r = 3\%$ per year.

With these data, we compute $d_1 = 0.9965$ and $d_2 = 0.9965 - 0.375\sqrt{4/12} = 0.7800$. This implies $N(d_1) = 0.8405$ and $N(d_2) = 0.7823$, and finally the call and put options' prices are given by the Black and Scholes formula:

$$\begin{aligned}\text{Call} &= 60 \times 0.8405 - 50 \times e^{-0.03\times(4/12)} \times 0.7823 \\ &= \$\ 11.7038, \qquad (9.55)\\ \text{Put} &= 50 \times e^{-0.03\times 4/12} \times (1 - 0.7823) - 60 \times (1 - 0.8405) \\ &= \$\ 1.2067. \qquad (9.56)\end{aligned}$$

Remark 2.2 It is important to notice that the underlying asset's expected rate of return μ doesn't affect the value of the options in the Black and Scholes formula.

Property 2.3 ***European options put-call parity***: *There exists a relation between the call and put option prices called the put-call parity.*

One can show it by constructing the following portfolio: buy one share of the stock and one European put option and sell one European call option. The two options have the same maturity T and the same underlying stock and strike price K.

At maturity, we have the following two cases: either $S < K$ or $S \geq K$. When $S < K$, the long stock gives the ex-dividend price (price just after dividends are announced) of the stock S plus the dividend received over the period, the long put gives $K - S$ and the short call gives 0, which sums up to K plus the dividend.

When $S \geq K$, the long stock gives S plus the dividend received over the period, the long put gives 0 and the short call gives $-(S - K)$, which sums up to K plus the dividend. In either case, the total payoff at date T is K plus the dividend. The law of one price requires the portfolio value today to be equal to the present value of K and the dividend, which yields the put-call parity relationship. This relation is defined as follows:

$$\text{Put} - \text{Call} + S = \text{Div} + Ke^{-rT}, \qquad (9.57)$$

where Div *is the discounted amount of dividend paid by the underlying asset.*

9.2.3 Hedging Ratios and the Sensitivity Coefficients

In hedging and pricing derivatives or contingent claims, the concept of Greeks or derivatives' risk factors is fundamental. Below we summarize some of these risk factors, also called Greeks. Note that these Greeks are computed using the Black and Scholes formula by applying the mathematical rules of partial differentiation of integrals or Leibnitz's rule.

DELTA

The hedge ratio DELTA measures the variation in the option's price with respect to a movement in the underlying asset's price. It can be computed as:

$$\Delta = \frac{\partial \text{Call}}{\partial S} = N(d_1) > 0, \tag{9.58}$$

where

$$d_1 = \frac{\ln(S/K) + rT}{\sigma\sqrt{T}} + \frac{1}{2}\sigma\sqrt{T}. \tag{9.59}$$

A portfolio containing a short proportion $-1/\Delta$ in the call option and a long position in one unit of the underlying asset gives a hedged portfolio, that is, a risk-free portfolio.

Similarly, the put option's hedge ratio DELTA is

$$\Delta = \frac{\partial \text{Put}}{\partial S} = N(d_1) - 1. \tag{9.60}$$

Example 2.4 We consider a call option and a put option on a stock S. These two options have the same strike price and the same maturity. Let a portfolio comprise of A stocks, a number Δ_{Call} of call options and a number Δ_{Put} of put options, that is

$$V = A \times S + \Delta_{\text{Call}} \times \text{Call} + \Delta_{\text{Put}} \times \text{Put}, \tag{9.61}$$

where S, Call and Put are the prices of the stock, the call option and the put option. The position Δ of portfolio V is

$$\begin{aligned}\Delta &= \frac{\partial V}{\partial S} \\ &= A + \Delta_{\text{Call}} \times \frac{\partial \text{Call}}{\partial S} + \Delta_{\text{Put}} \times \frac{\partial \text{Put}}{\partial S} \\ &= A + \Delta_{\text{Call}} \times N(d_1) + \Delta_{\text{Put}} \times (N(d_1) - 1).\end{aligned} \tag{9.62}$$

Numerically, let 100 stocks ($A = 100$) and $N(d_1) = 0.7437$, then how many call options are needed in the portfolio in order to have $\Delta = 0$ if we assume that there is no put option in the portfolio ($\Delta_{\text{Put}} = 0$)? In this case,

$$\Delta = 0 = 100 + \Delta_{\text{Call}} N(d_1) \quad \Rightarrow \quad 100 = -\Delta_{\text{Call}} N(d_1). \tag{9.63}$$

Which implies

$$\Delta_{\text{Call}} = \frac{-100}{0.7437} = -134.46 \tag{9.64}$$

call options (short positions or short sales of call options).

VEGA

VEGA measures the sensitivity of the option's price to a movement in the volatility of the underlying asset's returns. It is equal to

$$\mathcal{V} = \frac{\partial \text{Call}}{\partial \sigma} = \frac{\partial \text{Put}}{\partial \sigma} = S\sqrt{T}N'(d_1) > 0, \tag{9.65}$$

where

$$d_1 = \frac{\ln(S/K) + rT}{\sigma\sqrt{T}} + \frac{1}{2}\sigma\sqrt{T} \tag{9.66}$$

and $N'(.)$ is the first derivative of $N(.)$.

GAMMA

GAMMA measures the sensitivity of the option's DELTA to a variation in the asset price. It is the second derivative of the option's price with respect to the price of the underlying asset and is computed as

$$\Gamma = \frac{\partial^2 \text{Call}}{\partial S^2} = \frac{\partial^2 \text{Put}}{\partial S^2} = \frac{N'(d_1)}{S\sigma\sqrt{T}} > 0, \tag{9.67}$$

where

$$d_1 = \frac{\ln(S/K) + rT}{\sigma\sqrt{T}} + \frac{1}{2}\sigma\sqrt{T} \tag{9.68}$$

and $N'(.)$ is still the first derivative of $N(.)$.

With MATLAB, these coefficients are computed as follows:

```
function Greeks
%Function computing the sensitivity coefficients for
%a call option

%Parameters' initial values
r=0.03;
Strike=50;
S0=60;
sigma=0.375;
T=4/12;

%Computation of di's
d1=(log(S0/Strike)+(r+sigma^2/2)*T)/(sigma*sqrt(T));
d2=d1-sigma*sqrt(T);

%Computation of the coefficients
Delta=normcdf(d1)
Vega=S0*sqrt(T)*normpdf(d1)
Gamma=normpdf(d1)/(S0*sigma*sqrt(T))

end
```

> **Example 2.5** If we take the same parameters as in Example 2.1, then, for the call option, we find:
>
> $$d_1 = 0.9965$$
> $$\Delta = 0.8405$$
> $$\mathcal{V} = 8.4110$$
> $$\Gamma = 0.0187.$$

The other sensitivity coefficients

In addition to the three coefficients above, we can compute the sensitivity of the option's price to the strike price (KAPPA κ):

$$\kappa = \frac{\partial \text{Call}}{\partial K} = -e^{-rT} N(d_2) < 0, \tag{9.69}$$

the sensitivity of the option's price to the passage of time (THETA θ)

$$\theta = \frac{\partial \text{Call}}{\partial T} = \frac{S\sigma}{2\sqrt{T}} N'(d_1) + K e^{-rT} N(d_2) > 0, \tag{9.70}$$

and the sensitivity to the risk-free interest rate (RHO ρ)

$$\rho = \frac{\partial \text{Call}}{\partial r} = T K e^{-rT} N(d_2) > 0, \tag{9.71}$$

where

$$d_1 = \frac{\ln(S/K) + rT}{\sigma\sqrt{T}} + \frac{1}{2}\sigma\sqrt{T}, \qquad d_2 = d_1 - \sigma\sqrt{T}. \tag{9.72}$$

With MATLAB, these coefficients are computed as follows:

```
function Greeks2
%Function computing the coefficients Kappa, Theta, Rho
%for a call option

%Parameters' initial values
r=0.03;
Strike=50;
S0=60;
sigma=0.375;
T=4/12;

%Computation of di's
d1=(log(S0/Strike)+(r+sigma^2/2)*T)/(sigma*sqrt(T));
d2=d1-sigma*sqrt(T);

%Computation of the sensitivity coefficients
Kappa=-exp(-r*T)*normcdf(d2)
Theta=S0*sigma/(2*sqrt(T))*normpdf(d1)+Strike*exp(-r*T)*normcdf(d2)
Rho=T*Strike*exp(-r*T)*normcdf(d2)

end
```

Example 2.6 For the same parameters as those used in Example 2.1, for the call option, we find:

$$\begin{aligned}d_1 &= 0.9965\\ d_2 &= 0.7800\\ \frac{\partial \text{Call}}{\partial K} &= -0.7745\\ \frac{\partial \text{Call}}{\partial T} &= 43.4578\\ \frac{\partial \text{Call}}{\partial r} &= 12.9089.\end{aligned}$$

9.3 DERIVATION OF THE BLACK-SCHOLES FORMULA USING THE RISK-NEUTRAL VALUATION PRINCIPLE

This section characterizes the probabilistic approach to the valuation of contingent claims which seeks to solve systems of stochastic differential equations. This approach is also known as risk-neutralized or equivalent martingale.

9.3.1 The Girsanov Theorem and the Risk-Neutral Probability

Theorem 3.1 *(Girsanov) Let $W(t)$ be a Brownian motion vector having dimension d in the probability space*

$$(\Omega, \mathbf{F}, \mathcal{P}), \tag{9.73}$$

where Ω is the sample space of results, $\mathbf{F}$ is the set of all possible events and $\mathcal{P}$ is the set of probability measures.

Let $q(t) = (q_1(t), q_2(t), \cdots, q_d(t))$ be a vector of adapted processes (we have discussed this concept in Chapter 8) satisfying

$$\int_0^T (q_i(t))^2 dt < \infty \quad \forall i \qquad a.s. \tag{9.74}$$

We define

$$M_q(t) = \exp\left(\sum_{i=1}^{d} \int_0^t q_i(s) dW_i(s) - \frac{1}{2}\int_0^t \|q(s)\|^2 ds\right). \tag{9.75}$$

If $M_q(t)$ is a martingale, then the process

$$d\widetilde{W}(t) = dW(t) - q(t)dt \tag{9.76}$$

is a Brownian motion of dimension d defined on the probability space $(\Omega, \mathbf{F}, \mathcal{Q})$ where $\mathcal{Q}$ is the equivalent probability given by $d\mathcal{Q} = M_q d\mathcal{P}$.

By virtue of this theorem, if S is a diffusion process defined by

$$dS(t) = \mu(S(t), t)dt + \sigma(S(t), t)dW(t), \tag{9.77}$$

where μ and σ satisfy Lipschitz's continuity condition, then

$$dS(t) = (\mu(S(t), t) + \sigma(S(t), t)q(t))dt + \sigma(S(t), t)d\widetilde{W}(t). \tag{9.78}$$

More specifically, assuming that S follows a geometric Brownian motion

$$dS(t) = \mu S(t)dt + \sigma S(t)dW(t), \tag{9.79}$$

if we make the assumption that the risk-free interest rate r is constant, we can choose

$$q = \frac{r - \mu}{\sigma}. \tag{9.80}$$

In this case, we can easily show that the process

$$M_q(t) = \exp\left(\int_0^t q dW(t) - \frac{1}{2}\int_0^t q^2 dt\right) \tag{9.81}$$

is a martingale. From Girsanov's Theorem 3.1 above, the process

$$\begin{aligned} d\widetilde{W}_t &= dW_t - qdt \\ &= dW_t - \frac{r-\mu}{\sigma}dt \end{aligned} \tag{9.82}$$

is a Wiener process under the probability measure $\mathcal{Q}$. The process S is thus

$$\begin{aligned} dS(t) &= \left(\mu S(t) + \sigma S(t)\frac{r-\mu}{\sigma}\right)dt + \sigma S(t)d\widetilde{W}(t) \\ &= rS(t)dt + \sigma S(t)d\widetilde{W}(t). \end{aligned} \tag{9.83}$$

The probability $\mathcal{Q}$ is called the risk-neutral probability. Under this measure, the asset has an expected rate of return equivalent to the risk-free rate. More generally, in a risk-neutralized world, the expected return of any asset is the risk-free rate r.

9.3.2 Derivation of the Black and Scholes Formula Under The Risk Neutralized or Equivalent Martingale Principle

Under the risk-neutral probability, the asset's price can be rewritten under the form

$$S(T) = S(0)e^{(r-\frac{\sigma^2}{2})T + \sigma\widetilde{W}(T)}. \tag{9.84}$$

We consider a European call option on the underlying asset S with strike price K and maturity T. Under the risk neutralized principle, the option's price is

$$\text{Call} = E^{\mathcal{Q}}[e^{-rT}\max(0, S(T) - K)], \tag{9.85}$$

where $E^{\mathcal{Q}}[.]$ is the expectation operator under the risk-neutral probability $\mathcal{Q}$.

To obtain the analytical formula for the option price, we compute this expectation which is in fact the computation of an integral.

$$\begin{aligned} \text{Call} &= E^{\mathcal{Q}}[e^{-rT}\max(0, S(T) - K)] \\ &= e^{-rT}\int_K^{\infty}(S(T) - K)f_{S(T)}(s)ds, \end{aligned} \tag{9.86}$$

where $f_{S(T)}(.)$ is the probability density function of $S(T)$ under the risk-neutral probability.

For the $S(T)$ process, since $\widetilde{W}_T$ is a Wiener process, we can rewrite it as $\sqrt{T}X$ where X follows a Gaussian law with zero mean and unit variance, $N(0, 1)$.

With this transformation, the call price is:

$$\text{Call} = e^{-rT} \int_{d_2^*}^{\infty} (S(0)e^{(r-\frac{\sigma^2}{2})T+\sigma\sqrt{T}x} - K) f_X(x)dx, \tag{9.87}$$

where d_2^* is obtained by:

$$K \leq S(T) < \infty \Longrightarrow K \leq S(0)e^{(r-\frac{\sigma^2}{2})T+\sigma\sqrt{T}X} < \infty, \tag{9.88}$$

which implies

$$d_2^* = \frac{\ln(K/S(0)) - rT + \frac{\sigma^2 T}{2}}{\sigma\sqrt{T}} \leq X < \infty. \tag{9.89}$$

Now, set $Y = -X$, this way,

$$\begin{aligned} -\infty &\leq Y \\ &< \frac{\ln(S(0)/K) + rT - \frac{\sigma^2 T}{2}}{\sigma\sqrt{T}} \\ &= \frac{\ln(S(0)/K) + rT}{\sigma\sqrt{T}} - \frac{\sigma\sqrt{T}}{2} \\ &\equiv d_2. \end{aligned} \tag{9.90}$$

And since Y and X have the same distribution, then

$$\begin{aligned} \text{Call} &= e^{-rT} S(0)e^{(r-\frac{\sigma^2}{2})T} \int_{-\infty}^{d_2} e^{-\sigma\sqrt{T}y} f_Y(y)dy - e^{-rT} K \int_{-\infty}^{d_2} f_Y(y)dy \\ &= e^{-rT} S(0)e^{(r-\frac{\sigma^2}{2})T} \int_{-\infty}^{d_2} e^{-\sigma\sqrt{T}y} f_Y(y)dy - e^{-rT} K N(d_2). \end{aligned} \tag{9.91}$$

To arrive at the final formula, we must compute the following integral:

$$\begin{aligned} I &\equiv \int_{-\infty}^{d_2} e^{-\sigma\sqrt{T}y} f_Y(y)dy \\ &= \frac{1}{\sqrt{2\pi}} \int_{-\infty}^{d_2} e^{-\sigma\sqrt{T}y} e^{-y^2/2} dy. \end{aligned} \tag{9.92}$$

We can write this integral as:

$$I = \frac{1}{\sqrt{2\pi}} \int_{-\infty}^{d_2} e^{-(y+\sigma\sqrt{T})^2/2+\sigma^2 T/2} dy. \tag{9.93}$$

Making the following change of variable $z = y + \sigma\sqrt{T}$, then

$$-\infty < z - \sigma\sqrt{T} \leq d_2 \Longrightarrow -\infty < z \leq d_2 + \sigma\sqrt{T} = d_1 \tag{9.94}$$

which implies

$$\begin{aligned} I &= \frac{1}{\sqrt{2\pi}} \int_{-\infty}^{d_1} e^{-z^2/2} dz e^{\sigma^2 T/2} \\ &= e^{\sigma^2 T/2} N(d_1). \end{aligned} \tag{9.95}$$

Substituting this expression in the equation for the option's price, we obtain the desired formula

$$\text{Call} = S(0)N(d_1) - e^{-rT} K N(d_2), \tag{9.96}$$

where

$$d_1 = \frac{\ln(S(0)/K) + rT}{\sigma\sqrt{T}} + \frac{1}{2}\sigma\sqrt{T}, \qquad d_2 = d_1 - \sigma\sqrt{T}. \tag{9.97}$$

This technique of computing the value of a contingent claim using a change of variable is very useful when working with a single underlying derivative depending only on one state variable. For contingent claims depending on two state variables, we must work with the bivariate normal density. However, most common problems in finance are multivariate and necessitate the use of the probabilistic approach or equivalent martingale approach described above. The use of Monte Carlo simulation techniques is probably the best tool to implement the probabilistic or equivalent martingale approaches. We extensively use the Monte Carlo method in the following chapters to value complex contingent claims.

Notes and Complementary Readings

For a complementary review of literature about the valuation of contingent claims, see Bajeux-Besnainou and Portait (1992), Bjork (1999), Bryis, Bellalah, Mai and de Varenne (1998), Clewlow and Strickland (1998), Dana and Jeanblanc-Picqué (2003), Duffie (2001), Haug (1998), Hull (2005), Luenberger (1998), McDonald (2003), Merton (1992), Musiela and Rutkowski (1997), Neftci (2000), Quittard-Pinon (2003), Taleb (1997), Wilmott (1998).

It is important to note that there exists a vast literature on the valuation of contingent claims using the numerical approach of solving partial differential equations. For this methodology, the reader could consult Seydel (2002), Tavella (2002) and Wilmott (1998).

The reader could also consult the following classic articles: Black and Scholes (1973), Cox and Ross (1976), Cox, Ross and Rubinstein (1979), Géman, El Karoui and Rochet (1995), Harrison and Kreps (1979), Harrison and Pliska (1981), Merton (1973).

For a pedagogic introduction to the risk-neutral pricing or equivalent martingale concept, one can read Sundaram (1997), Baxter and Rennie (1996), and Chapter 25 of Hull (2005).

For extensions of the basic Black-Scholes-Merton (1973) model of valuing options to multivariate forms, one can read: Margrabe (1978), Stultz (1982) for complex options, Fouque, Papanicolaou and Sircar (2000), Heston (1993), Hofman, Platen and Schweizer (1992), Hull and White (1987), Romano and Touzi (1997) for options with stochastic volatility, Bensaid, Lesne, Pagès and Scheinkman (1992), Hoggard, Whalley and Wilmott (1994), Leland (1985) for the valuation of options with transaction costs.

10 Pricing Options using Monte Carlo Simulations

Since the seminal works of Black-Scholes-Merton (1973) on European options valuation, a great number of derivative products have been engineered. However, in most cases it is difficult to find closed form formulas for the pricing of these commonly encountered complex options. Monte Carlo simulation techniques have proved to be a flexible and handy alternative to price these options.

In this chapter, we proceed as follows. First, we start by valuing simple options called plain vanilla options, and then we introduce stochastic interest rates and/or stochastic volatilities.

Second, we estimate the value of American options using the Least-Square Linear Regression Method of Longstaff and Schwartz (2001) and the Dynamic Programming Technique with Stratified States Aggregation of Barraquand and Martineau (1995).

Third, we value Asian and barrier options using the approaches developed by Kemna and Vorst (1990) and El Babsiri and Noel (1998). Finally, to estimate the sensitivity coefficients of options or the Greeks, we discuss the pathwise derivatives and the likelihood ratio techniques proposed by Broadie and Glasserman (1996) and present the retrieval of volatility method of Cvitanic, Goukassian and Zapatero (2002).

10.1 PLAIN VANILLA OPTIONS: EUROPEAN PUT AND CALL

10.1.1 Simple Simulations

We assume that the asset $S(t)$ follows the stochastic differential equation (Geometric Brownian Motion) we have studied in Chapter 8 under the risk-neutral probability:

$$dS(t) = rS(t)dt + \sigma S(t)d\widetilde{W}(t), \tag{10.1}$$

where $\widetilde{W}$ is the Brownian motion under the risk-neutral probability. We will simulate 10 batches of 5000 paths each (*NbTraj* = 5000) to price a European put as well as a call. The option value corresponds to the average value of its discounted future payoffs under the risk-neutral probability. We will therefore reproduce the dynamics of future prices of the underlying asset using computers, and calculate next the future payoffs to be obtained by the option holder. The sample mean of these discounted payoffs is the value of the option contract. We use constant interest rate $r = 0.05$ and volatility $\sigma = 0.2$. In addition, we assume the underlying asset pays no dividend. Let's show how to simulate the asset process $S(t)$ in MATLAB and determine the value of European call and put options. To simulate a batch, we proceed as follows:

```
function OptionMC(S0,K,T)
%Function to calculate the prices of European Put and Call options
%using Monte Carlo simulations.
```

```
%S0: Initial price of the asset
%K: Exercise price of the options
%T: Time to maturity of the options

%Initial parameters
sigma=0.2;
r=0.05;
NbTraj=5000;
NbPas=100;
DeltaT=T/NbPas;

%Vector of asset prices
SPresent=S0*ones(NbTraj,1);
SNext=zeros(NbTraj,1);

%Loop to simulate the paths
for i=1:NbPas
  dW=sqrt(DeltaT)*randn(NbTraj,1);
  SNext=SPresent+(r)*SPresent*DeltaT+sigma*SPresent.*dW;
  SPresent=SNext;
end

%Calculation of the options prices
Call = exp(-r*T)*mean(max(0,SPresent-K));
Put = exp(-r*T)*mean(max(0,K-SPresent));

end
```

We executed the program for the 10 batches using 5000 paths ($NbTraj = 5000$) and 100 time steps ($NbPas = 100$). Tables 10.1 and 10.2 present the results.

In the tables, BS denotes the prices obtained from the Black-Scholes formula discussed in Chapter 9. The errors shown in the tables are the standard deviation of the vector of the 10 batches. These values are large. We could improve the simulations' accuracy by performing more simulations. However, as we discussed earlier, other variance reduction techniques can be used. The results obtained using antithetic and control variables follow.

Table 10.1 Price of a call option using simple simulations

Call option					
Parameters			BS	Monte Carlo	
$S(0)$ \$	K \$	T years	Price \$	Price \$	Error \$
90	100	1	5.09	5.04	0.15
90	100	2	9.91	9.95	0.26
100	100	1	10.45	10.41	0.15
100	100	2	16.13	16.10	0.38
110	100	1	17.66	17.66	0.23
110	100	2	23.59	23.45	0.32

Table 10.2 Price of a put option using simple simulations

Put option					
Parameters			BS	Monte Carlo	
$S(0)$ \$	K \$	T years	Price \$	Price \$	Error \$
90	100	1	10.21	10.28	0.11
90	100	2	10.39	10.42	0.12
100	100	1	5.57	5.60	0.12
100	100	2	6.61	6.58	0.17
110	100	1	2.79	2.74	0.08
110	100	2	4.07	4.10	0.11

10.1.2 Simulations with Antithetic Variables

We will simulate again the process for $S(t)$ with 10000 paths (5000 + 5000 antithetic) for each batch. For each generated $\widetilde{W}(t)$, we use $-\widetilde{W}(t)$ to obtain the second path. We slightly modified the previous program to incorporate this variance reduction technique.

```
function OptionMCAnti(S0,K,T)
%Function to calculate the prices of European Put and Call options
%using Monte Carlo simulations with antithetic variables.
%S0: Initial price of the asset
%K: Exercise price of the options
%T: Time to maturity of the options

%Initial parameters
sigma=0.2;
r=0.05;
NbTraj=5000;
NbPas=100;
DeltaT=T/NbPas;

%Price vector of the asset
SPresent=S0*ones(2*NbTraj,1);
SNext=zeros(2*NbTraj,1);

%Loop to simulate the paths
for i=1:NbPas
   temp=sqrt(DeltaT)*randn(NbTraj,1);
   dW=[temp;-temp];
   SNext=SPresent+(r)*SPresent*DeltaT+sigma*SPresent.*dW;
   SPresent=SNext;
end

%Calculation of the options prices
Call = exp(-r*T)*mean(max(0,SPresent-K));
Put = exp(-r*T)*mean(max(0,K-SPresent));

end
```

Table 10.3 Price of a European call option using antithetic variables in the simulations (MC Anti.)

Call option					
Parameters			BS	MC Anti.	
$S(0)$ $	K $	T years	Price $	Price $	Error $
90	100	1	5.09	5.13	0.10
90	100	2	9.91	9.86	0.17
100	100	1	10.45	10.46	0.10
100	100	2	16.13	16.10	0.20
110	100	1	17.66	17.66	0.11
110	100	2	23.59	23.60	0.17

Table 10.4 Price of a European put option using antithetic variables in the simulations (MC Anti.)

Put option					
Parameters			BS	MC Anti.	
$S(0)$ $	K $	T years	Price $	Price $	Error $
90	100	1	10.21	10.21	0.07
90	100	2	10.39	10.40	0.09
100	100	1	5.57	5.57	0.06
100	100	2	6.61	6.59	0.06
110	100	1	2.79	2.80	0.04
110	100	2	4.07	4.10	0.08

Tables 10.3 and 10.4 present the simulation results obtained using this program. The error is again measured by the standard deviation of the 10 batches.

We observe from the tables that the precision of the results has been improved considerably. The prices obtained from the Monte Carlo simulations are more precise and the errors are smaller.

10.1.3 Simulations with Control Variates

Let's now use control variates to increase the precision of the results. Using the above notation, we know that

$$Y = S(T) \tag{10.2}$$

$$E[Y] = S(0)e^{rT}. \tag{10.3}$$

We can then use the difference $Y - E[Y]$ to improve our results. The program is a modified version of the Monte Carlo simulation program given previously.

```
function OptionMCControl(S0,K,T)
%Function to calculate the prices of European Put and Call options
%using Monte Carlo simulations with control variates.
%S0: Initial price of the underlying asset
%K: Exercise price of the options
%T: Time to maturity of the options

%Initial parameters
sigma=0.2;
r=0.05;
NbTraj=5000;
NbPas=100;
DeltaT=T/NbPas;

%Price vector of the asset
SPresent=S0*ones(NbTraj,1);
SNext=zeros(NbTraj,1);

%Loop to simulate the paths
for i=1:NbPas
   dW=sqrt(DeltaT)*randn(NbTraj,1);
   SNext=SPresent+(r)*SPresent*DeltaT+sigma*SPresent.*dW;
   SPresent=SNext;
end

%Using the control variates technique for the call option
X1=exp(-r*T)*max(0,SPresent-K);
EX1=mean(X1);
Y=SPresent;
EY=S0*exp(r*T);

cov1=((X1-EX1)'*(Y-EY))/(NbTraj-1);
var=((Y-EY)'*(Y-EY))/(NbTraj-1);
alpha1=-cov1/var;

%Calculation of the price of the call option
PriceControl1=X1+alpha1*(Y-EY);
repCall=sum(PriceControl1)/(NbTraj);

%Using the control variates technique for the put option
X2=exp(-r*T)*max(0,K-SPresent);
EX2=mean(X2);
Y=SPresent;
EY=S0*exp(r*T);

cov2=((X2-EX2)'*(Y-EY))/(NbTraj-1);
alpha2=-cov2/var;
```

```
%Calculation of the price of the put option
PriceControl2=X2+alpha2*(Y-EY);
repPut=sum(PriceControl2)/(NbTraj);

end
```

We can now run our simulations for European call and put options using the control variates technique. Tables 10.5 and 10.6 present the simulations results.

We observe that the prices obtained with Monte Carlo simulations are more precise and that the errors have been reduced. The choice of the control variables could be different. For example, we could use the sensitivity coefficients of options (the Greeks) as in Clewlow and Strickland (1997a). If one wishes to use the option sensitivity coefficient Δ, the control variable will look like

$$Y = \sum_{i=0}^{NbPas-1} \frac{\partial P(T - t_i, S(t_i))}{\partial S} \Delta S(t_i), \tag{10.4}$$

Table 10.5 Price of a European call option using control variates in the simulations

Call option					
Parameters			BS	MC (Control)	
$S(0)$ $	K $	T years	Price $	Price $	Error $
90	100	1	5.09	5.06	0.06
90	100	2	9.91	9.95	0.10
100	100	1	10.45	10.42	0.08
100	100	2	16.13	16.15	0.10
110	100	1	17.66	17.64	0.07
110	100	2	23.59	23.58	0.10

Table 10.6 Price of a European put option using control variates in the simulations

Put option					
Parameters			BS	MC (Control)	
$S(0)$ $	K $	T years	Price $	Price $	Error $
90	100	1	10.21	10.20	0.06
90	100	2	10.39	10.45	0.09
100	100	1	5.57	5.54	0.08
100	100	2	6.61	6.62	0.09
110	100	1	2.79	2.81	0.08
110	100	2	4.07	4.06	0.07

where $T - t_i = \tau_i$ represents the time to maturity at the ith step. Replacing the differential and subtracting the expectation, we obtain for a call option:

$$Y - E[Y] = \sum_{i=0}^{NbPas-1} N(d_1(T - t_i, S(t_i)))\sigma S(t_i) d\widetilde{W}(t_i), \tag{10.5}$$

and for a put option:

$$Y - E[Y] = \sum_{i=0}^{NbPas-1} (N(d_1(T - t_i, S(t_i))) - 1)\sigma S(t_i) d\widetilde{W}(t_i), \tag{10.6}$$

where $d_1(.,.)$ is an explicit function of the time to maturity and the asset price S. Here is the MATLAB program for the simulations using these control variates.

```
function OptionMCControl2(S0,K,T)
%Function to calculate the prices of European Put and Call options
%using Monte Carlo simulations with control variates.
%We use the value of the coefficient Delta as control variable.
%S0: Initial price of the asset
%K: Exercise price of the options
%T: Time to maturity of the options

%Initial parameters
sigma=0.2;
r=0.05;
NbTraj=5000;
NbPas=100;
Tau=T;
DeltaT=T/NbPas;

%Price vector of the asset
SPresent=S0*ones(NbTraj,1);
SNext=zeros(NbTraj,1);

%Vector of the control variables
Y1=zeros(NbTraj,1);
Y2=zeros(NbTraj,1);

%Loop to simulate the paths of the asset and the control variables
for i=1:NbPas
   dW=sqrt(DeltaT)*randn(NbTraj,1);
   if i<NbPas
       Tau=Tau-DeltaT;
       d1=(log(SPresent/K)+(r+sigma^2/2)*Tau)/(sigma*sqrt(Tau));
       Y1=Y1+(normcdf(d1)).*SPresent.*dW*sigma;
       Y2=Y2+(normcdf(d1)-1).*SPresent.*dW*sigma;
   end
   SNext=SPresent+(r)*SPresent*DeltaT+sigma*SPresent.*dW;
   SPresent=SNext;
end
```

```
%Using the control variates technique for the call option
X1=exp(-r*T)*max(0,SPresent-K);
EX1=sum(X1)/NbTraj;
EY1=0;

cov1=((X1-EX1)'*(Y1-EY1))/(NbTraj-1);
var1=((Y1-EY1)'*(Y1-EY1))/(NbTraj-1);
alpha1=-cov1/var1;

%Calculation of the price of the call option
PrixControl1=X1+alpha1*(Y1-EY1);
repCall=sum(PrixControl1)/(NbTraj);

%Using the control variates technique for the put option
X2=exp(-r*T)*max(0,K-SPresent);
EX2=sum(X2)/NbTraj;
EY2=0;

cov2=((X2-EX2)'*(Y2-EY2))/(NbTraj-1);
var2=((Y2-EY2)'*(Y2-EY2))/(NbTraj-1);
alpha2=-cov2/var2;

%Calculation of the price of the put option
PrixControl2=X2+alpha2*(Y2-EY2);
repPut=sum(PrixControl2)/(NbTraj);

end
```

Tables 10.7 and 10.8 present the simulations results using these new control variables.

We can clearly see from the tables that these new control variates produce more accurate results than $Y = S(T)$. Hence, it is important to choose the appropriate control variates for our simulations. It is also possible to use several variance reduction techniques at the same time, i.e., combine control variates with antithetic variables or use multiple control variates.

Table 10.7 Price of a European call option with the second control variate

Call option					
Parameters			BS	MC (Control)	
$S(0)$ $	K $	T years	Price $	Price $	Error $
90	100	1	5.09	5.10	0.01
90	100	2	9.91	9.89	0.03
100	100	1	10.45	10.45	0.02
100	100	2	16.13	16.11	0.04
110	100	1	17.66	17.66	0.03
110	100	2	23.59	23.61	0.06

Table 10.8 Price of a European put option with the second control variate

Put option					
Parameters			BS	MC (Control)	
$S(0)$ $	K $	T years	Price $	Price $	Error $
90	100	1	10.21	10.21	0.01
90	100	2	10.39	10.39	0.03
100	100	1	5.57	5.58	0.01
100	100	2	6.61	6.60	0.02
110	100	1	2.79	2.78	0.01
110	100	2	4.07	4.09	0.03

10.1.4 Simulations with Stochastic Interest Rate

In practice, it is often necessary to account for the stochastic nature of interest rates, and several interest rate models are available for that end. We discuss in more detail interest rate models in Chapter 11. Here, we present two models: Cox, Ingersoll and Ross (1985b) (CIR) and Vasicek (1977) (VAS). These two interest rate models are based on the following equation:

$$dr(t) = \kappa(\theta - r(t))dt + \sigma_r r(t)^\gamma d\widetilde{W}_r(t). \tag{10.7}$$

In the VAS model, $\gamma = 0.0$ and $\gamma = 0.5$ in the CIR model. In our simulations, we use the following values for the other parameters:

$$\begin{aligned} \kappa &= 0.25 \\ \theta &= 0.05 \\ \sigma_r &= 0.05 \\ r(0) &= 0.05. \end{aligned}$$

In addition, we assume that

$$\text{corr}(d\widetilde{W}_r(t), d\widetilde{W}_S(t)) = \rho_{r,S}, \tag{10.8}$$

where $d\widetilde{W}_S(t)$ is the Brownian motion characterizing the diffusion portion of the asset price process:

$$dS(t) = r(t)S(t)dt + \sigma S(t)d\widetilde{W}_S(t). \tag{10.9}$$

We need to generate

$$d\widetilde{W} = \begin{pmatrix} d\widetilde{W}_S \\ d\widetilde{W}_r \end{pmatrix} \sim N(0, \Lambda), \tag{10.10}$$

with

$$\Lambda = \begin{pmatrix} \Delta t & \rho_{r,S}\Delta t \\ \rho_{r,S}\Delta t & \Delta t \end{pmatrix}. \tag{10.11}$$

In order to do this, we calculate L knowing that $\Lambda = LL^\top$ and simulate $dZ \sim N(0, I_2)$ to obtain $d\widetilde{W} = LdZ$. We have split the option's time to maturity into 100 time steps. We use the quadratic resampling method to generate dZ, which will affect $d\widetilde{W}$ by construction. For this purpose, we will use the *ReQuadratic* program proposed in Chapter 5. Let's define m_Z and Λ_Z that are respectively the theoretical mean and covariance matrix of dZ. Hence, we have

$$m_Z = \begin{pmatrix} 0 \\ 0 \end{pmatrix}, \tag{10.12}$$

$$\Lambda_Z = \begin{pmatrix} 1 & 0 \\ 0 & 1 \end{pmatrix}. \tag{10.13}$$

We use these variables when generating our stochastic processes. The MATLAB program used to simulate European call and put option prices is the following.

```
function OptionIntStoch(S0,K,T,gamma)
%Function to calculate the prices of the European call and put
 options
%using Monte Carlo simulation and stochastic interest rate.
%S0: Initial price of the asset
%K: Exercise price of the options
%T: Time to maturity of the options
%gamma: Parameter of the interest rate

%Initial parameters
NbPas=100;
DeltaT=T/NbPas;
NbTraj=5000;
sigma=0.2;

%Parameters of the interest rate
kappa=0.25;
theta=0.05;
sigmaR=0.05;
r0=0.05;
rho=-0.2;

%Vectors of the interest rate values and the discount rates
r = r0*ones(NbTraj,1);
rAct = zeros(NbTraj,1);

%Vector of the asset price
S = S0*ones(NbTraj,1);

%Choleski Factorization of the covariance matrix
L = chol([DeltaT,rho*DeltaT;rho*DeltaT,DeltaT])';

%Loop to simulate the steps
for cptPas=1:NbPas
    DeltaZ = randn(2,NbTraj);
    DeltaZ = ReQuadratic(DeltaZ,zeros(2,1),eye(2));
```

```
    DeltaW = L*DeltaZ;
    S = S.*(1+r*DeltaT+sigma*DeltaW(1,:)');
    r = r+kappa*(theta-r)*DeltaT+sigmaR*(r.^gamma).*DeltaW(2,:)';
    rAct = rAct + r*DeltaT;
end
%Calculation of the price of the options
PriceCall = mean(max(0,S-K).*exp(-rAct));
PricePut = mean(max(0,K-S).*exp(-rAct));
end

function Rep=ReQuadratic(Sample, MoyTheo,CovTheo)
%Function performing the quadratic resampling.
%Sample: Simulated sample
%MoyTheo: Theoretical mean of the variables
%CovTheo: Theoretical covariance matrix of the variables

%Calculation of the sample distribution
CovEmp=cov(Sample');
MoyEmp=mean(Sample,2);
LEmp=chol(CovEmp)';

%Resampling based on the theoretical covariance matrix
LTheo=chol(CovTheo)';
Sample=LTheo*inv(LEmp)*(Sample-...
               repmat(MoyEmp,1,size(Sample,2)))+...
               repmat(MoyTheo,1,size(Sample,2));
Rep=Sample;
end
```

We simulate 100000 paths (20 batches of 5000 simulations each) and calculate the standard deviation of the 20 batches. We use $\rho_{r,S} = -0.20$ and $NbPas = 100$. Tables 10.9 and 10.10 present the simulations results for the CIR and VAS models.

As in the previous section, the reader can use antithetic and control variables to obtain more accurate results. One suggested control variable is the Black-Scholes expression. We leave this as an additional practice exercise for the reader.

Table 10.9 Price of a European call option with stochastic interest rates

Call option						
Parameters			VAS		CIR	
$S(0)$ \$	K \$	T years	Price \$	Error \$	Price \$	Error \$
90	100	1	4.96	0.11	5.09	0.08
90	100	2	9.66	0.12	9.80	0.12
100	100	1	10.29	0.10	10.42	0.12
100	100	2	15.84	0.18	16.01	0.16
110	100	1	17.59	0.08	17.64	0.10
110	100	2	23.31	0.16	23.50	0.16

Table 10.10 Price of a European put option with stochastic interest rates

Put option						
Parameters			VAS		CIR	
$S(0)$ \$	K \$	T years	Price \$	Error \$	Price \$	Error \$
90	100	1	10.16	0.07	10.18	0.06
90	100	2	10.38	0.07	10.32	0.06
100	100	1	5.49	0.08	5.52	0.06
100	100	2	6.58	0.08	6.56	0.06
110	100	1	2.71	0.07	2.75	0.07
110	100	2	4.03	0.07	4.00	0.06

10.1.5 Simulations with Stochastic Interest Rate and Stochastic Volatility

In Section 10.1.4, we introduced two stochastic interest rate models. Indeed, the price of an asset can depend on many stochastic parameters. Modeling implies many errors such as dimensionality errors, measurement errors, etc. All these errors can be captured or subsumed by a stochastic volatility process.

The object here is not to make an extensive treatment of different volatility processes and models or to study various related concepts (e.g., implicit volatility, volatility surface, volatility derivatives, etc.). Readers interested in these issues will find useful references in the notes and complementary readings section at the end of the chapter.

In this section, we present a stochastic volatility model and use it to price plain vanilla options using Monte Carlo simulations.

The volatility of an asset price will be a function of its value but will also be correlated with its return. We also assume a non-zero correlation between the stochastic interest rate and the asset volatility.

The dynamic of the asset volatility is as follows

$$d\sigma(t)^2 = \nu(\beta - \sigma(t)^2)dt + \sigma_\sigma \sigma(t) d\widetilde{W}_\sigma(t), \tag{10.14}$$

where dW_σ is a Wiener process such that

$$\operatorname{corr}(d\widetilde{W}_\sigma(t), d\widetilde{W}_S(t)) = \rho_{\sigma,S} = -0.5, \tag{10.15}$$
$$\operatorname{corr}(d\widetilde{W}_\sigma(t), d\widetilde{W}_r(t)) = \rho_{\sigma,r} = \rho_{\sigma,S}\rho_{S,r} = 0.1. \tag{10.16}$$

In the stochastic volatility equation, ν is the adjustment speed, β the long run mean of the process and σ_σ the standard deviation of the process. In order to price European call and put options, we use the following parameter values to run our simulations

$$\begin{aligned} \sigma_0 &= 0.20 \\ \nu &= 1.25 \\ \beta &= 0.04 \\ \sigma_\sigma &= 0.20. \end{aligned}$$

The following MATLAB program is a slightly modified version of the previous program in which, in addition of the stochastic interest rate models of CIR and VAS, we have added the stochastic volatility for the simulation.

```
function rep=OptionIntVolStoch(S0,Strike,T,gamma)
%Function to calculate the prices of the European call and put
 options
%using Monte Carlo simulations with stochastic interest rate
%and stochastic volatility.
%S0: Initial asset price
%K: Exercise price of the options
%T: Time to maturity of the options
%gamma: Parameter of the interest rate
%Initial parameters
NbStep=100;
DeltaT=T/NbStep;
NbTraj=5000;
rho=-0.2;
%Parameters of the stochastic interest rate
kappa=0.25;
theta=0.05;
sigmaR=0.05;
r0=0.05;
%Parameters of the stochastic volatility
nu=1.25;
beta=0.04;
sigma0=0.2;
sigmaSigma=0.2;
rho2=-0.5;
rho3=rho*rho2;
%Vectors of spot interest rates and discounted rates
r = r0*ones(NbTraj,1);
rAct = zeros(NbTraj,1);
%Vectors of asset and  volatility values
S = S0*ones(NbTraj,1)
sigma = sigma0*ones(NbTraj,1);
%Choleski Factorization
L=chol([DeltaT,rho*DeltaT,rho2*DeltaT;rho*DeltaT,DeltaT,rho3*
                   DeltaT;...rho2*DeltaT,rho3*DeltaT,DeltaT])';
%Simulation of the paths
for cptpas=1:NbPas
    DeltaZ = randn(3,NbTraj);
    DeltaZ = ReQuadratic(DeltaZ,zeros(3,1),eye(3));
    DeltaW = L*DeltaZ;
    S = S.*(1+r*DeltaT+sigma.*DeltaW(1,:)');
    r = r+kappa*(theta-r)*DeltaT+sigmaR*(r.^gamma).*DeltaW(2,:)';
    sigma = (sigma.^2+nu*(beta-sigma.^2)*DeltaT+...
             sigmaSigma*Sigma.*DeltaW(3,:)').^(0.5);
    rAct = rAct + r*DeltaT;
end
```

Table 10.11 Price of a European call option with stochastic interest rate and stochastic volatility

Call option						
Parameters			VAS		CIR	
$S(0)$ $	K $	T years	Price $	Error $	Price $	Error $
90	100	1	4.61	0.07	4.69	0.08
90	100	2	9.37	0.13	9.48	0.17
100	100	1	10.31	0.08	10.33	0.09
100	100	2	15.87	0.17	16.10	0.17
110	100	1	17.79	0.10	17.88	0.08
110	100	2	23.56	0.11	23.79	0.19

```
%Calculation of the prices of the European call and put options
PrixCall = mean(max(0,S-Strike).*exp(-rAct));
PrixPut = mean(max(0,K-Strike).*exp(-rAct));
end

function Rep=ReQuadratic(Sample, MoyTheo,CovTheo)
%Function performing the quadratic resampling
%Sample: Simulated sample
%MoyTheo: Theoretical mean of the variables
%CovTheo: Theoretical covariance matrix of the variables
%Calculation of the parameters of the sample distribution
CovEmp=cov(Sample');
MoyEmp=mean(Sample,2);
LEmp=chol(CovEmp)';
%Resampling based on the theoretical covariance matrix
LTheo=chol(CovTheo)';
Sample=LTheo*inv(LEmp)*(Sample-...
               repmat(MoyEmp,1,size(Sample,2)))+...
               repmat(MoyTheo,1,size(Sample,2));
Rep=Sample;
end
```

This program is used to estimate European call and put option prices. Tables 10.11 and 10.12 present the simulations results. The error is measured by the standard deviation of the result vector of the 20 batches.

As in the section above, the reader can use antithetic and control variables to obtain more accurate results. One suggested control variable is the Black-Scholes formula. We leave this as an additional practice exercise for the reader.

10.2 AMERICAN OPTIONS

The feature of an American option is that it can be exercised at any time before its maturity. Given the fact that these options offer more flexibility to their holders, their price should be higher than the price of their equivalent counterpart European options. However, for a call

Table 10.12 Price of a European put option with stochastic interest rate and stochastic volatility

Put option						
Parameters			VAS		CIR	
$S(0)$ $	K $	T years	Price $	Error $	Price $	Error $
90	100	1	9.77	0.08	9.81	0.06
90	100	2	10.06	0.10	9.98	0.09
100	100	1	5.46	0.06	5.49	0.08
100	100	2	5.60	0.09	6.55	0.10
110	100	1	2.98	0.09	3.01	0.07
110	100	2	4.33	0.13	4.29	0.10

option on a non-dividend-paying stock, the American and European options are worth the same; there's no advantage in early exercise of a call in this case.

There exists no simple formula to price American options. One may use binomial trees and examine at each node if it is optimal to exercise the option immediately or not. This simple approach can take a considerable amount of calculation time to obtain an adequate precision for options on several underlying assets.

We present next two approaches to price American options. These two approaches use Monte Carlo simulations instead of binomial trees. The approaches are the Least-Squares Method of Longstaff and Schwartz (2001) and the Dynamic Programming Technique with Stratified States Aggregation of Barraquand and Martineau (1995).

10.2.1 Simulations Using The Least-Squares Method of Longstaff and Schwartz (2001)

When dealing with American options, it is not always easy to decide whether to exercise them immediately or keep them in the portfolio until their expiration date. The optimal strategy would be to exercise the option if the immediate payment is larger than the expected future payments, otherwise it should be kept. Let's assume that the price of the stock is $S(t)$ and the payoff function is $\widetilde{P}(S(t), t)$. Then the optimal strategy at time $t = t_1$ is

$$\text{Exercise} = \begin{cases} \text{Yes if } \widetilde{P}(S(t_1), t_1) > E_{t_1}\left[\widetilde{P}(S(t_2), t_2)|\mathcal{F}_{t_1}\right] \\ \text{No if } \widetilde{P}(S(t_1), t_1) < E_{t_1}\left[\widetilde{P}(S(t_2), t_2)|\mathcal{F}_{t_1}\right] \end{cases}, \tag{10.17}$$

where $E_{t_1}[\widetilde{P}(S(t_2), t_2)|\mathcal{F}_{t_1}]$ is the expectation of future payments (of time $t_2 > t_1$) at time $t = t_1$, and $\mathcal{F}_{t_1}$ represents the available information set at $t = t_1$. It is therefore essential to "know" the expected value of future payments in order to make an accurate evaluation of an American option. The Least-Squares method is a technique that enables us to perform this exercise.

We start by generating M paths for the underlying stock price S. Next, for each path, we need to regress the future payoffs on basis functions F_i, which depend on the stock price S. Let Y be the vector of future payoffs for the M paths and $1, F_1(S)$ and $F_2(S)$ be the basis functions. We regress Y on these basis functions, which yields the expression

$$E[Y|S] = \alpha + \beta F_1(S) + \gamma F_2(S). \tag{10.18}$$

Table 10.13 Simulation paths

Number	$t = 0$	$t = 1$	$t = 2$	$t = 3$
1	1.00	1.07	1.53	1.95
2	1.00	0.76	0.78	0.71
3	1.00	0.85	0.69	0.76
4	1.00	0.96	1.01	0.97
5	1.00	0.95	1.06	1.28
6	1.00	1.59	1.26	1.07
7	1.00	1.28	1.23	0.97
8	1.00	1.11	1.57	1.89

This expression gives us an estimation of the expected value of future payoffs as a function of S. This expected value is effectively the value of holding on to the option. From this expression, we can decide if it is preferable to exercise the option immediately or to wait one more period. This procedure is reproduced backward from the maturity date to time $t = 0$. For each path, we find the optimal exercise date of the option. The price of the option is therefore the average of all discounted payoffs.

To better illustrate the method, we use it to price an American put option. We assume $S(0) = \$\,1.0$, the exercise price is $K = \$\,1.10$, the time to maturity of the option is 3 years and the option's potential exercise dates are 1, 2 and 3 years. If $S(0) \neq \$\,1.0$, it is better to normalize the initial price to $S(0) = \$\,1.0$ as the exercise price becomes $K/S(0)$ to reduce the estimation errors in the regressions. We also assume the risk free interest rate to be $r = 6\%$ and $M = 8$ paths for simplification. Table 10.13 presents the simulation values of S.

To use the Least-Squares Method, we need to start at maturity and go backward until we reach the initial time $t = 0$. At time $t = 3$, the holder of the option exercises it only if he gains from it. The payoffs matrix at time $t = 3$ is given by Table 10.14.

This matrix shows the realized payoffs of an equivalent European option. Now we need to determine for which paths it is preferable to exercise the option at date $t = 2$. For $t = 2$, only 4 paths must be considered since the other 4 paths would result in zero payoffs. The results are presented in Table 10.15 (Y represents the discounted expected payoffs).

We use $1, S$ and S^2 as the basis functions. We therefore need to regress Y on these functions, which yields:

$$E[Y|S] = -2.71 + 7.81S - 4.96S^2. \tag{10.19}$$

Table 10.14 Payoffs at $t = 3$

Number	$t = 1$	$t = 2$	$t = 3$
1	–	–	0.00
2	–	–	0.39
3	–	–	0.34
4	–	–	0.13
5	–	–	0.00
6	–	–	0.03
7	–	–	0.13
8	–	–	0.00

Table 10.15 Variables for the first regression

Number	S	Y
1	–	–
2	0.78	0.39*0.9418 = 0.3673
3	0.69	0.34*0.9418 = 0.3202
4	1.01	0.13*0.9418 = 0.1224
5	1.06	0.00*0.9418 = 0.0000
6	–	–
7	–	–
8	–	–

To obtain the regression coefficients, we only need to compute the following matrix product

$$(\mathbf{X}^\top\mathbf{X})^{-1}\mathbf{X}^\top Y = (-2.7077, 7.8084, -4.9566)^\top, \tag{10.20}$$

where

$$\mathbf{X} = \begin{pmatrix} 1 & 0.78 & 0.78^2 \\ 1 & 0.69 & 0.69^2 \\ 1 & 1.01 & 1.01^2 \\ 1 & 1.06 & 1.06^2 \end{pmatrix} \text{ and } Y = \begin{pmatrix} 0.3673 \\ 0.3202 \\ 0.1224 \\ 0 \end{pmatrix}. \tag{10.21}$$

From the regression equation, we evaluate the function $E[Y|S]$ for different values of S at time $t = 2$.

$$\begin{aligned} E[Y\,|S = 0.78] &= 0.3672 \\ E[Y\,|S = 0.69] &= 0.3202 \\ E[Y\,|S = 1.01] &= 0.1225 \\ E[Y\,|S = 1.06] &= -0.0001. \end{aligned}$$

We then compare these values to the payoffs resulting from an immediate exercise of the option (see Table 10.16).

We note that it is preferable to exercise the option at date 2 for paths 3 and 5. For simulations 2 and 4, the expected payoffs are higher when the option is not exercised. Then, taking into

Table 10.16 Exercise decision at time $t = 2$

Number	Exercise	Continuation
1	–	–
2	0.32	0.36
3	0.41	0.32
4	0.09	0.12
5	0.04	0.00
6	–	–
7	–	–
8	–	–

Table 10.17 Payoffs at date $t = 2$

Number	$t = 1$	$t = 2$	$t = 3$
1	–	0.00	0.00
2	–	0.00	0.39
3	–	0.41	0.00
4	–	0.00	0.13
5	–	0.04	0.00
6	–	0.00	0.03
7	–	0.00	0.13
8	–	0.00	0.00

Table 10.18 Variables for the second regression

Number	S	Y
1	1.07	0.00
2	0.76	$0.39{*}0.9418^2 = 0.3459$
3	0.85	$0.41{*}0.9418 = 0.3861$
4	0.96	$0.13{*}0.9418^2 = 0.1153$
5	0.95	$0.04{*}0.9418 = 0.0377$
6	–	–
7	–	–
8	–	–

Table 10.19 Exercise decision at date $t = 1$

Number	Exercise	Continuation
1	0.03	−0.04
2	0.34	0.38
3	0.25	0.26
4	0.14	0.11
5	0.15	0.13
6	–	–
7	–	–
8	–	–

account the payoffs of paths 3 and 5 at time 2, we obtain the following payoff matrix in Table 10.17.

We need to follow the same steps to obtain the payoffs at time $t = 1$. For $t = 1$, only 3 paths provide values of S greater than 1.10 (number 6, 7 and 8). We then need to consider all other 5 paths in the regression, which yields Table 10.18.

The regression gives:

$$E[Y\,|\,S] = 1.38 - 1.28S - 0.04S^2. \tag{10.22}$$

Then we have to compare the immediate payoffs if the option is exercised and the expected payoffs if not. Table 10.19 presents the results.

Here we observe that it is preferable to exercise the option immediately for paths 1, 4 and 5. We can therefore complete the option exercise decision table. Table 10.20 presents the results.

Table 10.20 Payoffs at $t = 1$

Number	$t = 1$	$t = 2$	$t = 3$
1	0.03	0.00	0.00
2	0.00	0.00	0.39
3	0.00	0.41	0.00
4	0.14	0.00	0.00
5	0.15	0.00	0.00
6	0.00	0.00	0.03
7	0.00	0.00	0.13
8	0.00	0.00	0.00

The price of the American put option is obtained by taking the average value of all discounted payoffs. We obtain an option price of 0.1406. If the option was European, its price would have been 0.1065. The Least-Squares Method allows us to price the early exercise flexibility feature associated with American options; the value of that flexibility is $0.1406 - 0.1065 = 0.0341$.

This method can be used in many other option pricing cases with early exercise possibility. In addition, it is possible to use many basis functions, which improve the precision. For example, Longstaff and Schwartz (2001) suggest using the Laguerre, Hermite, Legendre, Chebychev polynomials among others.

MATLAB Program

The MATLAB program to implement the algorithm of the Least-Squares Method is given below. This program includes a function to generate the paths and another function to perform the regression and price the option in a backward manner (one step at a time).

```
function LSM
%Function to calculate the price of an American option
%using the Least-Squares method.

T=1; %Maturity
TimePresent=T; %Time to maturity
NbStep=50; %Number of steps.
K=40; %Exercise price
sigma=0.2; %Volatility of the asset
NbTraj=50000; %Number of paths
DeltaT=T/NbStep;
SqDeltaT=sqrt(DeltaT);
r=0.06;
SBegin=36; %Initial price of the asset

%To increase the precision of the regression,
%we use an initial price of 1
%and we decrease the exercise price consequently
S0=1; %
Strike=K/SBegin;
```

```
%We generate the paths of the asset price
S=GeneratePaths(NbTraj,NbStep,DeltaT,SqDeltaT,r,sigma,S0);

%Payoff is a vector formed of the largest cash flows
%using the optimal strategy
Payoff=zeros(2*NbTraj,1);
Payoff(:,1)=max(0,Strike-S(:,NbStep+1));

%Loop for backwardation by step from the maturity
for cptStep=1:NbStep-1
   %Discounting of the payoff vector
   Payoff=exp(-r*DeltaT)*Payoff;

   TimePresent=TimePresent-DeltaT;

   %Calculation of the new payoff vector by deciding if it is
    optimal
   %to exercise the option immediately.
   Payoff=BackwardStep(Payoff,Strike,TimePresent,NbTraj,r,DeltaT,...
                        S(:,NbStep+1-cptStep));
end

%Calculation of the option price
Price=mean(exp(-r*DeltaT)*Payoff);

%Calculation of the option price with the initial price of the
 asset
disp(Price*SBegin);

end

function S=GeneratePaths(NbTraj,NbStep,DeltaT,SqDeltaT,r,sigma,S0);
%Function to simulate the paths of the asset price

   dW=SqDeltaT*randn(NbTraj,NbStep);
   dW=cat(1,dW,-dW);

   Increments=(r-(sigma^2)/2)*DeltaT+sigma*dW;
   LogPaths=cumsum([log(S0)*ones(2*NbTraj,1),Increments],2);
   S=exp(LogPaths);
end

function Payoff=BackwardStep(Payoff,Strike, TimePresent,
                             NbTraj,r, ... DeltaT,S)
%Function using the Least-Squares method to determine
%if it is preferable to exercise immediately the option.
%Payoff: Old vector of Payoff at time t+1
%Strike: Exercise price of the option
%TimePresent: time t
```

```
%NbTraj: Number of paths
%r: interest rate
%DeltaT
%S: Vector of asset prices at time t

   %Vector containing the paths where the price of the
    asset is lower than
   %the exercise price (otherwise it is preferable to exercise)
   SelectedPaths=(Strike>S);

   %Matrix of regressors
   X=[ones(2*NbTraj,1).*SelectedPaths,(S.*SelectedPaths),...
           (S.*SelectedPaths).^2];

   %Vector of expected payoffs
   Y=Payoff.*SelectedPaths;

   %Regression to determine the coefficients
   A=inv(X'*X)*X'*Y;

   %Calculation of the payoffs values when the option is not
    exercised
   Continuation=(X*A).*SelectedPaths;

   %Values when the option is exercised immediately
   Exercise=max(0,Strike-S);

   %Paths, exercise decision and update of the Payoff vector.
   for i=1:(2*NbTraj)
       if ((Exercise(i,1)>0)&(Exercise(i,1)>Continuation(i,1)))
           Payoff(i,1)=Exercise(i,1);
       end
   end

end
```

We use this program to calculate the value of an American put option. We use 100 000 paths including 50 000 antithetic, 50 time steps per year (hence 50 possible exercise dates per year), a risk-free rate of 6% as well as an exercise price of 40$ and an initial price $S(0)$ in $\{38, 40, 42\}$. In Table 10.21, we show the results and compare them to those of the finite difference method presented in Longstaff and Schwartz (2001).

Least-Squares Method with Multiple Underlying Assets

The previous section introduced the Least-Squares Method for the case of one dimension. With only one underlying asset, it is relatively easy to understand the approach. However, this method is also useful for cases featuring several underlying assets and complex cash flows. We use the Least-Squares Method to price an American call option written on three underlying

Table 10.21 Prices of an American put option with the Least-Squares Method

$S(0)$ $	σ	T years	Finite difference $	Least-Squares $
38	0.2	1	3.250	3.244
38	0.2	2	3.745	3.725
38	0.4	1	6.148	6.129
38	0.4	2	7.670	7.675
40	0.2	1	2.314	2.310
40	0.2	2	2.885	2.878
40	0.4	1	5.312	5.302
40	0.4	2	6.920	6.895
42	0.2	1	1.617	1.618
42	0.2	2	2.212	2.211
42	0.4	1	4.582	4.574
42	0.4	2	6.248	6.239

assets. Let's consider the following processes for the underlying assets prices

$$\frac{dS_1(t)}{S_1(t)} = 0.05dt + 0.2d\widetilde{W}_1(t), \tag{10.23}$$

$$\frac{dS_2(t)}{S_2(t)} = 0.05dt + 0.3d\widetilde{W}_2(t), \tag{10.24}$$

$$\frac{dS_3(t)}{S_3(t)} = 0.05dt + 0.2d\widetilde{W}_3(t), \tag{10.25}$$

with initial values $S_i(0) = 40$. The *payoff* function for the American call option at time t is given by

$$\max(0, S_1(t) - 40, S_2(t) - 40, S_3(t) - 40). \tag{10.26}$$

Now we need to choose the basis functions to perform the regressions. There exists an infinite number of functions we could have used. Here we choose basis functions leading to polynomials of order less than or equal to 4.

$$\begin{array}{ccccc}
1 & S_1 & S_2 & S_3 & (S_1)^2 \\
(S_2)^2 & (S_3)^2 & S_1S_2 & S_1S_3 & S_2S_3 \\
(S_1)^3 & (S_2)^3 & (S_3)^3 & (S_1)^2S_2 & (S_1)^2S_3 \\
(S_2)^2S_1 & (S_2)^2S_3 & (S_3)^2S_1 & (S_3)^2S_2 & (S_1)^4 \\
(S_2)^4 & (S_3)^4 & (S_1)^3S_2 & (S_1)^3S_3 & (S_2)^3S_1 \\
(S_2)^3S_3 & (S_3)^3S_1 & (S_3)^3S_2 & (S_1)^2(S_2)^2 & (S_1)^2(S_3)^2 \\
(S_2)^2(S_3)^2 & & & &
\end{array} \tag{10.27}$$

The MATLAB program used to obtain the results shown in Table 10.22 is given below.

```
function Least2
%Function to calculate the price of an American call option
%using the Least-Squares method.
%Here the underlying asset is a basket of assets.
```

Table 10.22 Prices of an American call option on three underlying assets with the Least-Squares Method

Exercise price ($)	T (year)	Option price ($)
38	0.25	7.7555
	0.50	10.4924
40	0.25	5.9368
	0.50	8.7276
42	0.25	4.3501
	0.50	7.0876

```
%SBegin: Vector of initial prices
SBegin=40;
%T: Maturity of the option
T=0.25;
%K: Exercise price of the option
K=38;

%Initial parameters
TimePresent=T;
NbStep=12;
NbTraj=100000;
DeltaT=T/NbStep;
SqDeltaT=sqrt(DeltaT);
r=0.05;
S0=1;
Strike=K/SBegin;

%Vectors to store the paths of then three underlying assets
S1=GeneratePaths(NbTraj,NbStep,DeltaT,SqDeltaT,r,0.2,S0);
S2=GeneratePaths(NbTraj,NbStep,DeltaT,SqDeltaT,r,0.3,S0);
S3=GeneratePaths(NbTraj,NbStep,DeltaT,SqDeltaT,r,0.4,S0);

%Payoff is a vector formed by the highest cash flows
%using the optimal strategy
Payoff=zeros(2*NbTraj,1);
Payoff(:,1)=max([S1(:,NbStep+1)-Strike,S2(:,NbStep+1)-Strike,...
                S3(:,NbStep+1)-Strike,zeros(2*NbTraj,1)]')';

%Loop for the backwardation by steps starting from the maturity
for cptStep=1:NbStep-1
   %Discounting of the vector Payoff
   Payoff=exp(-r*DeltaT)*Payoff;

   TimePresent=TimePresent-DeltaT;

   %Calculation of the new vector Payoff with respect to the
    exercise
   % decision.
```

```
   Payoff=BackwardStep(Payoff,Strike,TimePresent,NbTraj,r,DeltaT,...
                   S1(:,NbStep+1-cptStep),S2(:,NbStep+1-
                   cptStep),...
                   S3(:,NbStep+1-cptStep));
end

%Calculation of the price and the standard deviation
std(exp(-r*DeltaT)*Payoff);
Price=mean(exp(-r*DeltaT)*Payoff);

%Calculation of the option price with the departure
 value of the asset
disp(Price*SBegin);

end

function S=GenerePaths(NbTraj,NbStep,DeltaT,SqDeltaT,r,sigma,S0);
%Function to simulate the paths of the asset price

   dW=SqDeltaT*randn(NbTraj,NbStep);
   dW=cat(1,dW,-dW);

   Increments=(r-(sigma^2)/2)*DeltaT+sigma*dW;
   LogPaths=cumsum([log(S0)*ones(2*NbTraj,1),Increments],2);
   S=exp(LogPaths);
end

function Payoff=BackwardStep(Payoff,Strike, TimePresent, NbTraj,...
                          r,DeltaT,S1,S2,S3)
%Function using the Least-Squares method to determine
%if it is preferable to exercise immediately.
%Payoff: Old vector Payoff at time t+1
%Strike: Exercise price of the option
%TimePresent: Time t
%NbTraj: Number of paths
%r: Interest rate
%DeltaT
%S1 S2 S3: Vectors of assets prices at time t

   %Vector containing the paths where the asset price is less than
   %the exercise price (otherwise it is not preferable to exercise
   % the option)
   SelectedPaths=(max([S1-Strike,S2-Strike,S3-Strike]')'>0);
   S1Temp=S1.*SelectedPaths;
   S2Temp=S2.*SelectedPaths;
   S3Temp=S3.*SelectedPaths;

   %Matrix of regressors
   X=[ones(2*NbTraj,1).*SelectedPaths,S1Temp,S1Temp.^2,S1Temp.^3,...
       S2Temp,S2Temp.^2,S2Temp.^3,S3Temp,S3Temp.^2,S3Temp.^3,...
       S1Temp.*S2Temp,S1Temp.*S3Temp,S2Temp.*S3Temp,...
```

```
        S1Temp.^2.*S2Temp,S1Temp.^2.*S3Temp,S2Temp.^2.*S1Temp,...
        S2Temp.^2.*S3Temp,S3Temp.^2.*S1Temp,S3Temp.^2.*S2Temp,...
        S1Temp.^4,S2Temp.^4,S3Temp.^4,S1Temp.^3.*S2Temp,...
        S1Temp.^3.*S3Temp,S2Temp.^3.*S1Temp,S2Temp.^3.*S3Temp,...
        S3Temp.^3.*S1Temp,S3Temp.^3.*S2Temp,S1Temp.^2.*S2Temp.^2,...
        S1Temp.^2.*S3Temp.^2,S2Temp.^2.*S3Temp.^2];

    %Vector of expected values
    Y=Payoff.*SelectedPaths;

    %Regression to find the coefficients
    A=inv(X'*X)*X'*Y;

    %Calculation of the expected values when the option is not
     exercised
    Continuation=(X*A).*SelectedPaths;

    %Values when the option is exercised immediately
    Exercise=max([zeros(2*NbTraj,1),S1-Strike,S2-Strike,
    S3-Strike]')';

    %Paths, exercise decision and updating of the vector Payoff.
    for i=1:(2*NbTraj)
        if ((Exercise(i,1)>0)&(Exercise(i,1)>Continuation(i,1)))
            Payoff(i,1)=Exercise(i,1);
        end
    end

end
```

10.2.2 Simulations Using The Dynamic Programming Technique of Barraquand and Martineau (1995)

The Dynamic Programming Technique has been developed to price American options written on n underlying assets

$$S = (S_1, S_2, \ldots, S_n). \tag{10.28}$$

The fundamental idea of this method is to divide the approximation space (dimension n) into cells. Next, we assume that the payoff function and the optimal strategy are constant over each cell. Finally, we need to evaluate the price of the option on this partitioned space. The steps of the algorithm to be implemented are presented below.

Since the option is written on n underlying assets, the payoff function is given by:

$$\begin{aligned} \widetilde{P} : \mathbb{R}^n \times \mathbb{R} &\longrightarrow \mathbb{R} \\ (S, t) &\longrightarrow \widetilde{P}(S, t). \end{aligned} \tag{10.29}$$

We divide the time to maturity of the option according to $\{0, \Delta t, \ldots, T\}$. If we have a partition $\mathcal{Q}$ of $\mathbb{R}$, then we can construct a partition of $\mathbb{R}^n \times t$ given as follows

$$\text{Partition}_i(t) = \{S \in \mathbb{R}^n | \widetilde{P}(S, t) \in \mathcal{Q}_i(t)\}. \tag{10.30}$$

We assume the partition $\mathcal{Q}$ to be composed of k sets. The intervals $\mathcal{Q}_i(t)$ will be given by

$$\mathcal{Q}_i(t) =]A(t)e^{B(t)(i-2)}, A(t)e^{B(t)(i-1)}] \tag{10.31}$$

for $i \in [2, k-1]$ and by

$$\mathcal{Q}_1(t) =]-\infty, A(t)], \tag{10.32}$$
$$\mathcal{Q}_k(t) =]A(t)e^{B(t)(k-2)}, +\infty[. \tag{10.33}$$

We will then have the following cells:

$$\text{Partition}_i(t) = \{S \in \mathbb{R}^n | A(t)e^{B(t)(i-2)} < \widetilde{P}(S, t) \leq A(t)e^{B(t)(i-1)}\} \tag{10.34}$$

for $i \in [2, k-1]$ and

$$\text{Partition}_1(t) = \{S \in \mathbb{R}^n | \widetilde{P}(S, t) \leq A(t)\} \tag{10.35}$$
$$\text{Partition}_k(t) = \{S \in \mathbb{R}^n | \widetilde{P}(S, t) > A(t)e^{B(t)(k-2)}\}. \tag{10.36}$$

We choose $A(t)$ and $B(t)$ such that

$$\text{Prob}(S(t) \in \text{Partition}_1(t)) \approx \text{Prob}(S(t) \in \text{Partition}_k(t)) \approx 0.1\%. \tag{10.37}$$

The choice of 0.1% is somewhat arbitrary; it will depend on the dispersion of our paths and the problem under study. Let's denote by $S^1(t), \ldots, S^M(t)$ the M generated paths of the process $S(t)$. We then define

$$\alpha_i(t) = \text{Card}\{m \in [1, M] | S^m(t) \in \text{Partition}_i(t)\}, \tag{10.38}$$
$$\beta_{i,j}(t) = \text{Card}\{m \in [1, M] | S^m(t) \in \text{Partition}_i(t),\ S^m(t + \Delta t) \in \text{Partition}_j(t + \Delta t)\}, \tag{10.39}$$
$$\gamma_i(t) = \sum_{S^m \in \text{Partition}_i(t)} \widetilde{P}(S^m(t), t), \tag{10.40}$$

where Card stands for the cardinal or the number of elements in the set. These numbers will be useful because

$$\frac{\gamma_i(t)}{\alpha_i(t)} \tag{10.41}$$

is the average value of payoffs on cell $\text{Partition}_i(t)$ and

$$\frac{\beta_{i,j}(t)}{\alpha_i(t)} \tag{10.42}$$

is an approximation of the conditional probability of moving to cell $\text{Partition}_j(t + \Delta t)$ when we are already in cell $\text{Partition}_i(t)$. We can therefore use the following algorithm to calculate the price of the American option.

1. At time T, we calculate

$$\text{Price}(i, T) = \frac{\gamma_i(T)}{\alpha_i(T)}. \tag{10.43}$$

2. At time $T - \Delta t$, for each $i \in [1, k]$ we have

$$\text{Price}(i, T - \Delta t) = \max\left(\frac{\gamma_i(T - \Delta t)}{\alpha_i(T - \Delta t)}, \sum_{j=1}^{k} \text{Price}(j, T)\frac{\beta_{i,j}(T - \Delta t)}{\alpha_i(T - \Delta t)}\right). \tag{10.44}$$

3. We apply the previous step recursively to calculate Price($i, T - 2\Delta t$), ... , Price(1, 0).
4. Since we buy the option at time $-\Delta t$ so that the exercise decision period begins at time $t = 0$, we can obtain the final price by calculating

$$e^{-r\Delta t}\text{Price}(1, 0). \tag{10.45}$$

MATLAB Program

We propose a MATLAB program that was used to implement the algorithm presented above on the Dynamic Programming approach. The method has been applied to calculate the price of an American option written on three underlying assets. The payoff of the equivalent European option is given by:

$$\text{Payoff} = \max(0, S_1(T) - K, S_2(T) - K, S_3(T) - K). \tag{10.46}$$

```
function SSA
%Function to calculate the price of an American option
%underwritten on 3 underlying assets and
%using the dynamic programming technique of Barraquand and
 Martineau.
%T: Maturity
T=1/12;
%Strike: Exercise price
Strike=35;

%%%%%%%%%%%%%%%%%%%%%%%%%%%%%%
%Initial parameters %%%%%%%%%
%%%%%%%%%%%%%%%%%%%%%%%%%%%%%%
k=100;                    %Number of cells
NbTraj=100000;            %Number of paths
NbStep=10;                 %Number of time steps
n=3;                      %Number of underlying assets
mu=ones(n,1)*0.00;        %Dividend yield on the underlying assets
r=0.05;                   %Risk-free rate
DeltaT=T/NbStep;           %Time step
sqDeltaT=sqrt(DeltaT);

%The vector partition keeps in memory the cell containing the asset
%The first column indicates the cell at time t and
%the second column indicates the cell at time t+1.
%partition is initialized as a vector of un, meaning that
%the 3 underlying assets start in cell P1(0).
partition=[ones(NbTraj,1),zeros(NbTraj,1)];
```

```
%The vector payoff stores the cash flows if the option is
 exercised.
payoff=zeros(NbTraj,1);

%The vectors a, b and gamma represent the parameters of the
%Barraquand and Martineau technique, we need to calculate them.
a=zeros(k,NbStep);
b=zeros(k,k,NbStep);
gamma=zeros(k,NbStep);

v=diag([0.2,0.3,0.5]);      %Matrix of the standard deviations
kappa=v*(v');               %variance-covariance matrix
                            %(independent assets)

%x0 is the vector of initial values of the assets
%(40 is the initial value)
x0=40*ones(NbTraj,n);

%x1 is the vector of the assets values at time t and x2 at time t+1
x1=x0;
x2=zeros(NbTraj,n);
%%%%%%%%%%%%%%%%%%%%%%%%%%%%%%
%End of the initialization %%%
%%%%%%%%%%%%%%%%%%%%%%%%%%%%%%

%%%%%%%%%%%%%%%%%%%%%%%%%%%%%%%%%%%%%%%%%%%%%%%%
%Calculation of a, b and gamma for the time t=0%
%%%%%%%%%%%%%%%%%%%%%%%%%%%%%%%%%%%%%%%%%%%%%%%%
%a_1(0) = M, the others are zero since there is only one cell
aInit=NbTraj;
%Calculation of gamma_1(0) alone since a_1(0) is the only non null
 element
gammaInit=exp(-r*DeltaT)*sum(Payoff(x1,NbTraj,Strike,DeltaT,r));
%%%%%%%%%%%%%%%%%%%%%%%%%%%%%%%%%%%%%%%%%%%%%%%%%%%
%End of the calculation of a, b and gamma for t=0%%
%%%%%%%%%%%%%%%%%%%%%%%%%%%%%%%%%%%%%%%%%%%%%%%%%%%

%%%%%%%%%%%%%%%%%%%%%%%%%%%%%%%%%
%Loop for each time step%%%%%%%%%
%%%%%%%%%%%%%%%%%%%%%%%%%%%%%%%%%
for cptStep=1:NbStep

    %Calculation of x2 by simulating one time step
    x2=NextStep(x1,kappa,v,sqDeltaT,DeltaT,mu,NbTraj,n,r);

    %Calculation of the cash flows if the option is exercised
     immediately
    payoff=Payoff(x2,NbTraj,Strike,DeltaT,r);

    %Determination of the partition and classification of the paths
    %with respect to the cash flows
    partition(:,2)=Partition(payoff,NbTraj,k);
```

```
    %Calculation of the values of a, b and c to determine
    %the probabilities
    [a(:,cptStep),b(:,:,cptStep),gamma(:,cptStep)]=...
                          Prob(partition,NbTraj,k,payoff,r,DeltaT);

    %The new partition and the x2 become the old
    %partition and the old x for the next time step
    partition(:,1)=partition(:,2);
    x1=x2;

end

%Initialization of the Calli to compute the price of the call
Call1=zeros(k,1);
Call2=zeros(k,1);

%We initialize Call2 and avoid the division by zero
Call2=gamma(:,NbStep)./max(1,a(:,NbStep));

%Loop starting at the maturity and proceeding backward
 by the time step
for cptStep=1:NbStep-1

    %Calculation of Call1 and no division by zero
    Call1=max(gamma(:,NbStep-cptStep),b(:,:,NbStep-cptStep+1)
          *Call2)./...
            max(1,a(:,NbStep-cptStep));

    %The new Call1 becomes the old Call2 coming back by one step
    Call2=Call1;

end

%Calculation of the option price
Price=max(gammaInit,b(:,:,1)*Call2)/aInit;
callssap=Price(1)

end
%%%%%%%%%%%%%%%%%%%%%%%%%%%%
%End of the main program%%%%
%%%%%%%%%%%%%%%%%%%%%%%%%%%%

%%%%%%%%%%%%%%%%%%%%%%%%%%%%%%%%%%%%%%%%%%%%%%
%Function to simulate the one time step %%%%%%
%%%%%%%%%%%%%%%%%%%%%%%%%%%%%%%%%%%%%%%%%%%%%%
function x2=NextStep(x1,kappa,v,sqDeltaT,DeltaT,mu,NbTraj,n,r)
%x1: Values of the assets at time t
%kappa: Variance-covariance matrix
%v: Matrix of the standard deviation
%spDeltaT: Square root of DeltaT
%DeltaT: Time step
```

```
%mu: Dividend yield
%NbTraj: Number of simulated paths
%n: Number of underlying assets
%r: Risk-free rate
%x2: Values of assets at time t+1

    %Initialization of x2
    x2=zeros(NbTraj,n);

    %Loop to simulate the assets prices at time t+1.
    for cptTraj=1:NbTraj
        x2(cptTraj,:)= SimUnderly(x1(cptTraj,:),kappa,v,sqDeltaT,...
                                          DeltaT,mu,n,r);
    end

end
%%%%%%%%%%%%%%%%%%%%%%%%%%%%%%%%%%
%End of the simulation%%%%%%%%%%%
%%%%%%%%%%%%%%%%%%%%%%%%%%%%%%%%%%

%%%%%%%%%%%%%%%%%%%%%%%%%%%%%%%%%%%%%%%%%%%%
%Function to simulate the underlying assets%
%%%%%%%%%%%%%%%%%%%%%%%%%%%%%%%%%%%%%%%%%%%%
function x2=SimUnderly(x1,kappa,v,sqDeltaT,DeltaT,mu,n,r)
%Same parameters as the previous function but for the paths

    z=randn(n,1);
    temp=v*sqDeltaT*z;

    %Initialization of x2 and simulation for each underlying asset
    x2=zeros(1,n);
    for cptUnderly=1:n
        x2(1,cptUnderly)=x1(1,cptUnderly)*exp((r-mu(cptUnderly,1)-
        ...
        kappa(cptUnderly,cptUnderly)/2)*DeltaT + temp
        (cptUnderly,1));
    end

end
%%%%%%%%%%%%%%%%%%%%%%%%%%%%%%%%%%%%%%%%%%%%%%%%
%End of the simulation of the underlying assets%
%%%%%%%%%%%%%%%%%%%%%%%%%%%%%%%%%%%%%%%%%%%%%%%%

%%%%%%%%%%%%%%%%%%%%%%%%%%%%%%%%%%%
%Function to calculate the payoffs%
%%%%%%%%%%%%%%%%%%%%%%%%%%%%%%%%%%%
function payoff=Payoff(x2,NbTraj,strike,DeltaT,r)
%x2: Values of the assets
%NbTraj: Number of paths
%Strike: Exercise price
```

```
%DeltaT
%r: Risk-free rate

    payoff=zeros(NbTraj,1);

    %For each path, we calculate the payoff if the option is
     exercised
    for cptTraj=1:NbTraj
        payoff(cptTraj,1)=exp(-r*DeltaT)*max(0,max(x2(cptTraj,:))-
        strike);
    end

end
%%%%%%%%%%%%%%%%%%%%%%%%%%%%%%%%%
%End of the payoffs calculations%
%%%%%%%%%%%%%%%%%%%%%%%%%%%%%%%%%

%%%%%%%%%%%%%%%%%%%%%%%%%%%%%%%%%%%%%%
%Function to classify the paths%%%%%%
%%%%%%%%%%%%%%%%%%%%%%%%%%%%%%%%%%%%%%
function partition=Partition(payoff,NbTraj,k)
%Function determining the partitioning of the cells and
%classify the path in the partition it belongs
%payoff: Vector of cash flows if the option is exercised
 immediately
%NbTraj: Number of paths
%k: Number of cells

    partition=zeros(NbTraj,1);

    %Ordering the payoffs to obtain the distribution
    temp=sort(payoff);

    %Keep only the non null elements
    tempNonZero=nonzeros(temp);

    %Calculation of the factor A to class the payoffs
    %(take the 0.1 percentile)
    %The function max is used to avoid a zero
    A=tempNonZero(max(1,floor(0.001*size(tempNonZero,1))));

    %Inscription of the number 1 for the paths in the first cell
    partition=partition+1*(payoff<=A);

    %Determination of the factor B to class the payoffs
    %(take the 99.9 percentile)
    B=log(temp(floor(0.999*NbTraj)-1)/A)/(k-2);

    %Inscription of the number k for the paths in the last cell
    partition=partition+k*(payoff>A*exp(B*(k-2)));
```

```
    %Inscription of the appropriate number for the other paths
    %by checking all the possible cells
    for cptPartition=2:k-1
        partition = partition + ...
            cptPartition*(payoff>A*exp(B*(cptPartition-2))).* ...
                            (payoff<=A*exp(B*(cptPartition-1)));
    end

end
%%%%%%%%%%%%%%%%%%%%%%%%%%%%%%%%%
%End of the classification of the paths%
%%%%%%%%%%%%%%%%%%%%%%%%%%%%%%%%%

%%%%%%%%%%%%%%%%%%%%%%%%%%%%%%%%%%%%%%%%%%
%Function to calculate the probabilities a,b,gamma%
%%%%%%%%%%%%%%%%%%%%%%%%%%%%%%%%%%%%%%%%%%
function [a,b,gamma]=Prob(partition,NbTraj,k,payoff,r,DeltaT)
%partition: Table indicating in which cell is located
%          the paths at time t and t+1
%NbTraj: Number of paths
%k: Number of cells
%payoff: Vector the cash flows if the option is exercised
%r: Risk-free rate
%DeltaT
%a, b and gamma: The numbers used to calculate the probabilities
%                 to move from one cell to another

    %Initialization of a, b and gamma
    a=zeros(k,1);
    b=zeros(k,k);
    gamma=zeros(k,1);

    %Discounting factor computed once
    act=exp(-r*DeltaT);

    %All the paths and incrementing the counters
    %a, b and gamma highlighted.
    for cptTraj=1:NbTraj
        a(partition(cptTraj,2),1)=a(partition(cptTraj,2),1)+1;
        b(partition(cptTraj,1),partition(cptTraj,2))=...
            b(partition(cptTraj,1),partition(cptTraj,2))+act;
        gamma(partition(cptTraj,2),1)=gamma(partition(cptTraj,2),1)
                                        + ... act*payoff(cptTraj,1);
    end

end
%%%%%%%%%%%%%%%%%%%%%%%%%%%%%%%%%%%%%%
%End of the calculation of the probabilities %
%%%%%%%%%%%%%%%%%%%%%%%%%%%%%%%%%%%%%%
```

Table 10.23 Prices of an American call option using the Dynamic Programming Technique

T (year)	K (\$)	Call_{PDE} (\$)	$\text{Call}_{\text{SSAP}}$ (\$)
	35	8.59	8.6051
1/12	40	3.84	3.7837
	45	0.89	0.9145
	35	12.55	12.5614
4/12	40	7.87	7.8971
	45	4.26	4.3071
	35	15.29	15.2957
7/12	40	10.72	10.6878
	45	6.96	7.0526

We compare the computed results ($\text{Call}_{\text{SSAP}}$) with those obtained with another pricing method (Call_{PDE}) given in Barraquand and Martineau (1995). The results are presented in Table 10.23.

The Barraquand and Martineau method is efficient and applicable to various problems.

10.3 ASIAN OPTIONS

This example follows the work of Kemna and Vorst (1990). We assume the price of the underlying asset to follow a geometric Brownian motion:

$$S(t+\Delta t) = S(t) + rS(t)\Delta t + \sigma S(t)\Delta\widetilde{W}(t). \tag{10.47}$$

The goal is to calculate the price of Asian options on arithmetic and geometric means.

10.3.1 Asian Options on Arithmetic Mean

Consider the following value for the option on the arithmetic mean:

$$E\left[e^{-rT}\max\left(\frac{1}{I}\sum_{i=1}^{I} S(iT/I) - K, 0\right)\right]. \tag{10.48}$$

For example, when $I = 3$, we have

$$E\left[e^{-rT}\max\left(\frac{S(T/3)+S(2T/3)+S(T)}{3} - K, 0\right)\right]. \tag{10.49}$$

Compute this value using the parameter values: $S(0) = \$\,100, K = \$\,100, \sigma = 0.30, r = 0.03$, $T = 1$ year with 250 time steps. We use $N = 50\,000$ simulations and $I = 1, 2, 5, 10, 25, 50$, 125.

Using the previously discussed methods, we save the simulated values. Next, we calculate the mean and the payoff of the option as follows:

```
function Rep=ArithOptCall(I)
%Function to calculate the price of the Asian option
%on arithmetic average.
%I: Number of days used to calculate the average
%Rep: Price of the option
I=3;
```

```
%Initial parameters
 S0=100;
 r=0.03;
 sigma=0.3;
 Strike=100;
 T=1;
 NbStep=250;
 DeltaT=T/NbStep;
 NbTraj=50000;

 %Number of days used to calculate the average
 NbDaysAverage=I;

 %Number of days between two days to calculate the average
 DaysBetween = NbStep/NbDaysAverage;

 %Vector used to keep the values needed to calculate the average
 A=zeros(NbTraj,1);

 %We compute each path
 for cptTraj=1:NbTraj
    Path=GenerePaths(S0,r,sigma,1,NbStep,DeltaT);
    %For each day used to calculate the average, we keep the
    %price of the asset
    for cptStep = DaysBetween:DaysBetween:NbStep
        A(cptTraj,1)=A(cptTraj,1) + Path(1,cptStep);
    end

    %Calculation of the arithmetic average
    A(cptTraj,1)=A(cptTraj,1)/NbDaysAverage;
 end

 %Calculation of the cash flows, the average and the standard
  deviation
 Payoff=exp(-r*T)*max(A-Strike,0);
 std(Payoff)/sqrt(NbTraj)
 Rep=mean(Payoff,1);

 end

 function Rep=GenerePaths(S0,r,sigma,NbTraj,NbStep,DeltaT)
 %Function to generate the paths.
 %S0: Initial price of the asset
 %r: Risk-free rate
 %sigma: Volatility
 %NbTraj: Number of simulated paths
 %NbStep: Number of time steps per paths
 %DeltaT: Delta T

 NuT = (r - sigma*sigma/2)*DeltaT;
 SqDelta = sqrt(DeltaT);
 DeltaW = SqDelta*randn(NbTraj, NbStep);
 Increments = NuT + sigma*DeltaW;
```

```
LogPaths = cumsum(cat(2,log(S0)*ones(NbTraj,1) , Increments) , 2);
Rep = exp(LogPaths);

end
```

Table 10.24 presents the simulations results.

10.3.2 Asian Options on Geometric Mean

Consider the following value for the option on the geometric mean:

$$E\left[e^{-rT}\max\left(\left(\prod_{i=1}^{I} S(iT/I)\right)^{1/I} - K, 0\right)\right]. \tag{10.50}$$

For example, when $I = 3$, we have

$$E[e^{-rT}\max((S(T/3)S(2T/3)S(T))^{1/3} - K, 0)]. \tag{10.51}$$

Calculate the value of the option using as parameter values: $S(0) = \$\ 100$, $K = \$\ 100$, $\sigma = 0.30$, $r = 0.03$, $T = 1$ year and 250 time steps. We run $N = 50\,000$ simulations and $I = 1, 2, 5, 10, 25, 50, 125$.

In this case, we use the same program as for the arithmetic mean above except that we need to insert a loop to calculate the geometric mean.

```
function Rep=GeomOptCall
%Function to calculate the price of an Asian option on
 geometric average.
%I: Number of days used to calculate the average
I=5;
%Rep: Price of the option

%Initial parameters
S0=100;
r=0.03;
sigma=0.3;
Strike=100;
T=1;
NbStep=250;
DeltaT=T/NbStep;
NbTraj=50000;

%Number of days used in the average calculation
NbDaysAverage=I;

%Number of days between two dates to calculate the average
DaysBetween = NbStep/NbDaysAverage;

%Vector used to keep the values needed to calculate the average
G=ones(NbTraj,1);

%We calculate each path
for cptTraj=1:NbTraj
```

```
    Path=GeneratePaths(S0,r,sigma,1,NbStep,DeltaT);

    %For each day used to calculate the average, we keep the
     asset price.
    for cptStep = DaysBetween:DaysBetween:NbStep
        G(cptTraj,1)=G(cptTraj,1)*Path(1,cptStep);
    end

    %Calculation of the geometric average
    G(cptTraj,1)=G(cptTraj,1)^(1/NbDaysAverage);
end

%Calculation of the cash flows, the average and the standard
 deviation
Payoff=exp(-r*T)*max(G-Strike,0);
std(Payoff)/sqrt(NbTraj)
Rep=mean(Payoff,1);

end

function Rep=GeneratePaths(S0,r,sigma,NbTraj,NbStep,DeltaT)
%Function generating the paths.
%S0: Initial price of the asset
%r: Risk-free rate
%sigma: Volatility
%NbTraj: Number of simulated paths
%NbStep: Number of time steps per path
%DeltaT: Delta T

NuT = (r - sigma*sigma/2)*DeltaT;
SqDelta = sqrt(DeltaT);
DeltaW = SqDelta*randn(NbTraj, NbStep);
Increments = NuT + sigma*DeltaW;
LogPaths = cumsum(cat(2,log(S0)*ones(NbTraj,1) , Increments) , 2);
Rep = exp(LogPaths);

end
```

Table 10.24 Prices of Asian call options

	Arithmetic ($)		Geometric ($)	
I	Estimation	Error	Estimation	Error
1	13.1329	0.0964	13.1329	0.0964
2	10.3149	0.0741	9.9840	0.0724
5	8.5887	0.0602	8.1774	0.0578
10	8.0379	0.0569	7.6164	0.0543
25	7.7484	0.0542	7.3241	0.0516
50	7.5742	0.0532	7.1500	0.0505
125	7.4971	0.0529	7.0780	0.0501

The results are also summarized in Table 10.24 where the errors are obtained by dividing the standard deviation by the square root of the number of simulations.

We note that the geometric mean is lower than the arithmetic mean, which was expected.

10.4 BARRIER OPTIONS

This example stems from El Babsiri and Noel (1998). We assume that the price of the asset follows a geometric Brownian process:

$$S(t + \Delta t) = S(t) + rS(t)\Delta t + \sigma S(t)\Delta \widetilde{W}(t). \tag{10.52}$$

The goal is to calculate the prices of barrier options. There are several types of barrier options. Here, we focus on *knock-in* options: *Up-And-In* and *Down-And-In* call options. The payoff of a *Down-And-In* call option is the following

$$\begin{array}{rl} \max(S(T) - K, 0) & \text{if } \min_{t\in[0,T]} S(t) < H \\ 0 & \text{if } \min_{t\in[0,T]} S(t) > H \end{array} \tag{10.53}$$

and for an *Up-And-In* call option

$$\begin{array}{rl} \max(S(T) - K, 0) & \text{if } \max_{t\in[0,T]} S(t) > H \\ 0 & \text{if } \max_{t\in[0,T]} S(t) < H \end{array}, \tag{10.54}$$

where H is the barrier and K the exercise price. To calculate the payoff of these options, we need to know $S(T)$ and the minimum or the maximum of $S(t)$. It is possible to generate $\ln(S(T)/S(0))$ since we know that it has a normal distribution $N(rT, \sigma\sqrt{T})$. From El Babsiri and Noel (1998), one can show that

$$\text{Prob}\left(\min_{t\in[0,T]} \ln\left(\frac{S(t)}{S(0)}\right) \le y \;\middle|\; \ln\left(\frac{S(T)}{S(0)}\right) = x\right) = e^{\frac{2y(x-y)}{\sigma^2 T}}, \tag{10.55}$$

where $y \le x$ and $y \le 0$. If we consider the conditional distribution function F_Y of the minimum y of $\ln(\frac{S(T)}{S(0)})$, then we know that $F_Y(y)$ follows a uniform distribution over the interval [0, 1]. Hence, denoting $u = F_Y(y)$ and inverting this equation, we obtain

$$y = \frac{x - \sqrt{x^2 - 2\sigma^2 T \ln(u)}}{2}. \tag{10.56}$$

Note that y is non-positive since u is drawn from a uniform distribution between 0 and 1.

To perform the simulation of a *Down-And-In* barrier option, we simulate $\ln(S(T)/S(0))$ and a uniform random variable u. Then we find the minimum y and obtain the payoff of the option. Here is the MATLAB program for the method.

```
function DownAndInCall
%Function to calculate the value of an exotic call option Down
 And In.
```

```
S0=100;
Strike = 100;
Barrier = 90;
InterestRate = 0.05;
Dividend = 0.02;
T = 1;
sigma = 0.30;
NbTraj = 1000000;
Mu = InterestRate-Dividend;

%Simulation of the final value of the paths.
Paths = exp(log(S0)+(Mu-sigma*sigma/2)*T+ ...
                      randn(NbTraj,1)*sigma*sqrt(T));

%Calculation of the value x in the article of El Babsiri and Noel.
x=log(Paths/S0);

%Simulation of the minimum of the paths
Uniform = rand(NbTraj,1);
Minimum=(x-sqrt(x.*x-2*sigma^2*T*log(Uniform)))/2;

%Calculation of the payoffs at the maturity
PayoffPV=exp(-InterestRate*T)*max(Paths-Strike,0).* ...
             (Minimum<log(Barrier/S0));

%Presentation of the mean and the standard deviation of the
 payoffs.
disp('Estimation');
disp(mean(PayoffPV,1));
disp('Error');
disp(std(PayoffPV)/sqrt(NbTraj));
end
```

For an *Up-And-In* option, we have

$$\text{Prob}\left(\max_{t\in[0,T]} \ln\left(\frac{S(t)}{S(0)}\right) \leq y \quad | \quad \ln\left(\frac{S_T}{S(0)}\right) = x\right) = 1 - e^{\frac{2y(x-y)}{\sigma^2 T}} \tag{10.57}$$

and also

$$y = \frac{x + \sqrt{x^2 - 2\sigma^2 T \ln(1-u)}}{2}. \tag{10.58}$$

In this case, $y \geq x$ and $y \geq 0$. The program is almost the same as in the *Down-And-In* option case. Just like El Babsiri and Noel, we use the following parameter values $S(0) = \$\ 100$, $K = \$\ 100$, $r = 0.05$, dividend $= 0.02$, $NbTraj = 1000000$, and $T = 1$. Table 10.25 presents the results obtained from the program.

Table 10.25 Simulated prices of the barrier options

	Down-And-In ($H = 90$) ($)		*Up-And-In* ($H = 110$) ($)	
σ	Estimation	Error	Estimation	Error
0.10	0.0725	0.0007	4.7942	0.0073
0.15	0.6081	0.0028	7.0977	0.0105
0.20	1.6384	0.0055	9.1173	0.0139
0.25	2.9936	0.0086	11.1010	0.0176
0.30	4.4904	0.0119	12.9615	0.0215

10.5 ESTIMATION METHODS FOR THE SENSITIVITY COEFFICIENTS OR GREEKS

In this section, we present some methods to estimate the option sensitivity coefficients. Several procedures can be used. We discuss the pathwise derivative estimates method, the likelihood ratio method and the retrieval of volatility method.

A simple method consists of calculating the differential numerically over discrete intervals. Let's consider a security or a derivative product, $\widetilde{P}$, depending on the parameter X. We have

$$\begin{aligned}\frac{d\widetilde{P}}{dX} &\approx \lim_{\Delta X \to 0} \frac{\Delta \widetilde{P}}{\Delta X} \\ &= \lim_{\Delta X \to 0} \frac{\widetilde{P}(X+\Delta X) - \widetilde{P}(X)}{\Delta X}.\end{aligned} \tag{10.59}$$

There are some problems with this method. First, to obtain more precise results, we need to use small increments ΔX. However, a very small ΔX will lead to approximation errors and the results will be erroneous. Second, we could use a larger ΔX and simulate several paths to calculate the coefficient and then average the obtained results. It has been shown that with this method the estimator is biased. We can run as many simulations as possible, and we will always experience bias. That's why other techniques have been developed to mitigate these problems.

10.5.1 Pathwise Derivative Estimates

The estimation technique for sensitivity coefficients has been introduced, for instance by Broadie and Glasserman in 1996. It is based on the structure of the derivative of the payoff function. Let $\widetilde{P}$ be this payoff function (discounted payoff). We know that the price P of an option is given by

$$P = E\left[\widetilde{P}\right]. \tag{10.60}$$

Assuming the derivative of an expectation is equivalent to the expectation of the derivative, we can calculate

$$\frac{dP}{dX} = \frac{dE\left[\widetilde{P}\right]}{dX} \approx E\left[\frac{d\widetilde{P}}{dX}\right]. \tag{10.61}$$

For simplicity, we assume the necessary and sufficient conditions to be satisfied for this equality to hold. Therefore, we will only posit that if the payoff function $\widetilde{P}$ is continuous with respect to the path $X(t)$ then this equality holds.

From this equation, we see that we can evaluate the derivative dP/dX using an expectation. We start by calculating the derivative $d\widetilde{P}/dX$, then simulate the underlying and finally calculate the expectation. Example 5.1 illustrates the method.

Example 5.1 We use the pathwise derivative estimates method to calculate the sensitivity coefficient DELTA of a call option. In this case, we have

$$\widetilde{P} = e^{-rT} \max(0, S(T) - K). \tag{10.62}$$

Hence, we calculate

$$\frac{d\widetilde{P}}{dS(0)} = e^{-rT} 1_{\{S(T) \geq K\}} \frac{S(T)}{S(0)} \tag{10.63}$$

and we can estimate DELTA (Δ) using Monte Carlo simulation techniques by simulating the underlying asset S (and possibly the interest rate too) and averaging the obtained results.

We present some estimators for a relatively simple payoff function. In the case of an Asian call option for which the average of the prices is observed over the last m days

$$\bar{S} = \frac{1}{m} \sum_{i=1}^{m} S(t_i) = \frac{1}{m} \sum_{i=1}^{m} S(T - i\Delta t), \tag{10.64}$$

$$\widetilde{P} = e^{-rT} \max(0, \bar{S} - K) \tag{10.65}$$

and assuming the underlying asset price to be log-normally distributed:

$$S(T) = S(0)e^{(r-\sigma^2/2)T + \sigma\sqrt{T}Z}, \tag{10.66}$$

then we obtain the following estimators:

$$\Delta = \frac{dP}{dS} = e^{-rT} 1_{\{\bar{S} \geq K\}} \frac{\bar{S}}{S(0)}, \tag{10.67}$$

$$\mathcal{V} = \frac{dP}{d\sigma} = e^{-rT} 1_{\{\bar{S} \geq K\}} \frac{1}{m\sigma} \sum_{i=1}^{m} S(t_i)(\log(S(t_i)/S(0)) - (r - \delta + \sigma^2/2)t_i), \tag{10.68}$$

$$\Gamma = \frac{d^2P}{dS^2} = e^{-rT} \left(\frac{K}{S(0)}\right)^2 mg(S_{m-1}, w(t_m), \Delta t), \tag{10.69}$$

$$\rho = \frac{dP}{dr} = 1_{\{\bar{S} \geq K\}} e^{-rT} \left(\frac{1}{m} \sum_{i=1}^{m} S(t_i)t_i - T \max(\bar{S} - K, 0)\right), \tag{10.70}$$

where

$$w(t_m) = m(K - \bar{S}) + S(t_m), \tag{10.71}$$

$$g(u, v, t) = 1_{\{v \geq 0\}} \frac{n(d(u, v, t))}{v\sigma\sqrt{t}}, \tag{10.72}$$

$$d(u, v, t) = \frac{\log(v/u) - (r - \delta - \sigma^2/2)t}{\sigma\sqrt{t}}, \tag{10.73}$$

where $n(.)$ is the probability density function of the normal distribution, u and v are dummy variables, and δ is the dividend yield.

The following program is used to calculate the sensitivity coefficients DELTA and GAMMA of an Asian option (arithmetic mean) with the pathwise derivative estimates technique.

```
function rep = AsiPath

r=0.1;          %Risk-free rate
k=100;          %Strike price
sigma=0.25;     %Stock return volatility
div=0.03;       %Dividend yield = delta
T=0.2;          %Maturity (years)
S0=90;          %Stock initial value

%DELTA and GAMMA estimations for an Asian arithmetic option
%with pathwise derivatives estimates

NStep = floor(T*365.25); %Number of time step
DeltaT = 1/365.25;        %Length of a step
NTraj = 100000;          %Number of paths
m = 30; %Number of days used to calculate the arithmetic average
Si = zeros(2*NTraj,m);% Storage of the values
SAve = zeros(2*NTraj,1);% Average values

%Parameters initialization
dW = zeros(2*NTraj,1);
S = S0*ones(2*NTraj,1);
dW=sqrt(DeltaT)*randn(NTraj,NStep);
dW=cat(1,dW,-dW);
%End of parameters initialization

%Storing the simulation values
j=1;
   for i=1:NStep
       S = S + S.*((r-div)*DeltaT + sigma*dW(:,i));
       if i > NStep - m
           Si(:,j) = S;
           j=j+1;
       end
   end
%End of Storing the simulation values

%Computing the average value
SAve = sum(Si,2)/m;

%Estimation of DELTA
EstimDel = exp(-r*T)*(SAve>=k).*SAve/S0;

Del = sum(EstimDel)/(2*NTraj);
DelError = sqrt((EstimDel -Del)'*(EstimDel -
Del)/(2*NTraj))/sqrt(NTraj);
```

```
%Printing the result for DELTA
fprintf('\n Option''s DELTA: %f', Del);
fprintf('\n Standard error: %f', DelError);
%End of Estimation of DELTA

%Estimation of GAMMA
d = zeros(2*NTraj,1);
g = zeros(2*NTraj,1);
w = m*(k - SAve) + Si(:,m);
for i=1:2*NTraj
   if (w(i,1)>0)
        d(i,1) =(log(w(i,1)/Si(i,m-1))-(r-div-0.5*sigma^2)
                   *DeltaT)/...
                        (sigma*sqrt(DeltaT));
        g(i,1) = normpdf(d(i,1))/(w(i,1)*sigma*sqrt(DeltaT));
   end
end
EstimGam = exp(-r*T)*(k/S0)^2*m*g;

Gam = sum(EstimGam)/(2*NTraj);
GamError = sqrt((EstimGam -Gam)'*(EstimGam -Gam)/(2*NTraj))/
           sqrt(NTraj);

% Printing the result for GAMMA
fprintf('\n Option''s GAMMA: %f', Gam);
fprintf('\n Standard error: %f', GamError);
%End of Estimation of GAMMA

rep = 1;
```

We run this MATLAB program by changing the initial stock price and keeping the other parameter values constant. The simulations' results are given in Table 10.26.

10.5.2 Likelihood Ratio Method

This estimation method of the sensitivity coefficients is based on the structure of the probability density function. We know that the price of an option is given by the expectation of its future cash flows $\widetilde{P}$. We therefore have the following formula:

$$P = E\left[\widetilde{P}\right] = \int_0^\infty \widetilde{P}(s) f(s) ds, \tag{10.74}$$

Table 10.26 Estimation of DELTA and GAMMA of an Asian option

Greeks	$S(0) = \$ 90$	Error (\$)	$S(0) = \$ 100$	Error (\$)	$S(0) = \$ 110$	Error (\$)
Δ	0.174	0.0013	0.561	0.0017	0.867	0.0012
Γ	0.029	0.0015	0.040	0.0016	0.020	0.0010

where $f(s)$ is the probability density function of the variable $S(T)$. Assuming that the function $\widetilde{P}$ does not depend on the parameter X, we have

$$\begin{aligned}\frac{dP}{dX} &= \frac{d\int_0^\infty \widetilde{P}(s)f(s)ds}{dX}\\ &\approx \int_0^\infty \widetilde{P}(s)\frac{df(s)}{dX}ds\\ &= \int_0^\infty \widetilde{P}(s)\frac{df(s)}{dX}\frac{f(s)}{f(s)}ds\\ &= \int_0^\infty \widetilde{P}(s)\frac{d\log f(s)}{dX}f(s)ds\\ &= E\left[\widetilde{P}(S(T))\frac{d\log f(s)}{dX}\Big|_{S(T)}\right].\end{aligned} \tag{10.75}$$

Note that we have interchanged the differential with the integral, but we will not discuss further the complex details associated with this operation. We only assert that it can be done when the probability density function f is smooth enough. In general, if the function is continuous, we can calculate the likelihood ratio estimator using this approach. Let's now illustrate the approach with an application case on European call options. From

$$S(T) = S(0)e^{(r-\sigma^2/2)T+\sigma\sqrt{T}Z}, \tag{10.76}$$

we deduce that $S(T)$ is log-normally distributed and that

$$f(x) = \frac{1}{x\sigma\sqrt{T}}n(d(x)), \tag{10.77}$$

where

$$n(z) = \frac{1}{\sqrt{2\pi}}e^{-z^2/2} \tag{10.78}$$

$$d(x) = \frac{\ln(x/S(0)) - (r-\sigma^2/2)T}{\sigma\sqrt{T}}. \tag{10.79}$$

Assume that we use the technique for a European call option. The payoff function is $\widetilde{P} = e^{-rT}\max(S(T)-K,0)$. We then have

$$\begin{aligned}\frac{dP}{dS(0)} &= E\left[e^{-rT}\max(S(T)-K,0)\frac{d\log(f(x))}{dS(0)}|_{S(T)}\right]\\ &= E\left[e^{-rT}\max(S(T)-K,0)\frac{\log\left(\frac{S(T)}{S(0)}\right)-(r-\delta-\sigma^2/2)T}{S(0)\sigma^2T}\right].\end{aligned} \tag{10.80}$$

We found an estimator for the DELTA of a European call option. An interesting remark here is that, unlike the re-simulation technique, this is an unbiased estimator. For a European call option, we find the following estimators:

$$\Delta = E\left[e^{-rT}\max(S(T)-K,0)\frac{1}{S(0)\sigma^2 T}(\log(S(T)/S(0)) - (r-\delta-\sigma^2/2)T)\right], \quad (10.81)$$

$$\mathcal{V} = E\left[e^{-rT}\max(S(T)-K,0)\left(-d(S(T))\frac{\partial d(S(T))}{\partial \sigma} - \frac{1}{\sigma}\right)\right], \quad (10.82)$$

$$\Gamma = E\left[e^{-rT}\max(S(T)-K,0)\frac{d(S(T))^2 - d(S(T))\sigma\sqrt{T} - 1}{S(0)^2\sigma^2 T}\right], \quad (10.83)$$

$$\rho = E\left[e^{-rT}\max(S(T)-K,0)\left(-T + \frac{d(S(T))\sqrt{T}}{\sigma}\right)\right]. \quad (10.84)$$

It is possible to find estimators for other options with the likelihood ratio method. However, the estimators obtained with the method converge slowly. Moreover, some of these estimators are difficult to calculate. We would therefore like to have an easy and practical method that can be used for most types of options.

Here is a MATLAB program to compute the DELTA and GAMMA of a European option using the likelihood ratio method.

```
function rep = EurLik

r=0.1;        %Risk-free rate
k=100;        %Strike price
sigma=0.25;   %Stock return volatility
delta=0.03;   %Dividend yield
T=0.2;        %Maturity
S0=110;       %Initial stock price

NStep = floor(T*365.25);  %Number of time step
Delta = 1/365.25;         %Length of a step
NTraj = 100000;           %Number of paths

%Simulation of paths
dW = zeros(2*NTraj,1);
S = S0*ones(2*NTraj,1);
Temp =zeros(NTraj,1); dW = cat(1,Temp, -Temp);

for i=1:NStep
   Temp = sqrt(Delta)*randn(NTraj,1);
   dW = cat(1,Temp,-Temp);
   S = S + S.*((r-delta)*Delta + sigma*dW);
end
%End of Simulation of paths

%Computation of the values used in the estimators formulae
d = (log(S/S0) - (r - delta - 0.5*sigma^2)*T)/(sigma*sqrt(T));
ddsig= (log(S0) - log(S) + (r - delta +0.5*sigma^2)*T)/(sigma^2
*sqrt(T));
```

```
%Estimation of DELTA
EstimDel = exp(-r*T)*max(S-k,0).*1/(S0*sigma^2*T).*(log(S/S0) -...
             (r -delta - 0.5*sigma^2)*T);

Del = sum(EstimDel)/(2*NTraj);
DelError = sqrt((EstimDel -Del)'*(EstimDel -Del)/(2*NTraj))/
           sqrt(NTraj);

%Printing the result for DELTA
fprintf('\n DELTA of the option: %f', Del);
fprintf('\n Standard error: %f', DelError);
%End of Estimation of DELTA


%Estimation of GAMMA
EstimGam = exp(-r*T)*max(S-k,0).*(d.*d - d*sigma*sqrt(T) -1)/...
            (S0^2*sigma^2*T);

Gam = sum(EstimGam)/(2*NTraj);
GamError = sqrt((EstimGam -Gam)'*(EstimGam -Gam)/(2*NTraj))/
           sqrt(NTraj);

%Printing the result for GAMMA
fprintf('\n GAMMA of the option: %f', Gam);
fprintf('\n Standard error: %f', GamError);
%End of Estimation of GAMMA

rep = 1;
```

We run this program by changing the initial stock price and the simulation results are shown in Table 10.27.

10.5.3 Retrieval of Volatility Method

This method suggested by Cvitanic, Goukassian and Zapatero (2002) allows us to find the volatility of an entire portfolio without having to determine the volatility of all individual

Table 10.27 Estimation of DELTA and GAMMA for a European option

Greeks	$S(0) = \$\ 90$	Error (\$)	$S(0) = \$\ 100$	Error (\$)	$S(0) = \$\ 110$	Error (\$)
Δ						
Exact	0.222		0.568		0.844	
Likelihood	0.221	0.0025	0.564	0.0041	0.848	0.0055
Γ						
Exact	0.030		0.035		0.019	
Likelihood	0.029	0.0005	0.034	0.0007	0.019	0.0008

assets composing the portfolio. As usual, we assume that $S(t)$ satisfies the equation

$$\frac{dS(t)}{S(t)} = r(t)dt + \sigma(t)d\widetilde{W}(t) \tag{10.85}$$

and the risk-free asset satisfies the equation

$$dB(t) = B(t)r(t)dt. \tag{10.86}$$

We start by assuming that the market uncertainty is captured by a single Brownian motion $d\widetilde{W}(t)$. If $\widetilde{P}(t)$ is the payoff function at time t (non-discounted amounts), then the value of the portfolio $P(t)$ is given by

$$P(t) = E_t\left[e^{-\int_t^T r(u)du}\widetilde{P}(T)\right]. \tag{10.87}$$

The value of the portfolio follows a stochastic differential equation of the form

$$dP(t) = \alpha(t)dt + \nu(t)d\widetilde{W}(t), \tag{10.88}$$

where $\nu(t)$ is an adapted process. In discrete time, we obtain

$$\Delta P(t) = \alpha(t)\Delta t + \nu(t)\Delta\widetilde{W}(t). \tag{10.89}$$

Hence, we have

$$\begin{aligned} E[\Delta P(t) - \alpha(t)\Delta t]^2 &= E\left[\nu(t)\Delta\widetilde{W}(t)\right]^2 \\ &\approx E\left[\int_t^{t+\Delta t} \nu(t)d\widetilde{W}(t)\right]^2 \\ &= \int_t^{t+\Delta t} \nu(u)^2 du \\ &= \nu(t)^2\Delta t, \end{aligned} \tag{10.90}$$

where the second line is obtained from the first line using the Ito isometry. From these calculations, we can deduce the following expression for $\nu(t)$

$$\begin{aligned} \nu(t) &= \left(\lim_{\Delta t\to 0} E\left[\frac{(\Delta P(t) - \alpha(t)\Delta t)^2}{\Delta t}\right]\right)^{1/2} \\ &= \left(\lim_{\Delta t\to 0} E\left[\frac{(\Delta P(t))^2}{\Delta t}\right]\right)^{1/2}. \end{aligned} \tag{10.91}$$

The term $\alpha(t)\Delta t$ disappears since its square value is negligible. A second approach allows us to find an expression for $\nu(t)$ which is more efficient for simulation purposes.

$$\begin{aligned} E[\Delta P(t)\Delta\widetilde{W}(t)] &= E[(\Delta P(t) - \alpha(t)\Delta t)\Delta\widetilde{W}(t)] \\ &= E\left[\int_t^{t+\Delta t} \nu(u)du\right] \\ &\approx \nu(t)\Delta t. \end{aligned} \tag{10.92}$$

Thus

$$\nu(t) = \lim_{\Delta t\to 0} E\left[\frac{\Delta P(t)\Delta\widetilde{W}(t)}{\Delta t}\right]. \tag{10.93}$$

We can now write an algorithm to calculate the volatility of a portfolio.

Step 1 Calculate $P(t)$ using Monte Carlo simulations.
Step 2 Generate $\Delta\widetilde{W}(t)^i, i = 1, \ldots, NbTraj$ where *NbTraj* is the number of simulations.
Step 3 Move one step ahead for all parameters, i.e. calculate

$$S(t + \Delta t)^i = S(t)(1 + r(t)\Delta t + \sigma(t)\Delta\widetilde{W}(t)^i) \tag{10.94}$$

and the other stochastic parameters.
Step 4 Evaluate $P(t + \Delta t)^i$ using Monte Carlo simulations (M simulations) with starting value $S(t + \Delta t)^i$.
Step 5 Calculate

$$\nu(t) = \frac{1}{NbTraj} \sum_{i=1}^{NbTraj} \frac{(P(t + \Delta t)^i - P(t))\Delta\widetilde{W}(t)^i}{\Delta t}. \tag{10.95}$$

With this technique, it is possible to dynamically hedge our position. We only need to short a number

$$\frac{\nu(t)}{\sigma(t)S(t)} \tag{10.96}$$

of stocks S to hedge the portfolio. Indeed, we have

$$\frac{\nu(t)}{\sigma(t)S(t)} dS(t) = \frac{\nu(t)r(t)}{\sigma(t)} dt + \nu(t)d\widetilde{W}(t) \tag{10.97}$$

and hence we can eliminate the portfolio risk by shorting this number of stocks (because the stochastic parameters offset each other).

Here is a MATLAB program to apply the retrieval of volatility method. We start by writing the function used to calculate the value of the call option.

```
function rep=PriceCall(T,NbTraj,NbStep,S,r,sigma, DeltaT)
%Simple function to calculate the value of an European call option.
%T: Maturity
%NbTraj: Number paths to simulate
%NbStep: Number of time steps by path
%S: Initial price of the stock
%r: Risk-free interest rate
%sigma: Volatility of the underlying stock price
%DeltaT: Time step

%Initial parameters
K=90;
S = S*ones(2*NbTraj,1);
r = r*ones(2*NbTraj,1);
sigma = sigma*ones(2*NbTraj,1);

%Loop to simulate the paths at each time step
for i=1:NbStep
    Temp = sqrt(DeltaT)*randn(NbTraj,1);
    dW = cat(1,Temp,-Temp);
    S = S + S.*(r*DeltaT+sigma.*dW);
```

```
    r = r + 0.0824*(0.06-r)*DeltaT - 0.0364*sqrt(r).*dW;
    sigma = sigma + 0.695*(0.1-sigma)*DeltaT + 0.21*dW;
end

%Calculation of the option price
Price = exp(-r*DeltaT*NbStep).*max(S - K,0);
rep=mean(Price,1);

end
```

We can then write the rest of the program.

```
function rep=Retrieval
%Function to retrieve the volatility of a financial instrument
%based on the method proposed by Cvitanic et al.
%Here, the financial instrument is a call option.

%Initial parameters
S0 = 100;
Sig0 = 0.1;
R0 = 0.06;
T = 0.3;
NbTraj=10000;
NbStep=100;
NbTrajSim2=100; %Value of M in the theory
DeltaT=T/NbStep;

%Calculation of the price of the option at time t=0.
PriceZero=PriceCall(T,NbTraj,NbStep,S0,R0,Sig0,DeltaT);

%Simulation of the first time step to find the values of the option
%at time t=DeltaT
Temp=sqrt(DeltaT)*randn(NbTraj,1);
dW1 = cat(1,Temp,-Temp);
SOne = S0 + S0.*(R0*DeltaT+Sig0.*dW1);
rOne = R0 + 0.0824*(0.06 - R0)*DeltaT - 0.0364*sqrt(R0).*dW1;
sigmaOne = Sig0 + 0.695*(0.1 - Sig0)*DeltaT + 0.21*dW1;

%Vector to store the option prices at time t=DeltaT
PriceOne=zeros(2*NbTraj,1);

%Calculation of the prices at time t=DeltaT
for j=1:2*NbTraj
   PriceOne(j,1)=PriceCall(T-DeltaT,NbTrajSim2,
                 NbStep-1,SOne(j,1),...
                         rOne(j,1),sigmaOne(j,1),DeltaT);
end

%Calculation of the volatility using the method presented.
rep=mean((PriceOne-PriceZero).*dW1,1)/(DeltaT);

end
```

Table 10.28 DELTA coefficient calculated using the retrieval of volatility method (RVM)

	$T = 0.1$ year		$T = 0.3$ year		$T = 0.5$ year	
	DELTA	Price ($)	DELTA	Price ($)	DELTA	Price ($)
$K = \$\,90$						
BS	0.9998	10.5385	0.9887	11.6272	0.9744	12.7303
RVM	0.9918	10.5389	1.0053	11.6282	0.9755	12.7301
$K = \$\,100$						
BS	0.5814	1.5794	0.6391	3.1731	0.6771	4.5027
RVM	0.5894	1.5736	0.6358	3.1781	0.6774	4.4940
$K = \$\,110$						
BS	0.0025	0.0023	0.0831	0.2035	0.1872	0.7022
RVM	0.0025	0.0024	0.0831	0.1985	0.1868	0.7050

For a call option, using Black and Scholes, we have:

$$d\text{Call} = \left(\frac{\partial \text{Call}}{\partial t} + \frac{\partial \text{Call}}{\partial S} Sr + \frac{1}{2}\frac{\partial^2 \text{Call}}{\partial S^2} S^2\sigma^2\right) dt + \frac{\partial \text{Call}}{\partial S} S\sigma d\widetilde{W}. \tag{10.98}$$

Hence, $\frac{\nu}{S\sigma} = \frac{\partial \text{Call}}{\partial S}$ is the DELTA of the call option. We compare the simulations results with analytical values. Table 10.28 compares the values obtained using the Black and Scholes formula (BS) and the results obtained using the retrieval of volatility method (RVM) described above in a constant interest rate and volatility regime.

The advantage of this technique is that it is always applicable no matter what the number of stochastic parameters. For example, we run simulations with several stochastic variables. Table 10.29 exhibits the simulations' results of the retrieval of volatility method (RVM) with stochastic interest rate and stochastic volatility.

Multi-factors

The retrieval of volatility method can also be applied when there are two sources of uncertainty in the economy. Assume we have

$$dS_i(t) = S_i(t)(r(t)dt + \sigma_{i1}(t)d\widetilde{W}_1(t) + \sigma_{i2}(t)d\widetilde{W}_2(t)), \tag{10.99}$$

Table 10.29 DELTA coefficient with stochastic interest rate and stochastic volatility

	$T = 0.1$ year		$T = 0.3$ year		$T = 0.5$ year	
	DELTA	Price ($)	DELTA	Price ($)	DELTA	Price ($)
$K = \$\,90$						
RVM	1.0049	10.5325	0.9626	11.6146	0.9548	12.6831
$K = \$\,100$						
RVM	0.7101	1.5501	0.7936	3.1465	0.8230	4.5295
$K = \$\,110$						
RVM	0.0693	0.0787	0.3336	0.8989	0.5006	1.9349

for $i = 1, 2$. Thus, the portfolio P composed of many financial instruments have the following process

$$dP(t) = P(t)(r(t)dt + \nu_1(t)d\widetilde{W}_1(t) + \nu_2(t)d\widetilde{W}_2(t)). \tag{10.100}$$

We can estimate

$$\nu_i(t) = \frac{1}{N}\sum_{j=1}^{N}\frac{(P(t+\Delta t)^j - P(t))\Delta\widetilde{W}_i(t)^j}{\Delta t} \tag{10.101}$$

and, to replicate the dynamic of our portfolio, we need to invest $-M_1\$$ in the first asset and $-M_2\$$ in the second asset, where

$$\begin{pmatrix} M_1 \\ M_2 \end{pmatrix} = \begin{pmatrix} \sigma_{11}(t) & \sigma_{12}(t) \\ \sigma_{21}(t) & \sigma_{22}(t) \end{pmatrix}^{-1} \begin{pmatrix} \nu_1(t) \\ \nu_2(t) \end{pmatrix}. \tag{10.102}$$

Example 5.2 For example, if we use this method with two underlying assets and the following parameter values: $S_1(0) = S_2(0) = \$\ 100$, $K = \$\ 90$, $T = 0.1$, $r = 0.06$, $\sigma_{11}(0) = 0.1$, $\sigma_{12}(0) = 0.2$, $\sigma_{21}(0) = 0.3$ and $\sigma_{22}(0) = 0.1$, we find the approximation

$$\nu = \begin{pmatrix} 18.5289 \\ 14.1397 \end{pmatrix}. \tag{10.103}$$

We then have

$$\begin{pmatrix} M_1 \\ M_2 \end{pmatrix} = \begin{pmatrix} 19.50 \\ 82.89 \end{pmatrix}. \tag{10.104}$$

So we need to short 0.1950 stock S_1 and 0.8289 stock S_2 to hedge our position.

Notes and Complementary Readings

To complement the topics covered in this chapter, the reader will find the following books useful: Clewlow and Strickland (1998), Glasserman (2003), Jäckel (2002), Tavella (2002).

Regarding the classics, see Boyle (1977) for the pricing of European options using Monte Carlo simulations and Barraquand (1995) for the quadratic resampling.

The articles by Boyle, Broadie and Glasserman (1997) and Fu, Laprise, Madan, Su and Wu (2001) provide good summaries of Monte Carlo simulation techniques.

For simulation techniques developed to price American options, see Broadie and Detemple (1996) for a general overview, Barraquand and Martineau (1995) for the dynamic programming with Stratified States Aggregation technique, Longstaff and Schwartz (2001) for the Least-Squares Method.

For numerical evaluation methods of Asian options with control variables, see Kemna and Vorst (1990), and for barrier options with extreme values simulation technique, see El Babsiri and Noel (1998). For treatments on exotic options, see Jarrow (1995), Clewlow and Strickland (1997a), Zhang (1998).

To estimate options sensitivity coefficients (or the Greeks), see Broadie and Glasserman (1996) and the retrieval of volatility method (RVM) of Cvitanic, Goukassian and Zapatero (2002).

For references on volatility models, the reader can consult the articles by Poon and Granger (2003, 2005) and the books by Gatheral (2006), Rebonato (2004), Poon (2005) and Javaheri (2005).

11

Term Structure of Interest Rates and Interest Rate Derivatives

To compute the present value of cash flows, one requires interest rates. However, interest rates are far from being constant, which makes them very difficult to analyze. In the last decades, we have witnessed the development of many models that depict the evolution of interest rates in financial markets. Generally, the curve representing the evolution of interest rates obtained from zero coupon government bonds with different maturities constitutes what we call the term structure of interest rates. An interest rate derivative is a contingent claim having as underlyings the interest rates or different assets whose prices depend principally on interest rates.

Term structure of interest rates and interest rate derivatives' models can be classified into two categories: arbitrage-free models and general equilibrium models. In this chapter, we present some main classical interest rate models as well as their uses in the valuation of bonds and interest rate derivatives. We begin by first presenting the general modeling approach for the term structure of interest rates as of Vasicek (1977), then we review the general equilibrium approach of Cox, Ingersoll and Ross (1985b) and the affine model proposed by Duffie and Kan (1997). Market models of Heath, Jarrow and Morton (1992) and Brace, Gatarek and Musiela (1997) are also presented. These models are typical of those used for interest rates modeling in continuous time.

Since the mathematical complexity and the tediousness of the derivation of the models presented here will take us away from the objective of this chapter, which consists merely of providing the economics and analytical approaches of the topics covered, we will skip most details of the derivations of the results. The interested reader can consult the list of references provided at the end of the chapter.

In providing a useful framework for pricing bonds and interest rate derivatives, when necessary we make the link between the real world probability and the risk-neutral pricing by means of the market price of risk discussed in the previous chapter.

Since the market models are popular among practitioners, we spend more time on these models for which we propose more detailed MATLAB® programs. We must point out that the models summarized in this chapter are far from being exhaustive, and the reader looking for more breadth and depth could consult the references given at the end of the chapter.

11.1 GENERAL APPROACH AND THE VASICEK (1977) MODEL

11.1.1 General Formulation

Let $P(t, T)$ be the value at t of a bond paying \$1 at time T, that is $P(T, T) = 1$.

Definition 1.1 *The yield to maturity R(t, T) of the bond is the discount rate that makes the present value of the cash flows equal to the bond price at time t, and it is obtained by the following formula:*

$$P(t,T) = e^{-R(t,T)(T-t)}, \tag{11.1}$$

which implies

$$R(t,T) = -\frac{\ln(P(t,T))}{T-t}. \tag{11.2}$$

The function R(., T) can be used to describe the evolution of the interest rate of zero-coupon bonds with respect to maturity or the term structure of interest rates.

How many economic state variables do we need to generate $R(t, T)$, for all t? Intuition tells us that few state variables are needed if adjacent points are highly correlated. Vasicek (1977) proposes only one state variable. This variable is the risk-free interest rate $r(t)$ defined as:

$$r(t) = R(t,t) = \lim_{T\to t} R(t,T). \tag{11.3}$$

We suppose that $r(t)$ follows the process

$$dr(t) = \mu(r,t)dt + \sigma(r,t)dW(t), \tag{11.4}$$

where $W(t)$ is a Wiener process.

Today's price $P(t, T)$ (at time t) of \$1 payable at time T is only a function of time t and the spot interest rate r.

Remark 1.2 This condition means that bonds' instantaneous returns for different maturities are perfectly correlated.

Therefore, from Ito's lemma, we can express a bond price as follows:

$$\begin{aligned} dP(t,T) &= \frac{\partial P}{\partial r}dr(t) + \frac{\partial P}{\partial t}dt + \frac{1}{2}\frac{\partial^2 P}{\partial r^2}(dr(t))^2 \\ &= \left(\frac{\partial P}{\partial r}\mu(r,t) + \frac{\partial P}{\partial t} + \frac{1}{2}\sigma(r,t)^2\frac{\partial^2 P}{\partial r^2}\right)dt \\ &\quad + \frac{\partial P}{\partial r}\sigma(r,t)dW(t) \end{aligned} \tag{11.5}$$

or also

$$dP(t,T) = P(t,T)\left[\mu_P(t,T,r)dt + \sigma_P(t,T,r)dW(t)\right], \tag{11.6}$$

with

$$\mu_P(t,T,r) = \frac{\frac{\partial P}{\partial r}\mu(r,t) + \frac{\partial P}{\partial t} + \frac{1}{2}\sigma(r,t)^2\frac{\partial^2 P}{\partial r^2}}{P(t,T)}, \tag{11.7}$$

$$\sigma_P(t,T,r) = \frac{\frac{\partial P}{\partial r}\sigma(r,t)}{P(t,T)}. \tag{11.8}$$

We consider a portfolio composed of two bonds with maturities T_1 and T_2, and proportions $(\omega, 1-\omega)$ invested respectively in the two bonds. The return on this portfolio is

$$\begin{aligned}&\omega[\mu_P(t,T_1,r)dt + \sigma_P(t,T_1,r)dW(t)]\\ &\quad+(1-\omega)[\mu_P(t,T_2,r)dt + \sigma_P(t,T_2,r)dW(t)].\end{aligned} \tag{11.9}$$

We choose ω such that the portfolio is riskless, this implies

$$\omega\mu_P(t,T_1,r) + (1-\omega)\mu_P(t,T_2,r) = r(t) \tag{11.10}$$

and

$$\omega\sigma_P(t,T_1,r) + (1-\omega)\sigma_P(t,T_2,r) = 0. \tag{11.11}$$

So,

$$\frac{\mu_P(t,T_1,r) - r(t)}{\sigma_P(t,T_1,r)} = \frac{\mu_P(t,T_2,r) - r(t)}{\sigma_P(t,T_2,r)}. \tag{11.12}$$

This equation is called the fundamental equation. Since this result is valid for all T_1 and T_2, then it is independent of T. Finally, we get

$$-\frac{(\mu_P(t,T,r) - r(t))}{\sigma_P(t,T,r)} = q(t,r), \qquad \forall T \geq t, \tag{11.13}$$

representing the market price of risk. Substituting this expression into equation (11.7), we get

$$\frac{\partial P}{\partial t} + (\mu(r,t) + \sigma(r,t)q(t,r))\frac{\partial P}{\partial r} + \frac{1}{2}\sigma(r,t)^2\frac{\partial^2 P}{\partial r^2} = r(t)P(t,T), \tag{11.14}$$

with the boundary condition $P(T,T) = 1$. This equation is the basis equation of the term structure of interest rates.

The general solution of this equation is

$$P(t,T) = E_t\left[\exp\left(-\int_t^T r(\tau)d\tau\right)\exp\left(\int_t^T q(\tau,r(\tau))dW(\tau) - \frac{1}{2}\int_t^T q\left(\tau,r(\tau)\right)^2 d\tau\right)\right], \tag{11.15}$$

and

$$R(t,T) = -\frac{\ln(P(t,T))}{T-t}. \tag{11.16}$$

11.1.2 Risk Neutral Approach

Here we provide an alternative derivation of the results of the previous section.

In the absence of arbitrage opportunities, there exists a risk neutral probability

$$dQ = \exp\left(\int_t^T q(\tau, r(\tau))dW(\tau) - \frac{1}{2}\int_t^T q(\tau, r(\tau))^2 d\tau\right) d\mathcal{P} \tag{11.17}$$

such that

$$d\widetilde{W}(t) = dW(t) - q(t, r)dt \tag{11.18}$$

is a Brownian motion under this probability Q. In this case:

$$\begin{aligned} dP(t, T) &= P(t, T)\left[\mu_P(t, T, r)dt + \sigma_P(t, T, r)dW(t)\right] \\ &= P(t, T)\left[r(t)dt + \sigma_P(t, T, r)d\widetilde{W}(t)\right]. \end{aligned} \tag{11.19}$$

Combining equations (11.18) and (11.19) shows that:

$$-\frac{(\mu_P(t, T, r) - r(t))}{\sigma_P(t, T, r)} = q(t, r), \qquad \forall T \geq t. \tag{11.20}$$

Note here that $q(.,.)$ representing the market price of risk is a function of many variables such as the state variable r, the time t and the time to maturity $T - t$, and then risk-neutral pricing does not necessarily imply q equal to zero. Sometimes one may set q equal to zero or constant for tractability.

The price of the bond under the risk neutral probability Q is

$$\begin{aligned} P(t, T) &= E_t^Q\left[\exp\left(-\int_t^T r(\tau)d\tau\right)\right] \\ &= E_t\left[\exp\left(-\int_t^T r(\tau)d\tau\right)\exp\left(\int_t^T q(\tau, r(\tau))dW(\tau) - \frac{1}{2}\int_t^T q(\tau, r(\tau))^2 d\tau\right)\right]. \end{aligned} \tag{11.21}$$

11.1.3 Particular Case: One Factor Vasicek Model

The general model doesn't help us very much. We consider the particular case where the risk-free interest rate follows the Ornstein-Uhlenbeck process:

$$dr(t) = \alpha(\gamma - r(t))dt + \sigma dW(t) \tag{11.22}$$

and the market price of risk q is set constant. In this process, γ represents the value towards which $r(t)$ is attracted: this property is called *mean reversion*. In this context

$$P(t, T) = E_t\left[\exp\left(-\int_t^T r(\tau)d\tau\right)\exp\left(\int_t^T q dW(\tau) - \frac{1}{2}\int_t^T q^2 d\tau\right)\right]. \tag{11.23}$$

Considering the Brownian motion under the risk neutral probability Q,

$$d\widetilde{W}(t) = dW(t) - q dt, \tag{11.24}$$

we obtain the following process for the interest rate

$$dr(t) = (\alpha\gamma + \sigma q - \alpha r(t))dt + \sigma d\widetilde{W}(t). \tag{11.25}$$

We see that $r(t)$ is normally distributed under probability Q. Thus

$$\begin{aligned}
P(t,T) &= E_t^Q\left[\exp\left(-\int_t^T r(\tau)d\tau\right)\right] \\
&= \exp\left(E^Q\left[-\int_t^T r(\tau)d\tau\right] + \frac{1}{2}Var^Q\left[-\int_t^T r(\tau)d\tau\right]\right) \\
&= \exp\left(\frac{1}{\alpha}(1 - e^{-\alpha(T-t)})(R(\infty) - r(t)) - (T-t)R(\infty) - \frac{\sigma^2}{4\alpha^3}(1 - e^{-\alpha(T-t)})^2\right),
\end{aligned} \tag{11.26}$$

with

$$R(\infty) = \gamma - \frac{\sigma q}{\alpha} - \frac{\sigma^2}{2\alpha^2}. \tag{11.27}$$

Thus

$$\begin{aligned}
R(t,T) &= -\frac{\ln(P(t,T))}{T-t} \\
&= R(\infty) + (r(t) - R(\infty))\frac{1}{\alpha(T-t)}\left(1 - e^{-\alpha(T-t)}\right) + \frac{\sigma^2}{4\alpha^3(T-t)}\left(1 - e^{-\alpha(T-t)}\right)^2.
\end{aligned} \tag{11.28}$$

The term structure yield curve can be flat, increasing or decreasing depending on values of $r(t)$ and other parameter values. We present the MATLAB code for such a simulation as well as a possible trajectory in Figure 11.1.

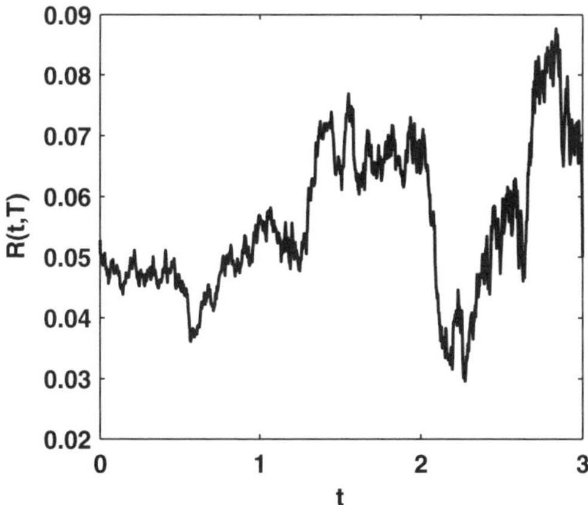

Figure 11.1 Simulation of the one factor Vasicek model

```
function Vasicek1Factor
%Function simulating the term structure using
%Vasicek model

%Parameters initial values for one factor Vasicek model
alpha=1.3;
gamma=0.05;
sigma=0.06;
q=-0.1;
Maturity=3;
rInit=0.05;
NbStep=1000;
DeltaT=Maturity/NbStep;

%Interest rates simulation
r=SimulRates(alpha,gamma,sigma,q,DeltaT,NbStep,rInit);

%Parameters of model to rate R.
RInfinity=RInf(alpha,gamma,sigma,q);

%Vector of time steps
t=[0:1:NbStep-1]*DeltaT;

%Computation of rates for the points represented in vector r
R=RInfinity + ...
   (r-RInfinity).*(1-exp(-alpha*(Maturity-t)))./(alpha*
     (Maturity-t))+ ...
   sigma^2.*((1-exp(-alpha*(Maturity-t))).^2)./(4*alpha^3*
     (Maturity-t));

%Graph of the interest rate as function of maturity
plot([t,Maturity],[R,rInit]);

end

function rep=RInf(alpha,gamma,sigma,q)
%Simple function computing parameter R(infinity) of
%Vasicek model

rep=gamma-sigma*q/alpha-sigma^2/(2*alpha^2);

end

function rep=SimulRates(alpha,gamma,sigma,q,DeltaT,NbStep,rInit)
%Fonction simulating the interest rates for Vasicek model
%alpha, gamma, sigma, q: Model parameters
%DeltaT: Time step
%NbStep: Number of steps
%rInit: Initial value of interest rate at time t=0.

%Initialisation of the answer vector
rep=zeros(1,NbStep);
rep(1)=rInit;

%For each step, we simulate the rate following the model
```

```
for i=2:NbStep
    rep(i)=rep(i-1)+alpha*(gamma-rep(i-1))*DeltaT+ ...
            sigma*sqrt(DeltaT)*randn(1);
end

end
```

11.2 THE GENERAL EQUILIBRIUM APPROACH: THE COX, INGERSOLL AND ROSS (CIR, 1985) MODEL

With the Ornstein-Uhlenbeck process proposed by Vasicek for the short term interest rate, negative values for r can result. However, based on a general equilibrium model, Cox, Ingersoll and Ross (CIR, 1985a) propose a one-factor model as follows:

$$r(t) = \delta \times Y(t), \tag{11.29}$$

where the short term interest rate is proportional to a stochastic state variable Y. Under a particular process for $Y(t)$, the short term interest rate process can be characterized as:

$$dr(t) = \kappa(\theta - r(t))dt + \sigma\sqrt{r(t)}dW(t) \tag{11.30}$$

with

$$2\kappa\theta \geq \sigma^2, \qquad \forall t \in [0, T]. \tag{11.31}$$

Without the restriction (11.31) on σ, r can reach zero. Note that in equation (11.30), the form of the volatility term prevents negative rates, which is not the case with the Ornstein-Uhlenbeck process suggested by Vasicek.

Comparing equations (11.4) with (11.30) and then substituting the values of $\mu(r, t)$ and $\sigma(r, t)$ into (11.14), assuming again that P is a function of r and t, the bond's price must satisfy the following partial differential equation:

$$\frac{1}{2}\sigma^2 r\frac{\partial^2 P}{\partial r^2} + (\kappa(\theta - r) - \lambda r)\frac{\partial P}{\partial r} + \frac{\partial P}{\partial t} - rP = 0, \tag{11.32}$$

with the market price of risk q given by

$$q(t, r) = -\frac{\lambda\sqrt{r(t)}}{\sigma}, \tag{11.33}$$

or

$$\lambda = -\frac{q(t, r)\sigma}{\sqrt{r(t)}}. \tag{11.34}$$

The constant λ is the 'market' risk parameter. These specifications allow us to reconcile the valuation partial differential equation (11.32) and equation (11.14).

Finally, it can be shown after lengthy calculations that the solution of equation (11.32) is

$$P(t, T) = A(t, T)e^{-H(t,T)r(t)}, \tag{11.35}$$

with

$$A(t,T) = \left[\frac{2\gamma e^{[(\kappa+\lambda+\gamma)(T-t)]/2}}{(\gamma+\kappa+\lambda)(e^{\gamma(T-t)}-1)+2\gamma}\right]^{2\kappa\theta/\sigma^2}, \tag{11.36}$$

$$H(t,T) = \frac{2(e^{\gamma(T-t)}-1)}{(\gamma+\kappa+\lambda)(e^{\gamma(T-t)}-1)+2\gamma}, \tag{11.37}$$

$$\gamma = \sqrt{(\kappa+\lambda)^2+2\sigma^2}. \tag{11.38}$$

Thus, the term structure is given by

$$R(t,T) = -\frac{\ln(P(t,T))}{T-t} = \frac{r(t)H(t,T)-\ln(A(t,T))}{T-t} \tag{11.39}$$

and

$$R(t,\infty) = \frac{2\kappa\theta}{\gamma+\kappa+\lambda}. \tag{11.40}$$

When $r < R(t, \infty)$, the term structure yield curve is increasing, and when $r > \frac{\kappa\theta}{\kappa+\lambda}$, it is decreasing. For values of r between these two bounds, the curve isn't monotonic. With regards to the market price of risk q, Chan, Karolyi, Longstaff and Sanders (1992) estimated empirically this parameter for both Vasicek and CIR models and found negative values for q.

We once again present a program simulating a possible trajectory for the term structure. One trajectory is plotted in Figure 11.2.

```
function CIR
%Function simulating the term structure from the CIR model

%Parameters' initial values
Theta = 0.05;
Kappa = 1.3;
Sigma = 0.2;
```

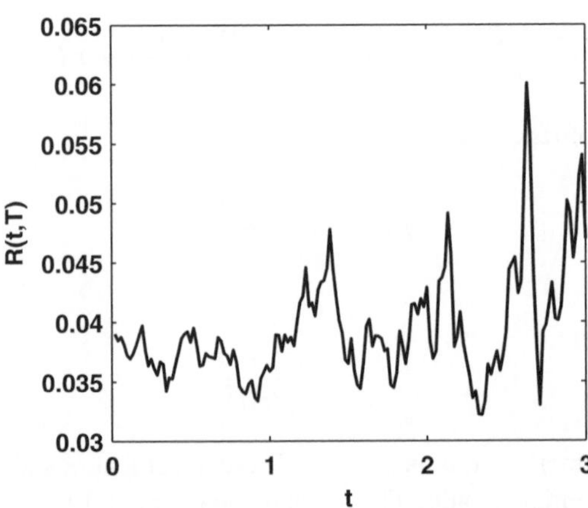

Figure 11.2 CIR model simulation

```
T=3;
NbSteps = 156;
DeltaT = T / NbSteps;
rInit = 0.05;
Lambda = 0.3;
Gamma = sqrt((Kappa+Lambda)^2+2*Sigma^2);
t=0;
r=rInit;

%Definition of vector R to keep the simulations results
R = zeros(NbSteps,1);

%For each step, we simulate the term structure for time t
for i=1:NbSteps

   %Computation of numerators and denominators in formula
     of A and H
   Temp1=(Gamma+Kappa+Lambda)*(exp(Gamma*(T-t))-1)+2*Gamma;
   Temp2=2*Gamma*exp((Gamma+Kappa+Lambda)*(T-t)/2);
   Temp3=2*(exp(Gamma*(T-t))-1);

   %Computation of A and H
   A = (Temp2/Temp1)^(2*Kappa*Theta/Sigma^2);
   H = Temp3/Temp1;

   %Rates' simulation
   r = r + Kappa*(Theta-r)*DeltaT + Sigma*sqrt(r)*sqrt
     (DeltaT)*randn(1);

   %Term structure computation at this time
   R(i,1) = (r*H-log(A))/(T-t);
   t=t+DeltaT;
end

%Graph of the term structure
plot([DeltaT:DeltaT:T], R);

end
```

11.3 THE AFFINE MODEL OF THE TERM STRUCTURE

In the absence of arbitrage opportunities, the price at time t of a zero coupon bond maturing at T is given by the following formula:

$$P(t, t+\tau) = E_t^Q\left[e^{-\int_t^{t+\tau} r(s)ds}\right], \tag{11.41}$$

where E^Q is the risk neutral probability Q expectation operator.

From the Cox, Ingersoll and Ross (CIR, 1985a) general equilibrium model, or the Heath, Jarrow and Morton (HJM, 1992) arbitrage model, described in Section 11.4, we can deduce a multi-factor linear model for the short term interest rate. Indeed, we can posit an N factor affine model for the term structure under the assumption that the short term interest rate $r(t)$ is an affine combination of N state variables $\mathbf{Y}(t) = (Y_1(t), Y_2(t), \ldots, Y_N(t))$. Thus, we can write the short term interest rate as:

$$r(t) = \delta_0 + \sum_{i=1}^{N} \delta_i Y_i(t) = \delta_0 + \delta_y^\top \mathbf{Y}(t), \tag{11.42}$$

with the vector $Y(t)$ having an "affine diffusion" that is defined as:

$$d\mathbf{Y}(t) = \mathbf{K}(\theta - \mathbf{Y}(t))dt + \Sigma\sqrt{\mathbf{S}(t)}dW(t), \tag{11.43}$$

where W is a vector of independent Brownian motions under probability Q, $\mathbf{K}$ and Σ are matrices of dimensions $N \times N$, and $\mathbf{S}$ is a diagonal matrix whose element on the ith diagonal is

$$[\mathbf{S}(t)]_{ii} = \alpha_i + \beta_i^\top \mathbf{Y}(t). \tag{11.44}$$

With these specifications, Duffie and Kan (1996) proved that the bond price given in (11.41) can be written as:

$$P(t, t+\tau) = P(t, T) = e^{A(\tau) - \mathbf{H}^\top(\tau)\mathbf{Y}(t)}, \tag{11.45}$$

where $A(\tau)$ and $\mathbf{H}(\tau)$ satisfy the following ordinary differential equations:

$$\frac{dA(\tau)}{d\tau} = \theta^\top \mathbf{K}^\top \mathbf{H}(\tau) + \frac{1}{2}\sum_{i=1}^{N} [\Sigma^\top \mathbf{H}(\tau)]_i^2 \alpha_i - \delta_0, \tag{11.46}$$

$$\frac{d\mathbf{H}(\tau)}{d\tau} = -\mathbf{K}^\top \mathbf{H}(\tau) - \frac{1}{2}\sum_{i=1}^{N} [\Sigma^\top \mathbf{H}(\tau)]_i^2 \beta_i + \delta_y. \tag{11.47}$$

These ordinary differential equations can be solved using numerical integration techniques with initial conditions $A(0) = 0$ and $\mathbf{H}(0) = 0_{N\times 1}$ and the specifications given by equations (11.41), (11.42), (11.43) and (11.44).

The term structure is given by

$$R(t, T) = -\frac{\ln(P(t, T))}{T - t} = \frac{\mathbf{H}^\top(T - t)\mathbf{Y}(t) - A(T - t)}{T - t}. \tag{11.48}$$

11.4 MARKET MODELS

11.4.1 The Heath, Jarrow and Morton (HJM, 1992) Model

This model was developed by Heath, Jarrow and Morton (HJM, 1992). It uses forward rates to generate the complete term structure of interest rates.

We consider a continuous time economy on interval $[0, T]$. The zero coupon bond price at t paying 1\$ at future date T is $P(t, T)$, with

$$P(T, T) = 1. \tag{11.49}$$

The instantaneous forward rate, f, at time t for maturity T is

$$f(t,T) = -\frac{\partial \ln(P(t,T))}{\partial T} \tag{11.50}$$

or also

$$P(t,T) = \exp\left(-\int_t^T f(t,s)ds\right). \tag{11.51}$$

Term Structure Movements

We consider the following process for forward rates

$$f(t,T) = f(0,T) + \int_0^t \alpha(s,T)ds + \sum_{i=1}^{n} \int_0^t \sigma_i(s,T)dW_i(s), \tag{11.52}$$

where $\{W_i\}_{i=1,\ldots,n}$ are independent Brownian motions. The spot interest rate at date t, $r(t)$, can be seen as being the instantaneous forward rate at t, that is $r(t) = f(t, t)$, hence we can find the spot rate process as follows

$$r(t) = f(t,t) = f(0,t) + \int_0^t \alpha(s,t)ds + \sum_{i=1}^{n} \int_0^t \sigma_i(s,t)dW_i(s). \tag{11.53}$$

From equation (11.51), we have that

$$\ln(P(t,T)) = -\int_t^T f(t,s)ds. \tag{11.54}$$

Using equations (11.53) and (11.54) in conjunction with a key corollary provided in the appendix of Heath, Jarrow and Morton (1992), and after tedious algebra, we get

$$\begin{aligned} \ln(P(t,T)) = \ln(P(0,T)) &+ \int_0^t \big(r(s) + b(s,T)\big)ds \\ &-\frac{1}{2}\sum_{i=1}^{n} \int_0^t a_i(s,T)^2 ds + \sum_{i=1}^{n} \int_0^t a_i(s,T)dW_i(s), \end{aligned} \tag{11.55}$$

with

$$a_i(t,T) = -\int_t^T \sigma_i(s,T)ds \tag{11.56}$$

and

$$b(t,T) = -\int_0^t \alpha(t,s)ds + \frac{1}{2}\sum_{i=1}^{n} a_i(t,T)^2. \tag{11.57}$$

Using Ito's formula, we find the following process for the bond:

$$dP(t,T) = \big(r(s) + b(s,T)\big)P(t,T)dt + \sum_{i=1}^{n} a_i(t,T)P(t,T)dW_i(t). \tag{11.58}$$

Valuation in the absence of arbitrage opportunities and the market price of risk

Let's define $B(t)$ as being the value at time t of \$1 invested at time 0

$$B(t) = \exp\left(\int_0^t r(s)ds\right). \tag{11.59}$$

Then we build the relative price process of the zero coupon bond with maturity T by

$$\frac{P(t,T)}{B(t)}. \tag{11.60}$$

Applying Ito's formula to $\ln(P(t,T)/B(t))$ leads to:

$$\ln\left(\frac{P(t,T)}{B(t)}\right) = \ln\left(\frac{P(0,T)}{B(0)}\right) + \int_0^t b(s,T)ds - \frac{1}{2}\sum_{i=1}^{n}\int_0^t a_i(s,T)^2 ds$$
$$+ \sum_{i=1}^{n}\int_0^t a_i(s,T)dW_i(s). \tag{11.61}$$

The price variables $\{P(t,T_1)/B(t), \ldots, P(t,T_n)/B(t); 0 < T_1 < \ldots < T_n\}$ are martingales if and only if there exists an equivalent martingale measure Q, which means the existence of market prices of risk

$$\{q_i(t;T_1,\ldots,T_n)\}_{i\in[1,n]}$$

satisfying the following system of equations:

$$\begin{pmatrix} 0 \\ \vdots \\ 0 \end{pmatrix} = \begin{pmatrix} a_1(t,T_1) & \ldots & a_n(t,T_1) \\ & \vdots & \\ a_1(t,T_n) & \ldots & a_n(t,T_n) \end{pmatrix} \begin{pmatrix} q_1(t;T_1,\ldots,T_n) \\ \vdots \\ q_n(t;T_1,\ldots,T_n) \end{pmatrix} + \begin{pmatrix} b(t,T_1) \\ \vdots \\ b(t,T_n) \end{pmatrix}. \tag{11.62}$$

So

$$b(t,T) = -\sum_{i=1}^{n} a_i(t,T)q_i(t;T_1,\ldots,T_n), \quad 0 < t < T_1 < \ldots < T_n < T. \tag{11.63}$$

Using the Girsanov theorem, we can prove that under risk neutral probability Q defined by

$$dQ = \exp\left(\sum_1^n \int_0^{T_1} q_i(t;T_1,\ldots,T_n)dW_i(s) - \frac{1}{2}\sum_1^n \int_0^{T_1} q_i(t;T_1,\ldots,T_n)^2 ds\right) d\mathcal{P}, \tag{11.64}$$

processes

$$\widetilde{W}_i(t) = W_i(t) - \int_0^t q_i(t; T_1, \ldots, T_n)ds, \qquad i = 1, \ldots, n, \tag{11.65}$$

are Brownian motions. The risk neutral probability uniqueness implies that matrix

$$\begin{pmatrix} a_1(t, T_1) & \ldots & a_n(t, T_1) \\ & \vdots & \\ a_1(t, T_n) & \ldots & a_n(t, T_n) \end{pmatrix} \tag{11.66}$$

is nonsingular.

Heath, Jarrow and Morton (1992) demonstrated the following proposition essential to asset valuation under the arbitrage-free argument.

Proposition 4.1 *The following conditions are equivalent*

1. *Q is the unique equivalent martingale measure such that $P(t, T)/B(t)$ is a martingale.*
2. *The arbitrage-free valuation condition is*

$$q_i(t; T_1, \ldots, T_n) = q_i(t; T_1', \ldots, T_n'), \qquad i = 1, \ldots, n, \tag{11.67}$$

$\forall \ T_1, \ldots, T_n, \ T_1', \ldots, T_n'$, *with*

$$0 \le T_1 < \ldots < T_n \le T \quad \text{and} \quad 0 \le T_1' < \ldots < T_n' \le T. \tag{11.68}$$

3. *The restriction on the drift of the forward rate process is*

$$\alpha(t, T) = -\sum_{i=1}^{n} \sigma_i(t, T)\left(q_i(t) - \int_t^T \sigma_i(t, s)ds\right), \tag{11.69}$$

with $q_i(t) = q_i(t; T_1, \ldots, T_n)$.

With condition (11.69) of the above proposition, we can show that the bond price is defined by

$$dP(t, T) = P(t, T)\Big[r(t)dt + \sum_i^n a_i(t)d\widetilde{W}_i(t)\Big], \tag{11.70}$$

where $\widetilde{W}_i$ is Wiener process under the risk-neutral probability. Following Harrison and Kreps (1979) and Harrison and Pliska (1981), given a financial asset X paying \$ 1 at date T, its price at any moment t ($t \le T$) can be obtained using the risk neutral probability Q as follows:

$$X(t) = E^Q\left[\frac{X(T)}{B(T)}\Big|\mathcal{F}_t\right] \times B(t). \tag{11.71}$$

Using this expression, we obtain the zero coupon bond price

$$\begin{aligned}
P(t,T) &= E^Q\left[e^{-\int_t^T r(s)ds}\middle|\mathcal{F}_t\right]\\
&= E^Q\left[\frac{B(t)}{B(T)}\middle|\mathcal{F}_t\right]\\
&= B(t)E\left[\frac{\exp\left(\sum_{i=1}^n \int_0^T q_i(t)dW_i(t) - \frac{1}{2}\sum_{i=1}^n \int_0^T q_i(t)^2 dt\right)}{B(T)}\middle|\mathcal{F}_t\right]. \quad (11.72)
\end{aligned}$$

Remark 4.2 In this last expression, the bond's price depends on the value of the market prices of risk $\{q_i(t)\}$ under the real world probability, and $1/B(T)$, the discount factor. These two quantities contain: the forward rate $\{f(0, T)\}$'s initial term structure, the forward rate's drift $\{\alpha(., T)\}$ and the forward rate's volatility $\{\sigma_i(., T), i = 1, .., n\}$.

The market prices of risk will allow us to make the bridge between the real world probability and the risk-neutral pricing.

The HJM model allows us to derive many other interest rate models using specific calibration of forward rates' process. Here are some of these.

The Ho and Lee (1986) Model

To have the Ho and Lee (1986) continuous time term structure model, we use the following formulation for the forward rate:

$$f(t,T) = f(0,T) + \int_0^t \alpha(s,T)ds + \int_0^t \sigma dW(s), \quad (11.73)$$

with α satisfying the arbitrage-free condition defined by the following restriction on the forward rates' parameters as follows:

$$\alpha(t,T) = -\sigma q(t) + \sigma^2(T - t). \quad (11.74)$$

The forward rate formulation (11.73) is a special case of (11.52) with one factor and constant σ, therefore (11.74) follows from (11.69). Then, under risk neutral probability Q, we can rewrite the forward rate's process as:

$$f(t,T) = f(0,T) + \sigma^2\left(T - \frac{t}{2}\right) + \sigma\widetilde{W}(t) \quad (11.75)$$

and the spot interest rate's process

$$r(t) = f(0,T) + \sigma\widetilde{W}(t) + \sigma^2\frac{t}{2}. \quad (11.76)$$

We must note that from these two processes, r and f can be negative with strictly positive probability.

Equations (11.75) and (11.51) give the following zero coupon bond's price

$$P(t,T)=\frac{P(0,T)}{P(0,t)}\exp\left(-\frac{\sigma^2}{2}Tt(T-t)-\sigma(T-t)\widetilde{W}(t)\right). \tag{11.77}$$

Now consider a European call on this zero coupon bond, $P(t,T)$, with strike price K and maturity T' with $0\le t\le T'\le T$. From equation (11.71), we can deduce the call price as

$$\begin{aligned}\text{Call}(t)&=E^Q\left[\frac{\max(P(T',T)-K,0)}{B(T')}B(t)\middle|\mathcal{F}_t\right]\\&=P(t,T)N(h)-KP(t,T')N\big(h-\sigma(T-T')\sqrt{T'-t}\big),\end{aligned} \tag{11.78}$$

with

$$h=\frac{\ln\left(\frac{P(t,T)}{KP(t,T')}\right)+\frac{1}{2}\sigma(T-T')^2(T'-t)}{\sigma(T-T')\sqrt{T'-t}}. \tag{11.79}$$

The Two-Factor Model

Now consider the following two-factor forward rate process

$$df(t,T)=\alpha(t,T)dt+\underbrace{\sigma_1 dW_1(t)}_{\text{long term factor}}+\underbrace{\sigma_2 e^{-\frac{\lambda}{2}(T-t)}dW_2(t)}_{\text{short term factor}}, \tag{11.80}$$

where W_1 is the long term factor and W_2 is the spread between the short and long term factors. In this case, the arbitrage-free condition satisfied by the forward rate's parameters is

$$\alpha(t,T)=-\sigma_1 q_1(t)-\sigma_2 e^{-\frac{\lambda}{2}(T-t)}q_2(t)+\sigma_1^2(T-t)-2\frac{\sigma_2^2}{\lambda}e^{-\frac{\lambda}{2}(T-t)}\big(e^{-\frac{\lambda}{2}(T-t)}-1\big). \tag{11.81}$$

Under the risk neutral probability, the forward rate's process is

$$\begin{aligned}f(t,T)&=f(0,T)+\sigma_1^2 t\left(T-\frac{t}{2}\right)-2\left(\frac{\sigma_2}{\lambda}\right)^2\left[e^{-\lambda T}(e^{\lambda t}-1)-2e^{-\frac{\lambda}{2}T}\big(e^{\frac{\lambda}{2}t}-1\big)\right]\\&\quad+\sigma_1\widetilde{W}_1(t)+\sigma_2\int_0^t e^{-\frac{\lambda}{2}(T-s)}d\widetilde{W}_2(s)\end{aligned} \tag{11.82}$$

and the spot interest rate is

$$\begin{aligned}r(t)&=f(0,t)+\sigma_1^2\frac{t^2}{2}-2\left(\frac{\sigma_2}{\lambda}\right)^2\left[(1-e^{-\lambda t})-2\big(1-e^{-\frac{\lambda}{2}t}\big)\right]\\&\quad+\sigma_1\widetilde{W}_1(t)+\sigma_2\int_0^t e^{-\frac{\lambda}{2}(t-s)}d\widetilde{W}_2(s).\end{aligned} \tag{11.83}$$

In this case, the price of a call having as underlying the zero coupon bond $P(t, T)$ with strike price K and maturity T' with $0 \leq t \leq T' \leq T$, is given by:

$$\text{Call}(t) = P(t, T)N(h) - KP(t, T')N(h - v), \tag{11.84}$$

with

$$h = \frac{\ln\left(\frac{P(t,T)}{KP(t,T')}\right) + \frac{1}{2}v^2}{v} \tag{11.85}$$

and

$$v^2 = \sigma_1^2(T - T')^2(T' - t) + \frac{4\sigma_2^2}{\lambda^3}\left(e^{-\frac{\lambda}{2}T} - e^{-\frac{\lambda}{2}T'}\right)^2(e^{\lambda T'} - e^{\lambda t}). \tag{11.86}$$

The CIR Model Revisited

In section 11.2, we presented the Cox, Ingersoll and Ross (CIR, 1985) model. Here, the objective is to show how one may obtain the CIR general equilibrium model as a special case of the HJM arbitrage-free model with a specific forward rate process.

Recall that the term structure model proposed by Cox, Ingersoll and Ross (CIR, 1985) follows from a general equilibrium model. In the one variable case, CIR obtain the following term structure process:

$$dr(t) = \kappa(\theta(t) - r(t))dt + \sigma\sqrt{r(t)}dW(t), \tag{11.87}$$

with

$$2\kappa\theta(t) \geq \sigma^2, \qquad \forall t \in [0, T]. \tag{11.88}$$

Which implies a bond price process of the following form

$$dP(t, T) = r(t)[1 - \lambda H(t, T)]P(t, T)dt - H(t, T)\sigma\sqrt{r(t)}P(t, T)dW(t), \tag{11.89}$$

where

$$H(t, T) = \frac{2(e^{\gamma(T-t)} - 1)}{(\gamma + \kappa + \lambda)(e^{\gamma(T-t)} - 1) + 2\gamma}, \tag{11.90}$$

$$\gamma = \sqrt{(\kappa + \lambda)^2 + 2\sigma^2}, \tag{11.91}$$

and λ is constant.

In this context, we showed that the market price of risk is given by

$$q(t) = -\frac{\lambda\sqrt{r(t)}}{\sigma}. \tag{11.92}$$

From the bond's price process, CIR deduce the following forward rate process:

$$f(t, T) = r(t)\left(\frac{\partial H(t, T)}{\partial T}\right) + \kappa\int_t^T \theta(s)\left(\frac{\partial H(s, T)}{\partial T}\right)ds. \tag{11.93}$$

CIR suggest to reverse this equation to implicitly determine the spot interest rate parameters.

Remark 4.3 The CIR model is not coherent with all initial forward rate curves since we must have $2\kappa\theta(t) \geq \sigma^2$.

However, from the HJM model, to obtain the term structure of interest rates proposed by CIR, we start from the following forward rate process

$$df(t,T) = r(t)\kappa\Big(\frac{\partial^2 H(t,T)}{\partial t \partial T} - \frac{\partial H(t,T)}{\partial T}\Big)dt + \Big(\frac{\partial H(t,T)}{\partial T}\Big)\sigma\sqrt{r(t)}dW(t), \tag{11.94}$$

with

$$r(t) = \frac{\Big[f(t,T) - \kappa \int_t^T \theta(s)\Big(\frac{\partial H(t,T)}{\partial T}\Big)ds\Big]}{\frac{\partial H(t,T)}{\partial T}}. \tag{11.95}$$

Remark 4.4 The CIR model fixes a specific market price of risk and endogenously derives the forward rate process; the HJM model takes a given stochastic process for the forward rate and prices the contingent claims from this process. The HJM model is more general than the one obtained from an equilibrium model such as CIR.

11.4.2 The Brace, Gatarek and Musiela (BGM, 1997) Model

We present next a model known as the Brace, Gatarek and Musiela (BGM 1997) market model. The principle consists of describing the market rates process from an already existing model such as the one of Heath, Jarrow and Morton (1992).

BGM describe the LIBOR rates' process observed on swaps' markets with the HJM model. They then define the different conditions satisfied by these processes.

The HJM Model Revisited and Notations

Let $f(t, t+x)$ be the instantaneous continuously compounded forward rate at t for future date $t+x$. Thus for all $T > 0$, the process

$$P(t,T) = \exp\left(-\int_t^T f(t,u)du\right), \quad 0 \leq t \leq T \tag{11.96}$$

describes the price evolution of a zero coupon bond with maturity T. The temporal evolution of the discounting function is

$$x \mapsto P(t,t+x) = \exp\left(-\int_t^{t+x} f(t,u)du\right). \tag{11.97}$$

We consider the following forward rate process:

$$df(t,t+x) = \left(\frac{\partial f(t,t+x)}{\partial x} + \frac{1}{2}\frac{\partial \|\sigma(t,t+x)\|^2}{\partial x}\right)dt + \frac{\partial \sigma^\top(t,t+x)}{\partial x}d\widetilde{W}(t), \tag{11.98}$$

where for all $x \geq 0$, the volatility vector process $\{\sigma(t, t+x); t \geq 0\}$ is an adapted process with values in $\mathbb{R}^d$, while $\|\cdot\|$ stands for the norm. This process of the forward rate is consistent with the free-arbitrage conditions in the HJM model. The process:

$$B(t) = \exp\left(\int_0^t r(s)ds\right), \quad t \geq 0 \tag{11.99}$$

is the accumulated value at $t \geq 0$ of one dollar invested at time 0. We know that

$$\{P(t,T)/B(t); \quad 0 \leq t \leq T\} \tag{11.100}$$

is a martingale, which implies the no arbitrage possibility. With these definitions, we can show that

$$\frac{P(t,T)}{B(t)} = P(0,T)\exp\left(-\int_0^t \sigma^\top(s,T)d\widetilde{W}(s) - \frac{1}{2}\int_0^t \|\sigma(s,T)\|^2 ds\right). \tag{11.101}$$

This implies

$$dP(t,T) = P(t,T)\big(r(t)dt - \sigma^\top(t,T)d\widetilde{W}(t)\big). \tag{11.102}$$

This can be related back to equation (11.70).

The LIBOR Rate Process

To characterize the volatility $\sigma(t, t+x)$ process in the above forward rate equation (11.98), we suppose the time period $\delta > 0$ (for example $\delta = 0.25$ year or one quarter). δ represents the payment frequency of the LIBOR rate. We then consider the LIBOR rate process $\{\text{LIBOR}(t, x); t \geq 0\}$, defined as:

$$1 + \delta\text{LIBOR}(t,x) = \exp\left(\int_x^{x+\delta} f(t, t+u)du\right). \tag{11.103}$$

This process has a log-normal volatility structure, that is:

$$d\text{LIBOR}(t,x) = (\cdot)dt + \text{LIBOR}(t,x)\gamma^\top(t,x)d\widetilde{W}(t). \tag{11.104}$$

Ito's lemma applied to expression (11.103) gives:

$$\begin{aligned} d\text{LIBOR}(t,x) &= \frac{1}{\delta}d\exp\left(\int_x^{x+\delta} f(t,t+u)du\right) \\ &= \left[\frac{\partial\text{LIBOR}(t,x)}{\partial x} + \frac{1}{\delta}\big(1+\delta\text{LIBOR}(t,x)\big)\sigma^\top(t,t+x+\delta)\right. \\ &\quad \left.\times\big(\sigma(t,t+x+\delta) - \sigma(t,t+x)\big)\right]dt \\ &\quad + \frac{1}{\delta}\big(1+\delta\text{LIBOR}(t,x)\big)\big(\sigma(t,t+x+\delta) - \sigma(t,t+x)\big)^\top d\widetilde{W}(t). \end{aligned} \tag{11.105}$$

Comparing this expression to equation (11.104), we have

$$\sigma(t, t+x+\delta) - \sigma(t, t+x) = \frac{\delta \text{LIBOR}(t, x)}{1+\delta \text{LIBOR}(t, x)} \gamma(t, x). \tag{11.106}$$

So the expression of LIBOR(t, x) becomes

$$\begin{aligned} d\text{LIBOR}(t, x) = & \left(\frac{\partial \text{LIBOR}(t, x)}{\partial x} + \text{LIBOR}(t, x)\gamma^{\top}(t, x)\sigma(t, t+x+\delta) \right) dt \\ & + \text{LIBOR}(t, x)\gamma^{\top}(t, x) d\widetilde{W}(t). \end{aligned} \tag{11.107}$$

From equations (11.106) and (11.107), we can show that $\{\text{LIBOR}(t, x);\ t \geq 0\}$ must satisfy:

$$\begin{aligned} d\text{LIBOR}(t, x) = & \left(\frac{\partial \text{LIBOR}(t, x)}{\partial x} + \text{LIBOR}(t, x)\gamma^{\top}(t, x)\sigma(t, t+x) \right. \\ & \left. + \frac{\delta \text{LIBOR}^2(t, x)}{1+\delta \text{LIBOR}(t, x)} \|\gamma(t, x)\|^2 \right) dt + \text{LIBOR}(t, x)\gamma^{\top}(t, x) d\widetilde{W}(t), \end{aligned} \tag{11.108}$$

with σ and γ linked by the relation defined by the following equation:

$$\sigma(t, t+x) = \begin{cases} 0 & \text{if} \quad 0 \leq x < \delta \\ \sum_{k=1}^{\text{Int}(\frac{x}{\delta})} \frac{\delta \text{LIBOR}(t, x-k\delta)}{1+\delta \text{LIBOR}(t, x-k\delta)} \gamma(t, x-k\delta); & \text{if} \quad \delta \leq x \end{cases}, \tag{11.109}$$

where $\text{Int}(\frac{x}{\delta})$ is the integer part of $\frac{x}{\delta}$.

We have described modern modeling approaches for the term structure of interest rates and also summarized the most widely known models used by practitioners. In the following section, we propose simulation programs to illustrate the implementation of the BGM market model. For this purpose, we provide programs to evaluate interest rate derivative products such as caps, floors and swaptions. The reader could start from these basic programs to make extensions into more sophisticated market models.

Pricing Interest Rate Caps and Floors

A cap is a call option on an interest rate or, equivalently, a put option on the bond's price. A floor is a put option on the interest rate or, equivalently, a call on the bond's value.

We consider a cap having a strike price of K, resetting at dates $T_j = T_0 + j\Delta t$, $j = 1, \ldots, n$, on a principal of \$ 1. For any principal A, the value will be multiplied by the principal value A.

The cap is a portfolio of n ($j = 1, \ldots, n$) caplets. The LIBOR rate received at date T_j is fixed at T_{j-1} from equation (11.103) at level

$$\text{LIBOR}(T_{j-1}, 0) = \frac{1}{\Delta t}\left(P(T_{j-1}, T_j)^{-1} - 1\right). \tag{11.110}$$

The $(j-1)^{th}$ caplet gives at date T_j a payment equal to:

$$\Delta t \max\left(\text{LIBOR}(T_{j-1}, 0) - K, 0\right). \tag{11.111}$$

The cap's price is obtained at $t \le T_0$ by taking the expectations under the risk-neutral measure:

$$\begin{aligned}\text{cap}(t) &= E^Q\left[\sum_{j=1}^{n} \frac{B(t)}{B(T_j)}(\text{LIBOR}(T_{j-1}, 0) - K)^+ \Delta t \middle| \mathcal{F}_t\right] \\ &= \sum_{j=1}^{n} P(t, T_j) E^Q_{T_j}\left[(\text{LIBOR}(T_{j-1}, 0) - K)^+ \Delta t \middle| \mathcal{F}_t\right]. \end{aligned} \tag{11.112}$$

Theorem 4.5 *BGM show that the cap's price at date $t \le T_0$ is obtained by the following formula*

$$\begin{aligned}\text{cap}(t) = \sum_{j=1}^{n} \Delta t P(t, T_j)\Big[&\text{LIBOR}(t, T_{j-1} - t) N\big(h(t, T_{j-1})\big) \\ &- KN\big(h(t, T_{j-1}) - \sigma_j\sqrt{T_{j-1} - t}\big)\Big],\end{aligned} \tag{11.113}$$

with

$$h(t, T_{j-1}) = \frac{\left[\ln\big(\text{LIBOR}(t, T_{j-1} - t)/K\big) + \frac{1}{2}\sigma_j^2 (T_{j-1} - t)\right]}{\sigma_j\sqrt{T_{j-1} - t}} \tag{11.114}$$

and

$$\sigma_j^2 = \frac{1}{T_{j-1} - t}\int_t^{T_{j-1}} \|\gamma(s, T_{j-1} - s)\|^2 ds. \tag{11.115}$$

We implement this approach to evaluate a cap. First, we get the $P(0, T_j)$ from different LIBOR rates observed on markets using linear interpolation. We suppose in the program these values are known. Second, we specify a function $\gamma(t, x) = \gamma(x)$. For this, we consider a 2 dimensional function γ. This function is constant over the intervals of length $\Delta t = 0.25$. Here is the program:

```
function AnsBGM=CapBGM
%Function computing a cap's value from the BGM model.
%Strike: The strike price.
Strike=0.03;

%Initial parameters
NbStep=20;
DeltaT=0.25;

%Specification of a gamma function
Gamma=[0.00, 0.00; 0.09, 0.12; 0.08, 0.05;
       0.08, 0.05; 0.23, 0.09; 0.23, 0.09;
       0.19, 0.03; 0.19, 0.03; 0.08, 0.01;
       0.08, 0.01; 0.19, 0.01; 0.19, 0.01;
       0.14, -0.01; 0.14, -0.01; 0.14, -0.01;
```

```
      0.14, -0.01; 0.09, -0.05; 0.09, -0.05;
      0.09, -0.05; 0.09, -0.05; 0.14, -0.04];

%Forward rates' specification
P=[1; 0.9830; 0.9652; 0.9464; 0.9271; 0.9076;
   0.8882; 0.8688; 0.8497; 0.8308; 0.8123; 0.7942;
   0.7764; 0.7596; 0.7435; 0.7274; 0.7112; 0.6954;
   0.6797; 0.6644; 0.6491];

%Vector storing the values of LIBOR L computed.
L=zeros(NbStep,1);

%For each time steps, we compute the correspondent value for L
for i=1:NbStep
   L(i,1)=(P(i,1)/P(i+1,1)-1)/DeltaT;
end

%Vector of computed sigma values
Sigma=zeros(NbStep,1);

%For each time steps, we compute the value of sigma at this moment
for k=2:NbStep
   Sigma(k,1)=(Sigma(k-1,1)*(k-2)*DeltaT+norm(Gamma(k,:),2)^2
                  *DeltaT)/...((k-1)*DeltaT);
end

%Vector storing the values of h computed
h=zeros(NbStep,1);

%For each time step, we computed the corresponding values of h
for j=1:NbStep-1
   h(j,1)=(log(L(j+1,1)/Strike)+0.5*Sigma(j+1,1)*(j*DeltaT))/...
                  sqrt(Sigma(j+1,1)*(j*DeltaT));
end

%Vector storing the caplets' prices at each time t
Caplet=zeros(NbStep,1);

%For each time, we compute the corresponding caplet's value
for l=2:NbStep
   Caplet(l,1)=DeltaT*P(l,1)*(L(l,1)*normcdf(h(l-1,1))-...
              Strike*normcdf(h(l-1,1)-sqrt(Sigma(l,1)*
              (l-1)*DeltaT)));
end

%Cap's value from the BGM model is the sum of caplets' values
AnsBGM=sum(Caplet,1);

%For comparison, we present the cap's price computed
%from Black's model. For this, we must specify
%a sigma, here it is chosen to be near the
```

```
%average value of sigma computed in the BGM model
CapletBlack=zeros(NbStep,1);
sigma=0.15;
for m=1:NbStep
  d1=(log(L(m,1)/Strike)+sigma^2*DeltaT*m/2)/(sigma*sqrt(m*DeltaT));
  d2=d1-sigma*sqrt(m*DeltaT);
  CapletBlack(m,1)=DeltaT*P(m+1,1)*(L(m,1)*normcdf(d1)-...
                      Strike*normcdf(d2));
end

%Black cap's price is equal to the sum of caplets' prices
AnsBlack=sum(CapletBlack,1)

end
```

At the end of the program, we add a code that prices the cap using Black's (1976) risk neutral valuation. In that part, we suppose a constant volatility equal to 0.15. Table 11.1 shows the results obtained with different strike prices.

Theorem 4.6 *Similarly, it is possible to obtain a floor price with the following formula*

$$\text{floor}(t) = \sum_{j=1}^{n} \Delta t P(t, T_j)\Big[KN\big(-h(t, T_{j-1}) + \sigma_j\sqrt{T_{j-1} - t}\big) - \text{LIBOR}(t, T_{j-1} - t)N\big(-h(t, T_{j-1})\big)\Big], \tag{11.116}$$

with

$$h(t, T_{j-1}) = \frac{\Big[\ln\big(\text{LIBOR}(t, T_{j-1} - t)/K\big) + \frac{1}{2}\sigma_j^2(T_{j-1} - t)\Big]}{\sigma_j\sqrt{T_{j-1} - t}} \tag{11.117}$$

and

$$\sigma_j^2 = \frac{1}{T_{j-1} - t}\int_t^{T_{j-1}} \|\gamma(s, T_{j-1} - s)\|^2 ds. \tag{11.118}$$

Table 11.1 BGM cap prices ($)

Strike	BGM Price	Black price
0.03	0.2248	0.2296
0.04	0.1860	0.1891
0.05	0.1475	0.1490
0.06	0.1104	0.1099
0.07	0.0763	0.0746
0.08	0.0493	0.0477
0.09	0.0310	0.0292

Table 11.2 BGM floor prices ($)

Strike	BGM price	Black price
0.06	0.0021	0.0017
0.07	0.0069	0.0069
0.08	0.0187	0.0204
0.09	0.0392	0.0423
0.10	0.0663	0.0710
0.11	0.0977	0.1043
0.12	0.1319	0.1405

Since the program computing the floor price is almost identical, except for the signs in the summation, we only report the results. We also give floor prices evaluated in a risk neutral world with constant volatility using Black's model. Table 11.2 presents the results.

Pricing a Swaption

A swaption is an option on an interest rate swap. It gives its owner the right to enter into an interest rate swap contract at a specific date in the future. Of course, the owner of a swaption is not obliged to exercise it. Recall that a swap contract is a commitment between two counterparties to exchange cash flows in the future that will be determined according to a predetermined formula.

We consider a swaption with strike price K and maturity T_0. If settlement dates are: $T_j = T_0 + j\Delta t, j = 1, \ldots, n$. Then the price at $t \leq T_0$ is

$$\text{swaption}(t) = \Delta t \sum_{j=1}^{n} P(t, T_j) E_{T_j}^{Q}\left[(\text{LIBOR}(T_0, T_{j-1} - T_0) - K)\mathbf{1}_{\{\sum_{j=1}^{n} C_j P(T_0, T_j) \leq 1\}} \middle| \mathcal{F}_t\right], \tag{11.119}$$

with

$$C_j = K\Delta t, \quad j = 1, \ldots, n-1, \quad C_n = 1 + K\Delta t. \tag{11.120}$$

Theorem 4.7 *BGM showed that a swaption price at date $t \leq T_0$ could be obtained from the following approximate formula*

$$\text{swaption}(t) = \Delta t \sum_{j=1}^{n} P(t, T_j)\Big[\text{LIBOR}(t, T_{j-1} - t)N(-s_0 - d_j + \Gamma_j) - KN(-s_0 - d_j)\Big], \tag{11.121}$$

with s_0 computed from

$$\sum_{k=1}^{n} C_k \left(\prod_{i-1}^{k}\left(1 + \Delta t \text{LIBOR}(t, T_{i-1} - t)\exp(\Gamma_i(s_0 + d_i) - \frac{1}{2}\Gamma_i^2)\right)\right)^{-1} = 1, \tag{11.122}$$

where

$$C_k = K\Delta t, \quad k = 1, \ldots, n-1, \quad C_n = 1 + K\Delta t, \tag{11.123}$$

and Γ_i *and* d_i *are determined by*

$$\Delta_{lj} = \Gamma_l \Gamma_i = \int_t^{T_0} \gamma^\top(s, T_{l-1} - s)\gamma(s, T_{i-1} - s)ds \tag{11.124}$$

and

$$d_i = \sum_{l=1}^{i} \frac{\Delta t \text{LIBOR}(t, T_{l-1} - t)}{1 + \Delta t \text{LIBOR}(t, T_{l-1} - t)} \Gamma_l, \quad l \geq 1, \quad d_0 = 0. \tag{11.125}$$

We present a simple program showing the procedure to follow to find the price of a swap contract. We suppose that the values of LIBOR, P, γ and Δt (for the MATLAB program *spread*) are already known. Here are the programs in the case where the strike price is 0.06:

```
function AnsBGM=SwaptionBGM
%Function computing the swaption value from the BGM model

%Initial parameters
Strike=0.06;
NbStep=20;
DeltaT=0.25;
%Already specified gamma function
gamma = [0; 0.0750; 0.0472; 0.0472; 0.1235; 0.1235;
         0.0962; 0.0962; 0.0403; 0.0403; 0.0951; 0.0951;
         0.0702; 0.0702; 0.0702; 0.0702; 0.0515; 0.0515;
         0.0515; 0.0515];

%Zero coupon bonds prices vector
P=[1; 0.9830; 0.9652; 0.9464; 0.9271; 0.9076;
    0.8882; 0.8688; 0.8497; 0.8308; 0.8123; 0.7942;
    0.7764; 0.7596; 0.7435; 0.7274; 0.7112; 0.6954;
    0.6797; 0.6644; 0.6491];

%Vector storing the LIBOR rates
L=zeros(NbStep,1);

%For each step, we computed the LIBOR rate
for i=1:NbStep
   L(i,1)=(P(i,1)/P(i+1,1)-1)/DeltaT;
end

%Vector storing the values of di
d=zeros(NbStep,1);
%For each time steps, we compute the value of di
```

```
for n=1:NbStep
   temp=0;
   for o=1:n
       temp=temp+DeltaT*L(o)/(1+DeltaT*L(o))*gamma(o);
   end
   d(n)=temp;
end

%Vector storing the value of Ck computed
C=ones(NbStep,1)*Strike*DeltaT;

%Only the last of Ck is different
C(NbStep,1)=1+Strike*DeltaT;


s=fsolve(@spread,0.01);

function ans=spread(s)
%Function used in the computation of spread. We must find
%the value of s that cancels the spread.

%Variable storing the sum of elements
temp1=0;
for k=1:NbStep
   temp2=1;
   for i=1:k
       temp2=temp2*(1+DeltaT*L(i)*exp(gamma(i)
              *(s+d(i))-gamma(i)^2/2));
   end
   temp1=temp1+C(k)/temp2;
end

%Return temp1-1 since we want to find s such that temp1=1.
ans=temp1-1;

end

%Vector storing the swaption value at each time step
Swaption=zeros(NbStep,1);
%Swaption's price computation
for p=1:n
   Swaption(p)=P(p+1)*DeltaT*(L(p)*normcdf(-s-d(p)+gamma(p))-...
                Strike*normcdf(-s-d(p)));
end
%The swap's value is the sum of swaptions
AnsBGM=sum(Swaption,1);
end
```

With a strike price of 0.06, the BGM model gives us a swap value of \$ 0.1082. Table 11.3 shows the results using different strike prices.

Table 11.3 Evaluation of a swap using the BGM model ($)

Strike	BGM price
0.05	0.1487
0.06	0.1082
0.07	0.0678
0.08	0.0286
0.09	0.0046

Notes and Complementary Readings

For the reader looking for more details on interest rates term structure models and interest rate derivatives, the following books would be relevant: Hull (2005), James and Webber (2000), McDonald (2003), Neftci (2004), Rebonato (1998, 2002, 2004).

As stated in the introduction, the term structure of interest rates and interest rate derivatives literature can be classified into two categories: the arbitrage-free models and the equilibrium models. The arbitrage-free models can be studied in Vasicek (1977), Hull and White (1990), Heath, Jarrow and Morton (1992), the market models in Brace, Gatarek and Musiela (1997), Jamshidian (1997), Miltersen, Sandmann and Sondermann (1997). Equilibrium models have been introduced in the paper by Cox, Ingersoll and Ross (1985a). A theoretical reference for affine models is the paper of Duffie and Kan (1996). The first empirical applications of affine models have been given by Dai and Singleton (2000) and Duffie and Singleton (1999).

For an overview of the term structure of interest rates, see Courtadon (1985), Gibson-Asner (1987), Chapman and Pearson (2001), Yan (2001). For application papers, see for instance Hull and White (2000) for the implementation of Brace, Gatarek and Musiela (1997)'s market model, Clewlow and Strickland (1997a) for an interesting application of simulation techniques in the valuation of interest rate derivatives.

12

Credit Risk and the Valuation of Corporate Securities

Credit risk results in losses incurred by lenders following a counterparty's default. It is a component of risk from debt and represents one of the major risks that must face most financial institutions. There are also many other sources of risk related to the activities and operations of a firm or a bank. Add to this the advent of Basle II which is scheduled to be effective in 2007, and the quantification and management of credit risk becomes of paramount importance.

Credit derivatives' markets have constantly grown at rapid paces in the past few years. Investors increasingly resort to these financial products, more complex and but also more flexible, for the risk management of their activities. Indeed, any investor who wants to eliminate or reduce a risk that he doesn't want to assume or is unable to control can use derivative products in order to transfer this risk to other counterparties which are able to manage or willing to absorb it.

There are two modern fundamental approaches for the measurement and management of credit risk: the structural approach and the reduced-form approach. Merton's (1973, 1974) structural model will allow us to value risky debts issued by a risky firm. This approach lays down the foundation of corporate securities valuation and in particular of the capital structure in corporate finance studied by Modigliani and Miller (1958). We must also note that this approach is the basis of many recent commercial models built for the quantification and management of credit risk, such as the popular Moody's KMV credit risk management model.

In this chapter, we begin by presenting Merton's model for risky debt valuation and the intuitive properties of the term structure of credit risk. Then we explain how a risky debt can be associated with a risk-free debt (issued by a risk-free institution such as a government) minus a put option. This put option constitutes the total loss or the risk premium. This analysis of credit risk using a put option will be used in the following chapter to illustrate the simulation techniques' application from previous chapters to evaluate the total losses and the financial guarantee in the context of a portfolio exposed to default risk from many counterparties.

We end the chapter with an introduction to the reduced-form approach for the valuation of a risky debt. This approach is simple to implement since it only needs an estimation of default rates which are being calibrated from market data. However, its weakness emerges from the difficulty of studying the interaction properties between counterparties involved in the debt contracts.

12.1 VALUATION OF CORPORATE RISKY DEBTS: THE MERTON (1974) MODEL

The value of any debt issued by a firm is a function of three factors:

1. The rates offered on risk free debts (government bonds or high quality corporate bonds);
2. The characteristics and covenants stipulated in the debt contract: maturity, coupon rate, sinking fund, debt's seniority, etc;

3. The probability that the firm reneges partially or fully on its commitments: this is the probability of default.

These are the three essential factors that determine the cost of debt for the borrower which is the interest rate required by the lender.

While there are many theoretical and empirical studies about the term structure of interest rates, Merton (1974) is the first to develop a theory for the valuation of debts with default risk using contingent claims analysis. He analytically derived the term structure of credit spreads as a function of endogenous factors of the firm (its state variables). These models of credit risk analysis are known as structural models.

12.1.1 The Black and Scholes (1973) Model Revisited

Under the usual assumptions of a complete and perfect market, the dynamics of the value of a firm represented by its total assets A through time follows a stochastic diffusion process given by:

$$dA(t) = \mu A(t)dt + \sigma A(t)dW(t), \tag{12.1}$$

with μ being the instantaneous expected rate of return for the firm, σ the instantaneous volatility of the firm's returns, and W a standard Wiener process.

Let $Y = P(A, t)$ be a financial asset whose market value is a function of the firm value A and time t. We can write the dynamics of asset Y in the following differential form:

$$dY(t) = \mu_Y Y(t)dt + \sigma_Y Y(t)dW(t). \tag{12.2}$$

By Ito's lemma, we obtain

$$dY(t) = \frac{\partial P}{\partial A}dA(t) + \frac{1}{2}\frac{\partial^2 P}{\partial A^2}(dA(t))^2 + \frac{\partial P}{\partial t}dt. \tag{12.3}$$

Replacing dA by its expression (1.1) into equation (12.3), we find:

$$dY(t) = \left[\frac{1}{2}\sigma^2 A(t)^2\frac{\partial^2 P}{\partial A^2} + \mu A(t)\frac{\partial P}{\partial A} + \frac{\partial P}{\partial t}\right]dt + \sigma A(t)\frac{\partial P}{\partial A}dW(t). \tag{12.4}$$

The equality of the terms in equations (12.1) and (12.4) brings us to the following system of equations:

$$\begin{cases} \mu_Y Y = \frac{1}{2}\sigma^2 A^2\frac{\partial^2 P}{\partial A^2} + \mu A\frac{\partial P}{\partial A} + \frac{\partial P}{\partial t} \\ \sigma_Y Y = \sigma A\frac{\partial P}{\partial A} \end{cases}. \tag{12.5}$$

We now consider a portfolio V, composed with two assets: the firm's asset and asset Y. The portfolio is composed of a long position in asset Y and a short position of the firm's asset with proportion $\frac{\partial P}{\partial A}$.

$$V(t) = Y(t) - \frac{\partial P}{\partial A}A(t). \tag{12.6}$$

The proportions invested in each asset are such that any stochastic component is removed from the portfolio V:

$$dV(t) = dY(t) - \frac{\partial P}{\partial A} dA(t)$$
$$= \frac{\left(\frac{\partial P}{\partial t} + \frac{1}{2}\frac{\partial^2 P}{\partial A^2}\sigma^2 A(t)^2\right)}{V(t)} V(t)dt. \quad (12.7)$$

This is equivalent of saying that portfolio V's variation is deterministic. Then, in the absence of arbitrage opportunities, the return on the portfolio is equal to the risk-free rate r:

$$dV(t) = V(t)r dt. \quad (12.8)$$

Comparing equations (12.7) and (12.8), we have the following partial differential equation:

$$\frac{1}{2}\sigma^2 A^2 \frac{\partial^2 P}{\partial A^2} + rA\frac{\partial P}{\partial A} + \frac{\partial P}{\partial t} - rP = 0. \quad (12.9)$$

This relation represents the well known partial differential equation of Black-Scholes-Merton. This is a parabolic partial differential equation satisfied by all asset $Y = P(A, t)$ such that the value at each time is a function of A and t.

In order to determine the expression of $P(A, t)$, we must specify the boundary constraints of the problem as well as an initial condition. These constraints allow us to differentiate between the expression of a firm's debt and its equity, for example.

As we have seen in Chapter 9, note the absence of the firm's expected rate of return or any expression related to investors' preferences and expectations. In an arbitrage-free framework, all investors assign the same price to a claim on an asset, given that they agree on the asset's value and volatility.

12.1.2 Application of the Model to the Valuation of a Risky Debt

Merton (1974) adapted the Black-Scholes-Merton (1973) model described above for the valuation of a debt security.

Under the standard assumptions of a complete and perfect market, we consider a firm financed by a unique and homogeneous class of debt and with stocks. The debt consists of issuing a zero-coupon bond with maturity T and face value F.

In the case of a partial or total default, debtors seize all the firm's assets. The firm's shareholders will only recover the residual value of the assets after the debt has been paid.

The firm cannot issue new senior debt nor can it issue a debt of the same rank as the actual debt and pay dividends as long as the debt has not reached maturity.

Consider $P(A, \tau)$ with $\tau = T - t$ the time to maturity, since $\frac{\partial P}{\partial \tau} = -\frac{\partial P}{\partial t}$, the debt value which is the contingent claim must satisfy equation (12.9):

$$\frac{1}{2}\sigma^2 A^2 \frac{\partial^2 P}{\partial A^2} + rA\frac{\partial P}{\partial A} - \frac{\partial P}{\partial \tau} - rP = 0. \quad (12.10)$$

Merton (1974) showed that in the absence of corporate taxes and bankruptcy cost, Modigliani and Miller (1958)'s theorem still holds for a risky firm whose default probability before maturity is positive.

If we define $S(A, t)$ as the shareholders' value at any time t, referred to as the firm's equity, we can express the whole value of the firm as the sum of the shareholders' value and the debt value:

$$A(t) = P(A, \tau) + S(A, t), \tag{12.11}$$

with the constraints $P(0, \tau) = S(0, t) = 0$, and $P(A, \tau) \leq A$, $\forall t$ and $\tau = T - t$. Condition $P(0, \tau) = S(0, t) = 0$ is a condition assuring that P and S take positive values and condition $P(A, \tau) \leq A$ is another constraint ensuring that the debt's value at all time is smaller that the firm's total value.

At the maturity of the debt, if the firm's total value $A(T)$ is higher than F, the debt will be fully reimbursed. In the other case, debtors will only recover the firm's value $A(T)$. Then the debt's value at maturity is

$$P(A, 0) = \min(A, F). \tag{12.12}$$

In order to get an expression for the debt $P(A, \tau)$ at date t, we first determine the value of the firm's equity that we associate with a call on the firm's value as in the Black-Scholes (1973) model.

Equations (12.10) and (12.11) bring us to the following equity valuation equation:

$$\frac{1}{2}\sigma^2 A^2 \frac{\partial^2 S}{\partial A^2} + rA\frac{\partial S}{\partial A} + \frac{\partial S}{\partial t} - rS = 0, \tag{12.13}$$

with boundary conditions:

$$\begin{aligned} S(A, T) &= A - P(A, 0) \\ &= \max(A - F, 0), \\ S(0, t) &= 0, \\ S(A, t) &\leq A. \end{aligned}$$

We find the expression of a European call option written on the firm's value A held by shareholders and whose strike price is F. The counterparty for this contingent claim is the debtor. Black and Scholes's (1973) formula gives us the following expression for the firm's equity:

$$S(A, t) = AN(x_1) - Fe^{-r(T-t)}N(x_1 - \sigma\sqrt{T-t}), \tag{12.14}$$

where

$$x_1 = \frac{\ln(A/F) + (r + \sigma^2/2)(T-t)}{\sigma\sqrt{T-t}} \tag{12.15}$$

and

$$N(x) = \frac{1}{\sqrt{2\pi}} \int_{-\infty}^{x} e^{-\frac{1}{2}z^2} dz \tag{12.16}$$

is the standard normal cumulative distribution function.

Since $P(A, T - t) = A - S(A, t)$, we can show from equation (12.14) that the debt's value is :

$$P(A, T-t) = Fe^{-r(T-t)}N(x_1 - \sigma\sqrt{T-t}) + AN(-x_1). \tag{12.17}$$

After algebraic manipulations, we get the following form:

$$P(A, T - t) = Fe^{-r(T-t)}\Big[N(x_1 - \sigma\sqrt{T-t}) + \frac{1}{d^*}N(-x_1)\Big], \tag{12.18}$$

with

$$d^* = \frac{Fe^{-r(T-t)}}{A} \tag{12.19}$$

also called quasi-debt ratio.

The expected loss EL is given by:

$$\begin{aligned} \text{EL} &= Fe^{-r(T-t)} - P(A, T - t) \\ &= N(-x_1 + \sigma\sqrt{T-t}) \times Fe^{-r(T-t)} \times \Big[1 - \frac{1}{d^*}\frac{N(-x_1)}{N(-x_1 + \sigma\sqrt{T-t})}\Big]. \end{aligned} \tag{12.20}$$

From this expression we find the widely used expressions in credit risk models, such as KMV-Moodys', as well as in recent capital regulations of Basle. These expressions are: the probability of default PD equal to

$$\text{PD} = N(-x_1 + \sigma\sqrt{T-t}), \tag{12.21}$$

the exposure at default EAD given by

$$\text{EAD} = Fe^{-r(T-t)}, \tag{12.22}$$

and finally the loss given default LGD which is equal to

$$\text{LGD} = \Big[1 - \frac{1}{d^*}\frac{N(-x_1)}{N(-x_1 + \sigma\sqrt{T-t})}\Big]. \tag{12.23}$$

In this expression for LGD, the term

$$\frac{1}{d^*}\frac{N(-x_1)}{N(-x_1 + \sigma\sqrt{T-t})} \tag{12.24}$$

represents the recovery rate. As we can see, the recovery rate depends on the assets' value, the debt ratio and the asset returns' volatility. We can show that the recovery rate is correlated with the firm's probability of default.

Since the debt's value can also be written in terms of a risk premium, we set:

$$P(A, T - t) = Fe^{-R(t,T)(T-t)}. \tag{12.25}$$

Then $R(t, T)$ is called the yield to maturity and the expression $R(t, T) - r$ is the default risk premium. The credit spread's term structure, $R(t, T) - r$, is defined by the following equation:

$$R(t, T) - r = -\frac{1}{T-t}\ln\Big(N(x_1 - \sigma\sqrt{T-t}) + \frac{1}{d^*}N(-x_1)\Big). \tag{12.26}$$

Thus, Merton (1974) valued a risky debt and its credit risk premium. At each time t, we define $N(x_1 - \sigma\sqrt{T-t})$ as being the probability that at maturity the debt will be totally reimbursed and $N(-x_1 + \sigma\sqrt{T-t}) = 1 - N(x_1 - \sigma\sqrt{T-t})$ as the probability of default. These probabilities are expressed in a risk neutral world.

As we can see in Figures 12.1 and 12.2, at each time t, and for a given maturity, the risk premium or the credit spread is a function of two variables: the assets' volatility and the ratio

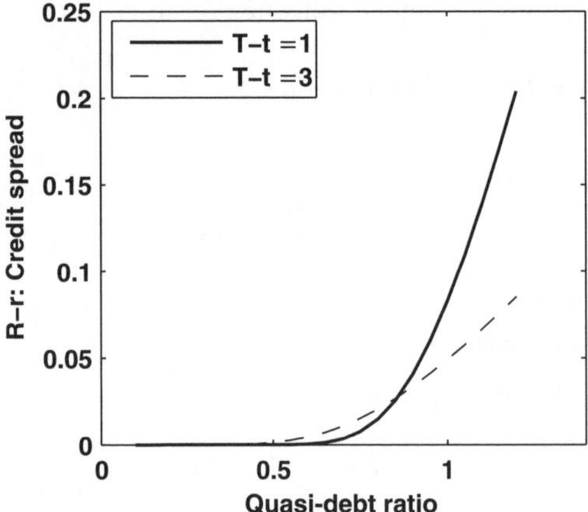

Figure 12.1 Evolution of the risk premium or credit spread as a function of the quasi-debt ratio

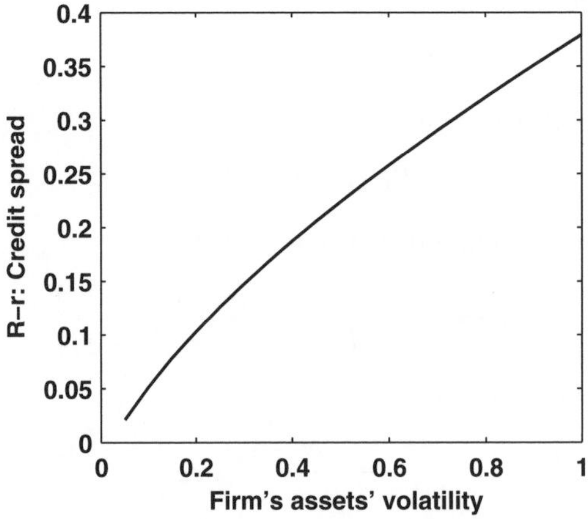

Figure 12.2 Evolution of the risk premium or credit spread as a function of the assets' volatility

of the debt's present value (discounted at the risk free rate) to the firm's value, the quasi-debt ratio.

These figures can be built in calling the MATLAB® function below with a vector $d*$ of quasi-debt ratios (for Figure 12.1) and a vector σ of the firm's asset volatilities (for Figure 12.2) as its parameters.

```
function RiskPremium=RiskPremium(tau,d,A,sigma,r)
%Function computing the risk premium for a risky bond
%Tau: Time to maturity.
%d: Quasi-debt ratio.
%A: Initial value of the firm's assets.
%sigma: Volatility of the firm's assets.
%r: Risk-free interest rate.

%Computing debt with given parameters.
```

```
F = d.*A.*exp(r*tau);

%Computation of parameter x1.
x1 = (log(A./F)+(r+sigma.^2/2).*tau)./(sigma.*sqrt(tau));

%Computation of risk premium.
RiskPremium = -(1./tau).*log(normcdf(x1-sigma.*sqrt(tau))+ ...
              (1./d).*normcdf(-x1));

end
```

We see that the risk premium or credit spread required by lenders is an increasing function of the quasi-debt ratio and the volatility of the firm's value. The assets' volatility stems both from systematic and non-systematic factors.

12.1.3 Analysis of the Debt Risk

Merton (1974) was interested in the analysis of debt's risk relative to the firm's global risk. The variable ν measures this relative risk:

$$\nu(d^*, T-t) = \frac{\sigma_Y}{\sigma}, \tag{12.27}$$

where σ_Y represents the debt's volatility and σ the volatility of firm's assets. From equation (12.5), we get:

$$\nu(d^*, T-t) = A\frac{\partial P/\partial A}{P} = \frac{N(-x_1)}{N(-x_1) + d^* N(x_1 - \sigma\sqrt{T-t})}. \tag{12.28}$$

Since $0 \leq N(.) \leq 1$ and $0 < d*$, we see that $0 \leq \nu \leq 1$. A firm's debt can never be more risky (volatile) than the firm itself. Figures 12.3 and 12.4 show the variations of debt's risk level as a function of the firm's volatility and quasi-debt ratio. These figures have been plotted using the following MATLAB program.

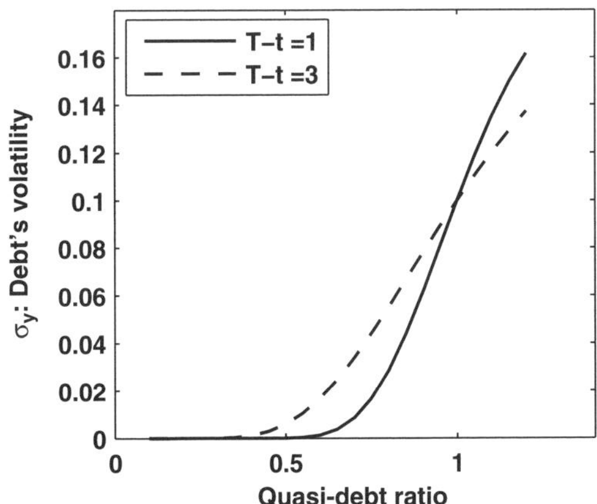

Figure 12.3 Debt volatility as a function of the quasi-debt ratio

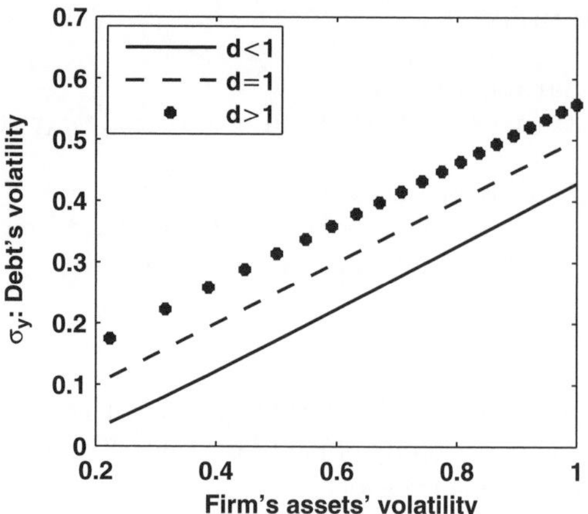

Figure 12.4 Debt volatility as a function of the firm's assets' volatility

```
function VolDebt = VolatilityDebt(tau,d,A,sigma,r)
%Function computing the risky debt volatility
%Tau: Time before maturity.
%d: Quasi-debt ratio.
%A: Firm's assets initial value.
%sigma: Firm's assets volatility.
%r: Risk-free interest rate.

%Determination of the debt value from initial parameters.
F = d.*A.*exp(r*tau);

%Computation of parameter x1.
x1 = (log(A./F)+(r+sigma.^2/2).*tau)./(sigma.*sqrt(tau));

%Computation of debt volatility.
VolDebt = sigma.*normcdf(-x1)./(norm(-x1)+ ...
                        d.*normcdf(x1-sigma.*sqrt(tau)));

end
```

When the quasi-debt ratio becomes very large, that is, when the ratio of the present value of the promised payment F relative to the firm's value becomes very large, we see that the risky debt's price P goes to the firm's value. In that case, the firm's probability of default at maturity goes to one. Similarly, the debt risk σ_Y goes to its superior limit which is the global risk of the firm. Thus we have the following limit conditions

$$\lim_{d^* \to +\infty} P(A, T-t) = A \quad \text{and} \quad \lim_{d^* \to +\infty} \nu(d^*, T-t) = 1. \tag{12.29}$$

When the quasi-debt ratio goes to its inferior limit of 0, the present value of the future payment is very small compared to the firm's market value. Then, the firm is almost certain to

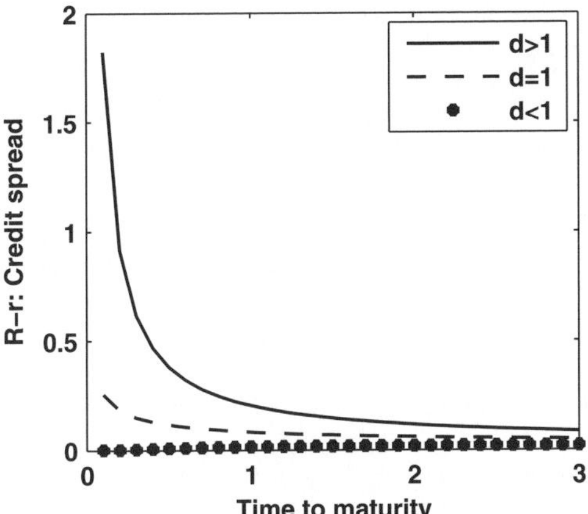

Figure 12.5 Credit spread as a function of the debt maturity

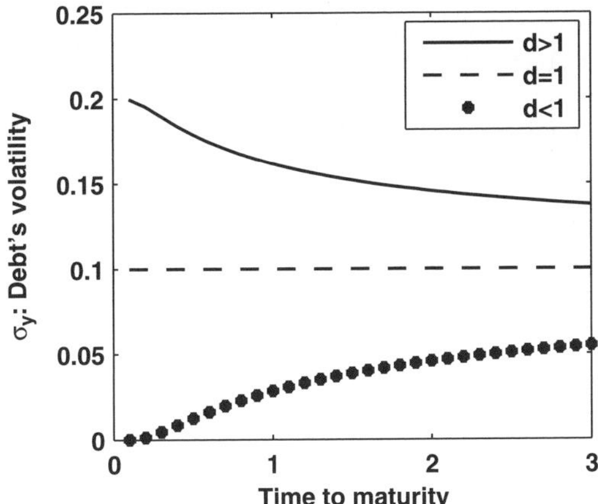

Figure 12.6 Debt's volatility as a function of the debt maturity

honor its payments to its lenders. Thus we get the following limit conditions

$$\lim_{d^*\to 0} P(A, T-t) = Fe^{-r(T-t)} \quad \text{and} \quad \lim_{d^*\to 0} \nu(d^*, T-t) = 0. \tag{12.30}$$

Figures 12.5 and 12.6 show the credit spread and the debt's volatility as a function of time to maturity for different debt ratio levels. To generate these graphs, we use the following program:

```
function Graphs
%Function plotting the credit spread and the debt's volatility
%as a function of different factors.

%ta is the vector of time steps where we want to
%compute the spread and the volatility.
ta=0.1:.1:3;
```

```
%Initial parameters.
d0=0.8;
sigma=0.2;
A=1;
r=0.05;

%Computation of the spread and volatility with d=0.8.
Rmro=RiskPremium(ta,d0,A,sigma,r);
SigmaYo=VolatilityDebt(ta,d0,A,sigma,r);

%Computation of the spread and volatility with d=1.0.
d0=1;
Rmr=RiskPremium(ta,d0,A,sigma,r);
SigmaY=VolatilityDebt(ta,d0,A,sigma,r);

%Computation of the spread and volatility with d=1.2.
d0=1.2;
Rmrs=RiskPremium(ta,d0,A,sigma,r);
SigmaYs=VolatilityDebt(ta,d0,A,sigma,r);

%Then we plot the graphs.
figure
hold on
plot(ta,Rmrs,'k',ta,Rmr,'k--',ta,Rmro,'k*');
xlabel('Time to maturity');
ylabel('R-r: Spread');
legend('d>1', 'd=1','d<1');
hold off

figure hold on
plot(ta,SigmaYs,'k',ta,SigmaY,'k--',ta,SigmaYo,'k*');
ylabel('\sigma_y: debt's volatility');
xlabel('Time to maturity');
legend('d>1','d=1','d<1');
hold off

end
```

12.1.4 Relation Between The Firm's Asset Volatility and Its Equity Volatility

When computing risky debt value, we considered a contingent claim having the firm's value as underlying. This implies that the firm's volatility is an important variable for the valuation of different corporate securities. Unfortunately, since most or all of a firm's assets are generally not traded, it is difficult to directly determine the volatility of the firm's total assets.

However, from market data it is possible to determine the firm's equity volatility if its shares are traded on a stock exchange. In establishing the relation between the equity value and the call option, Ito's lemma allows us to get a system of equations linking the market value and volatility of equity to the market value and volatility of the firm's total assets that cannot be directly observed. Then, from the equity market's data of the traded firm, we can determine the volatility and the market value of the firm's total assets.

As we previously demonstrated, the firm's equity can be seen as a call option owned by shareholders on the firm's total assets with the face value of the debt as its strike price. If we respectively note A and σ_A as the market value and the volatility of the firm's total assets, S and σ_S the market value and the volatility of the firm's equity, and F the debt's face value, then the equity value can be expressed as the price of a call option as follows:

$$S = AN(x) - Fe^{-r\tau}N(x - \sigma_A\sqrt{\tau}), \tag{12.31}$$

where

$$x = \frac{\ln(A/F) + (r + \sigma_A^2/2)\tau}{\sigma_A\sqrt{\tau}}. \tag{12.32}$$

The two volatilities can be linked by the following relation:

$$\sigma_S = \frac{A}{S}\frac{\partial S}{\partial A}\sigma_A, \tag{12.33}$$

which implies

$$\sigma_S = \frac{A}{S}N(x)\sigma_A, \tag{12.34}$$

or

$$\sigma_A = \frac{\sigma_S S}{AN(x)}. \tag{12.35}$$

In conclusion, if we know S and σ_S, using equations (12.31) and (12.35) simultaneously allows us to estimate the values of A and σ_A.

To find the values for A and σ_A we use MATLAB's function *fsolve*. This function is implemented to find the roots of a function. It allows us to find a value for y such that

$$f(y) = 0.$$

For our problem, we begin by building function *VolatilityAssets(y)*.

```
function VolAssets = VolatilityAssets(y)
%Function used in solving the non linear equation to
%estimate the volatility and firm's assets value.
%y(1,1): Assets' value.
%y(2,1): Assets' volatility.

%Extraction to input parameters
A = y(1,1);
sigmaA = y(2,1);

%Initial parameters
S = 100;
sigmaS = 0.3;
r = 0.03;
F = 60;
tau = 1;
```

```
%Computation of parameters x.
x = (log(A/F)+(r+sigmaA^2/2)*tau)/(sigmaA*sqrt(tau));

%Determination of outputs.
VolAssets(1,1) = S-A*normcdf(x)+F*exp(-r*tau)* ...
                        normcdf(x-sigmaA*sqrt(tau));
VolAssets(2,1) = sigmaA-sigmaS*S/(A*normcdf(x));

end
```

Now we use function *fsolve*:

```
%These lines solve simultaneously the two equations.

%Initial value for y0.
y0 = [100;0.3];

%Setting the options for function fsolve.
options = optimset('Display','iter');

%Call of function fsolve to solve the equations.
[y] = fsolve(@VolatilityAssets,y0,options);
```

Using MATLAB's *options* function in this manner, we can see the number of iterations performed by function *fsolve* and the value of the variable *VolatilityAssets* at each iteration. With the values used in the program, we find:

$$A = 158.2267$$
$$\sigma_A = 0.1896.$$

12.2 INSURING DEBT AGAINST DEFAULT RISK

12.2.1 Isomorphism Between a Put Option and a Financial Guarantee

Because issuing a financial guarantee generates a liability or a cost for the guarantor, Merton (1977) derived a formula to value that cost.

Merton (1977) established an isomorphism between the financial guarantee on a loan and a put option in order to apply the Black-Scholes-Merton (1973) option pricing formula to the valuation of financial guarantees.

We consider a European put option written on an underlying asset of value S, with strike price K and maturity T. If at maturity the asset value is smaller than K, ($S(T) < K$), then the option holder exercises the option, and if the value is larger, ($S(T) > K$), the holder doesn't exercise it and will let it expire. In the first case, the option value is $K - S(T)$, and in the second case it is zero. The option's value at maturity date T is then equal to the maximum of zero and the difference $K - S(T)$:

$$\max(K - S(T), 0), \tag{12.36}$$

and its price at each time is determined by the Black and Scholes (1973) formula if the asset's value follows a geometric Brownian motion.

Now we consider a firm borrowing an amount F by issuing bonds. The firm promises to pay the amount F at the maturity date T.

We suppose that the dynamic of the firm's assets A follows a geometric Brownian motion:

$$dA(t) = \mu A(t)dt + \sigma A(t)dW(t), \tag{12.37}$$

with μ the expected instantaneous return on the firm's assets, σ the instantaneous volatility of returns on the firm's assets, and W a standard Wiener process.

If at maturity date T the firm's value $A(T)$ is superior to F, $(A(T)>F)$, then the bond's owner will receive F as promised. However, if the firm's value is inferior to F, $(A(T)<F)$, the firm defaults and the bond's owner seizes the firm's assets; thus the bond's owner will only receive $A(T)$. The debt value $D(T)$ (or equivalently $P(A, 0)$ in equation (12.12)) can therefore be written as

$$D(T) = \min(A(T), F) \tag{12.38}$$

and the value of equity is

$$\max(A(T) - F, 0). \tag{12.39}$$

If the probability of event $\{A(T) - F < 0\}$ is greater than zero, then there is a risk of default, that is, the debt having face value F is risky.

Now suppose that a third counterparty guarantees the loss without default, for example, a government endorser. At the maturity of the debt, if $A(T) < F$, the value of the debt redeemed will be F with the difference $F - A(T)$ being paid by this third counterparty. However, if $A(T) > F$, the firm doesn't need the help of the third counterparty and the contribution of the endorser will therefore be zero. Finally, the amount paid by the endorser will be equal to the maximum of zero and the difference $F - A(T)$:

$$G(T) = \max(F - A(T), 0). \tag{12.40}$$

We can then establish an identity between the financial guarantee and the put option, supposing that F is equal to the strike price K, and A is equal to the value of asset S. When guaranteeing the debt, the endorser is actually issuing a put option that is owned by the firm's shareholders. This option gives the firm the right to sell its assets to the endorser for an amount F at the debt's maturity date T.

If $A(T)>F$, the firm will not exercise its right and the financial guarantee will be zero; however, if $A(T) < F$, it will exercise its right and the financial guarantee's value will be $F - A(T)$. From the isomorphism between the put option and the financial guarantee, the value of the guarantee is determined by the Black and Scholes (1973) formula.

The value of the guarantee G at time t is given by:

$$G(t) = Fe^{-r(T-t)}N(-x_1 + \sigma\sqrt{T-t}) - A(t)N(-x_1), \tag{12.41}$$

where

$$x_1 = \frac{\ln(A(t)/F) + (r + \frac{\sigma^2}{2})(T-t)}{\sigma\sqrt{T-t}}, \tag{12.42}$$

with r the constant risk-free interest rate, F the bond's face value representing the amount of debt, A the value of the firm's assets, $N(.)$ the Gaussian cumulative distribution function, and σ the volatility of the returns on the firm's assets.

12.2.2 Insuring The Default Risk of a Risky Debt

Following Merton's (1974, 1977) work, Babbel (1989) qualitatively sketched an insurance strategy for a bank.

The proposed strategy for the bank is to buy a put option on the firm's assets with an exercise price F corresponding to the debt's face value and a maturity T, the same as the debt's maturity.

Equation (12.17) giving the risky debt's value reported below,

$$P(A, \tau) = Fe^{-r\tau}N(x_1 - \sigma\sqrt{\tau}) + AN(-x_1), \tag{12.43}$$

is modified and rewritten under the following form:

$$\begin{aligned} P(A, \tau) &= Fe^{-r\tau} - [Fe^{-r\tau}N(-x_1 + \sigma\sqrt{\tau}) - AN(-x_1)] \\ &= Fe^{-r\tau} - \text{Put}(A, \tau), \end{aligned} \tag{12.44}$$

with

$$x_1 = \frac{\ln(A/F) + (r + \sigma^2/2)\tau}{\sigma\sqrt{\tau}}. \tag{12.45}$$

This formulation of the debt's value shows that it is equivalent to an identical risk-free debt minus the put option's value Put(A, τ).

Since equities are a call option on the firm's assets, the debt is represented by the difference between the firm's value and the value of its equity. Figure 12.7 shows the bank's payoff function when it takes a position in the previous put option.

From the bank's point of view, owning the firm's risky debt corresponds to having a long position in a risk-free asset and a short position in the put option.

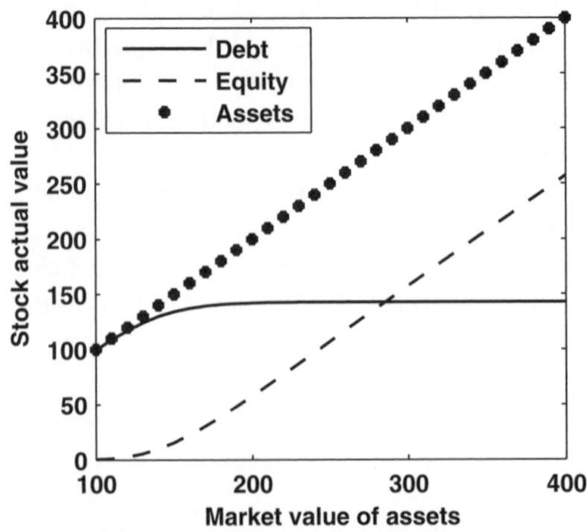

Figure 12.7 Debt, equity and assets' payoffs

To hedge its risky debts portfolio – that is, to eliminate the risky component corresponding to the short position in the put option – the bank must close its position in the put. It must therefore enter into a long position in an identical put option to hedge its portfolio.

By buying this option, or by synthetically creating it, the bank buys an insurance policy on the risky debt, which guarantees the recovery of the face value at maturity, regardless of the fate of the firm.

At maturity T, the put option's value will be

$$\text{Put}(A, 0) = \max(0, F - A), \tag{12.46}$$

added to the risky debt's value $P(A, 0) = \min(A, F)$, the bank is assured that the combination of these two values (risky debt portfolio and put option) gives F:

$$P(A, 0) + \text{Put}(A, 0) = \min(A, F) + \max(0, F - A) = F. \tag{12.47}$$

Because the final payoff of the portfolio composed of long positions in the risky debt and the insured put option is a sure payoff, that is there is no risky component. In an arbitrage-free world, the expected return of the debt asset net of the insurance strategy cost will not be larger than the risk-free rate.

If the bank seeks to make a return superior to the risk-free rate, it must not totally eliminate the risky component of its debt. Its insurance strategy must be adjusted to keep only the risk's portion that it is ready to bear and realize the consequent expected return.

One way to achieve this is to adjust the put option's strike price in function of the floor value of its insurance strategy. Since the new strike price is lower, the bank is only partially hedged and the price of its new put option is inferior to the price of the total insurance option.

To illustrate this idea with an example, we consider the case where the bank wants to insure the recovery of at least a fraction α of the debt. The floor value chosen by the bank would therefore be αF. To achieve that goal, it must get a put option with a strike price of αF.

With this strategy, the bank would be ready to take a maximal loss of $(1 - \alpha)F$. Figure 12.8 illustrates this partial insurance strategy. We used the following parameters: $F = \$\,200$ and $\alpha = 0.75$.

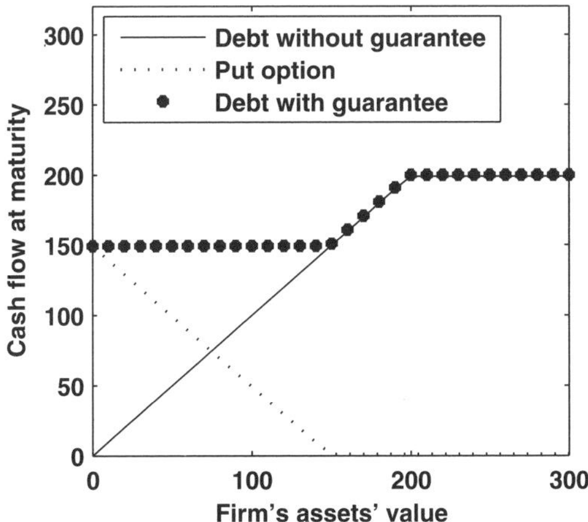

Figure 12.8 Illustration of a loan guarantee

12.2.3 Establishing a Lower Bound for the Price of the Insurance Strategy

In the context of a portfolio of loans, which will be covered in more detail in Chapter 13, suppose that a bank is interested in synthetically replicating a put option on the whole portfolio instead of creating a portfolio of put options for each debt. The reason for this choice is that the strategy in the first case costs less for the same hedge level.

Moreover, the efficiency of the synthetic put option depends on the underlying asset or portfolio of assets of this option. Also, the strike price (the floor value) is very important for the effectiveness of this strategy.

Many aspects must be considered to determine the fraction α to cover. First, we must recognize the possibility that many firms default because of specific conditions rather than systematic risk. This type of risk is on the one hand diversifiable and on the other hand recovered with the risk premium requested from each borrower. Thus, integrating this risk factor in the hedging strategy with the put option would be redundant and would constitute an additional cost for the bank. To avoid this situation, the lender must fix the floor value below the total face value of the debt F.

Recall that when the bank increases the number of loans to independent borrowers (not perfectly correlated), it can predict with more confidence the loss rate on the loans and absorb default cases due to micro-factors, and that is because of the diversification effect.

On the other hand, when a variation of economic factors brings many simultaneous defaults by corporations, there will always be some firms that will be only slightly hit by these factors and honor their contracts.

Even if the systematic risk factor affects all firms, its impact will still be unique to each firm since the degrees of market risk exposition are different. Thus, it is important that the put option's strike price takes this into consideration.

Babbel (1989) determined that the chosen fraction α for decreasing the option's floor value will depend on parameters such as the financial leverage and the borrower's activities. The optimal α parameter can be found using actuarial treatment based on important economic criteria.

In the insurance portfolio context, Leland (1980) and Brennan and Solanki (1981) showed that, generally, the optimal insurance strategy would be to hold a portfolio of options, written on the same asset but with strike prices fixed at different levels $\alpha_i F$ (where $0 < \alpha_i \leq 1$ for $i = 1, \ldots, n$, and n is the number of options).

12.3 VALUATION OF A RISKY DEBT: THE REDUCED-FORM APPROACH

The reduced-form approach has been initially proposed by Jarrow, Lando and Turnbull (1997) and later extended by Duffie and Singleton (1999). We present the works of Duffie and Singleton (1999) in this family of reduced-form approaches.

12.3.1 The Discrete Case with a Zero-Coupon Bond

Before presenting the result in the general case, for the sake of intuition we present the discrete case with a zero-coupon bond. Our goal is to show that in a risk neutral context, the price of a zero coupon bond paying X at maturity is given by

$$P(t,T) = E_t^Q\left[\exp\left(-\int_t^T R(u,T)du\right)X\right], \tag{12.48}$$

where $R(t, T) = r(t) + h(t)L(t)$, with $r(t)$ the short-term risk-free interest rate, $h(t)$ the hazard rate for default at date t and $L(t)$ the expected loss on market value in case of default at date t. Because there is a default probability, quantity $h \times L$ is qualified as the risk-neutral-mean loss rate. $E_t^Q[\,.\,]$ is the expectation under risk neutral probability Q.

We look at a bond whose issuer promises to pay an amount X at maturity without intermediate payments before maturity. In this case, we can write the bond's price the following way:

$$P(t,T) = h(t)e^{-r(t)}E_t^Q[\varphi(t+1)] + (1-h(t))e^{-r(t)}E_t^Q[P(t+1,T)], \tag{12.49}$$

where $h(t)$ is the default probability, $\varphi(t+1)$ is the bond value after default, and $P(t+1, T)$ is the bond value if there is no default. This equation means that the bond's price is equal to the discounted value of payments received between t and $t+1$ in case of default plus the discounted value of price $P(t+1, T)$, in the absence of default.

Suppose that

$$E_t^Q[\varphi(t+1)] = (1-L(t))E_t^Q[P(t+1,T)], \tag{12.50}$$

then

$$P(t,T) = [h(t)(1-L(t)) + (1-h(t))]e^{-r(t)}E_t^Q[P(t+1,T)]. \tag{12.51}$$

And since

$$P(t,T) = e^{-R(t,T)}E_t^Q[P(t+1,T)], \tag{12.52}$$

then $R(t, T)$ is defined as follows

$$e^{-R(t,T)} = h(t)(1-L(t))e^{-r(t)} + (1-h(t))e^{-r(t)}. \tag{12.53}$$

Which implies the following expression for the credit spread

$$R(t,T) - r(t) = -\ln\big(h(t)(1-L(t)) + (1-h(t))\big) = -\ln\big(1-h(t)L(t)\big), \tag{12.54}$$

or

$$R(t,T) \simeq r(t) + h(t)L(t). \tag{12.55}$$

12.3.2 General Case in Continuous Time

Now we consider the general case – that is in continuous time and with the possibility of intermediate payments. For this approach, the default event is generally a jump process modeled by a process $\mathcal{H}(t) = \mathbf{1}_{\{t \geq \tau\}}$. The first date when a jump occurs is τ. The random variable $\mathcal{H}(t)$ takes value 1 if there is a default and zero in the opposite case. We can decompose the expression for $\mathcal{H}$ using $\mathcal{H} = I + M$, with

$$I(t) = \int_0^{\tau \wedge t} h(u)du = \int_0^t h(u)\mathbf{1}_{\{u<\tau\}}du, \quad t \geq 0 \tag{12.56}$$

and M is a martingale. Variable h is interpreted as being the hazard rate under the risk neutral probability.

We look at a bond with a possibility of default. Under the risk neutral probability, the bond's price can be written as:

$$P(t,T) = E_t^Q\left[\int_t^\tau \exp\left(-\int_t^{\tau\wedge s} r(u)du\right)dC(\tau\wedge s)\right], \tag{12.57}$$

or equivalently

$$P(t,T) = E_t^Q\left[\int_t^T \exp\left(-\int_t^{s} R(u,T)du\right)dC(s)\right], \tag{12.58}$$

with $C(t)$ representing the cumulative coupons payments, τ the time of default, and $\tau \wedge s = \min(\tau, s)$. The credit spread is the difference $R(t, T) - r(t)$.

If we suppose that in the case of a default at date t, the amount paid X' using the asset is proportional to its price just before default with a proportionality factor $1 - L(t)$:

$$X' = (1 - L(t))P(t_-, T) \quad \text{with} \quad P(t_-, T) = \lim_{s\uparrow t} P(s, T), \tag{12.59}$$

to have an equality between equations (12.57) and (12.58) for all $t \leq \tau$, then it is possible to show that the following relation must be satisfied:

$$R(t,T) = r(t) + \underbrace{h(t)L(t)}_{\text{spread}}, \tag{12.60}$$

with h the hazard rate and L the expected loss proportion as a percentage of the asset's market value.

Notes and Complementary Readings

Complementary references on this chapter's subjects are: Das (2005), Duffie and Singleton (2003), Lando (2004), Schonbucher (2003).

Generally, this large literature can be classified into two categories: structural approach and reduced-form approach. For the structural approach, seminal papers are Black and Scholes (1973), Merton (1973, 1974, 1977), Black and Cox (1976) and many others. For the reduced-form approach, basic papers are Duffie and Singleton (1999), Jarrow, Lando and Turnbull (1997) and many others.

13

Valuation of Portfolios of Financial Guarantees

Nowadays, credit risk management is a very important and challenging task for all financial institutions. Many institutions manage portfolios composed of many financial assets. To assess, manage and control risks, risk managers need to quantify their portfolio's risk level. For the purpose of credit risk assessment, in the previous chapter we have presented the structural model for the valuation of risky debts.

Financial guarantees are financial instruments which facilitate the management of risks linked to credit portfolios held by institutions. In this chapter, we propose two valuation cases of financial guarantees and credit insurance portfolios using the simulation techniques studied in previous chapters. The first application case presents a portfolio of loan guarantees held by a vulnerable guarantor. In the second case, we again analyze a portfolio of credit insurances but this time using stochastic interest rates and asset volatilities.

These application cases are practice exercises, in the credit risk context, for the simulation techniques covered in this book. For each application case, we provide the MATLAB® program.

13.1 VALUATION OF A PORTFOLIO OF LOAN GUARANTEES

This section is an adaptation of the work by Gendron, Lai and Soumaré (2002). The goal of this study is to use contingent claims analysis (CCA) or option pricing theory to evaluate portfolios of vulnerable private loan guarantees.

To analyze private loan guarantee portfolios, we first consider the value of single guarantees that we aggregate into portfolios. Merton (1977) has established the isomorphism between a single default-free guarantee and a put option. Since we are dealing with private guarantees, this put becomes a complex option on both the value of the guaranteed firm and the guarantor. Under the standard Merton (1974) framework, we first describe the dynamics of the firm and the guarantor, then evaluate the loss per unit of face value, and finally calculate the value of the private loan guarantee.

We use the standard CCA assumptions (e.g. perfect markets, frictionless markets, no taxes, no transaction costs, no asymmetric information, continuous trading, etc.). So, there is no moral hazard (hidden action) and no adverse selection (hidden information). We suppose no violation of the absolute priority rule. When there is violation of the absolute priority rule in bankruptcy situations, senior claimants concede to junior claimants (e.g., manager and shareholders) part of the assets they are entitled to. We also ignore potential agency problems inherent in financial contracting resulting from the conflict of interest between shareholders and debtholders. For each firm, we also assume a simple capital structure consisting of only one zero-coupon bond and equity under a constant interest rate regime.

The insured portfolio consists of N guaranteed firms ($N \geq 2$). There are no cash outflows from the firms (e.g. dividends) before the bonds mature. All the bonds mature at the same time and we assume no other senior debt.

13.1.1 Firms' and Guarantor's Dynamics

As in Merton (1974), the firm's asset follows a continuous diffusion process with constant instantaneous mean return and volatility. Since we have N borrowing firms correlated, the dynamics of the firms' asset values $\{A_i, i = 1, \ldots, N\}$ are given by the following stochastic differential equations:

$$dA_i(t) = \mu_i A_i(t)dt + \sigma_i A_i(t)dW_i(t), \quad i = 1, \ldots, N \tag{13.1}$$

where A_i is firm i's total asset value, μ_i is the instantaneous mean of firm i's assets returns and σ_i is the instantaneous volatility of firm i's asset returns. $\{W_i, i = 1, \ldots, N\}$ are standard Wiener processes correlated as follows

$$\rho_{ij}dt = E[dW_i dW_j], \quad \forall i, j = 1, \ldots, N. \tag{13.2}$$

Or under the risk-neutral probability,

$$dA_i(t) = rA_i(t)dt + \sigma_i A_i(t)d\widetilde{W}_i(t), \quad i = 1, \ldots, N \tag{13.3}$$

where r is the constant risk-free interest rate and $\{\widetilde{W}_i, i = 1, \ldots, N\}$ are standard Wiener processes under the risk-neutral probability.

The firms borrow money by issuing zero-coupon bonds with the same maturities and face values $\{F_i, i = 1, \ldots, N\}$. We assume the existence of a single guarantor.

The guarantor's total asset is also assumed to follow a continuous diffusion process. Let A_G denote the value of the guarantor's total assets. The dynamics of the guarantor are then described by the following process:

$$dA_G(t) = \mu_G A_G(t)dt + \sigma_G A_G(t)dW_G(t), \tag{13.4}$$

or under the risk-neutral probability,

$$dA_G(t) = rA_G(t)dt + \sigma_G A_G(t)d\widetilde{W}_G(t), \tag{13.5}$$

where A_G is the value of the guarantor's assets available for the guarantee, μ_G is the instantaneous mean of the guarantor's assets returns, and σ_G is the instantaneous volatility of the guarantor's assets returns. W_G is a standard Wiener process and its correlations with the sources of risk of the firms' returns are

$$\rho_{iG}dt = E[dW_i dW_G], \quad \forall i = 1, \ldots, N. \tag{13.6}$$

$\widetilde{W}_G$ is a standard Wiener process under the risk-neutral probability.

The above equations describe the dynamics and the interaction of each borrowing firm with the other firms and the guarantor. A firm is influenced not only by its own characteristics (i.e. the instantaneous asset returns' mean and volatility), but also by the dynamics of the other firms and the guarantor.

13.1.2 Value of Loss Per Unit of Debt

The loss per unit of debt measures the average portfolio risk level. It represents the total portfolio risk to be covered by the guarantor. The value of loss per unit of debt, $L_i(T)$, to the debtholders of firm i at maturity T is given by:

$$L_i(T) = \frac{\max(0, F_i - A_i(T))}{F_i}, \tag{13.7}$$

where $A_i(T)$ is firm i's asset value at maturity T and F_i is the face value of the debt issued by firm i. The numerator of this equation denotes the payoff at maturity of a put on the underlying asset A_i, with exercise price F_i. Rewriting the equation as $\max(0, 1 - A_i(T)/F_i)$, it is clear that the loss is a function of the Merton's (1974) pseudo debt-asset ratio F_i/A_i.

At maturity T, the value of loss per unit of debt $L(T)$ for the portfolio is the weighted average of $L_i(T)$:

$$L(T) = \sum_{i=1}^{N} \alpha_i \times L_i(T), \tag{13.8}$$

where α_i is the portfolio weight for firm i and is defined as the relative contribution of firm i to the total portfolio debt value, i.e.,

$$\alpha_i = \frac{F_i}{\sum_{k=1}^{N} F_k}. \tag{13.9}$$

Using the equivalent martingale argument via the expectation $E^Q[.]$, the present value of the portfolio loss per unit of debt is the expected value of loss per unit at maturity discounted at the constant risk-free interest rate r, or:

$$\begin{aligned} L(t) &= E^Q\left[e^{-r(T-t)} L(T)\right] \\ &= E^Q\left[e^{-r(T-t)} \sum_{i=1}^{N} \frac{F_i}{\sum_{k=1}^{N} F_k} \times \frac{\max(0, F_i - A_i(T))}{F_i}\right] \\ &= E^Q\left[e^{-r(T-t)} \sum_{i=1}^{N} \frac{\max(0, F_i - A_i(T))}{\sum_{k=1}^{N} F_k}\right]. \end{aligned} \tag{13.10}$$

Note the similarity between the portfolio loss per unit $L(t)$ and the loss given default LGD seen in section 12.1.2.

MATLAB program

```
function rep=MeanPremium
%Function computing the average insurance premium in the case
%of a guarantor and three firms.

%Initial parameters
T=1;
NbStep=52;
NbTraj=100000;
```

```
r=0.05;
mu=r;            %Instantaneous rate of return for
                 %firms under risk-neutral probability
DeltaT=T/NbStep;

%Initial values for the firms
A1=30*ones(NbTraj,1);
A2=40*ones(NbTraj,1);
A3=50*ones(NbTraj,1);

%Initial value of guarantor
AG=80*ones(NbTraj,1);

%Covariance matrix construction
Rho12=0.1;
Rho13=0.5;
Rho23=-0.3;
sigma1=0.2;
sigma2=0.3;
sigma3=0.5;
sigmaG=0.25;
MatrixCov=DeltaT*[1,Rho12,Rho13,0;Rho12,1,Rho23,0;Rho13,Rho23,1,0;
                  ...0,0,0,1];
MatrixL=chol(MatrixCov)';

%Face values of the firms' debts
Debt1=20;
Debt2=30;
Debt3=30;

%Vector of theoretical means of the Brownian motions.
MatrixMean=zeros(4,1);

%For each step, we simulate the firms's prices and the guarantor's
 value.
for i=1:NbStep

   %Use of the quadratic resampling technique.
   Temp=MatrixL*randn(4,NbTraj);
   dW=ReQuadrac(Temp,MatrixMean,MatrixCov)';

   A1=A1.*(1+mu*DeltaT*ones(NbTraj,1)+sigma1*dW(:,1));
   A2=A2.*(1+mu*DeltaT*ones(NbTraj,1)+sigma2*dW(:,2));
   A3=A3.*(1+mu*DeltaT*ones(NbTraj,1)+sigma3*dW(:,3));
   AG=AG.*(1+mu*DeltaT*ones(NbTraj,1)+sigmaG*dW(:,4));

end

%Sum of losses divided by the total of debts.
LossPayOff=(max(0,Debt1-A1)+max(0,Debt2-A2)+max(0,Debt3-A3))/ ...
                                                (Debt1+Debt2+Debt3);
```

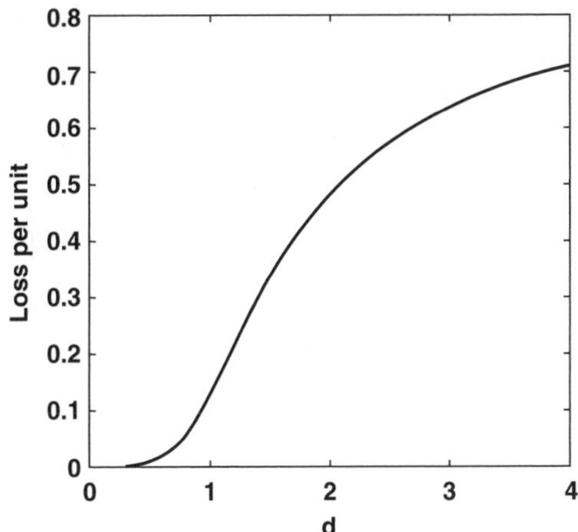

Figure 13.1 Loss per unit of debt as a function of the quasi-debt ratio d^*

```
%Discounting
Premium=exp(-r*T)*mean(LossPayOff,1);

rep=Premium;

end
```

Figure 13.1 plots the loss per unit of debt as a function of the quasi-debt ratio. Recall from Chapter 12 that the quasi-debt ratio is defined by:

$$d^* = \frac{e^{-rT} F_i}{A_i}.$$

We begin the simulation with the following initial assets values $A_1(0) = A_2(0) = A_3(0) = \$\,50$. We compute the amount of debt using the quasi-debt ratio (which is equal for each firm). Then we run a simulation of 50 000 trajectories for each value of d^* from 0.02 to 4.00. The result is plotted in Figure 13.1.

13.1.3 Value of Guarantee Per Unit of Debt

Since a private guarantor can default, the value of the guarantee at maturity is bounded by the value at maturity of the guarantor, $A_G(T)$. Hence, the value of the private guarantee at maturity per unit of debt, $G(T)$, will be the minimum of the expected loss and the residual value of the guarantor.

$$\begin{aligned} G(T) &= \min\left(\sum_{i=1}^{N} \frac{\max(0, F_i - A_i(T))}{\sum_{k=1}^{N} F_k}, \frac{A_G(T)}{\sum_{k=1}^{N} F_k}\right) \\ &= \frac{1}{\sum_{k=1}^{N} F_k} \min\left(\sum_{i=1}^{N} \max(0, F_i - A_i(T)), A_G(T)\right). \end{aligned} \tag{13.11}$$

Again, using the equivalent martingale argument, we obtain the following equation for the present value of the guarantee:

$$G(t) = E^Q\left[e^{-r(T-t)}\frac{1}{\sum_{k=1}^{N} F_k}\min\left(\sum_{i=1}^{N}\max(0, F_i - A_i(T)), A_G(T)\right)\right]. \tag{13.12}$$

This expression can be interpreted as a complex option on a portfolio of puts and on the value of the guarantor.

Given the curse of dimensionality due to the large number of underlying assets involved in the problem, we use the Monte Carlo simulations technique studied in previous chapters to evaluate these guarantees.

Matlab Program

The program simulating the guarantee per unit of debt is similar to the last one except for the payoff line.

```
function rep=GuaranteePremium
%Function computing the average guarantee premium in the case of
%one guarantor and three firms
%Initial parameters
T=1;
NbStep=52;
NbTraj=100000;
r=0.05;
mu=r;                    %Instantaneous return for the firms
DeltaT=T/NbStep;
%Initial values of the firms
A1=30*ones(NbTraj,1);
A2=40*ones(NbTraj,1);
A3=50*ones(NbTraj,1);
%Initial value of the guarantor
AG=80*ones(NbTraj,1);
%Construction of the covariance matrix.
Rho12=0.1;
Rho13=0.5;
Rho23=-0.3;
sigma1=0.2;
sigma2=0.3;
sigma3=0.5;
sigmaG=0.25;
MatrixCov=DeltaT*[1,Rho12,Rho13,0;Rho12,1,Rho23,0;Rho13,Rho23,1,0;
          ... 0,0,0,1];
MatrixL=chol(MatrixCov)';

%Face value of the firms' debts
Debt1=20;
Debt2=30;
Debt3=30;
%Vector of theoretical average of Brownian motions
```

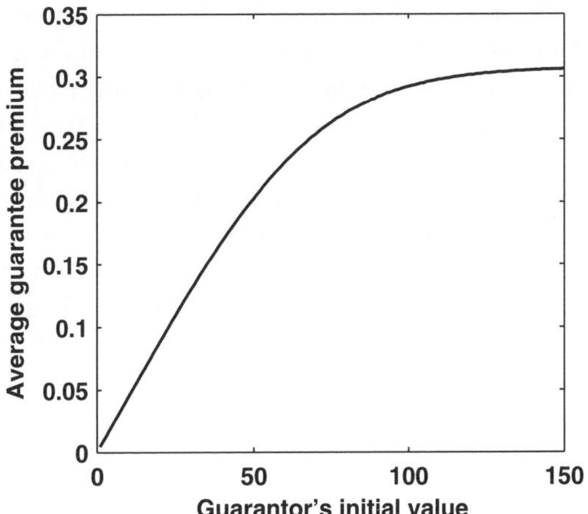

Figure 13.2 Guarantee per unit of debt as a function of the guarantor's asset value

```
MatrixMean=zeros(4,1);
%For each step, we simulate the firms' prices and the
 guarantor's value.
for i=1:NbStep
   %Use of quadratic resampling technique.
   Temp=MatrixL*randn(4,NbTraj);
   dW=ReQuadratic(Temp,MatrixMean,MatrixCov)';
   A1=A1.*(1+mu*DeltaT*ones(NbTraj,1)+sigma1*dW(:,1));
   A2=A2.*(1+mu*DeltaT*ones(NbTraj,1)+sigma2*dW(:,2));
   A3=A3.*(1+mu*DeltaT*ones(NbTraj,1)+sigma3*dW(:,3));
   AG=AG.*(1+mu*DeltaT*ones(NbTraj,1)+sigmaG*dW(:,4));

end
%Computation of the the mean guarantee premium
PremiumPayOff=min(max(0,Debt1-A1)+max(0,Debt2-A2)+...
                  max(0,Debt3-A3),AG)/(Debt1+Debt2+Debt3);
%Discounting
Premium=exp(-r*T)*mean(PremiumPayOff,1);
rep=Premium;
end
```

We run this program with initial assets values $A_i(0) = \$\,50$ and debt face value $F_i = \$\,75$. We vary the guarantor's initial value from \$ 1 to \$ 150. The results are illustrated in Figure 13.2.

13.2 VALUATION OF CREDIT INSURANCE PORTFOLIOS USING MONTE CARLO SIMULATIONS

This section is based on the work by Gendron, Lai and Soumaré (2006 a and b). The objective of this study is to investigate the effect of multiyear risk-management decisions on credit insurance portfolios. For this purpose, we contrast portfolio risk diversification with increased insurer's capital in a multiyear contractual environment. Using equivalent martingale measures (EMMs) in Harrison and Pliska (1981), we measure the value of credit insurance through the market value of vulnerable financial guarantees, which accounts for all shortfalls, clients' and insurers' specific risks, and capital as well as the correlations between the parties.

From an insurance company's viewpoint, portfolios of financial guarantees are complex because of their risk distribution structure and the systematic nature of credit risk, which underscores the importance of multiyear management.

The model presented below captures different types of risks inherent to portfolios of credit insurances through stochastic cash flows of the policyholders, net-assets of the insurer, stochastic interest rate and stochastic volatilities. In addition, default before the maturity of the debt is triggered by missing on a coupon payment.

13.2.1 Stochastic Processes

We make the standard assumptions of no-arbitrage pricing of Merton (1974) and Harrison and Kreps (1979), i.e., perfect, frictionless markets in which securities are traded in continuous time, with no tax, no transaction costs, no asymmetric information, and so on.

Assume a complete probability space $(\Omega, \mathbf{F}, Q)$ where $\mathbf{F} = \{\mathcal{F}_t; t \geq 0\}$ is the filtration, $\mathcal{F}_t$ is the set of information available at time t and Q the risk-neutral probability measure.

We consider a portfolio of N credit insurance contracts. Each credit contract consists of insuring one debt. Let us denote by A_i the cash flows available for loan repayment by the policyholder i ($i = 1, \ldots, N$). The process describing the cash flows are

$$dA_i(t) = r(t)A_i(t)dt + \sigma_i(t)A_i(t)d\widetilde{W}_i(t), \quad i = 1, \ldots, N, \tag{13.13}$$

where r is the short-term interest rate, $\{\sigma_i; i = 1, \ldots, N\}$ are the instantaneous volatilities of the cash flows' returns described below (see equation (13.16) for the volatilities and equation (13.17) for the interest rate). $\{\widetilde{W}_i; i = 1, \ldots, N\}$ are Wiener processes under the risk-neutral probability.

Let ASSET be the total assets of the insurer and LIABILITIES the current existing liabilities. The total net-assets available to the insurance company to support credit insurance claims is denoted by A_G:

$$A_G(t) = \max(\text{ASSET}(t) - \text{LIABILITIES}(t), 0). \tag{13.14}$$

This equation links conceptually the insurer's net-asset, capital, and insuring capacity. It is assumed to follow the Ito diffusion process

$$dA_G(t) = r(t)A_G(t)dt + \sigma_G(t)A_G(t)d\widetilde{W}_G(t), \tag{13.15}$$

where σ_G is the instantaneous volatility of the insurer's total net-assets described below in equation (13.16) and $\widetilde{W}_G$ a Brownian motion under the risk-neutral probability.

The volatilities of the cash flows $\{A_i, \quad i = 1, \ldots, N\}$ and the insurer's total net-assets (A_G) are stochastic and their processes are given as follows:

$$d\sigma_k^2(t) = v_k\big(\beta_k - \sigma_k^2(t)\big)dt + \phi_k\sigma_k(t)(\rho_{k\sigma}d\widetilde{W}_k(t) + \sqrt{1 - \rho_{k\sigma}^2}\,d\widetilde{W}'_k(t)), \tag{13.16}$$

for $k = 1, \ldots, N, G$, where $\widetilde{W}'_k$, $k = 1, \ldots, N, G$ are Wiener processes. The coefficients $\{v_k, \beta_k, \phi_k;\ k = 1, \ldots, N, G\}$ are respectively the speed of adjustment, the long-run mean and the variation of the diffusion volatility, and the constants $\{\rho_{k\sigma};\ k = 1, \ldots, N, G\}$ represent the correlations between the variables and their volatilities. Note that the volatility risk is rewarded in the sense that it earns a risk premium and it is incorporated into the stochastic process through the speed of adjustment parameter.

The dynamic of the stochastic interest rate is

$$dr(t) = \kappa(\theta - r(t))dt + \sigma_r r(t)^{\gamma} d\widetilde{W}_r(t), \tag{13.17}$$

where κ is the speed of adjustment, θ is the long-run mean. σ_r is the volatility of the interest rate changes which is set to a constant, and $\widetilde{W}_r$ is a Wiener process. Note that, as discussed in Chapter 11, the interest rate risk is rewarded by way of its market price of risk. Here, this is implicitly reflected in equation (13.17) and adjusted through κ.

The Cox, Ingersoll and Ross (CIR, 1985b) and Vasicek (1977) interest rate processes are particular cases of this process, with γ equal to 0.5 for the CIR (1985) process and 0 for the Vasicek (1977) process.

The Brownian motions satisfy the following conditions

$$E_t^Q[d\widetilde{W}_k(t)d\widetilde{W}_l(t)] = \rho_{kl}dt, \quad \forall k, l \in \{1, \ldots, N, G, r\}, \quad k \neq l, \tag{13.18}$$

$$E_t^Q[d\widetilde{W}_k(t)d\widetilde{W}_l'(t)] = 0, \quad \forall (k, l) \in \{1, \ldots, N, G, r\} \times \{1, \ldots, N, G\}, \tag{13.19}$$

$$E_t^Q[d\widetilde{W}_k'(t)d\widetilde{W}_l'(t)] = 0, \quad \forall k, l = \{1, \ldots, N, G\}, \quad k \neq l. \tag{13.20}$$

13.2.2 Expected Shortfall and Credit Insurance Valuation

The debt underwritten on the contract of policyholder i is represented by a coupon paying bond with coupon C_i at each interval Δt of time and face value F_i at maturity date T_i. The coupon payments are made semiannually and subtracted from the policyholder's cash flows' value denoted by A_i. The insurer seizes the policyholder's remaining cash flows at the first default date.

Again, we use a no-arbitrage argument similar to Harrison and Kreps (1979) and Harrison and Pliska (1981); therefore the debts are priced using the equivalent martingale measure (EMM) Q as follows.

In absence of default, the bond price at any time τ is

$$D_i(\tau) = E_t^Q\left[\sum_{k=0}^{\frac{T-\tau}{\Delta t}} \exp\left(-\int_{\tau}^{\tau+k\Delta t} r(s)ds\right) C_i + \exp\left(-\int_{\tau}^{T} r(s)ds\right) F_i\right]. \tag{13.21}$$

From this formula, the default-free coupon bond price at time τ is the expected present value of all future payments until maturity. The first part of the expectation expression is the present value of all remaining coupons and the second part is the present value of the final payment.

The policyholder i defaults on its debt service if the cash flow A_i drops below the required payment. This occurs at the first exit time τ_i:

$$\tau_i = \inf\{t \text{ such that } A_i(t) < C_i \text{ or } A_i(t) < C_i + F_i \text{ if } t = T_i\}. \tag{13.22}$$

Hence, the price of the risky debt at time zero without guarantee, $D_{i,NG}(0)$, is

$$D_{i,NG}(0) = E_0^Q\left[\sum_{k=1}^{[\frac{\tau_i}{\Delta t}]-1} \exp\left(-\int_0^{k\Delta t} r(s)ds\right) C_i + \exp\left(-\int_0^{\tau_i} r(s)ds\right) A_i(\tau_i)\right]. \tag{13.23}$$

Intuitively, from equation (13.23), in the absence of a credit insurance, all future payments are lost upon default at time τ_i. The risky debt price is the expectation (under the risk-neutral probability Q) of the present value at time zero of all coupons received prior to default plus the value $A_i(\tau_i)$. Here, the default trigger date is random and can be any coupon date. For a zero-coupon bond, the default trigger date has no random component, corresponding exactly to the maturity date of the debt.

Credit insurance enhances the value of the risky debt. The price at time zero of the insured debt, $D_{i,G}(0)$, is

$$\begin{aligned} D_{i,G}(0) &= D_{i,NG}(0) \\ &\quad + E_0^Q\left[\exp\left(-\int_0^{\tau_i} r(s)ds\right)\min(\alpha_i A_G(\tau_i), D_i(\tau_i) - A_i(\tau_i))\right], \end{aligned} \tag{13.24}$$

where α_i is the allocation percentage of the insurer's wealth to policyholder i.

In equation (13.24), the price of the insured debt is equal to the price of the risky debt without credit insurance plus an additional amount representing the value of the credit insurance. Upon default at time τ_i, if the insurer's contribution ($\alpha_i A_G(\tau_i)$) combined with the value of the cash flows ($A_i(\tau_i)$) is sufficient to cover all remaining payments on the debt, then the lender receives full payment. Otherwise, the insurer can only provide partial payment.

The total expected shortfall on the loan is measured by the difference between the value of the default-free debt and the noninsured debt: $D_i(0) - D_{i,NG}(0)$. In the spirit of Merton (1977), the difference between the default-free debt and the insured risky debt comes from the fact that insurance companies can default. Some government debt can practically be considered as default-free. The value of credit insurance is the difference between the insured risky debt and the noninsured risky debt:

$$\begin{aligned} D_{i,G}(0) - D_{i,NG}(0) = E_0^Q\Bigg[&\exp\left(-\int_0^{\tau_i} r(s)ds\right) \\ &\times \min(\alpha_i A_G(\tau_i), D_i(\tau_i) - A_i(\tau_i))\Bigg]. \end{aligned} \tag{13.25}$$

In a portfolio context, our key variables are the total expected shortfall (ES) and the credit insurance (CI) per unit of total risk-free debt value and are given by

$$\text{ES} = \frac{\sum_{i=0}^{N}(D_i(0) - D_{i,NG}(0))}{\sum_{i=0}^{N} D_i(0)}, \tag{13.26}$$

$$\text{CI} = \frac{\sum_{i=0}^{N}(D_{i,G}(0) - D_{i,NG}(0))}{\sum_{i=0}^{N} D_i(0)}. \tag{13.27}$$

ES captures not only the stochastic cash flows and insurer's net-assets risks, but also the interest-rate risk and the correlation risks among these sources of uncertainty. The difference between ES and CI represents what is not covered by the risky insurer. For a riskless insurer, e.g., government corporations, this difference is zero.

13.2.3 MATLAB Program

Here is the MATLAB program to value portfolios of credit insurances.

```
function Guarantee(NbCoupons,VG,d)
%Function simulating the guaranteed debt and debt without guarantee
%for three firms.
%NbCoupons: Number of coupons of the debts.
%AG: Initial value of the guarantor.
%d: Quasi debt ratio initial for all firms.
%Initial parameters
T=NbCoupons/2;
NbSteps=NbCoupons;
NbTraj=5000;
DeltaT=T/NbSteps;
%Cholesky decomposition.
MatrixL=CreateMatrixChol(DeltaT);
%Vectors keeping information on different
%debts for computing the mean on all trajectories.
DebtNoGuaranteeMean=zeros(3,1);
DebtGuaranteeMean=zeros(3,1);
DebtNonRiskyMean=zeros(3,1);
%Vectors keeping information on total loss
%expected and credit insurance.
Es=zeros(NbTraj,1);
Ci=zeros(NbTraj,1);
%For each trajectories we compute the debts' values
for j=1:NbTraj
    %We initialize to 0 the information vectors
    [r,A,Sigma,sigmaGuarant,Default,ValueDefault,...
    ValueDefaultGuarant,RateBeforeDefault,RateAfterDefault,...
    ValueDebt,ValuePaid,DebtNoGuarantee,DebtGuarantee]=...
    InitializeToZero;
    %Simulation of brownian motion, interest rate and variance.
    dW=GenerateVariable(MatrixL,NbSteps);
    r=SimulationRates(dW,r,NbSteps,DeltaT);
    Sigma=SimulationSigma(dW,Sigma,NbSteps,DeltaT);
    %Computation of debts' value by discounting
    Debt=A*d*exp(sum(r)*DeltaT);
    %Computation of the guarantor allocated to each debt.
    alpha=ComputeAlpha(Debt);
    %Coupon rate of debts.
    Coupon=[5;5;5];
    %Initialization of the guarantor's value.
    Guarant=AG;
    %Computation of the risk free debt
    DebtNonRisky=ComputeDebtNonRisky(r,Coupon,Debt,DeltaT, ...
                                                    NbSteps);
    %Addition of non risky debt to computation of the mean
    DebtNonRiskyMean=DebtNonRiskyMean+DebtNonRisky;
    %For each step, we simulate firms' defaults and store
```

```
information.
  for i=1:NbSteps-1
     %Vector storing the discounting rate from time 0 until
      default.
     RateBeforeDefault=RateBeforeDefault+DeltaT*r(1,i) ...
                                       *(ones(3,1)-Default);
     %Simulation of firms and guarantor's value
     A = max(A.*(1+r(1,i)*DeltaT + Sigma(1:3,i).*dW(1:3,i)),0);
     Guarant=Guarant*(1+r(1,i)*DeltaT+Sigma(4,i)*dW(4,i));
     %Temp keeps in memory firms defaulting at time
     Temp=(A<Coupon).*(1-Default);
     %Vector keeping in memory the firm's value at default time
     ValueDefault=ValueDefault+Temp.*A;
     %Vector keeping the guarantor's value when a firm defaults
     ValueDefaultGuarant=ValueDefaultGuarant+alpha.*Guarant.*Temp;
     %Vector keeping in memory which firm defaulted since
     time 0.
     Default=Default|Temp;
     %Vector keeping the value of remaining debt a time of
     default.
     ValueDebt=ValueDebt+Temp.*ComputeValueDebt(i,NbSteps,r, ...
                                   Debt,Coupon,Temp.*A,DeltaT);
     %Vector keeping the value paid by guarantor when a default
      occurs.
     ValuePaid=ValuePaid+min(Guarant*alpha, ValueDebt).*Temp;
     %Amount paid are deducted from the guarantor assets's value
     Guarant=Guarant-sum(ValuePaid.*Temp);
     %Computation of debt without guarantee
     DebtNoGuarantee = DebtNoGuarantee + ...
         exp(-RateBeforeDefault).*min(Coupon,A).*(1-Default+
         Temp);
     %Initialization of debt of the firms in default
     Debt=Debt-Debt.*Temp;
     %Computation of new alpha
     alpha=ComputeAlpha(Debt);
     %Computation of firms values when paying coupon.
     A=A-min(Coupon,A);
  end
  %For the last step, we make computation outside principal loop.
  RateBeforeDefault=RateBeforeDefault+ ...
          DeltaT*r(1,NbSteps)*(ones(3,1)-Default);
  A = max(0,A.*(1+r(1,NbSteps)*DeltaT + Sigma(1:3,NbSteps).*...
            dW(1:3,NbSteps)));
  Guarant=Guarant*(1+r(1,NbSteps)*DeltaT+Sigma(4,NbSteps)*...
                    dW(4,NbSteps));
  Temp=(A<Coupon+Debt).*(1-Default);
  ValueDefault=ValueDefault+Temp.*A;
  ValueDefaultGuarant=ValueDefaultGuarant+Guarant.*Temp;
  Default=Default|Temp;
  DebtNoGuarantee = DebtNoGuarantee + ...
   exp(-RateBeforeDefault).*min(Coupon+Debt,A).*(1-Default+Temp);
```

```
    ValueDebt=ValueDebt+Temp.*(Coupon+Debt-A);
    ValuePaid=ValuePaid+min(Guarant*alpha, ValueDebt).*Temp;
    %Computation of guaranteed debt's value
    DebtGuarantee=DebtGuarantee+exp(-RateBeforeDefault).*ValuePaid;
    %Deducting the amounts paid from the firms' values
    A=A-min(Coupon+Debt,A);
    %Computation of expected loss and credit insurance.
    Es(j) = sum(DebtNonRisky-DebtNoGuarantee)/sum(DebtNonRisky);
    Ci(j) = sum(DebtGuarantee)/sum(DebtNonRisky);
    %Addition of the debt guarantee and debt non guarantee for the
    mean.
    DebtNoGuaranteeMean=DebtNoGuaranteeMean+DebtNoGuarantee;
    DebtGuaranteeMean=DebtGuaranteeMean+DebtGuarantee;
end
%Computation of expected loss and credit insurance for
 computing the mean.
EsMoy=mean(Es)
CiMoy=mean(Ci)
end

function MatrixL=CreateMatrixChol(DeltaT)
%Function computing Cholesky decomposition of the covariance
 matrix.
    %Correlations
    Rho12=0.1; Rho13=0.5; Rho23=-0.3;
    Rho1G=0.2; Rho2G=0.2; Rho3G=0.2;
    Rho1r=0.1; Rho2r=0.1; Rho3r=0.1;
    RhoGr=0.1;
    %Construction of the covariance matrix
    MatrixCov=DeltaT*[1,Rho12,Rho13,Rho1G, Rho1r, 0, 0, 0, 0;
        Rho12,1,Rho23, Rho2G, Rho2r, 0, 0, 0, 0;
        Rho13,Rho23,1,Rho3G, Rho3r, 0, 0, 0, 0;
        Rho1G, Rho2G, Rho3G, 1, RhoGr, 0, 0, 0, 0;
        Rho1r, Rho2r, Rho3r, RhoGr, 1, 0, 0, 0, 0;
        0,0,0,0,0,1,0,0,0;
        0,0,0,0,0,0,1,0,0;
        0,0,0,0,0,0,0,1,0;
        0,0,0,0,0,0,0,0,1];
    %Cholesky decomposition
    MatrixL=chol(MatrixCov)';
end

function dW=GenerateVariable(MatrixL,NbSteps)
%Function generating brownian motions.
%MatrixL: Cholesky decomposition matrix
%NbSteps: Number of time steps.
       dW=MatrixL*randn(9,NbSteps);
end

function  r=SimulationRates(dW,r0, NbSteps,DeltaT);
%Function simulating the interest rate.
```

```
%dW: Brownian motion
%r0: Interest rate at time t=0.
%NbSteps: Number of time steps.
%DeltaT
    r=zeros(1,NbSteps);
    r(1,1)=r0;
    %Simulation of interest rate avoiding negative rates.
    for j=1:NbSteps-1
        r(1,j+1)=max(r(1,j)+0.02*(0.05-r(1,j))*DeltaT+ ...
                                    0.2*r(1,j)^(0.5)*dW(5,j),0);
    end
end

function Sigma=SimulationSigma(dW,Sigma0,NbSteps,DeltaT)
%Function simulating the firms' volatilities.
%dW: Brownian motions
%Sigma0: Initial volatility
%NbSteps: Number of time steps
%DeltaT
    %Parameters
    nu=0.5;
    beta=Sigma0.^2;
    phi=0.15;
    rho=0.1;
    Sigma=zeros(4,NbSteps);
    Sigma(:,1)=Sigma0;
    %Simulation of volatilities avoiding negative volatilities.
    for j=1:NbSteps-1
        Sigma(:,j+1)=(max(0,Sigma(:,j).^2+nu*(beta- ...
                     Sigma(:,j).^2)*DeltaT+ ...
                     phi*Sigma(:,j).*(rho*dW(1:4,j)+ ...
                     (1-rho)^0.5*dW(6:9,j)))).^0.5;
    end
end

function Alpha=ComputeAlpha(Debt)
%Function computing the guarantor's proportion allocated to each
debt
%Debt: Remaining debts vector.
    %Computation of alpha avoiding dividing by zero.
    if sum(Debt,1)~=0
        Alpha=Debt/(sum(Debt,1));
    else
        Alpha=0*Debt;
    end
end

function ValueDebt=ComputeValueDebt(i,NbSteps,r,Debt,Coupon,A, ...
                                             DeltaT);
%Function computing the debt's value and remaining debt when
there is
```

```
%default before maturity.
%i: Time of default
%NbSteps: Number of time steps
%r: Risk free interest rate
%Debt: Firms debts' values
%Coupon: Each debt coupon
%A: Firms' values
%DeltaT
    %The remaining debt comprises the coupon's unpaid part
    ValueDebt=Coupon-A;
    %Addition of coupons that would have been paid if there were...
    % no default.
    for j=i+1:NbSteps-1
        ValueDebt=ValueDebt+exp(-sum(r(i+1:j))*DeltaT)*Coupon;
    end
    %Addition of last payment comprises the facial value.
    ValueDebt=ValueDebt+exp(-sum(r(i+1:NbSteps))*DeltaT)*(Coupon+
    Debt);
end

function DebtNonRisky=ComputeDebtNonRisky(r,Coupon,Debt, ...
                                                       DeltaT,NbSteps)
%Function computing the debts' value if they were risk free.
%r: Interest rate
%Coupon: Coupon rate
%Debt: Face values of debts.
%DeltaT
%NbSteps: Number of time steps.
%Initialization of the risk free debt.
DebtNonRisky=zeros(3,1);
%For each coupon, we discount at risk free rate.
for j=1:NbSteps-1
    DebtNonRisky=DebtNonRisky+exp(-sum(r(1:j))*DeltaT)*Coupon;
end
%Addition of last coupon and face value of debt.
DebtNonRisky=DebtNonRisky+ ...
                       exp(-sum(r(1:NbSteps))*DeltaT)*(Coupon+Debt);
end

function [r,A,Sigma,sigmaGuarant,Default,ValueDefault,...
  ValueDefaultGuarant,RateBeforeDefault,RateAfterDefault,...
  ValueDebt,ValuePaid,ValueNoGuarantee,DebtGuarantee]=Initialize
  ToZero
%Function initializing parameters and vectors to their initial
 values.
    r=0.05;
    A=[50;50;50];
    Sigma=[0.2;0.3;0.5;0.25];
    sigmaGuarant=0.25;
    Default=zeros(3,1);
    ValueDefault=zeros(3,1);
```

```
    ValueDefaultGuarant=zeros(3,1);
    RateBeforeDefault=zeros(3,1);
    RateAfterDefault=zeros(3,1);
    ValueDebt=zeros(3,1);
    ValuePaid=zeros(3,1);
    ValueNoGuarantee=zeros(3,1);
    DebtGuarantee=zeros(3,1);
end
```

We use the program to compute the total expected shortfall or total loss per unit of debt ES and the value of the credit insurance per unit of debt CI. Figure 13.3 plots these values as a function of time to maturity T.

Since the guarantor has limited wealth, we can see on the graph the maximum level of its insuring capacity. Indeed, when maturity increases, the number of coupons increases and the

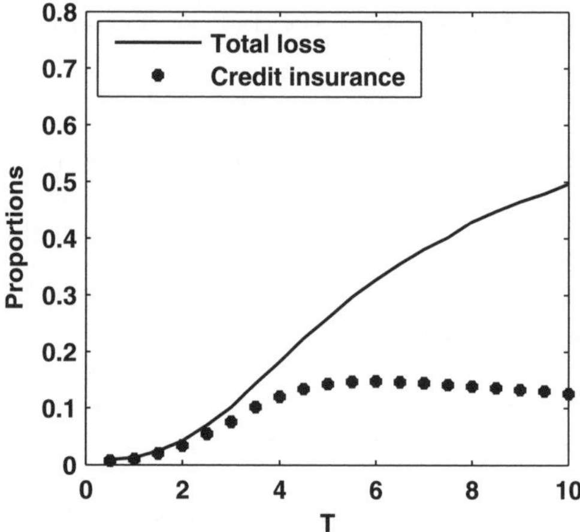

Figure 13.3 Total loss and credit insurance as a function of maturity

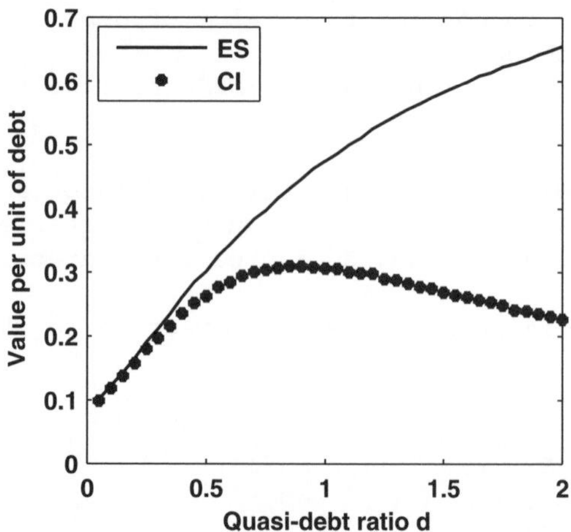

Figure 13.4 Total loss and credit insurance as a function of the quasi-debt ratio

guarantor hits its insuring capacity limit. After this maximum insuring capacity, the value of the credit insurance per unit decreases since the credit insurance value is at its maximum and at the same time the risk-free debt continues to increase, which decreases the credit insurance per unit of debt.

We present a second graph that shows the evolution of ES and CI as a function of the quasi-debt ratio. The initial asset values for the firms are \$ 50, the initial net-asset value of the guarantor is \$ 100, the maturity of the debts is 5 years and coupons of \$ 5 are required from each firm every six months. With these parameters values, we obtain Figure 13.4.

Notes and Complementary Readings

Complementary readings on financial guarantees are Merton (1974, 1977), Merton and Bodie (1992), Lai (1992), Lai and Gendron (1994), Lai and Yu (1999), Gendron, Lai and Soumaré (2002, 2006 a and b), Lai and Soumaré (2005) and Angoua, Lai and Soumaré (2008).

14

Risk Management and Value at Risk (VaR)

Risk management is very important for both individuals and corporate entities (e.g., institutional investors, pension funds, insurance companies, asset managers and, particularly, banks). Under its widest scope, risk management includes market risk, liquidity risk, credit risk, insurance risk, operational risk, legal risk, and so on.

Nowadays, we observe that financial and non financial institutions own complex portfolios composed of many financial contracts (for example, futures, options, swaps and other complex derivatives) and non financial products (for example, insurance contracts, contractual clauses, and structured finance). Moreover, the different financial disasters (Barings, Bear Stearns, Enron, Long Term Capital Management, Orange County, WorldCom, etc.) that occurred during recent decades have brought to the fore the crucial necessity and importance for all parties to implement efficient methods for measuring and controlling risk in order to sustain the firm's competitive advantage, and to assure the survival of institutions and the stability of the financial systems. All stakeholders have an interest in monitoring risks in the economy since the financial health of the economy depends on it.

Given that managers like simple concepts and measures that provide a global idea of all the risks their institutions face, the "snapshot" Value at Risk (VaR) fits the bill. Indeed, in order to quantify and manage risks, many institutions use the Value at Risk. The Value at Risk is defined as an aggregate risk measure which gives the expected extreme loss of owning a portfolio or an asset for a given period of time given a specific confidence level. The VaR gives a unique value reflecting the risk level of a portfolio when considering the financial leverage, the diversification and the multidimensional nature and interdependence of risks.

Computation approaches for the VaR can be classified into two groups: parametric approaches and non parametric approaches. However, the VaR presents many limitations which can be circumvented by conditional VaR models. In this chapter, we limit ourselves to a presentation of the basic elements related to the computation of the market risk VaR (MarketVaR and no other risk such as credit risk VaR or CreditVaR and operational risk VaR or OpVaR) using Monte Carlo simulations.

The remainder of this chapter is structured as follows. We begin by describing each type of risk. Then we give a formal definition of the VaR computation. After this, we discuss the Basle regulatory environment and the concepts of stress testing and back testing. Then we describe the different VaR computation approaches. Finally, since our objective is to provide ingredients for the VaR computation using Monte Carlo simulations, we give two examples of such calculations.

In Chapter 8, we characterized the dynamics of asset prices. In Chapter 4, we showed how to generate correlated random variables. We apply those concepts studied in Chapters 4 and 8 in the context of VaR computations.

The next chapter gives examples where we apply the Quasi Monte Carlo simulation techniques and the Principal Components Analysis technique to evaluate a bond portfolio's VaR.

14.1 TYPES OF FINANCIAL RISKS

We present a very brief and non exhaustive taxonomy of the risks that both financial and non financial institutions have to face.

14.1.1 Market Risk

Market risk corresponds to the risks generated by market variables' fluctuations such as interest rates, exchange rates, stock prices, and commodity prices on the financial results and the economic value of an institution or a portfolio of assets.

14.1.2 Liquidity Risk

The goal of liquidity risk management is to ensure that a financial institution is able to obtain rapidly and efficiently all monetary amounts to meet its short term obligations even during a crisis. Liquidity risk management is essential to ensure the confidence of clients, suppliers, depositors and creditors as well as the survival of the institution.

14.1.3 Credit Risk

Credit risk is the risk that a counterparty (a borrower, an endorser, an issuer, a guarantor or an institution) defaults on its commitments (for example principal or interest payments). For banks, this risk represents a major source of risk and a significant part of their capital requirements.

14.1.4 Operational Risk

Operational risk can be defined as the financial loss or loss in terms of public image following malfunctionings or inefficiencies of organizational, procedures and logistics. It includes losses resulting from defaults or any inefficiencies of internal processes and systems, individuals, external events, defaults in the command chain, bad supervision, human errors and frauds.

14.2 DEFINITION OF THE VALUE AT RISK (VaR)

The first commercial model for computing VaR was launched in 1994 by J.P. Morgan. VaR, an aggregate measure of risk, can be defined as the expected extreme loss emerging from the ownership of a portfolio or an asset during a specific period of time given a specific confidence level. Generally, the time period is one or 10 days. The VaR provides a unique value reflecting the risk level of the portfolio taking into account financial leverage and diversification.

For example, if a portfolio has a daily VaR of $ 10 million with a confidence level of 99%, it means that the total potential loss on this portfolio will be on average more than 10 million one day out of 100 days of successive transaction days, or two or three days during the year. Using VaR, we do not answer the question "How much could I lose on my portfolio during a specific period of time?" but "What will be the maximal loss on a given period with a small probability (for example 1%)?". In other words, VaR models developed by banks try to measure the maximum potential loss for a fixed probability on a given period of time. The

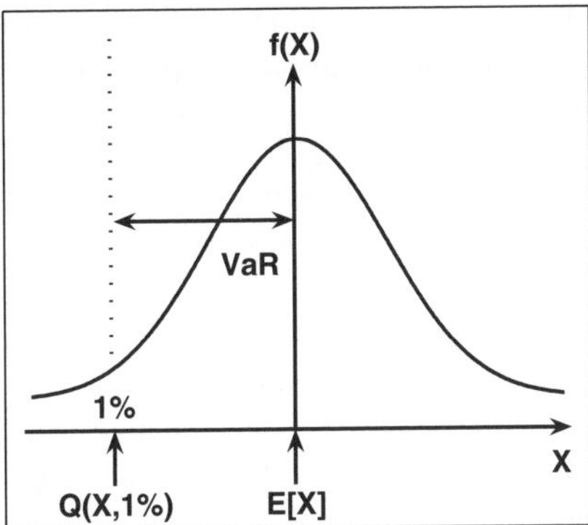

Figure 14.1 Value at Risk (VaR) with $\alpha = 1\%$

VaR of a market position is thus a sole number measuring and summarizing this position's risk for a given confidence level.

If we denote by ΔP the random variable representing the variation in the portfolio value (variation for a period of j days), then we determine a number or VaR, such that:

$$\text{Prob}(\Delta P < -\text{VaR}) = \alpha, \tag{14.1}$$

with $\alpha = 1\%$, 5% or 10%. We clearly see that the VaR is the percentile of order $\alpha \times 100$. In this case $1 - \alpha$ represents the VaR's confidence level. Figure 14.1 provides an illustration.

14.3 THE REGULATORY ENVIRONMENT OF BASLE

We offer below a general overview of the different Basle accords regarding the use of VaR.

In 1988, the Basle committee introduced the Basle Capital Accord I with the major impetus from the Bank of International Settlement (BIS) to fix a minimum equity capital requirement for the banks (8% for corporate loans and 4% for non-insured residential mortgages) in order to avoid the risk of insolvency.

In 1996, this same committee approved an approach allowing banks to use their own models of internal risk management but still in conformity with specific quantitative and qualitative criteria defined by the Basle Committee on Bank Supervision. Table 14.1 presents the main quantitative and qualitative criteria that internal VaR models have to comply with.

Table 14.1 Quantitative and qualitative criteria for internal VaR models

Quantitative criteria	Qualitative criteria
• VaR must be computed daily on a time horizon of 10 days. • Confidence level is 99%. • These models must take into account the impact of time variations of volatilities on derivative products prices.	• Perform stress-tests for their portfolio to measure the impact of extreme market conditions. • Must have independent risk management units directly linked to the top management. • Analyze internal risk management systems using internal and/or external auditors.

The New Basle II accord follows the same objectives as the Basle I accord with the addition of new guidelines for the treatment and control of operational risk. The Basle II accord is based on the following three pillars:

Pillar 1: Minimal capital requirement derived from the composition of risks of all assets and liabilities: risk-weighted assets are the sum of assets weighted by market, credit and operational risks.

Pillar 2: Supervisory review process ensures that banks follow rigorous procedures, measure their risk exposures correctly, and have sufficient capital to cover their risks.

Pillar 3: Market discipline introduces a radical change which imposes the disclosure of information on risks to investors in order to apply a market discipline that discourages inappropriate and excessive risk taking. It allows the disclosure of information, as well as the transparency and viability of the financial system.

To gain control over their risks and to follow regulatory directives, Basle allows institutions to use their own internal VaR models but they must perform the following two tests, stress testing and back testing, which we briefly describe in the next two sub-sections.

14.3.1 Stress Testing

This approach is being used to partially answer some of the following questions: "What will happen in extreme market conditions?"; "What will be the probable loss level when the VaR limit is reached?" We can subdivide the stress testing process into three principal steps.

1. The process begins with a set of extreme market scenarios. These scenarios are based on the historical crises that the market has gone through (Asian crisis, Russian crisis, etc.), or are simply hypothetical, such as supposing a market movement equivalent to 10 times its standard deviation.
2. For each scenario, we evaluate the variation in the portfolio's value.
3. We prepare a report of the principal results summarizing the gains and losses for each extreme scenario and point out sectors and industries that would be more affected.

14.3.2 Back Testing

Back testing is a procedure used to validate the efficiency of internal VaR computation systems. It can be defined as a simple statistical technique which determines the number of times that real losses exceeded the levels predicted by the VaR.

It consists of comparing the VaR distributions with realized losses where the elements to consider are: (i) Find the value of cash flows to be compared with the VaR. The VaR must be compared to static profits and losses, since the VaR supposes a static position over one or 10 days. (ii) Test the model validity: it consists of computing the probability frequencies of losses greater than the estimated level by the VaR model.

14.4 APPROACHES TO COMPUTE VaR

As we mentioned in the introduction to this chapter, many approaches exist to compute a VaR. Here we present some of these approaches.

14.4.1 Non-Parametric Approach: Historical Simulations

The non-parametric VaR is obtained from the distribution of historical data and doesn't necessarily imply the computation of parameters from a theoretical distribution.

This approach relies on the use of past daily series of risk factors influencing the portfolio value, and valuation model or price function linking the variations of the portfolio's value to the risk factors' variations. It is then possible, from the portfolio's actual composition, to simulate the empirical distribution of the portfolio's change in value, and thus to obtain the VaR. Although this approach is easy to understand, it suffers from many limitations such as:

- the assumption that the past predicts the immediate future;
- data sample size that require a lot of observations;
- considerable results sensibility to the time horizon and the time period;
- consistency of collected data.

14.4.2 Parametric Approaches

The parametric approach supposes that returns are derived from a given theoretical distribution, like a Gaussian distribution. For this class of approach, we present the delta-normal or variance-covariance method and the Monte Carlo simulations method.

Delta-normal method or variance-covariance method

This is a parametric method which uses historical data to determine the market returns' distribution. Among the advantages of this approach, we note that it is flexible and simple. However this approach suffers from weaknesses related to the following restrictive assumptions:

- the linearity of portfolios' returns;
- the normality of market factors changes;
- the existence of a covariance matrix that characterizes historical data. However, it is often hard to estimate and forecast these matrices.

The assumption of the normality of short-term returns is generally not satisfactory in spite of its simplicity of computations. Indeed, these distributions are often leptokurtic, which implies more frequent extreme events. Moreover, methods based on the covariance underestimate a portfolio's risk when the distribution is flatter and highly skewed to the left.

A practical application of the variance-covariance method is the commercial model RiskMetrics developed by J.P. Morgan and made public in 1994. This model postulates the shape of the risk factors' distribution. Once this is defined, it is necessary to determine the risk factors' variance-covariance matrix on the historical observation period.

The delta-normal method can be improved to take into account the convexity of returns using an extension of this method: the delta-gamma method.

Monte Carlo simulations method

The risk factors' scenarios are directly taken from the past in the variance-covariance approach and in the historical simulations approach, but in the Monte Carlo approach, these are simulated through the mathematical modeling of a stochastic process for each factor.

In practice, portfolios include several financial assets which are themselves influenced by many financial risk sources. Even relatively simpler assets such as bonds can depend on a combination of two or more stochastic variables.

In the following, we describe the Monte Carlo simulations method for the case which includes many sources of risk. We also provide two application examples of this approach.

14.5 COMPUTING VaR BY MONTE CARLO SIMULATIONS

14.5.1 Description of the Procedure

We consider a portfolio P composed of N assets of prices X_j, $j = 1, \ldots, N$. The description of the asset prices' processes is based on the stochastic differential equations theory seen in Chapter 8. We assume the asset prices processes to follow an Ito process defined as:

$$\Delta X_j(t) = X_j(t-1)(\mu_j \Delta t + \sigma_j \sqrt{\Delta t} Z_j(t)), \quad j = 1, \ldots, N, \tag{14.2}$$

where the values of Z_j are taken from a standard Gaussian distribution.

In Chapter 4, we described how to generate correlated random variables. We will apply concepts seen in that chapter to the VaR computation context. Indeed, if variables Z_j are not correlated between themselves, then the sampling can be generated independently for each variable. But generally, the variables are correlated, and to consider these correlations, we begin by generating a set of variables Y which will then be transformed into Z. We described the process of transforming variables Y into Z in Chapter 4. This transformation procedure requires the Cholesky decomposition and/or the eigenvalues decomposition.

To compute our portfolio's VaR, we perform a large number of simulations, for example 100 000 simulations (the number of simulations depends on the desired precision) of the prices of the assets for the VaR computation period. For each simulation, we compute the portfolio's value. Thus, we obtain 100 000 simulated values for our portfolio. Finally, for a given level of confidence $1 - \alpha = 99\%$ (that is $\alpha = 1\%$), the VaR is the value of the portfolio exceeded by $99\% \times 100\,000$ simulated values or the $1\% \times 100\,000^{\text{th}}$ smallest value.

We note that the procedure used in VaR estimation by Monte Carlo simulations is similar to the one employed for complex options valuation, but in the VaR case, there is no discounting.

14.5.2 Application: VaR of a Simple Bank Account

This example is inspired by Marrison (2002), but with modifications. We suppose that our savings account balance is described by the following stochastic process

$$P(t + \Delta t) = P(t) + P(t)\left(0.1 + \frac{0.1}{0.035} r_{3m}(t) + \frac{0.05}{0.040} r_{1y}(t) + \frac{0.1}{\sqrt{\Delta t}} Z_V(t)\right) \Delta t, \tag{14.3}$$

where Z_V follows a Gaussian distribution $N(0, 1)$. r_{3m} and r_{1y} are respectively three month and one year interest rates driving this process. We suppose then that our account's value is explicitly affected by the three month and one year interest rates.

Our objective is to compute the VaR of this bank account. We therefore characterize the term structure of interest rates as studied in Chapter 11. For this purpose, we assume that the three month and one year interest rates are correlated as well as correlated with the five year interest rate. We respectively consider the following processes for the three month, one year and five year interest rates:

$$r_{3m}(t+\Delta t) = r_{3m}(t) + 0.25(0.035 - r_{3m}(t))\Delta t + 0.07(r_{3m}(t))^{0.5}\sqrt{\Delta t}Z_{3m}(t), \quad (14.4)$$
$$r_{1y}(t+\Delta t) = r_{1y}(t) + 0.26(0.040 - r_{1y}(t))\Delta t + 0.05(r_{1y}(t))^{0.25}\sqrt{\Delta t}Z_{1y}(t), \quad (14.5)$$
$$r_{5y}(t+\Delta t) = r_{5y}(t) + 0.27(0.060 - r_{5y}(t))\Delta t + 0.05(r_{5y}(t))^{0.25}\sqrt{\Delta t}Z_{5y}(t), \quad (14.6)$$

where variables Z_{3m}, Z_{1y}, Z_{5y}, drawn from a Gaussian distribution $N(0, 1)$, satisfy the following correlation structure:

$$\rho_{3m,1y} = \text{corr}(Z_{3m}, Z_{1y}) = 0.10, \quad (14.7)$$
$$\rho_{3m,5y} = \text{corr}(Z_{3m}, Z_{5y}) = 0.20, \quad (14.8)$$
$$\rho_{1y,5y} = \text{corr}(Z_{1y}, Z_{5y}) = 0.50. \quad (14.9)$$

We note that the interest rate processes follow mean reverting processes, for example the Cox, Ingersol and Ross (1985) process described in Chapter 11.

Simulating the interest rates processes

With initial values, $r_{3m}(0) = 0.035, r_{1y}(0) = 0.040, r_{5y}(0) = 0.060$, simulate these three interest rates on a monthly basis for a 3 year period. We must note that in this exercise, we generate the term structure of interest rates for a horizon of 3 years. However, the VaR will be computed according to a shorter horizon. Here is the code used to obtain the simulation results.

```
function RatesGenerate
%Function generating interest rates for 3 months, 1 year
%and 5 years satisfying the specified correlations.

%Initial parameters
T=3;
NbSteps=36;
DeltaT=T/NbSteps;
sqDeltaT=sqrt(DeltaT);

%Cholesky decomposition of the covariance matrix.
CovTheo=[1,0.1,0.2;0.1,1,0.5;0.2,0.5,1];
MatrixL=chol(CovTheo)';

%Initial rates
r0=[0.035;0.04;0.06];

%Vector storing the historical rates
r=cat(2,r0,zeros(3,NbSteps));

%Rates dynamic parameters
Speed=[0.25;0.26;0.27];
Factor=[0.07;0.05;0.05];
Exponent=[0.5;0.25;0.25];

%Loop simulating the rates for each time
for i=1:NbSteps
```

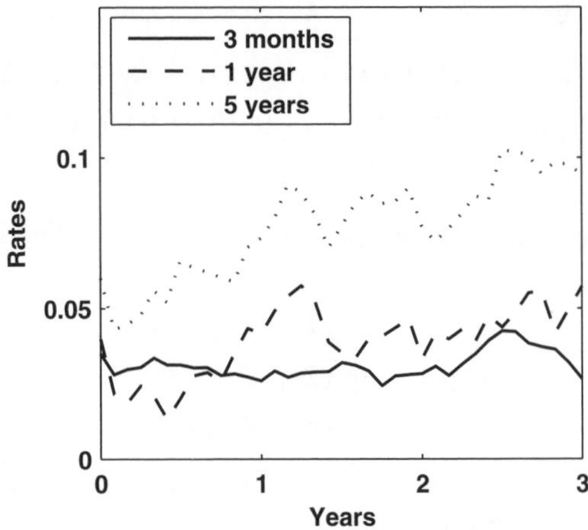

Figure 14.2 Possible scenario for the interest rates evolution

```
    dW=MatrixL*randn(3,1);
    r(:,i+1)=r(:,i) + Speed.*(r0-r(:,i))*DeltaT + ...
                Factor.*r(:,i).^Exponent*sqDeltaT.*dW;
end

%We plot the graphs for the rates.
plot([0:DeltaT:T],r)

end
```

One possible scenario for the interest rates' paths is presented in Figure 14.2.

Computing the VaR of a bank account

We are required to compute the VaR of this bank account for a horizon of 1 year with a confidence level of 99%.

To compute the VaR, we simulate M scenarios for the bank account from equation (14.3) with the interest rates simulated over one year. Then, we compute the VaR by taking the $0.01M^{\text{th}}$ smallest value. In Table 14.2 we present the VaR results and the estimation error for $M = 1000, 10\,000, 100\,000, 1\,000\,000$.

Table 14.2 99% Value at Risk for a bank account

M	VaR ($)	Error ($)
1000	33.082	0.032
10 000	35.779	0.010
100 000	35.336	0.003
1 000 000	35.261	0.001

Here is the program that has been used to obtain these results.

```
function VaRAccount(N)
%Function computing the value at risk for one year of a bank ac-
count.
%N: Number of simulations to do
%Vector storing the balance in the account for all the simulations.
Account=zeros(N,1);
%Initial balance in the account.
InitialBalance=100;
%For each simulation we compute the account's balance
for j=1:N
    Balance=InitialBalance;
    Account(j,1)=BalanceAccount;
end
%Sorting of the balances
Account=sort(Account);
%Value at risk computation.
VaR=mean(Account)-Account(floor(0.01*N),1);

function rep=BalanceAccount
%Function generating the balance in an account
  %Initial parameters
  T=1;
  NbSteps=12;
  DeltaT=T/NbSteps;
  sqDeltaT=sqrt(DeltaT);
  %Cholesky decomposition of the covariance matrix.
  CovTheo=[1,0.1,0.2;0.1,1,0.5;0.2,0.5,1];
  MatrixL=chol(CovTheo)';
  %Initial interest rates
  r0=[0.035;0.04;0.06];
  %Vector storing the historical rates
  r=cat(2,r0,zeros(3,NbSteps));
  %Parameters of the rates' dynamics
  Speed=[0.25;0.26;0.27];
  Factor=[0.07;0.05;0.05];
  Exponent=[0.5;0.25;0.25];
  %Loop generating the interest rates for each step
  for i=1:NbSteps
      dW=MatrixL*randn(3,1);
      r(:,i+1)=max(0,r(:,i) + Speed.*(r0-r(:,i))*DeltaT +...
                   Factor.*r(:,i).^Exponent*sqDeltaT.*dW);
      Balance=max(0,Balance+Balance*(0.1+0.1/0.035*r(1,i+1)+...
                   0.05/0.04*r(2,i+1)+0.1/sqDeltaT*randn(1))*DeltaT);
 end
 rep=Balance;
 end
 end
```

14.5.3 Application: VaR of a Portfolio Composed of One Domestic Stock and One Foreign Stock

We consider a Canadian investor investing CAD 100 000 in two market indices in equal weights on 25 January 2006. The indices are the Toronto stock exchange composite index S&P/TSX of the Canadian market and the EuroNext index.

The exercise consists in computing the portfolio's VaR for a horizon of 1 year with a confidence interval of 99% using Monte Carlo simulations.

For the Monte Carlo simulations, we will use the following processes for the indices and the exchange rate.

S&P/TSX Index:

$$\frac{dS(t)}{S(t)} = \mu_S dt + \sigma_S \sqrt{dt} dZ_1(t), \tag{14.10}$$

EuroNext Index:

$$\frac{dS^*(t)}{S^*(t)} = \mu_{S^*} dt + \sigma_{S^*} \sqrt{dt} dZ_2(t), \tag{14.11}$$

Exchange rate EURCAD, i.e., 1 EUR = CAD x.xx

$$\frac{de(t)}{e(t)} = \mu_e dt + \sigma_e \sqrt{dt} dZ_3(t). \tag{14.12}$$

We also assume that we have the following correlations:

$$\text{corr}(dZ_1, dZ_2) = \rho_{12} \tag{14.13}$$

$$\text{corr}(dZ_1, dZ_3) = \rho_{13} \tag{14.14}$$

$$\text{corr}(dZ_2, dZ_3) = \rho_{23}. \tag{14.15}$$

Parameters μ_i and σ_i are the instantaneous average rates (drifts) and average volatilities of the composite index S&P/TSX returns, the EuroNext index returns and the returns of the exchange rate EURCAD. Correlations ρ_{ij} are the correlations between these variables returns. In this case, the coefficients are estimated roughly from the descriptive statistics of the data using the statistical mean and standard deviation of the sample.

From daily data between 12 December 2005 and 25 January 2006 (see Table 14.3), estimate the different parameters for the processes using the empirical means, standard deviations and correlations.

From these data, we can compute the parameters' values.

$$\begin{aligned}
\mu_S &= 0.1763\% \\
\sigma_S &= 0.005909 \\
\mu_{S^*} &= 0.2292\% \\
\sigma_{S^*} &= 0.005295 \\
\mu_e &= 0.0794\% \\
\sigma_e &= 0.005754 \\
\rho_{12} &= 0.47424 \\
\rho_{13} &= 0.09901 \\
\rho_{23} &= -0.16983.
\end{aligned}$$

Table 14.3 Daily data for the indices and exchange rate

	TSX	Return TSX	EuroNext	Return EuroN.	Exchange rate e	Return e
25Jan06	11675.16		1466.24		1.4078	
24Jan06	11692.35	−0.15%	1452.10	0.97%	1.4147	−0.49%
23Jan06	11733.37	−0.35%	1448.32	0.26%	1.4139	0.06%
20Jan06	11605.67	1.10%	1450.90	−0.18%	1.3983	1.12%
19Jan06	11692.97	−0.75%	1450.15	0.05%	1.4074	−0.65%
18Jan06	11554.49	1.20%	1438.28	0.83%	1.4170	−0.68%
17Jan06	11689.61	−1.16%	1445.22	−0.48%	1.4084	0.61%
16Jan06	11720.97	−0.27%	1458.08	−0.88%	1.4030	0.38%
13Jan06	11604.82	1.00%	1455.37	0.19%	1.4082	−0.37%
12Jan06	11595.18	0.08%	1463.86	−0.58%	1.3987	0.68%
11Jan06	11621.03	−0.22%	1455.24	0.59%	1.4049	−0.44%
10Jan06	11597.61	0.20%	1444.99	0.71%	1.4056	−0.05%
09Jan06	11565.21	0.28%	1452.29	−0.50%	1.4115	−0.42%
06Jan06	11620.46	−0.48%	1448.21	0.28%	1.4157	−0.30%
05Jan06	11507.68	0.98%	1441.30	0.48%	1.4059	0.70%
04Jan06	11501.48	0.05%	1438.04	0.23%	1.3908	1.09%
03Jan06	11441.58	0.52%	1423.64	1.01%	1.3884	0.17%
30Dec05	11272.26	1.50%	1401.57	1.57%	1.3763	0.88%
29Dec05	11296.29	−0.21%	1402.99	−0.10%	1.3782	−0.14%
28Dec05	11261.20	0.31%	1394.64	0.60%	1.3782	0.00%
23Dec05	11245.37	0.14%	1387.96	0.48%	1.3841	−0.43%
22Dec05	11255.39	−0.09%	1383.37	0.33%	1.3841	0.00%
21Dec05	11247.25	0.07%	1381.86	0.11%	1.3809	0.23%
20Dec05	11180.63	0.60%	1373.63	0.60%	1.3906	−0.70%
19Dec05	11154.28	0.24%	1373.39	0.02%	1.4038	−0.94%
16Dec05	11136.58	0.16%	1373.45	0.00%	1.3928	0.79%
15Dec05	11092.81	0.39%	1368.44	0.37%	1.3882	0.33%
14Dec05	11095.81	−0.03%	1367.46	0.07%	1.3829	0.38%
13Dec05	11137.44	−0.37%	1370.03	−0.19%	1.3733	0.70%
12Dec05	11099.26	0.34%	1372.60	−0.19%	1.3764	−0.23%

Investing \$50 000 in each index means that at time $t = 0$ the investor owns

$$\frac{50000}{11675.16} = 4.2826$$

times the S&P/TSX index and

$$\frac{50000}{1466.24 * 1.4147} = 24.1046$$

times the EuroNext index. Here is the MATLAB program generating M value trajectories over a 1 year horizon and computing the VaR given by the $0.01 \times M^{\text{th}}$ smallest portfolio value.

```
function VaRPortfolio(NbTraj)
%Function computing the portfolio's value at risk.
%Initial values of the indices and the exchange rate.
```

```
STSX = 11675.16;
SEuroNext = 1466.24;
e=1.4147;
%Computation of the indices proportions that we buy.
NbTSX = 50000/STSX;
NbEuroNext = 50000/(e*SEuroNext);
%250 working days per year
NbSteps=250;
DeltaT=1;
%Cholesky decomposition of the covariance matrix.
L=chol([1,0.47424,0.09901;0.47424,1,-0.16983;0.09901,-0.16983,1])';
%Vector keeping the simulated values for the portfolio.
PortfolioValue=zeros(NbTraj,1);
%Loop simulating the trajectories.
for i=1:NbTraj
   %Re-initialization of the indices values and exchange rate.
   STSX = 11675.16;
   SEuroNext = 1466.24;
   e=1.4147;
   %Loop simulating the indices and exchange rates dynamic.
   for k=1:NbSteps
       Z=L*randn(3,1);
       STSX=STSX*(1+0.001763+0.005909*Z(1,1));
       SEuroNext = SEuroNext*(1+0.002292+0.005295*Z(2,1));
       e = e*(1+0.000794+0.005754*Z(3,1));
   end
   %Computation of the portfolio's final value.
   PortfolioValue(i,1)=NbTSX*STSX+NbEuroNext*SEuroNext*e;
end
%Sorting of the final value of the portfolio and computation of the
%value at risk.
PortfolioValue=sort(PortfolioValue);
VaR=mean(PortfolioValue) - PortfolioValue(floor(NbTraj*0.01),1);
disp(VaR);
end
```

After running the program, we compile in Table 14.4 the values at risk of the portfolio at the 99% confidence level for different values of M.

Table 14.4 99% Value at Risk for the portfolio

M	VaR ($)	Error ($)
1000	35811	0.032
10 000	35893	0.010
100 000	35671	0.003
1000 000	35428	0.001

Notes and Complementary Readings

For complementary readings on risk management and Value at Risk (VaR), the reader could refer to the following works: Alexander (1998), Crouhy, Galai and Mark (2001), Holton (2003), Hull (2005), Jorion (2000), Marrison (2002), Pearson (2002), Risk Publications (1997). The book by Dupire (1998) provides a state-of-the-art review of methods and application of Monte Carlo simulations to the pricing and management of risks. For VaR enhancements, we refer to Artzner, Delbaen, Eber and Heath (1999) and McNeil, Frey and Embrechts (2005).

The reader could consult the following standard papers on the VaR: Linsmeier and Pearson (2000), Duffie and Pan (1997) and Aït Sahalia and Lo (2000).

The reader could also refer to the following web site for recent papers about VaR: http://www.gloriamundi.org/.

For additional references on alternative risk transfer, the management of risk in insurance companies and notions of integrated risk management, we suggest the books by Banks (2004), Doherty (2000) and Lane (2002).

For more information about the accords and the regulatory standards of Basle, the reader is invited to read the Basle documents (1996, 2004), and visit the web site of the institution: www.bis.org. For commercial models and documents on application systems, the reader should visit the web sites and download papers from KMV-Moodys, J.P. Morgan, Credit Suisse, Morgan Stanley, Algorithmics, BNP Paribas, Société Générale, etc.

15 Value at Risk (VaR) and Principal Components Analysis (PCA)

In the previous chapter, we presented basic concepts on the Value at Risk (VaR) which is a widely used tool to measure and manage risks. In most cases, many factors influence our risk variables, which causes the computation of the VaR to be very complex, tedious and time consuming.

However, it is possible to combine the VaR computation method with other techniques such as the principal components analysis (PCA) and the Quasi Monte Carlo simulations (QMC), which is the subject of this chapter. The principal components analysis technique is based on notions of eigenvalues already presented in Chapter 4 while the Quasi Monte Carlo simulations method has been developed in Chapter 6. When appropriately used, these two methods (PCA and QMC) substantially reduce both the number of variables to analyze and the computation time and increase the precision. This chapter is an adaptation of the Lai, Sakni and Soumaré (2005) article.

We also use real data to derive the term structure of interest rates using the linear interpolation technique. Note that to analyze and measure the risk of a portfolio containing bonds (fixed income assets), one resorts extensively to the term structure of interest rates.

The remainder of this chapter is structured as follows. In the first part, we introduce the principal components analysis technique. This introduction is carried out by way of graphical and analytical illustrations. Then we illustrate its use with real data. In the second part, we apply the PCA, Monte Carlo and Quasi Monte Carlo simulations techniques to the estimation of a bond portfolio's VaR. Finally, the results of the PCA, the interest rates interpolation and the comparison of the VaR computations using Monte Carlo and Quasi Monte Carlo simulations are presented and analyzed.

15.1 INTRODUCTION TO THE PRINCIPAL COMPONENTS ANALYSIS

This section presents a brief description of the principal components analysis using simple graphical and analytical illustrations. At the end of this section, we illustrate the use of the technique by data.

15.1.1 Graphical Illustration

To illustrate schematically the principal components analysis (PCA) technique, let's consider two variables: X_1 and X_2. The principle remains the same for more than two variables. Figure 15.1 plots the data points in the X_1-X_2 plane.

Obviously, X_1 and X_2 are correlated. However, it is possible to rotate the lines in order to form two independent variables as shown in Figure 15.2.

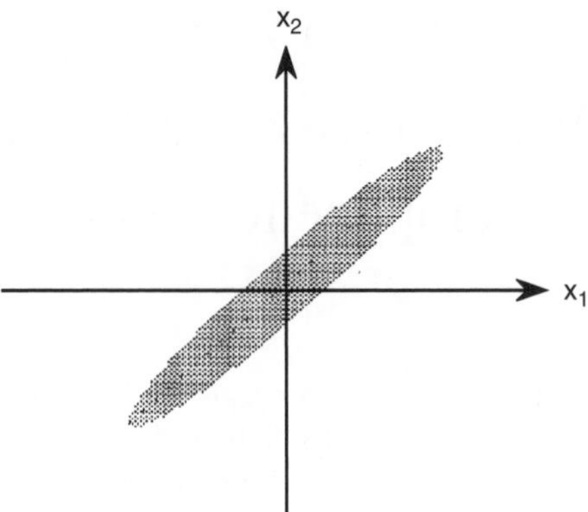

Figure 15.1 Data points in the two dimensional space (X_1, X_2)

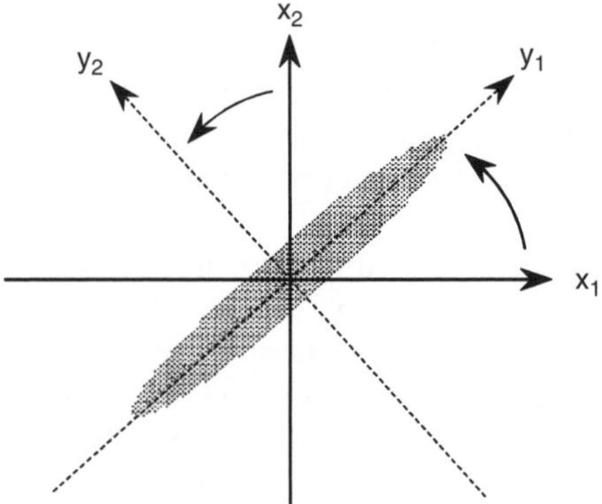

Figure 15.2 Data points with rotation of original axis

Y_1 and Y_2 are independent variables by construction and most of the data are clustered around the Y_1 axis. Two objectives have been met here. The two new axes corresponding to the components are not correlated. Moreover, the concentration on axis Y_1 is much stronger than the one on axis Y_2, and we can therefore say that the components are ordered. Thus Y_1 explains more of the variations in the data than Y_2. Therefore, Y_1 is the first principal component and Y_2 represents the second one. This is illustrated more clearly in Figure 15.3 in the Y_1-Y_2 plane.

15.1.2 Analytical Illustration

This part formalizes what we have previously described. It gives an analytical and theoretical formalization to the PCA.

We consider p vectors $(X_1, X_2, \ldots, X_p)$ of order n (standardized) representing the initial factors that explain the phenomenon under study, i.e., if the original data is represented by $\{D_i, i = 1, \ldots, p\}$, then the standardized variable X_i is obtained as follows: $X_i = \frac{D_i - \overline{D}_i}{\sigma(D_i)}$, where $\overline{D}_i$ and $\sigma(D_i)$ are respectively the sample mean and standard deviation of data D_i.

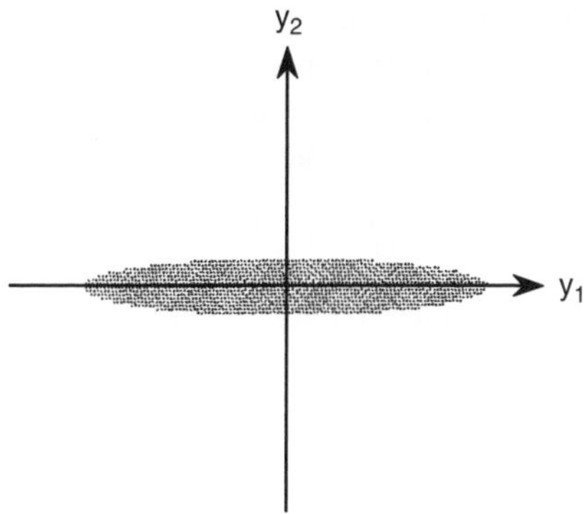

Figure 15.3 Data points in the new two dimensional space (Y_1, Y_2)

We can create new factors such as the first component for example Y_1 to be a linear combination of variables $X_1, X_2, X_3, \ldots, X_p$, (standardized) meaning

$$Y_1 = u_{11}X_1 + u_{21}X_2 + \cdots + u_{p1}X_p, \tag{15.1}$$

such that the variance of Y_1 is maximal. The second component Y_2 is constructed as a linear combination of the same initial variables

$$Y_2 = u_{12}X_1 + u_{22}X_2 + \cdots + u_{p2}X_p, \tag{15.2}$$

such that Y_2 has the maximal variance among all linear combinations uncorrelated with Y_1, $\sigma^2(Y_1) > \sigma^2(Y_2)$, and the correlation between Y_1 and Y_2 is zero, $\mathrm{corr}(Y_1, Y_2) = 0$. The same applies to all other components $Y_3, Y_4, \ldots, Y_p$, each one of them having maximal variance among all linear combinations of $X_1, X_2, X_3, \ldots, X_p$ and are not correlated with the previous components. In other words, each of the components explains a maximum of the residual variation.

Let $\mathbf{X}$ be the matrix built from standardized vectors $X_1, X_2, \ldots, X_p$. And let

$$\Lambda = \frac{1}{n-1}\mathbf{X}^\top\mathbf{X} \tag{15.3}$$

be the symmetric matrix of order p of the sample correlations between variables. Usually $|\Lambda| \neq 0$, except if there is perfect collinearity. Now the problem consists in finding linear combinations of the original vectors $X_1, X_2, \ldots, X_p$. Thus vector Y_i is obtained by

$$\begin{aligned} Y_i &= u_{1i}X_1 + u_{2i}X_2 + \cdots + u_{pi}X_p \\ &= \mathbf{X}U_i, \end{aligned} \tag{15.4}$$

where $U_i = (u_{1i}, u_{2i}, \ldots, u_{pi})^\top$.

The task consists of maximizing the sample variance of vector Y:

$$\begin{aligned} \sigma^2(Y) &= \frac{1}{n-1}Y^\top Y \\ &= U^\top\left(\frac{1}{n-1}\mathbf{X}^\top\mathbf{X}\right)U \\ &= U^\top\Lambda U, \end{aligned} \tag{15.5}$$

under the constraint that vector U has a norm of one, that is, $U^\top U = 1$. We must point out that, without the condition requiring a unit vector, there would be no solution, since one would need to take larger and larger elements of U to increase the variance of Y. With this normalization constraint $U^\top U = 1$, the Lagrangian of the above maximization problem is written as:

$$\mathcal{L} = U^\top \Lambda U - \lambda(U^\top U - 1), \tag{15.6}$$

where λ is the Lagrange multiplier. The first order condition of this maximization implies:

$$\begin{aligned}\frac{\partial \mathcal{L}}{\partial U} &= 2\Lambda U - 2\lambda U \\ &= 0,\end{aligned} \tag{15.7}$$

or simply

$$(\Lambda - \lambda I)U = 0. \tag{15.8}$$

This system of homogeneous linear equations has a non trivial solution ($U \neq 0$) if

$$|\Lambda - \lambda I| = 0. \tag{15.9}$$

Solving the characteristic equation $(\Lambda - \lambda I)U = 0$, first we obtain the eigenvalues of the symmetric matrix Λ that can be ordered the following way: $\lambda_1 > \lambda_2 > \ldots > \lambda_p$; and then the corresponding eigenvectors $U_1, U_2, \ldots, U_p$. Eigenvectors and eigenvalues satisfy the relation

$$(\Lambda - \lambda_i I)U_i = 0, \tag{15.10}$$

or, $\Lambda U_i = \lambda_i U_i$ with $U_i^\top U_i = 1$, for $i = 1, 2 \ldots, p$.

The elements of these eigenvectors are precisely the weights of variables $X_1, X_2, \ldots, X_p$ in order to build the linear combinations $Y_1, Y_2, \ldots, Y_p$ called components: $Y_i = \mathbf{X}U_i$. Since the ultimate goal of the principal components analysis is to reduce the problem's dimensionality, we will keep a reduced number of components to explain a large portion of the variance.

Indeed, since the vector is normalized to unity, the variance of Y_i is λ_i:

$$\begin{aligned}\sigma^2(Y_i) &= U_i^\top \Lambda U_i \\ &= U_i^\top \lambda_i U_i \\ &= \lambda_i.\end{aligned} \tag{15.11}$$

And since

$$\sum_{i=1}^{p} \lambda_i = \mathrm{trace}(\Lambda) = p, \tag{15.12}$$

the percentage of the variance that is explained by the first component is

$$\frac{\lambda_1}{p}, \tag{15.13}$$

by the first two components

$$\frac{\lambda_1 + \lambda_2}{p}, \tag{15.14}$$

by the first three components

$$\frac{\lambda_1 + \lambda_2 + \lambda_3}{p}, \tag{15.15}$$

and so on.

15.1.3 Illustrative Example of the PCA

Here is a simple example that enables us to apply the PCA method. We use historical data over two years on American Treasury bonds for maturities of 1 year, 2 years, 3 years and 5 years. These data, shown in Table 15.1, will be indexed by D_1, D_2, D_3 and D_4 respectively.

The steps for the principal components analysis are:

1. Enter data: D_1, D_2, D_3 and D_4.
2. Standardize variables D_1, D_2, D_3 and D_4, that is:

$$X_i = \frac{D_i - \overline{D}_i}{\sigma(D_i)}, \quad i = 1, 2, 3, 4, \tag{15.16}$$

   where $\overline{D}_i$ and $\sigma(D_i)$ are respectively the sample mean and standard deviation of data D_i.
3. Construct the covariance matrix of matrix $\mathbf{X}$ composed of X_1, X_2, X_3, X_4 as follows:

$$\Lambda = \frac{1}{n-1}\mathbf{X}^\top\mathbf{X}. \tag{15.17}$$

Table 15.1 American Treasury bonds yields

Date	1 year	2 years	3 years	5 years
10-2003	1.25	1.75	2.26	3.19
11-2003	1.34	1.93	2.45	3.29
12-2003	1.31	1.91	2.44	3.27
01-2004	1.24	1.76	2.27	3.12
02-2004	1.24	1.74	2.25	3.07
03-2004	1.19	1.58	2.00	2.79
04-2004	1.43	2.07	2.57	3.39
05-2004	1.78	2.53	3.10	3.85
06-2004	2.12	2.76	3.26	3.93
07-2004	2.10	2.64	3.05	3.69
08-2004	2.02	2.51	2.88	3.47
09-2004	2.12	2.53	2.83	3.36
10-2004	2.23	2.58	2.85	3.35
11-2004	2.50	2.85	3.09	3.53
12-2004	2.67	3.01	3.21	3.60
01-2005	2.86	3.22	3.39	3.71
02-2005	3.03	3.38	3.54	3.77
03-2005	3.30	3.73	3.91	4.17
04-2005	3.32	3.65	3.79	4.00
05-2005	3.33	3.64	3.72	3.85
06-2005	3.36	3.64	3.69	3.77
07-2005	3.64	3.87	3.91	3.98
08-2005	3.87	4.04	4.08	4.12
09-2005	3.85	3.95	3.96	4.01

4. Compute the eigenvalues and eigenvectors of Λ: $\lambda_1 > \lambda_2 > \lambda_3 > \lambda_4$ corresponding to eigenvectors V_1, V_2, V_3 and V_4.
5. Normalize the eigenvectors V_i as follows:

$$U_i = \frac{V_i}{\|V_i\|}, \quad \forall i = 1, 2, 3, 4. \tag{15.18}$$

6. Compute the principal components:

$$Y_i = \mathbf{X}U_i. \tag{15.19}$$

7. Compute the proportion of the variance that is explained by the components. The proportion explained by the first component is

$$\frac{\lambda_1}{\lambda_1 + \lambda_2 + \lambda_3 + \lambda_4}, \tag{15.20}$$

the proportion explained by the first two components is

$$\frac{\lambda_1 + \lambda_2}{\lambda_1 + \lambda_2 + \lambda_3 + \lambda_4}, \tag{15.21}$$

the proportion explained by the first three components is

$$\frac{\lambda_1 + \lambda_2 + \lambda_3}{\lambda_1 + \lambda_2 + \lambda_3 + \lambda_4}, \tag{15.22}$$

and the proportion explained by the four components is

$$\frac{\lambda_1 + \lambda_2 + \lambda_3 + \lambda_4}{\lambda_1 + \lambda_2 + \lambda_3 + \lambda_4} = 1. \tag{15.23}$$

The MATLAB program used to extract the components is given as follows:

```
function PCA
%Function extracting the principal components.
%Empirical data (can be imported from an external file).
Rates= [1.25 , 1.75 , 2.26 , 3.19 ;
 ...
 3.85 , 3.95 , 3.96 , 4.01];
%Computation of the average and standard deviation of rates.
Average=mean(Rates,1);
Deviation=std(Rates);
%Normalization of the rates to get a mean of zero and
%standard deviation of one.
for i=1:size(Rates,1)
   Rates(i,:) = (Rates(i,:)-Average)./Deviation;
end
%Interest rates covariance matrix.
CovRates=cov(Rates);
%Determination of the eigenvalues and eigenvectors.
[U,Lambda] = eigs(CovRates,4);
end
```

We obtain the following eigenvectors

$$U_1 = \begin{pmatrix} 0.4980 \\ 0.5074 \\ 0.5102 \\ 0.4839 \end{pmatrix}, U_2 = \begin{pmatrix} 0.5443 \\ 0.2672 \\ -0.0439 \\ -0.7940 \end{pmatrix},$$

$$U_3 = \begin{pmatrix} -0.6477 \\ 0.4056 \\ 0.5494 \\ -0.3379 \end{pmatrix}, U_4 = \begin{pmatrix} 0.1903 \\ -0.7118 \\ 0.6603 \\ -0.1456 \end{pmatrix},$$

and the following eigenvalues

$$\lambda_1 = 3.8379, \lambda_2 = 0.1602, \lambda_3 = 0.0017, \lambda_4 = 0.0002.$$

Now, if we want to compute the principal components, we just enter the MATLAB command

```
%Command for computing the principal components from the
eigenvectors.
Components=Rates*U;
```

The percentage of the variance that is explained by the first component is

$$\frac{3.8379}{3.8379 + 0.1602 + 0.0017 + 0.0002} = \frac{3.8379}{4} = 95.95\%,$$

by the first two components is 99.95%, by the first three components 99.995% and finally by the four components 100%.

15.2 COMPUTING THE VAR OF A BOND PORTFOLIO

In this section, we compute the VaR of a bond portfolio using the PCA technique and the Monte Carlo (MC) and Quasi Monte Carlo (QMC) simulations.

15.2.1 Sample Description and Methodology

To illustrate the approach, we use a portfolio composed of two coupon-paying bonds with the characteristics shown in Table 15.2. Even though, we use only two bonds to form our portfolio, the methodology can be easily adapted for portfolios of more than two bonds.

We use the Canadian market monthly spot interest rates over the period February 1996 to November 2003, i.e., 93 observations in total. The term structure of interest rates is represented by nine points defined by the spot rates of 1 month, 3 months, 6 months, 1 year, 2 years, 3 years, 5 years, 10 years and 30 years. We denote by $\{r_i, i = 1, \ldots, 9\}$ these initial variables with the subscript i being the maturity in years. For later use, the standardized values $\{X_i, i = 1, \ldots, 9\}$ of these initial spot rates are obtained as follows:

$$X_i = \frac{r_i - \bar{r}_i}{\sigma_i}, \tag{15.24}$$

where $\bar{r}_i$ is the sample average and σ_i is the sample standard deviation of the spot rate r_i.

Table 15.2 Characteristics of the two coupon-paying bonds portfolio

	Bond 1	Bond 2
Issue date	10 May 2003	10 November 2001
Maturity	3 years	7 years
Evaluation date	10 November 2003	
Weight	0.5	0.5
Coupon rate	0.06	0.08
Face value	$ 1000	
Coupon payment period	semi-annual	
Parameter for the QMC sequence		
1st prime number	2	
2nd prime number	5	

To compute the VaR of the portfolio, we use the principal components analysis (PCA) technique and Quasi Monte Carlo (QMC) simulations (see Chapter 6 for the description of this technique) or standard Monte Carlo (MC) simulations (used extensively in the previous chapters). The steps are described schematically in Diagram 15.1.

The steps described in Diagram 15.1 can be summarized as follows:

1. Obtain the principal component factors and extract a parsimonious number of k factors.
2. Represent the sample points in the k-dimensional cube with a uniform distribution based on QMC Low Discrepancy Sequences (please refer to Chapter 6 for a description of these sequences) or Monte Carlo pseudo-random numbers.

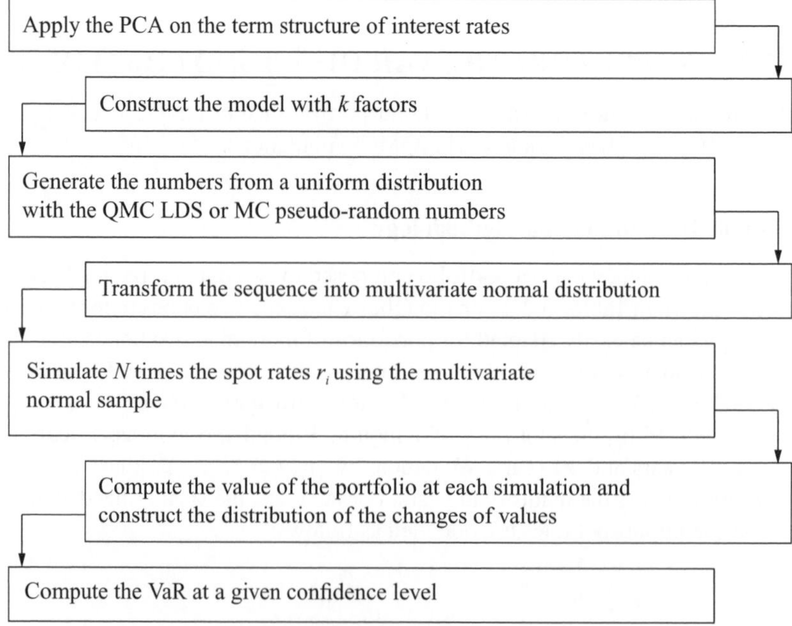

Diagram 15.1 Description of the VaR computation steps

3. Transforming the random numbers with uniform distribution into a k-dimensional vector with multivariate Gaussian distribution, we thus obtain the sample

$$Z = (Z_1, Z_2, \ldots, Z_k). \tag{15.25}$$

4. Simulate the spot rates using the k factors as follows:

$$r_i = r_{i0} + \sigma_i(U_{1i}\sqrt{\lambda_1}Z_1 + U_{2i}\sqrt{\lambda_2}Z_2 + \cdots + U_{ki}\sqrt{\lambda_k}Z_k), \tag{15.26}$$

where r_{i0} is the current spot rate, σ_i is the spot rate volatility over the VaR horizon, U_{ji} represents the ith element of the eigenvector j, λ_j is the jth eigenvalue. These variables are obtained from the principal components analysis described in the previous section. This last equation will give us simulated interest rates for each maturity.

5. From these rate processes, simulate N times the value of the portfolio. Then draw the distribution of the portfolio value. Finally, compute the VaR from the distribution at a specified confidence level $1 - \alpha$ by taking the αth-percentile as described in Chapter 14.

15.2.2 Principal Components Analysis (PCA)

Table 15.3 gives the results from the PCA. The table shows that the first factor explains 73.32% of the total variance. The first and second factors explain 97.56% of the total variation of the variance. And finally, the first three factors explain 99.34% of the variation in the total variance.

Since the first two components explain more than 97% of the total variance, we will then retain only these first two factors. Table 15.4 presents the sensitivity of the nine initial spot rates with respect to the first two principal components, which we name hereafter PC_1 and PC_2.

Thus variable X_i can be written as:

$$X_i = w_{i1}\text{PC}_1 + w_{i2}\text{PC}_2, \tag{15.27}$$

where X_i refers to the spot rate with maturity i. For example, for the one-month spot rate,

$$X_{1m} = 0.8480\text{PC}_1 - 0.4808\text{PC}_2, \tag{15.28}$$

for the three-year spot rate

$$X_{3y} = 0.9742\text{PC}_1 + 0.1638\text{PC}_2, \tag{15.29}$$

and finally for the thirty-year spot rate,

$$X_{30y} = 0.4334\text{PC}_1 + 0.8698\text{PC}_2. \tag{15.30}$$

Table 15.3 Results from the PCA

Factors	Eigen values	% of the variance explained	% of cumulative variance explained
1	6.599	73.318	73.318
2	2.182	24.241	97.559
3	0.160	1.777	99.337
4	0.045	0.498	99.835
5	0.009	0.099	99.934
6	0.003	0.039	99.973
7	0.001	0.011	99.984
8	0.001	0.009	99.993
9	0.001	0.007	100.00

Table 15.4 Loadings on the first two principal components

Variables	Components	
	PC_1	PC_2
1 month	0.8480	−0.4808
3 months	0.8805	−0.4568
6 months	0.9166	−0.3896
1 year	0.9579	−0.2566
2 years	0.9880	−0.0173
3 years	0.9742	0.1638
5 years	0.8822	0.4532
10 years	0.6746	0.7316
30 years	0.4334	0.8698

The numbers in Table 15.4 represent the square root of the eigenvalue times the corresponding eigenvector. From the table, we observe that the first factor loadings are almost similar for all spot rates except for long-term maturities (10 and 30 years). Therefore, any variation of the first factor (PC_1) will lead to a parallel shift in the term structure. For this reason, the first factor is commonly called the trend component of the zero-curve. In our sample, more than 73% of the total change in the term structure can be attributed to the parallel shift from the first factor.

The second factor loadings increase with the maturity of the spot rates. Thus, a positive shock on PC_2 will lead to a diminution of the short-term spot rates and an augmentation of the long-term spot rates. This second factor is called the tilt of the yield curve and accounts for almost 24% of the total variation of the yield curve in our sample.

The third factor loadings (which we omit from our analysis) have a U-shape, i.e., the loadings are positive and decreasing for short-term rates, they become negative for middle range rates, and increase and become positive for long-term rates. The third factor, PC_3, affects the convexity of the yield curve.

Figure 15.4 displays the trends of the first three factors (PC_1, PC_2 and PC_3) with respect to the maturity of the zero-coupon bonds.

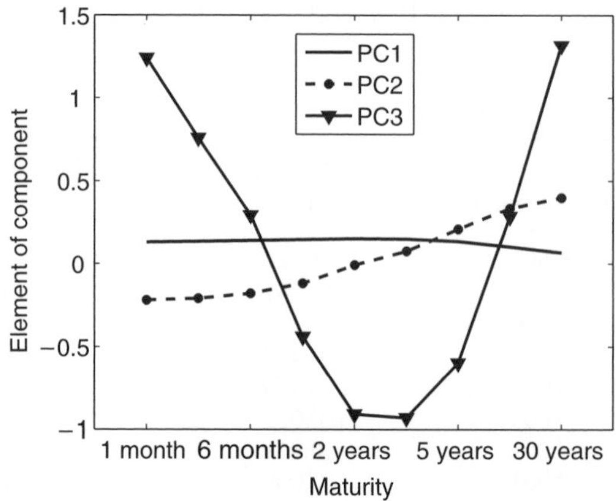

Figure 15.4 Trend of the first three principal components

15.2.3 Linear Interpolation or Bootstrapping for the Intermediate Spot Rates

Recall the portfolio is composed of coupon-paying bonds. The coupons are paid semi-annually. The initial nine spot rates are not enough to compute the price of the bonds in our portfolio since the intermediate spot rates are missing. We use the linear interpolation technique to obtain the other spot rates.

To illustrate the methodology, consider for example a yield on a zero-coupon bond maturing in eight months. Suppose that we know the six-month and twelve-month spot rates. The eight-month spot rate is obtained with a linear combination of the six-month and twelve-month rates such that the two portfolios have the same duration, i.e.,

$$\text{Duration}_{8m} = x\text{Duration}_{6m} + (1-x)\text{Duration}_{12m}, \tag{15.31}$$

with x the percentage of wealth invested in the six-month zero-coupon bond. Duration$_i$ stands for the duration of a zero-coupon bond with maturity i and represents the first derivative of the bond price with respect to the interest rate or its interest rate sensitivity coefficient. We need to find x. Since these are zero-coupon bonds, then

$$\text{Duration}_{6m} = \frac{1}{2} \tag{15.32}$$

and

$$\text{Duration}_{12m} = 1. \tag{15.33}$$

Thus,

$$\text{Duration}_{8m} = x\frac{1}{2} + (1-x), \tag{15.34}$$

which implies $x = \frac{2}{3}$.

The eight months spot rate is obtained with 2/3 of the six months spot rate and 1/3 of the one-year spot rate. We apply the same technique using the nine initial spot rates (1 month, 3 months, 6 months, 1 year, 2 years, 3 years, 5 years, 10 years and 30 years) and obtain the interpolated intermediate spot rates as follows:

$$\begin{aligned}
r_{1.5} &= \frac{1}{2}r_1 + \frac{1}{2}r_2, & r_{2.5} &= \frac{1}{2}r_2 + \frac{1}{2}r_3,\\
r_{3.5} &= \frac{3}{4}r_3 + \frac{1}{4}r_5, & r_4 &= \frac{1}{2}r_3 + \frac{1}{2}r_5,\\
r_{4.5} &= \frac{1}{4}r_3 + \frac{3}{4}r_5, & r_{5.5} &= \frac{9}{10}r_5 + \frac{1}{10}r_{10},\\
r_6 &= \frac{4}{5}r_5 + \frac{1}{5}r_{10}, & r_{6.5} &= \frac{7}{10}r_5 + \frac{3}{10}r_{10},\\
r_7 &= \frac{6}{10}r_5 + \frac{4}{10}r_{10}, & r_{7.5} &= \frac{1}{2}r_5 + \frac{1}{2}r_{10},\\
r_8 &= \frac{2}{5}r_5 + \frac{3}{5}r_{10}, & r_{8.5} &= \frac{3}{10}r_5 + \frac{7}{10}r_{10},\\
r_9 &= \frac{1}{5}r_5 + \frac{4}{5}r_{10}, & r_{9.5} &= \frac{1}{10}r_5 + \frac{9}{10}r_{10}.
\end{aligned}$$

To sum up, we use the initial term structure of interest rates data available, i.e., spot rates of 1, 3, 6 months, 1, 2, 3, 5, 10 and 30 years, and the other spot rates needed are obtained using the above linear interpolations.

15.2.4 Computing VaR by MC and QMC Simulations

We retain the first two factors for our analysis. Thus, the simulation equation will be:

$$r_i = r_{i0} + \sigma_i \left(U_{1i}\sqrt{\lambda_1} Z_1 + U_{2i}\sqrt{\lambda_2} Z_2 \right), \tag{15.35}$$

where r_{i0} is the current spot rate, σ_i is the spot rate volatility over the VaR horizon, and Z_i are distributed normally. This equation is used to generate the nine initial spot rates of the zero curve and the other rates are obtained by linear interpolation as described above in the previous sub-section.

Here is a program used to simulate the rates. For practical purposes, the spot rates' initial data will be kept in an EXCEL file and will later be converted into a text file (SpotRates.txt). The MATLAB program for the implementation of all the VaR computation steps described in this chapter is presented below. Note that the MATLAB program extracts data from a text file called SpotRates.txt.

```
function VaR=MC(NbTraj,p,alpha)
%Function computing the value at risk of a
%portfolio composed of two bonds.
%NbTraj: Number of simulations.
%p: Weight for each bond.
%alpha: Confidence level
%Identification of our data file
fid=fopen('SpotRates.txt','rt');
%Reading of the data from file SpotRates.txt
Data=fscanf(fid, '%f %f %f %f %f %f %f %f %f');
%Closing of source file.
fclose(fid);
%Partition of data into date and different rates
M1=Data(1:9:size(Data)); %spot rate 1 month
M3=Data(2:9:size(Data)); %spot rate 3 months
M6=Data(3:9:size(Data)); %spot rate 6 months
Y1=Data(4:9:size(Data)); %spot rate 1 year
Y2=Data(5:9:size(Data)); %spot rate 2 years
Y3=Data(6:9:size(Data)); %spot rate 3 years
Y5=Data(7:9:size(Data)); %spot rate 5 years
Y10=Data(8:9:size(Data)); %spot rate 10 years
Y30=Data(9:9:size(Data)); %spot rate 30 years
%Matrix of rates
Data1=[M1,M3,M6,Y1,Y2,Y3,Y5,Y10,Y30];
%Initial rates
ActualRates=Data1(size(Data1,1),:);
%Normalization of rates
for i=1:9
   Average(i)=mean(Data1(:,i));
   Deviation(i)=std(Data1(:,i));
   Data1(:,i)=(Data1(:,i)-Average(i))/Deviation(i);
end
```

```
%The standard deviation for a one month period.
%We want a value at risk for 10 days and we divide by
%sqrt(3) since 1 month = 3*10 days.
Deviation=Deviation/sqrt(3);
%Eigenvectors and eigenvalues of the covariance matrix
%Vector -Vi can also be returned by function
%eigs if Vi is an eigenvector.
[V,E]=eigs(cov(Data1),3);
%Components determination.
PC1=V(:,1);
PC2=V(:,2);
PC3=V(:,3);
%Graph of the principal components.
plot([1:1:9],sqrt(E(1,1))*PC1,'r',[1:1:9],sqrt(E(2,2))*PC2,'b', ...
     [1:1:9],sqrt(E(3,3))*PC3,'m');
Weight1=p;
Weight2=1-Weight1;
%Initial parameters
CouponRate1=0.06;
FaceValue1=1000;
CouponRate2=0.08;
FaceValue2=1000;
coupon1=CouponRate1*FaceValue1;
coupon2=CouponRate2*FaceValue2;
%Vectors for quasi random variables
u1=zeros(NbTraj,1);
u2=zeros(NbTraj,1);
%Simulation of quasi random numbers
for l=1:NbTraj
   u1(l)=norminv(VanDerCorput(l,3));
   u2(l)=norminv(VanDerCorput(l,5));
end
%Spot rates matrix
Rates=zeros(9,NbTraj);
%Loop generating the interest rates
for j=1:NbTraj
   for i=1:9
        %Computation of rates. We multiply by the sign of the first
        %element of the components to fix them positively. This will
         allow
        %us to replicate perfectly our results if needed.
        Rates(i,j)=ActualRates(1,i)+...
         Deviation(i)*(sqrt(E(1,1))*u1(j,1)*V(i,1)*sign(V(1,1))+...
         sqrt(E(2,2))*u2(j,1)*V(i,2)*sign(V(1,2)));
   end
end

%Spot rates initial values
M6=ActualRates(1,3);  %spot rate 6 months
Y1=ActualRates(1,4);  %spot rate 1 year
Y2=ActualRates(1,5);  %spot rate 2 years
Y3=ActualRates(1,6);  %spot rate 3 years
Y5=ActualRates(1,7);  %spot rate 5 years
```

```
%Linear interpolation
Y1_5=(Y1+Y2)/2;          %spot rate 1.5 years
Y2_5=(Y2+Y3)/2;          %spot rate 2.5 years
Y3_5=(3*Y3+Y5)/4;        %spot rate 3.5 years
Y4=(Y3+Y5)/2;             %spot rate 4 years
Y4_5=(3*Y5+Y3)/4;        %spot rate 4.5 years
%Determination of initial bonds' prices.
price1=(coupon1/2)/(1+(M6/100))^(1/2)+(coupon1/2)/(1+(Y1/100))^1+...
      (coupon1/2)/(1+(Y1_5/100))^(3/2)+(coupon1/2)/(1+(Y2/100))^2+...
      (FaceValue1+(coupon1/2))/(1+(Y2_5/100))^(5/2);
price2=(coupon2/2)/(1+(M6/100))^(1/2)+(coupon2/2)/(1+(Y1/100))^1+...
      (coupon2/2)/(1+(Y1_5/100))^(3/2)+(coupon2/2)/(1+(Y2/100))^2+...
      (coupon2/2)/(1+(Y2_5/100))^(5/2)+(coupon2/2)/(1+(Y3/100))^3+...
      (coupon2/2)/(1+(Y3_5/100))^(7/2)+(coupon2/2)/(1+(Y4/100))^4+...
      (coupon2/2)/(1+(Y4_5/100))^(9/2)+...
      (FaceValue2+(coupon2/2))/(1+(Y5/100))^5;
%Portfolio's initial price.
InitialPrice=Weight1*price1+Weight2*price2;
%Loop computing the possible evolution of the portfolio's price.
for k=1:NbTraj
   M6=Rates(3,k);   %Spot rate 6 months
   Y1=Rates(4,k);   %Spot rate 1 year
   Y2=Rates(5,k);   %Spot rate 2 years
   Y3=Rates(6,k);   %Spot rate 3 years
   Y5=Rates(7,k);   %Spot rate 5 years
   Y1_5=(Y1+Y2)/2;        %Spot rate 1.5 years
   Y2_5=(Y2+Y3)/2;        %Spot rate 2.5 years
   Y3_5=(3*Y3+Y5)/4;      %Spot rate 3.5 years
   Y4=(Y3+Y5)/2;           %Spot rate 4 years
   Y4_5=(3*Y5+Y3)/4;      %Spot rate 4.5 years
   %Valuation of two different bonds
   price1=(coupon1/2)/(1+(M6/100))^(1/2)+(coupon1/2)/(1+(Y1/100))^1+...
         (coupon1/2)/(1+(Y1_5/100))^(3/2)+(coupon1/2)/(1+(Y2/100))^2+...
         (FaceValue1+(coupon1/2))/(1+(Y2_5/100))^(5/2);
   price2=(coupon2/2)/(1+(M6/100))^(1/2)+(coupon2/2)/(1+(Y1/100))^1+...
         (coupon2/2)/(1+(Y1_5/100))^(3/2)+(coupon2/2)/(1+(Y2/100))^2+...
         (coupon2/2)/(1+(Y2_5/100))^(5/2)+(coupon2/2)/(1+(Y3/100))^3+...
         (coupon2/2)/(1+(Y3_5/100))^(7/2)+(coupon2/2)/(1+(Y4/100))^4+...
         (coupon2/2)/(1+(Y4_5/100))^(9/2)+...
         (FaceValue2+(coupon2/2))/(1+(Y5/100))^5;
%Computation of the portfolio's price for this scenario
PortfolioPrice=Weight1*price1+Weight2*price2;
vectPrice(k,1)= PortfolioPrice;
end
%Sorting the prices and VaR computation.
vectPrice=sort(vectPrice);
VaR=(InitialPrice-vectPrice(floor(alpha/100*NbTraj)));
end

function rep=VanDerCorput(n, b)
%Function generating the Van Der Corput sequence to build Halton
 sequence.
%n: Index of the sequence of elements.
```

```
%b: Basis for decomposition.
bn=0;
j=0;
while n~=0
   bn=bn+mod(n,b)/b^(j+1);
   n=floor(n/b);
   j=j+1;
end
rep=bn;
end
```

Table 15.5 compares the results for the portfolio VaR from MC and QMC simulations with respect to the number of simulations N and the confidence level (99% ($\alpha = 1\%$), 95% ($\alpha = 5\%$) or 90% ($\alpha = 10\%$)). It illustrates the convergence pattern for each simulation technique as the number of simulations increases. The standard deviation, σ, is used to measure the convergence and stationarity of the VaR for different numbers of simulations. For the QMC simulations, we use the Halton sequence.

For a confidence level of 99%, the standard deviation with MC is 1.491 and with QMC it is 0.125. Thus, the error of the VaR is on average 11.891 times higher with MC compared to QMC. With a confidence level of 95%, the standard deviation with MC is 0.648 and 0.151 with QMC. In this case, MC standard deviation is 4.304 times higher than that of QMC. With a 90% confidence level, the standard deviation obtained with MC is 0.274 and with QMC it is 0.205. The standard deviation of the VaR with MC is 1.335 times higher than that with QMC. These findings are illustrated in Figures 15.5, 15.6 and 15.7. The graphs show that

Table 15.5 Portfolio VaR with MC and QMC

	Portfolio VaR with MC and QMC ($)					
N	MC 10%	QMC 10%	MC 5%	QMC 5%	MC 1%	QMC 1%
500	21.46	21.16	26.22	28.38	34.53	39.43
800	22.25	21.37	27.84	28.28	41.31	39.43
1000	21.94	21.69	29.29	28.00	39.24	39.43
3000	21.74	21.74	28.04	27.92	37.81	39.22
5000	22.43	21.85	28.45	28.03	39.75	39.43
8000	21.73	21.85	27.84	28.00	38.71	39.43
10 000	21.45	21.76	27.40	28.00	37.98	39.43
30 000	22.03	21.84	28.07	27.91	39.62	39.21
50 000	22.04	21.82	28.09	27.92	39.27	39.17
80 000	21.76	21.83	27.96	27.91	39.38	39.22
100 000	21.83	21.83	27.77	27.91	39.11	39.22
150 000	21.63	21.82	27.73	27.90	39.00	39.17
200 000	21.80	21.82	27.81	27.90	39.16	39.17
250 000	21.78	21.82	27.80	27.89	39.20	39.16
σ	0.274	0.205	0.648	0.151	1.491	0.125
Ratio $\frac{\sigma_{MC}}{\sigma_{QMC}}$	1.335		4.304		11.891	

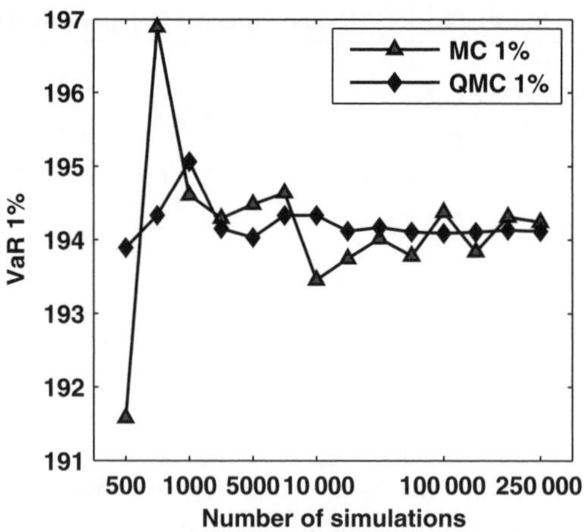

Figure 15.5 Convergence of simulations, 99% ($\alpha = 1\%$)

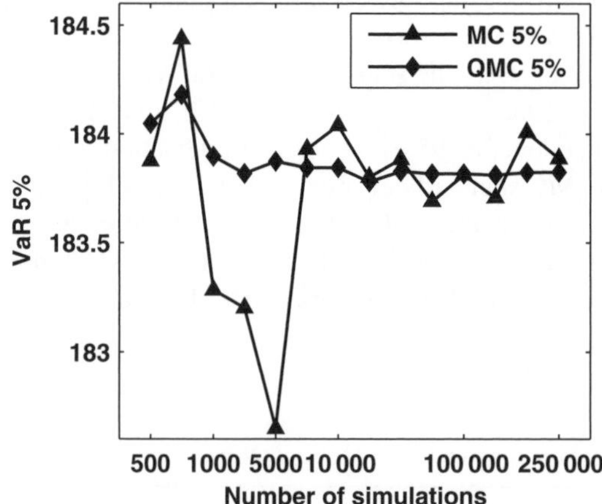

Figure 15.6 Convergence of simulations, 95% ($\alpha = 5\%$)

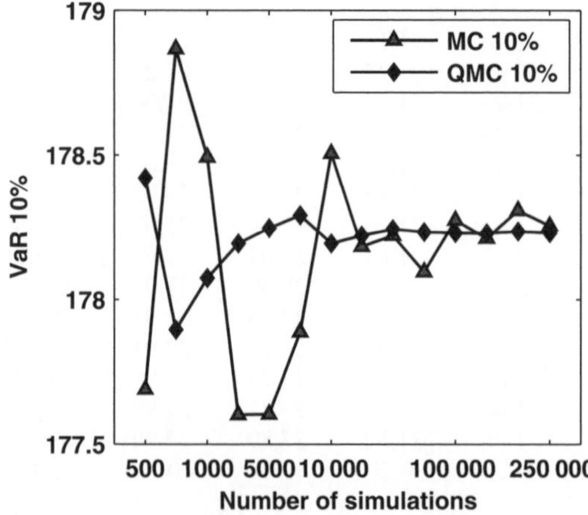

Figure 15.7 Convergence of simulations, 90% ($\alpha = 10\%$)

QMC converges quickly after 5000 simulations, with MC, the same results are obtained only after 150 000 simulations.

Notes and Complementary Readings

For further readings on the use of factor models in bond portfolio management, we refer the reader to papers by Litterman and Scheinkman (1991), Barber and Copper (1996), Kreinin, Merkoulovitch, Rosen and Zerbs (1998), Lai, Sakni and Soumaré (2005).

For a complementary reference on principal components analysis, consult the book by Dionne (2002).

Appendix A
Review of Mathematics

A.1 MATRICES

A matrix of order (n, m) is a rectangular array of $n \times m$ elements placed in n rows and m columns as follows:

$$A = \begin{pmatrix} a_{11} & a_{12} & \cdots & a_{1m} \\ a_{21} & a_{22} & \cdots & a_{2m} \\ \vdots & \vdots & \cdots & \vdots \\ a_{n1} & a_{n2} & \cdots & a_{nm} \end{pmatrix} \tag{A.1}$$

and we denote by $A = (a_{ij})_{n \times m}$, $1 \leq i \leq n$, $1 \leq j \leq m$ and $(A)_{ij} = a_{ij}$ is the element of matrix A at the intersection of row i and column j. In the following we suppose a_{ij} is a real number.

A matrix of order (n, m) is also called an n by m matrix or $n \times m$ matrix. When $n = m$, the matrix is a square matrix of order n. For such a matrix, elements $a_{11}, a_{22}, \ldots, a_{nn}$ form its principal diagonal.

Definition 1.1 *Two matrices* $\mathrm{A} = (\mathrm{a_{ij}})_{\mathrm{n \times m}}$ *and* $\mathrm{B} = (\mathrm{b_{ij}})_{\mathrm{p \times q}}$ *are equal if and only if:*

- *They have the same order (that is* $\mathrm{n = p}$ *and* $\mathrm{m = q}$*) and*
- $\mathrm{a_{ij} = b_{ij}}\ \forall\, \mathrm{i, j},\ 1 \leq \mathrm{i} \leq \mathrm{n = p},\ 1 \leq \mathrm{j} \leq \mathrm{m = q}$.

Example 1.2 The null matrix of order (2, 3) noted $\mathbf{0}_{2\times3}$ is the matrix

$$\mathbf{0}_{2\times3} = \begin{pmatrix} 0 & 0 & 0 \\ 0 & 0 & 0 \end{pmatrix},$$

while an order 3 identity square matrix is

$$I_3 = \begin{pmatrix} 1 & 0 & 0 \\ 0 & 1 & 0 \\ 0 & 0 & 1 \end{pmatrix},$$

matrix such that the elements on the principal diagonal are all equal to 1 and the elements off diagonal are zero. Generally, we can define a null matrix n by m and identity matrices of order n, where m and n are any integer number.

A.1.1 Elementary Operations on Matrices

The following elementary operations on matrices are summarized.

Multiplication by a Scalar

Let α be a real number and $A = (a_{ij})_{n\times m}$ a matrix $n \times m$. The product A by α, noted αA , is a matrix n by m obtained by multiplying each element of A by α, that is

$$\alpha A = \left(\alpha a_{ij}\right)_{n\times m}. \tag{A.2}$$

Addition and Substraction of Matrices

Let $A = (a_{ij})_{n\times m}$ and $B = (b_{ij})_{n\times m}$ be two n by m matrices. The sum of A and B denoted by $A+B$ is a matrix n by m whose element of row i and column j is obtained by summing elements of row i and column j of A and B. Then, we have $A + B = (a_{ij} + b_{ij})_{n\times m}$ or equivalently

$$(A + B)_{ij} = a_{ij} + b_{ij}. \tag{A.3}$$

The substraction of B from A is the matrix

$$A - B = A + (-1)B = \left(a_{ij} - b_{ij}\right)_{n\times m}. \tag{A.4}$$

Transpose of a Matrix

The transpose of an order (m, n) matrix A, denoted by $A^\top$ (or A'), is the matrix m by n whose element of row i and column j is the element of row j and column i of A:

$$\left(A^\top\right)_{ij} = a_{ji}, \quad 1 \le i \le n, \quad 1 \le j \le m. \tag{A.5}$$

Product of Two Matrices

Let $A = (a_{ij})_{n\times m}$ and $B = (b_{ij})_{m\times q}$ be two matrices. The product of A by B, noted AB is the matrix n by q whose element of row i and column j is given by:

$$(AB)_{ij} = \sum_{k=1}^{m} a_{ik} b_{kj}. \tag{A.6}$$

Product of Two Matrices Element by Element

For some computations, it can be important to define an elementwise product of two matrices $A = (a_{ij})_{n\times m}$ and $B = (b_{ij})_{n\times m}$ denoted by $A \odot B$, with:

$$(A \odot B)_{ij} = a_{ij} b_{ij}. \tag{A.7}$$

To define such product, the matrices must have the same order.

A.1.2 Vectors

A row vector X of order n is a 1 by n matrix, and a column vector Y of order n is a n by 1 matrix:

$$X = (x_1, x_2, \ldots, x_n) \tag{A.8}$$

and

$$Y = \begin{pmatrix} y_1 \\ y_2 \\ \vdots \\ y_n \end{pmatrix}. \tag{A.9}$$

Unless specified, a vector of order n will refer to a column vector of order n.

We define the usual scalar product of two vectors X and Y of order n, the real number

$$X^\top Y = x_1 y_1 + x_2 y_2 + \cdots + x_n y_n = \sum_{k=1}^{n} x_k y_k. \tag{A.10}$$

The norm of X is the real number denoted by $||X||$ with

$$||X|| = \sqrt{X^\top X} = \sqrt{\sum_{k=1}^{m} x_k^2}. \tag{A.11}$$

An n by m matrix is thus an array of n row vectors of order m, or equivalently an array of m column vectors of order n.

A.1.3 Properties

P1. Product of Two Matrices

Let $A = (a_{ij})_{n\times m}$ and $B = (b_{ij})_{m\times q}$ be two matrices. The product of A by B, denoted by AB is the n by q matrix whose element of row i and column j is obtained by computing the scalar product of row i of matrix A by column j of matrix B. We have

$$(AB)_{ij} = \sum_{k=1}^{m} a_{ik} b_{kj}. \tag{A.12}$$

P2. Inverse of a Matrix

A matrix $A = (a_{ij})_{n\times n}$ is said to be invertible if there exists a matrix B such that $AB = BA = I$, where I is the identity matrix of order n. In this case, B is the inverse matrix of A, and is denoted by A^{-1}.

P3. Triangular Matrix

A square matrix of order n,

$$A = \left(a_{ij}\right)_{n\times n} \tag{A.13}$$

is said to be upper triangular if $a_{ij} = 0$ for $i > j$; this is the case of the matrix

$$A = \begin{pmatrix} 1 & 5 & 6 \\ 0 & 2 & 9 \\ 0 & 0 & 3 \end{pmatrix}.$$

A matrix will be called lower triangular if $a_{ij} = 0$ for $i < j$, this is the case of matrix

$$B = \begin{pmatrix} 1 & 0 & 0 \\ 5 & 2 & 0 \\ 6 & 9 & 3 \end{pmatrix}.$$

A square matrix is called triangular if it is lower triangular or upper triangular.

P4. Diagonal Matrix

A square matrix that is upper triangular and lower triangular is a diagonal matrix. This is the case of matrix

$$D = \begin{pmatrix} 4 & 0 & 0 \\ 0 & 3 & 0 \\ 0 & 0 & 7 \end{pmatrix}.$$

P5. Symmetric Matrix, Positive and Definite Positive Matrix

A square matrix A of order n is symmetric if $A = A^\top$. It is positive if $X^\top AX \geq 0$ for all vector X of order n, and is called positive definite if $X^\top AX > 0$ for all vector X of order n different of zero ($X \neq \mathbf{0}_{n\times 1}$).

A.1.4 Determinants of Matrices

We associate to each square matrix A a real number called determinant and denoted by $|A|$ which has many applications as we will see below.

The determinant of a square matrix of order 2×2 noted

$$A = \begin{pmatrix} a_{11} & a_{12} \\ a_{21} & a_{22} \end{pmatrix} \tag{A.14}$$

is $|A| = a_{11}a_{22} - a_{12}a_{21}$. The determinant of matrix $\begin{pmatrix} 1 & 2 \\ 3 & 4 \end{pmatrix}$ is

$$\begin{vmatrix} 1 & 2 \\ 3 & 4 \end{vmatrix} = 1 \times 4 - 2 \times 3 = 4 - 6 = -2.$$

Definition 1.3 *Let* A = $(\mathrm{a_{ij}})_{\mathrm{n}\times\mathrm{n}}$ *be a square matrix of order* n. *We associate to each element* $\mathrm{a_{ij}}$ *of* A, *a sub-matrix of order* $(\mathrm{n}-1) \times (\mathrm{n}-1)$ *obtained by deleting row* i *and column* j *of* A. *The determinant of this sub-matrix called minor of* $\mathrm{a_{ij}}$ *constitutes* $\mathrm{A_{ij}}$.

Thus for

$$A = \begin{pmatrix} 2 & 0 & 3 \\ 4 & -1 & 1 \\ 0 & 1 & 2 \end{pmatrix}$$

the minor of $a_{11} = 2$ is

$$A_{11} = \begin{vmatrix} -1 & 1 \\ 1 & 2 \end{vmatrix} = (-1) \times 2 - 1 \times 1 = -3.$$

Definition 1.4 *The determinant of any matrix of order* n

$$A = \left(a_{ij}\right)_{n \times n} \tag{A.15}$$

is the real number

$$|A| = \sum_{j=1}^{n} (-1)^{1+j} a_{1j} A_{1j}. \tag{A.16}$$

Equivalently, we have

$$|A| = \sum_{i=1}^{n} (-1)^{i+j} a_{ij} A_{ij} \tag{A.17}$$

independently of row i *or column* j *used.*

For example, if

$$A = \begin{pmatrix} 2 & 0 & 3 \\ 4 & -1 & 1 \\ 0 & 1 & 2 \end{pmatrix},$$

then

$$\begin{aligned} |A| &= 2(-1)^{1+1} A_{11} + 0(-1)^{1+2} A_{12} + 3(-1)^{1+3} A_{13} \\ &= 2(-1)^{1+1} A_{11} + 4(-1)^{2+1} A_{21} + 0(-1)^{3+1} A_{31}, \end{aligned}$$

thus

$$\begin{aligned} |A| &= 2 \begin{vmatrix} -1 & 1 \\ 1 & 2 \end{vmatrix} + 0(-1)^{1+2} A_{12} + 3 \begin{vmatrix} 4 & -1 \\ 0 & 1 \end{vmatrix} \\ &= 2(-2-1) + 3(4) \\ &= -6 + 12 \\ &= 6. \end{aligned}$$

Properties of the Determinant

1. The determinant of a matrix with one null column or row is equal to zero.
2. The determinant of matrix B obtained from matrix A by multiplying a row or column by a scalar α is

$$|B| = \alpha\,|A|\,. \tag{A.18}$$

   It follows that the determinant of matrix αA is

$$|\alpha A| = \alpha^n\,|A|\,, \tag{A.19}$$

   where n is the dimension of matrix A.
3. The determinant of a square matrix of order n and upper or lower triangular, is the product of its elements on the main diagonal.
4. A matrix is invertible if and only if its determinant is different from zero.

A.2 SOLUTION OF A SYSTEM OF LINEAR EQUATIONS

A system of linear equations is an equation of the form $AX = B$, where A is an n by m matrix, X is a column vector of order m and B is a column vector of order n.

Example 2.1 Consider the system of linear equations

$$x - 3y = 1$$
$$2x - y = 3$$

equivalent to $AX = B$, where

$$A = \begin{pmatrix} 1 & -3 \\ 2 & -1 \end{pmatrix},$$
$$X = \begin{pmatrix} x \\ y \end{pmatrix}$$

and

$$B = \begin{pmatrix} 1 \\ 3 \end{pmatrix}.$$

For such a system, we look for the vector X for which $AX = B$. In the case of an invertible square matrix A, it is easy to see that $X = A^{-1}B$, since by multiplying by the inverse of A we have

$$A^{-1}AX = A^{-1}B, \tag{A.20}$$

and since $A^{-1}A = I$, we obtain $X = A^{-1}B$.

Case of an Upper Triangular Matrix

Consider the following linear system:

$$\begin{pmatrix} a_{11} & a_{12} & & a_{1n} \\ 0 & a_{22} & & a_{2n} \\ \vdots & 0 & \ddots & \vdots \\ & \vdots & & \\ 0 & \cdots & 0 & a_{nn} \end{pmatrix} \begin{pmatrix} x_1 \\ x_2 \\ \vdots \\ x_n \end{pmatrix} = \begin{pmatrix} b_1 \\ b_2 \\ \vdots \\ b_n \end{pmatrix}. \tag{A.21}$$

To solve this system, we just need to note that the last component of X is $x_n = \frac{b_n}{a_{nn}}$, and the penultimate row of the system gives us

$$\begin{aligned} x_{n-1} &= \frac{1}{a_{n-1\,n-1}} (b_{n-1} - a_{n-1\,n} x_n) \\ &= \frac{1}{a_{n-1\,n-1}} \left(b_{n-1} - a_{n-1n} \frac{b_n}{a_{nn}} \right). \end{aligned} \tag{A.22}$$

By going upwards, we can completely determine the vector X. Here is the principle. We begin by computing x_n. Once the value of x_n is known, we compute x_{n-1} as a function of x_n and we repeat this step. Knowing $x_n, \ldots, x_{k+1}$, we compute x_k as a function of $x_{k+1}, x_{k+2}, \ldots, x_n$ using row k of the system. Thus, we obtain:

$$x_n = \frac{b_n}{a_{nn}}, \tag{A.23}$$

$$x_{n-1} = \frac{1}{a_{n-1\,n-1}} (b_{n-1} - a_{n-1\,n} x_n), \tag{A.24}$$

$$\vdots = \vdots,$$

$$x_k = \frac{1}{a_{k\,k}} \left(b_k - \sum_{i=k+1}^{n} a_{ki} x_i \right), \tag{A.25}$$

for $k = 1, \ldots, n-2$.

This strategy can be used in the case of a lower triangular matrix, but one must compute from top to bottom. Beginning with x_1, we obtain the following solution:

$$x_1 = \frac{b_1}{a_{11}}, \tag{A.26}$$

$$x_2 = \frac{1}{a_{2\,2}} (b_2 - a_{2\,1} x_1), \tag{A.27}$$

$$\vdots = \vdots,$$

$$x_k = \frac{1}{a_{k\,k}} \left(b_k - \sum_{i=1}^{k-1} a_{ki} x_i \right), \tag{A.28}$$

$k = 3, \ldots, n$.

As we have just seen, it is easy to solve a linear system when the matrix is upper or lower triangular. Thus it can be interesting to find a triangular matrix T, and an appropriate second vector C such that the new system of linear equations $TY = C$ has exactly the same solutions as the initial system $AX = B$. Many approaches to performing this operation are available in the literature.

A.3 MATRIX DECOMPOSITION

LU *Decomposition*

Sometimes it is useful to decompose a square matrix A in a product of two square matrices L and U such that $A = LU$, where U is upper triangular and L is unit lower triangular. A triangular matrix is unit if all the entries on the main diagonal are 1. This decomposition enables us to easily solve the system of linear equations $AX = B$ by solving the equivalent following system $LUX = B$ that can be decomposed into two systems

$$\begin{aligned} LY &= B \\ UX &= Y. \end{aligned} \tag{A.29}$$

We solve the first system with the triangular matrix to get Y and knowing Y we can solve the second system to find X. We have $AX = LUX = LY = B$. The Gauss elimination method is one of the techniques used to perform a LU decomposition of any square matrix A. For more details, we refer the reader to any good linear algebra book.

Cholesky Decomposition

If matrix A is symmetric and invertible, then it has a decomposition $A = LDU$, where L is unit lower triangular, D is a diagonal matrix and U is unit upper triangular with $U = L^\top$. Moreover, if all elements on the diagonal of D are positive, then A has a decomposition $R^\top R$, where R is an invertible upper triangular matrix.

However, in practice, to find matrices U and L, a Gauss decomposition method or Crout method are often used.

A.4 POLYNOMIAL AND LINEAR APPROXIMATION

Definition 4.1 *A polynomial* P *of degree* n *is a function from* $\mathbb{R}$ *into* $\mathbb{R}$ *with the form*

$$\begin{aligned} P(x) &= a_0 + a_1 x^1 + a_2 x^2 + \cdots a_n x^n \\ &= \sum_{i=0}^{n} a_i x^i. \end{aligned} \tag{A.30}$$

Definition 4.2 *The Taylor series of degree* n *to approximate (in a neighborhood of* x_0*) the real function* f(x) *is the degree* n *polynomial in which all derivatives of order* k ($P^{(k)}$), $k \leq n$, *are such that*

$$P^{(k)}(x_0) = f^{(k)}(x_0) \text{ and} \tag{A.31}$$

$$P(x_0) = f(x_0). \tag{A.32}$$

Hence

$$P(x) = f(x_0) + \sum_{k=0}^{n} \frac{(x - x_0)^k}{k!} f^{(k)}(x_0) + O(x^{n+1}). \tag{A.33}$$

A.5 EIGENVECTORS AND EIGENVALUES OF A MATRIX

Definition 5.1 *Let* A *be a square matrix of order* n, *the real number* λ *is an eigenvalue of* A *if there exists a vector* $U \neq \mathbf{0}_{n\times 1}$ *of order* n *(called eigenvector associated to eigenvalue* λ*) such that* $AU = \lambda U$ *or equivalently*

$$(A - \lambda I_n)U = \mathbf{0}_{n\times 1}. \tag{A.34}$$

This is equivalent to $(A - \lambda I_n)$ *not invertible, or equivalently that its determinant is zero.*

Thus in order to find the eigenvalues of a matrix A, we can solve the equation $|A - \lambda I_n| = 0$, and knowing λ solve the equation $(A - \lambda I_n)U = \mathbf{0}_{n\times 1}$ to get U. Polynomial

$$P(\lambda) = |A - \lambda I_n| \tag{A.35}$$

is called characteristic polynomial of A, and its roots are the eigenvalues of A.

Example 5.2 With an order 4 matrix,

$$A = \begin{pmatrix} 1 & 1 & -1 & 2 \\ 2 & 1 & 2 & 1 \\ 3 & 2 & 3 & 6 \\ -1 & -1 & 2 & -4 \end{pmatrix},$$

we note

$$B = A - \lambda I_n = \begin{pmatrix} 1-\lambda & 1 & -1 & 2 \\ 2 & 1-\lambda & 2 & 1 \\ 3 & 2 & 3-\lambda & 6 \\ -1 & -1 & 2 & -4-\lambda \end{pmatrix}.$$

We compute the determinant of $B = A - \lambda I_n$ to obtain the characteristic polynomial of A:

$$|A - \lambda I_n| = 7 + 25\lambda - \lambda^3 - 25\lambda^2 + \lambda^4.$$

The roots of this polynomial are the eigenvalues of A. It is not always easy to find the exact values of the roots of this polynomial, so in such cases we proceed by approximation. With MATLAB, we obtain $\lambda_1 = -4.9764$, $\lambda_2 = 4.9643$, $\lambda_3 = -0.2284$ and $\lambda_4 = 1.2405$. The corresponding eigenvectors are

$$U_1 = \begin{pmatrix} 0.3675 \\ -0.1554 \\ 0.4857 \\ -0.7777 \end{pmatrix}, U_2 = \begin{pmatrix} 0.0297 \\ -0.4628 \\ -0.8737 \\ -0.1466 \end{pmatrix},$$

$$U_3 = \begin{pmatrix} -0.5608 \\ 0.8243 \\ 0.0707 \\ -0.0324 \end{pmatrix}, U_4 = \begin{pmatrix} -0.6586 \\ -0.5062 \\ 0.4086 \\ 0.3782 \end{pmatrix}.$$

Appendix B
MATLAB® Functions

A'	Transpose of matrix A.
$A. * B$	Product of 2 matrices or vectors, elementwise. Equivalent to the scalar product of 2 vectors.
$a\|b$	Logical OR operation between a and b. We can also use OR(a, b).
$\sim a$	$\sim$ is the logical NOT operator. We can also use NOT(a).
==	Verify if two expressions are equivalent.
!=	Verify if two expressions are different.
bitshift(a, k)	Shifts of k bits of integer number a. It is equivalent to multiply by 2^k and take the integer value of the result.
bitxor(a, b)	Performs the EXCLUSIVE OR operation between numbers a and b.
cat(*dim*, A, B)	Function that concatenates matrix B with matrix A according to the specified dimension *dim*.
ceil(x)	Returns the smallest integer greater or equal to x.
chol(A)	Cholesky decomposition. Returns matrix L such that $L^\top L = A$.
cov(X, X)	Function that computes the covariance between vectors X and Y.
cumsum(A, *dim*)	Computes the cumulative sum of elements of A following dimension *dim*.
disp(a), *disp*('text')	Displays the value of variable a or prints a text string.
doc function	Displays the MATLAB documentation on the command *function*.
eigs(A, k)	Called with outputs $[V, D] = eigs(A, k)$ returns the k greatest eigenvalues of A (ordered in matrix D) and the normalized eigenvectors associated (in matrix V).
floor(a)	Returns the integer value of a.
fclose(...)	Closes the file opened by function *fopen*.
figure	Creates a second graphical environment to display many figures in the same program.
fopen('files.txt')	Open file.txt for reading inputs in the file.
fscanf(...)	Extracts data stored in a file opened with function *fopen*.
fsolve(@*myFunction*,*x*0)	Solves the following non linear system: *myFunction*(x) = 0.
hold on ... *hold off*	Between these bounds, the curves plotted with command *plot* are added on the same graph.
inv(A)	Computes the inverse matrix of matrix A.
legend('Series 1', 'Series 2', ...)	Creates a legend in the last graph and names the first curve Series 1, the second curve Series 2, ...
lu(A)	*LU* decomposition of matrix A.
max(A, [], *dim*)	Returns a vector containing maximal elements following the selected dimension (*max*(X) returns the maximal element of vector X).
mean(A, *dim*)	Computes the mean of the elements in matrix A following the selected dimension.
mod(a, b)	Returns the value a modulo b.
nchoosek(n, k)	Computes the number of possibilities to draw k elements from a set of n elements.
normcdf(x)	Gives the cumulative distribution function of the normal distribution at point x.
norminv(x)	Gives the inverse of the cumulative distribution function of the normal distribution at point x.
normpdf(x)	Gives the probability density function of the normal distribution at point x.
ones(m, n)	Initializes a matrix $m \times n$ with all its elements equal to 1.

(continued)

plot(*A*, *B*)	Plots the curves defined by rows of A and B. For example, the first curve goes through coordinates $(A(1, i), B(1, i))$.
randn(*m*, *n*)	Generates a matrix $m \times n$ of standard Gaussian random variables.
rand(*m*, *n*)	Generates a matrix $m \times n$ of uniform random variables over the interval $[0, 1]$.
repmat(*A*, *m*, *n*)	Creates a matrix composed of many copies of matrix A m rows by n columns.
size(*A*, *dim*)	Gives the dimension of matrix A following dimension *dim*.
sort(*X*)	Sorts elements of vector X in increasing order.
sum(*A*, *dim*)	Computes the sum of elements of matrix A following the dimension *dim*.
tic ... *toc*	Returns the time needed to perform operations between bounds defined by *tic* and *toc*.
tinv(*x*)	Inverse function of the Student cumulative distribution function.
zeros(*m*, *n*)	Initializes a matrix $m \times n$ with all elements equal to 0.

References and Bibliography

Aït-Sahalia, Y. and A. W. Lo, "Nonparametric risk management and implied risk aversion", *Journal of Econometrics*, Vol. 94, 2000, pp. 9–51.

Alexander, C. (ed.), *Risk management and analysis*, John Wiley & Sons Ltd, 1998.

Angoua, P., V. S. Lai, and I. Soumaré, "Project risk choices under privately guaranteed debt financing", *The Quarterly Review of Economics and Finance*, Vol. 48, No. 1, 2008, pp. 123–152.

Artzner, P., F. Delbaen, J. M. Eber, and D. Heath, "Coherent measures of risk", *Mathematical Finance*, Vol. 9, 1999, pp. 203–228.

Babbel, D. F., "Insuring banks against systematic credit risk", *Journal of Futures Markets*, Vol. 9, 1989, pp. 487–505.

Bajeux-Besnainou, I. and R. Portait, "Méthodes probabilistes d'évaluation et modèles à variables d'état: Une synthèse", *Finance*, Vol. 13, No. 2, 1992, pp. 23–56.

Banks, E., *Alternative risk transfer: Integrated risk management through insurance, reinsurance, and the capital markets*, John Wiley & Sons Ltd, 2004.

Barber, J. R. and M. L. Copper, "Immunization using principal component analysis", *Journal of Portfolio Management*, Vol. 23, No. 1, 1996, pp. 99–105.

Barraquand, J., "Numerical valuation of high dimensional multivariate European securities", *Management Science*, Vol. 41, No. 12, 1995, pp. 1882–1891.

Barraquand, J. and D. Martineau, "Numerical valuation of high dimensional multivariate American securities", *Journal of Financial and Quantitative Analysis*, Vol. 30, No. 3, 1995, pp. 383–405.

Basle Committee on Banking Supervision, *Amendment to the capital accord to incorporate market risks*, Bank of International Settlements, 1996.

Basle Committee on Banking Supervision, *International convergence of capital measurement and capital standards*, Bank of International Settlements, 2004.

Baxter, M. and A. Rennie, *Financial calculus: An introduction to derivative pricing*, Cambridge University Press, 1996.

Bensaid, B., J. Lesne, H. Pagès, and J. Scheinkman, "Derivative asset pricing with transaction costs", *Mathematical Finance*, Vol. 2, 1992, pp. 63–86.

Bjork, T., *Arbitrage theory in continuous time*, Oxford University Press, 1999.

Black, F., "The pricing of commodity contracts", *Journal of Financial Economics*, Vol. 3, 1976, pp. 167–79.

Black, F. and J. Cox, "Valuing corporate securities: Some effects of bond indenture provisions", *Journal of Finance*, Vol. 31, No. 2, 1976, pp. 351–367.

Black, F. and M. Scholes, "The pricing of options and corporate liabilities", *Journal of Political Economy*, May–June 1973 pp. 637–654.

Borse, G. J., *Numerical methods with MATLAB*, PWS Publishing Company, 1997.

Boyle, P., "Options: A Monte Carlo approach", *Journal of Financial Economics*, May 1977, pp. 323–338.

Boyle, P., M. Broadie, and P. Glasserman, "Monte Carlo methods for security pricing", *Journal of Economic Dynamics and Control*, Vol. 21, No. 8–9, 1997, pp. 1267–1321.

Brace, A., D. Gatarek, and M. Musiela, "The market model of interest rate dynamics", *Mathematical Finance*, Vol. 7, No. 2, 1997, pp. 127–155.

Brennan, M. and E. Schwartz, "Corporate income taxes, valuation and the problem of optimal capital structure", *Journal of Business*, Vol. 51, 1978, pp. 103–114.

Brennan, M. and E. Schwartz, "A continuous-time approach to the pricing of bonds", *Journal of Banking and Finance*, Vol. 3, 1979, pp. 133–155.

Brennan, M. and R. Solanki, "Optimal portfolio insurance", *Journal of Financial and Quantitative Analysis*, Vol. 16, No. 3, 1981, pp. 279–300.

Broadie, M. and J. Detemple, "American option valuation: New bounds, approximations, and a comparison of existing methods", *Review of Financial Studies*, Winter 1996, pp.1211–1250.

Broadie, M. and P. Glasserman, "Estimating security price derivatives using simulation", *Management Science*, Vol. 42, No. 2, 1996, pp. 269–285.

Bryis, E., M. Bellalah, H. M. Mai and F. de Varenne, *Options, futures and exotic derivatives: Theory, application and practice*, John Wiley & Sons Ltd, 1998.

Chan, K. C., G. A. Karolyi, F. A. Longstaff and A. B. Sanders, "An empirical comparison of alternative models of the short-term interest rate", *The Journal of Finance*, Vol. 47, 1992, pp. 1209–1227.

Chang, C. C., V. S. Lai, and M. T. Yu, "Credit enhancement and loan default risk premiums", *Canadian Journal of Administrative Sciences*, Vol. 19, No. 3, 2002, pp. 301–312.

Chapman, D. and N. Pearson, "Recent advances in estimating term-structure models", *Financial Analysts Journal*, July–August 2001, pp. 77–95.

Choe, H., "Note sur le calcul différentiel stochastique", *Finance*, Vol. 4, 1983, pp. 55–78.

Clewlow, L. and C. Strickland, *Implementing derivatives models*, John Wiley & Sons Ltd, 1998.

Clewlow, L. and C. Strickland, *Exotic options: The state of the art*, Thomson Business Press, London, 1997a.

Clewlow, L. and C. Strickland, "Monte Carlo valuation of interest rate derivatives under stochastic volatility", *Journal of Fixed Income*, December 1997b, pp. 35–45.

Courtadon, G., "Une synthèse des modèles d'évaluation d'options sur obligations", *Finance*, Vol. 6, 1985, pp. 161–186.

Cox, J. C., J. E. Ingersoll, and S. A. Ross, "An intertemporal general equilibrium model of asset prices", *Econometrica*, Vol. 53, 1985(a), pp. 363–384.

Cox, J. C., J. E. Ingersoll, and S. A. Ross, "A theory of the term structure of interest rates", *Econometrica*, Vol. 53, 1985(b), pp. 385–407.

Cox, J. C. and S. A. Ross, "The valuation of options for alternative stochastic processes", *Journal of Financial Economics*, January–May 1976, pp. 145–166.

Cox, J. C., S. A. Ross, and M. Rubinstein, "Option pricing: A simplified approach", *Journal of Financial Economics*, September 1979, pp. 229–263.

Cox, J. and M. Rubinstein, *Option markets*, Prentice Hall, 1985.

Crouhy, M., D. Galai, and R. Mark, *Risk management*, McGraw-Hill, NewYork, 2001.

Cvitanic, J., L. Goukassian, and F. Zapatero, "Hedging with Monte Carlo simulation", in Kontoghiorghes, E., B. Rustem, and S. Siokos (eds.), *Computational methods in decision-making, economics and finance*, Kluwer Academic Publishers, 2002.

Cvitanic, J. and F. Zapatero, *Introduction to the economics and mathematics of financial markets*, MIT Press, 2004.

Dai, Q. and K. Singleton, "Specification analysis of affine term structure models", *Journal of Finance*, Vol. 60, 2000, pp. 1943–1978.

Dana, R. A. and M. Jeanblanc-Picqué, *Financial markets in continuous time*, Springer, 2003.

Das, D., *Credit derivatives: CDOs and structured credit products*, 3rd edition, John Wiley & Sons Inc., 2005.

Demange, G. and J. C. Rochet, *Méthodes mathématiques de la finance*, Economica, 2005.

Dionne, A., *Analyse des données multidimensionnelles*, Les Presses de l'Université Laval, 2002.

Doherty, N. A., *Integrated risk management: Techniques and strategies for reducing risk*, McGraw-Hill, Inc, 2000.

Duffie, D., *Dynamic asset pricing theory*, 3rd edition, Princeton University Press, 2001.

Duffie, D. and R. Kan, "A yield-factor model of interest rates", *Mathematical Finance*, Vol. 6, 1996, pp. 379–406.

Duffie, D. and J. Pan, "An overview of value at risk", *Journal of Derivatives*, Vol. 4, No. 3, Spring 1997, pp. 7–49.

Duffie, D., J. Pan, and K. Singleton, "Transform analysis and asset pricing for affine jump-diffusions", *Econometrica*, Vol. 68, 2000, pp. 1343–1376.

Duffie, D. and K. Singleton, "Modelling term structures of defaultable bonds", *Review of Financial Studies*, Vol. 12, 1999, pp. 687–720.

Duffie, D. and K. Singleton, *Credit risk: Pricing, measurement, and management*, Princeton University Press, 2003.

Dupire, B. (ed.), *Monte Carlo simulation: Methodologies and applications for pricing and risk management*, Risk Publications, 1998.

El Babsiri, M. and G. Noel, "Simulating path-dependent options: A new approach", *Journal of Derivatives*, Winter 1998, pp. 65–83.

Etter, D. and D. Kuncicky, *Introduction to Matlab 6*, Prentice-Hall, 2002.

El-Jahel, L., W. Perraudin and P. Sellin, "Value at Risk for derivatives", *Journal of Derivatives*, Spring 1999, pp. 7–26.

Flannery, B. P., W. H. Press, S. A. Teukolsky and W. T. Vetterling, *Numerical recipes in C++: The art of scientific computing*, 2nd edition, Cambridge University Press, 2002.

Fouque, J. P., G. Papanicolaou, and R. Sircar, *Derivatives in financial markets with stochastic volatility*, Cambridge UniversityPress, 2000.

Fu, M., S. Laprise, D. Madan, Y. Su, and R. Wu, "Pricing American options: A comparison of Monte Carlo simulation approaches", *Journal of Computational Finance*, Vol. 4, No. 3, 2001, pp. 39–98.

Galanti, S. and A. Jung, "Low-discrepancy sequences: Monte Carlo simulation of option prices", *Journal of Derivatives*, Fall 1997, pp. 63–83.

Gatheral, J., *The volatility surface: A practitioner's guide*, John Wiley & Sons Inc, 2006.

Géman, H., N. El Karoui, and J. C. Rochet, "Changes of numeraire, changes of probability measure and option pricing", *Journal of Applied Probability*, Vol. 32, No. 2, 1995, pp. 443–458.

Gendron, M., V. S. Lai, and I. Soumaré, "An analysis of private loan guarantee portfolios", *Research in International Business and Finance*, Financial Risk and Financial Risk Management, Vol. 16, 2002, pp. 395–415.

Gendron, M., V. S. Lai, and I. Soumaré, "An analysis of portfolios of insured debts", *Journal of Fixed Income*, Vol. 16, No.1, 2006a, pp. 55–64.

Gendron, M., V. S. Lai, and I. Soumaré, "Effects of maturity choices on loan guarantee portfolios", *Journal of Risk Finance*, Vol. 7, No. 3, 2006b, pp. 237–254.

Gibson-Asner, R., "Des modèles d'équilibre de la structure des taux d'intérêt: Un essai de synthèse", *Finance*, Vol. 8, No. 2, 1987, pp. 133–171.

Glasserman, P., *Monte Carlo methods in financial engineering*, Springer, 2003.

Glasserman, P., P. Heidelberger, and P. Shahabuddin, "Importance sampling in the Heath-Jarrow-Morton framework", *Journal of Derivatives*, Fall 1999, pp. 32–50.

Glasserman, P., P. Heidelberger, and P. Shahabuddin, "Variance reduction techniques for estimating Value-at-Risk", *Management Science*, Vol. 46, 2000, pp. 1349–1364.

Grant, D., G. Vora, and D. Weeks, "Path-dependent options: Extending the Monte Carlo simulation approach", *Management Science*, Vol. 43, No. 11, 1997, pp. 1589–1602.

Harrison, J. M. and D. M. Kreps, "Martingales and arbitrage in multiperiod securities markets", *Journal of Economic Theory*, Vol. 20, 1979, pp. 381–408.

Harrison, J. M. and S. R. Pliska, "Martingales and stochastic integrals in the theory of continuous trading", *Stochastic Processes and their Applications*, Vol. 11, 1981, pp. 215–260.

Haug, E. G., *The complete guide to option pricing formulas*, McGraw-Hill, 1998.

Heath, D., R. Jarrow, and A. Morton, "Bond pricing and the term structure of interest rates: A new methodology for contingent claim valuation", *Econometrica*, Vol. 60, No. 1, 1992, pp. 77–105.

Heston, S., "A closed-form solution for options with stochastic volatility with applications to bond and currency options", *Review of Financial Studies*, Vol. 6, No. 2, 1993, pp. 327–343.

Ho, T. S. Y., "Key rates durations: Measures of interest rate risks", *Journal of Fixed Income*, Vol. 2, No. 2, 1992, pp. 29–44.

Ho, T. and S. Lee, "Term structure movements and pricing interest rate contingent claims", *Journal of Finance*, Vol. 41, No. 5, 1986, pp. 1011–1029.

Hofmann, N., E. Platen, and M. Schweizer, "Option pricing under incompleteness and stochastic volatility", *Mathematical Finance*, Vol. 2, No. 3, 1992, pp. 153–187.

Hogg, R. V. and A. T. Craig, *Introduction to mathematical statistics*, 5th edition, Prentice Hall, 1995.
Hoggard, T., A. E. Whalley, and P. Wilmott, "Hedging options portfolios in the presence of transaction costs", *Advances in Futures and Options Research*, Vol. 7, 1994, pp. 21–35.
Holton, G., *Value at Risk*, Academic Press, 2003.
Hull, J. C., *Options, futures, and other derivatives*, 6th edition, Prentice-Hall, 2005.
Hull, J. and A. White, "The pricing of options on assets with stochastic volatility", *Journal of Finance*, Vol. 42, 1987, pp. 281–299.
Hull, J. and A. White, "Pricing interest-rate-derivative securities", *Review of Financial Studies*, Vol. 3, No, 4, 1990, pp. 573–592.
Hull, J. and A. White, "Forward rate volatilities, swap rate volatilities, and the implementation of the LIBOR market model", *Journal of Fixed Income*, Vol. 10, No. 3, September 2000, pp. 46–62.
Ingersoll, Jr., J. E., *Theory of financial decision making*, Rowman & Littlefields, 1987.
Jäckel, P., *Monte Carlo methods in finance*, John Wiley & Sons Ltd, 2002.
James, J. and N. Webber, *Interest rate modelling*, John Wiley & Sons Ltd, 2000.
Jamshidian, F., "The LIBOR and swap market models and measures", *Finance and Stochastics*, Vol. 1, No. 4, September 1997, pp. 293–330.
Jarrow, R. (ed.), *Over the rainbow: Developments in exotic options and complex swaps*, Risk Publications, 1995.
Jarrow, R. A., D. Lando, and S. M. Turnbull, "A Markov model for the term structure of credit spreads", *Review of Financial Studies*, Vol. 10, 1997, pp. 481–523.
Javaheri, A., *Inside volatility arbitrage: The secrets of skewness*, John Wiley & Sons Inc, 2005.
Johnson, H. and R. Stulz, "The pricing of options under default risk", *Journal of Finance*, Vol. 42, 1987, pp. 267–280.
Jones, E., S. Mason, and E. Rosenfeld, "Contingent claims analysis of corporate capital structures: An empirical investigation", *Journal of Finance*, Vol. 39, No. 3, 1984, pp. 611–625.
Jorion, P., *Value at Risk: The new benchmark for controlling market risk*, McGraw-Hill, 2000.
Joy, C., P. Boyle, and K. S. Tan, "Quasi-Monte Carlo methods in numerical finance", *Management Science*, Vol. 42, No. 6, June 1996, pp. 926–938.
Kemna, A. and A. Vorst, "A pricing method for options based on average values", *Journal of Banking and Finance*, Vol. 14, 1990, pp. 113–129.
Kloeden, P. E. and E. Platen, *Numerical solution of stochastic differential equations*, Springer, 1992.
Kloeden, P. E., E. Platen, and H. Schurz, *Numerical solution of SDE through computer experiments*, 2nd edition, Springer, 1997.
Knuth, D. E., *The art of computer programming*, Vol. 2, *Seminumerical algorithms*, 2nd edition, Addison-Wesley, 1981.
Kreinin, A., L. Merkoulovitch, D. Rosen, and M. Zerbs, "Principal component analysis in Quasi Monte Carlo Simulation", *Algo Research Quarterly*, Vol. 2, 1998, pp. 21–29.
Lai, V. S., "An analysis of private loan guarantees", *Journal of Financial Services Research*, September 1992, pp. 223–248.
Lai, V. S. and M. Gendron, "On financial guarantees insurance under stochastic interest rates", *Geneva Papers on Risk and Insurance Theory*, Vol. 19, 1994, pp. 119–137.
Lai, V. S., Y. Sakni, and I. Soumaré, "A simple method for computing Value at Risk using PCA and QMC", *Journal of Financial Decision Making*, Vol. 1, No. 2, 2005, pp. 1–13.
Lai, V. S. and I. Soumaré, "Investment incentives in project finance in the presence of partial loan guarantees", *Research in Finance*, Vol. 22, 2005, pp. 161–186.
Lai, V. S. and M. T. Yu, "An accurate analysis of vulnerable loan guarantees", *Research in Finance*, Vol. 17, 1999, pp. 103–137.
Lamberton, D. and B. Lapeyre, *Introduction au calcul stochastique appliqué à la finance*, Ellipse, 1992.
Lando, D., *Credit risk modeling: Theory and applications*, Princeton University Press, 2004.
Lane, M. (ed.), *Alternative risk strategies*, Risk Books, London, 2002.
Lapeyre, B., E. Pardoux, and R. Sentis, *Méthodes de Monte-Carlo pour les équations de transport et de diffusion*, Mathématiques et Applications 29, Springer, 1998.
Leland, H. E., "Who should buy portfolio insurance", *Journal of Finance*, Vol. 35, 1980, pp. 581–594.

Leland, H. E., "Option pricing and replication with transaction costs", *Journal of Finance*, Vol. 40, No. 5, 1985, pp. 1283–1301.

Linsmeier, J. T. and D. N. Pearson, "Value at Risk", *Financial Analyst Journal*, Vol. 56, No. 2, 2000, pp. 47–67.

Litterman, R. and J. Scheinkman, "Common factors affecting bond returns", *Journal of Fixed Income*, Vol. 1, No. 1, 1991, pp. 54–61.

Longstaff, F. and E. Schwartz, "Valuing American options by simulation: A simple least-squares approach", *Review of Financial Studies*, Spring 2001, pp. 113–147.

Luenberger, D. G., *Investment science*, Oxford University Press, 1998.

Malliaris, A. G. and W. A. Brock, *Stochastic methods in economics and finance*, North Holland, 1982.

Margrabe, W., "The value of option to exchange one asset for another", *Journal of Finance*, Vol. 33, 1978, pp. 177–186.

Marrison, C., *The fundamentals of risk measurement*, McGraw-Hill, 2002.

Martinez, W. L. and A. R. Martinez, *Computational statistics handbook with MATLAB*, Chapman & Hall/CRC, 2002.

McDonald, R., *Derivatives markets*, Addison Wesley, 2003.

McNeil, A. J., R. Frey, and P. Embrechts, *Quantitative risk management: Concepts, techniques, and tools*, Princeton University Press, 2005.

Merton, R. C., "Theory of rational option pricing", *Bell Journal of Economics and Management Science*, Spring 1973, pp. 141–183.

Merton, R. C., "On the pricing of corporate debt: The risk structure of interest rates", *Journal of Finance*, Vol. 2, 1974, pp. 449–470.

Merton, R. C. "Option pricing when underlying stock returns are discontinuous", *Journal of Financial Economics*, Vol. 3, 1976, pp. 125–44.

Merton, R. C., "An analytic derivation of the cost of deposit insurance and loan guarantees: An application of modern option pricing theory", *Journal of Banking and Finance*, June 1977, 3–11.

Merton, R. C., *Continuous-time finance*, Blackwell Publishers, 1992.

Merton, R. C. and Z. Bodie, "On the management of financial guarantees", *Financial Management*, Winter 1992, pp. 87–109.

Miltersen, K., K. Sandmann, and D. Sondermann, "Closed-form solution for term structure derivatives with log-normal interest rates", *Journal of Finance*, March 1997, pp. 409–430.

Modigliani, F. and M. Miller, "The cost of capital, corporation finance, and the theory of investment", *American Economic Review*, Vol. 48, June 1958, pp. 261–297.

Moler, C., "Random thoughts: 10^{435} years is a very long time", *MATLAB News & Notes*, Fall 1995, pp. 12–13.

Musiela, M. and M. Rutkowski, *Martingale methods in financial modelling*, Springer-Verlag, 1997.

Neftci, S., *Principles of financial engineering*, Academic Press, 2004.

Neftci, S., *An introduction to the mathematics of financial derivatives*, Academic Press, 2000.

Niederreiter, H., *Random number generation and Quasi Monte Carlo Methods*, SIAM, 1992.

Oksendal, B., *Stochastic differential equations*, 6th edition, Springer, 2003.

Papageorgiou, A. and S. Paskov, "Deterministic simulation for risk management, Quasi-Monte Carlo beats Monte Carlo for Value at Risk", *Journal of Portfolio Management*, Vol. 25, No. 5, 1999, pp. 122–127.

Pearson, N., *Risk budgeting: Portfolio problem with Value-at-Risk*, John Wiley & Sons Inc, 2002.

Poon, S-H., *A practical guide for forecasting financial market volatility*, John Wiley & Sons Ltd, 2005.

Poon, S-H. and C. Granger, "Forecasting volatility in financial markets: A review", *Journal of Economic Literature*, Vol. 41, 2003, pp. 478–539.

Poon, S-H. and C. Granger, "Practical issues in forecasting volatility", *Financial Analyst Journal*, Vol. 61, No. 1, 2005, pp. 45–56.

Pratap, R., *Getting started with Matlab*, Oxford University Press, 2002.

Press, W., S. Teukolsky, W. Vetterling, and B. Flannery, *Numerical recipes in C: The art of scientific computing*, Cambridge University Press, 1992.

Quittard-Pinon, F., *Marchés des capitaux et théorie financière*, Economica, 2003.

Raymar, S. and M. Zwecher, "Monte Carlo estimation of American call options on the maximum of several stocks", *Journal of Derivatives*, Fall 1997, pp. 7–23.
Rebonato, R., *Interest rate option models*, John Wiley & Sons Inc, 1998.
Rebonato, R., *Modern pricing of interest-rate derivatives: The LIBOR market model and beyond*, Princeton University Press, 2002.
Rebonato, R., *Volatility and correlation: The perfect hedger and the fox*, John Wiley & Sons Ltd, 2004.
Risk (ed.), *VAR: Understanding and applying Value-at-Risk*, Risk Publications, 1997.
Romano, M. and N. Touzi, "Contingent claims and market completeness in a stochastic volatility model", *Mathematical Finance*, Vol. 7, No. 4, October 1997, pp. 399–412.
Ronn, E. I. and A. K. Verma, "Pricing risk-adjusted deposit insurance: An option-based model", *Journal of Finance*, Vol. 41, 1986, pp. 871–895.
Ross, S. M., *A first course in probability*, 6th edition, Prentice Hall, 2002a.
Ross, S. M., *Introduction to probability models*, 8th edition, Academic Press, 2002b.
Rubinstein, R. Y., *Simulation and the Monte Carlo method*, John Wiley & Sons Inc, 1981.
Schonbucher, P. J., *Credit derivatives pricing models*, John Wiley & Sons Ltd, 2003.
Seydel, R., *Tools for computational finance*, Springer, 2002.
Shaefer, S. M. and E. S. Schwartz, "Time-dependent variance and the pricing of bonds", *Journal of Finance*, Vol. 42, No. 5, December 1987, pp. 1113–1128.
Stulz, R., "Options on the minimum or the maximum of two risky assets: Analysis and applications", *Journal of Financial Economics*, Vol. 10, 1982, pp. 161–185.
Sundaram, R., "Equivalent martingale measures and risk-neutral pricing: An expository note", *Journal of Derivatives*, Fall 1997, pp. 85–98.
Taleb, N. N., *Dynamic hedging: Managing vanilla and exotic options*, John Wiley & Sons Inc, 1997.
Tan, K. and P. Boyle, "Applications of randomized low discrepancy sequences to the valuation of complex securities", *Journal of Economic Dynamics and Control*, Vol. 24, 2000, pp. 1747–1782.
Tavella, D., *Quantitative methods in derivatives pricing*, John Wiley & Sons Inc, 2002.
Vasicek, O., "An equilibrium characterization of the term structure", *Journal of Financial Economics*, Vol. 5, 1977, pp. 177–188.
Wackerly, D. D., W. Mendenhall, and R. L. Scheaffer, *Mathematical statistics with applications*, 5th edition, Duxbury Press, 1996.
Wilmott, P., *Derivatives: The theory and practice of financial engineering*, John Wiley & Sons Ltd, 1998.
Williams, D., *Probability with martingales*, Cambridge Mathematical Textbooks, 1991.
Yan, H., "Dynamic models of the term structure", *Financial Analysts Journal*, July–August 2001, pp. 60–76.
Zhang, P. G., *Exotic options: A guide to second generation options*, 2nd edition, World Scientific, Singapore, 1998.

Index

Index compiled by Annette Musker